D1153186

THE WORLD'S GREATEST PLACES

ABOUT THIS BOOK

To collect photography is to collect the world - Susan Sontag

Human beings have become extremely mobile. It took Marco Polo years to reach the court of the Chinese Emperor, and Jules Verne journeyed "Around the World in 80 Days". Today, an airplane takes off every minute, unloading thousands of travelers on foreign continents in just hours. We visit the Antarctic, enjoy the beauty of Bali, go shopping in New York and Singapore, stay in Dubai's luxury hotels, travel the Garden Route and Highway 1, dream of Bora Bora, and sway along on the backs of elephants to visit the palaces of the last maharaja of Rajasthan. Human beings have been driven to travel the Blue Planet ever since Adam ate from the Tree of Knowledge – on a constant search for paradise lost and the most fascinating destinations in the world. But where do we find them?

More than anything, this book is an invitation to get more familiar with the world and its magnificent natural and cultural treasures. Arranged geographically according to country, its pages present a selection of destinations – many of which are UNESCO World Heritage Sites – illustrated with images from the world's best photographers and featuring loads of background information. The result is a "world tour" to the most important, impressive and attractive places on earth.

To see, to dream…to travel. "The world is a book," wrote St Augustine, "and those who do not travel read only one page of it."

We wish you an enjoyable journey…

The Publisher

Contents

Previous pages: St Lucia is often referred to as the "Helen of the West Indies". The mighty twin peaks of the Pitons on the south coast are the island's most famous landmarks. Michelangelo's world-famous statue of David, created between 1501 and 1504 in Florence, was exhibited by the town council on the Piazza della Signoria as a symbol of the city's liberty. Today a copy stands here; the original can be admired in the Galleria dell'Accademia.

Contents

The Golden Gate Bridge is a suspension bridge spanning the Golden Gate, the opening of the San Francisco Bay into the Pacific Ocean. The Golden Gate Bridge was the longest suspension bridge span in the world when it was completed during the year 1937, and has become one of the most internationally recognized symbols of San Francisco, California, and of the United States.

Contents

Contents

Minakshi-Sundareshvara Temple in Madurai in the southern Indian state of Tamil Nadu possesses formidable dimensions. The complex is dedicated to the "fish-eyed" goddess Minakshi, Shiva's bride. Shiva is honored here as Sunarshvara, the "Beautiful God".

Contents

The present city of Essaouira was founded in the year 1760 by Mohammed Ben Abdallah, wishing to reorient his kingdom towards the Atlantic for increased exchanges with European powers. He chose Essaouira as his key location.

Contents

The fjords and cliffs of Scandinavia, the rolling forest landscapes of Central Europe, the snow-covered peaks of the Alps, the sun-filled shores of the Mediterranean, the legacy of the ancient Greeks and Romans, the monumental Medieval cathedrals, the magnificent baroque castles ... Europe! For Pope Boniface VII, Tuscany (here the Val d'Orcia) was in fact "the quintessence of the world".

GODAFOSS

Location: North Iceland
Best time to travel:
May to September
www.world-of-waterfalls.com

Godafoss owes its name ("Waterfall of the Gods") to Thorgeir, the speaker of the Althing (Iceland's parliament) who converted to Christianity in the year 1000 (along with the rest of the island) and is said to have thrown the statues of the former pagan gods into the river. The Icelanders' decision was also a pragmatic one: King Olaf of Norway had threatened to cut off their supplies of timber, a move that would have meant the end of Iceland's vital shipbuilding industry.

Despite its modest height, the width and volume of the Godafoss make it one of the most impressive waterfalls in Iceland.

DETTIFOSS

Location: North Iceland
Best time to travel:
May to September
www.dettifoss.is

Dettifoss is by some margin the most powerful waterfall in Europe. This exceptional status is due neither to its height of 44 m (144 ft) nor its width of 100 m (328 ft); it is because of the sheer volume of water which plunges into the depths below. At its greatest, the flow approaches 1,500 cu m/s (53,000 cu ft/s) and the average flow is still an impressive 193 cu m/s (6,800 cu ft/s).

A path connecting all three waterfalls offers fantastic views of the 10-m (33-ft) high Selfoss, which lies to one side of the Dettifoss, and the approximately 27-m (89-ft) high Hafragilsfoss, which lies to the other.

MÝVATN

Location: North Iceland
Best time to travel: May to September
www.myv.is
www.myvatn.is

"Mosquito Lake", which lies roughly 30 km (17 mi) east of Godafoss, was formed by the escaping lava from two volcanic eruptions about 2,000 and 3,500 years ago respectively. The shallow eutrophic lake, which covers an area of 37 sq km (14 sq mi), is only 4 to 5 m (13 to 16 ft) deep and is fed by hot springs. A great variety of mosses, grasses, ferns, herbs, and birches grow along the lakeshore and on its numerous islands. Huge clouds of mosquitoes gather over the rapidly warming waters during the hot summer months, and along with the insect larvae in the water, these provide nutrition for bountiful fish stocks as well as the countless waterfowl which nest in the vast network of bays. Mývatn is considered to be one of Iceland's most spectacular landscapes because of its location in a zone of extreme volcanic activity. Strolling along the well-marked footpaths you will see an array of unusual lava formations.

The best view of the pseudocraters in and around Mývatn is to be had from the circular wall of the Hverfjall eruption crater, an ash cone about 170 m (560 ft) high.

KRAFLA

Location: North Iceland
Best time to travel:
May to mid-September
www.goiceland.org
www.visiticeland.com

Krafla is the name given to an area of volcanic activity near Myvatn which lies right on the junction of the slowly diverging Eurasian and North American continental plates. The gap created by this continental drift is continually being filled with lava, which bubbles up and causes the region's great variety of volcanic activity. Such activity is still centered on Krafla's main crater even though the name, which once included only the volcanic mountain, is now applied to the entire region. Believed for almost 2,000 years to be extinct, Krafla suddenly exploded to life at the beginning of the 18th century, smothering the region under a thick layer of lava and ash. What remained from the eruption was a sparkling, emerald-green crater lake measuring 320 m (1,050 ft) across at its widest point. Krafla erupted again in 1975, this time continuing for almost a decade, an impressive natural spectacle known today as the famous Krafla fires. Its sulfur mud pots, which have been bubbling and steaming ever since, are now a popular tourist attraction, as well as the most visible icon of Iceland's continuing volcanic activity.

Situated just to the north-east of Myvatn, the countryside around Krafla, an active, 818-m (2,684-ft) volcano, is tectonically one of the least stable regions in Iceland. Instead of the usual conical form, the main crater is a flattened depression riven with fissures aligned along a north–south axis, beneath which a giant magma chamber lurks. Krafla is one of Iceland's most spectacular and most active volcanoes.

VATNAJÖKULL

Location: South-east Iceland
Best time to travel: June–August
www.vatnajokull.is

Covering a vast area of roughly 12,000 sq km (4,632 sq mi), this national park has a variety of attractions: moors, swamps, birch groves, scree fields, and sandy terrain. The park is set against the magnificent backdrop of Vatnajökull ("water glacier"), which contains a larger volume of ice than all the glaciers in the Alps combined. The integration of the Skaftafell and Jökulsárgljúfur National Parks into the protected area in June 2008, made this the largest national park in Europe.

The mighty ice sheet of Vatnajökull, a giant among Europe's glaciers, can reach a thickness of up to 1,000 m (3,280 ft). It is Europe's greatest the 3rd biggest glacier of the world.

THINGVELLIR

Location: South-west Iceland
Best time to travel: mid-April to September
www.thingvellir.is

The Germanic tribes called the designated place in the open air where freemen assembled to debate the "Thing". The Thingvellir (literally, the "valley of the Thing") is the official place where Iceland's freemen have assembled to read out the law since 930, the time when land grabs ceased in Iceland and the Icelandic state was established. The Althing, which regularly sat for two weeks, is the oldest democratic body in the world.

The Thingvellir widens in places to form a valley covered with Arctic tundra. The Öxará river, which rises at the Botnssúlur volcano, flows through the national park.

BERGEN

Location: West Norway
Best time to travel: April–October
www.visitbergen.com
www.bergen-guide.com

The narrow alleys between the merchants' homes and warehouses still reek of tar and wood, and hatches open to reveal the pulleys which 500 years ago were used to load salt cod, fish oil, furs, beer, wine, salt, swords, and textiles. Even today a cog, the boat used to take these wares to the towns of the Hanseatic League, is moored in the historic port. From the 14th to the 16th centuries, it was mostly German merchants who controlled business dealings in the trading and port town of Bergen. The Germans ran the salt trade, an important ingredient needed to conserve the fish catches from the Norwegian Sea. In those days, salt fish

GEIRANGER-FJORD

Location: West Norway
Best time to travel: April–October
www.geirangerfjorden.net

Geirangerfjord is considered as one of the most impressive landscapes on the planet. The innermost arm of the Storfjord is roughly 120 km (75 mi) long and visited by more than 150 international cruise ships from around the world each year. There are a multitude of views, including three famous waterfalls: the Seven Sisters and the Suitor and the Bridal Veil. During the summer months, the Hurtigruten passenger ships dock in Geiranger, a small village of about 250 people.

The most spectacular viewpoint, the nearly vertical Flydalshornet, 1,112 m (3,648 ft) above the fjord, can only be reached on foot.

was sold as far away as the Mediterranean and, thanks to its extensive commercial ties, Bergen became one of the most important towns in the Hanseatic League. On the Tyske Bryggen Quay – which means German Bridge and is a clear reminder of its use by Hanseatic merchants – gabled warehouses bear witness to the former prosperity of this once mighty trading port. However, the 58 wooden houses that have been carefully preserved in the historic district do not actually date back to the Middle Ages; they were rebuilt in their original style after a fire in 1702. Fires have continued to cause damage in Bergen, which is still a major Norwegian port, with the most recent occurring in 1955.

The main attractions of Bergen are the picturesque yacht marina on the Byfjord and the unique Old Town.

SOGNEFJORD

Location: West Norway
Best time to travel: April–October
www.sognefjord.no
www.visitnorway.com

The Sognefjord is not only Europe's longest fjord at 204 km (127 mi), but also the world's deepest at 1,308 m (4,292 ft). The cruise ships and the Hurtigruten passenger boats which come here in summer are headed for the Nærøyfjord tributary fjord in Aurland; in places it is only 250 m (820 ft) wide. Both Nærøyfjord, flanked on both sides by rock cliffs up to 1,800 m (5,906 ft) high, and Aurlandfjord are arms at the southeastern end of Sognefjord. The local stave churches in their romantic settings are also worth a visit.

The waters of the Sognefjord reflect the clouds and mountains in the atmospheric light of dusk.

JOSTEDALSBREEN

Location: West Norway
Best time to travel: June–August
www.jostedalsbre.no

Jostedalsbreen is the largest glacier in mainland Europe. From the interior arms of the Sognefjord, this plateau glacier stretches about 100 km (328 mi) to the north-east, reaching widths of up to 15 km (9 mi). The ice is 500 m (1,640 ft) thick in places. In the middle of the glacier stands the Høgste Breakulen, a 1,957-m (6,421-ft) glacial cone covered in ice. Only a few rocky islands break through the ice cover, the highest of these being the Lodalskåpa at an impressive 2,083 m (6,834 ft). The best approach is to take Route 604 to the Jostedalen Valley, which runs for 50 km (31 mi) and contains a network of valleys with glacial fingers stretching toward the east. Brigsdalsbreen is the best-known glacier arm on the sunnier north-west side. The glacier has been in continual retreat for the last 200 years, although its arms have recently begun to grow again.

The Melkevollbreen, an arm of the largest glacier in continental Europe, flows into a valley above Oldevatnet, a lake in the Jostedalsbreen National Park, with the Briksdal Glacier in the distance.

DOVREFJELL-SUNNDALS-FJELLA

Location: Central Norway
Best time to travel: June–August
www.dovrefjellradet.no

It was once thought that the trim peak of Snøhetta 2,286 m (7,500 ft) was the highest point in Norway, but this is now known to be Galdhøppigen 2,469 m (8,100 ft). In the steep tributary valleys of the Sundalsfjord, the Vidda plateau descends to the valley as an impressive series of 100-m-high (328-ft) rock formations. The animal world is as diverse as the truly spectacular landscape here.

Along with moose and reindeer musk ox are just some of the species that roam the tundra of the national park. The ox is a recent arrival from Greenland.

JOTUNHEIMEN

Location: Central Norway
Best time to travel: June–August
www.visitnorway.com

Jotunheimen National Park, home to northern Europe's highest summits, is the most easily accessible hiking and mountain sports region in all of Norway. At 2,469 m (8,101 ft), Galdhøpiggen is the highest peak in Scandinavia, although more than two hundred further summits surpass the 2,000 m (6,562 ft) mark in this glacial mountain range. The landscape on the Vestland side is characterized by Alpine ruggedness while the Østland side features far gentler, undulating terrain.

In the mountainous Jotunheimen National Park, whose name means "Home of the Giants", you are more likely to meet sheep than giants.

VESTERÅLEN

Location: Northern Norway
Best time to travel:
May–September
www.visitvesteralen.com

The Vesterålen archipelago off the coast of Troms extends for 150 km (93 mi), and in the south merges almost seamlessly with the Lofoten archipelago. The Raftsund strait and the Trollfjord on the Lofoten side are considered the dividing line. The landscape resembles that of Lofoten. The main islands of this region are Hinnøya, the largest island in Norway covering 2,205 sq km (851 sq mi), Langøya and Andøya. In 2003, the lakes and highlands on Hinnøya island were protected as the Møysalen National Park.

Blooming fireweed transforms the moors of the Vesterålen island of Hinnøya into a sea of pink.

LOFOTEN

Location: Northern Norway
Best time to travel:
May–September
www.lofoten.com

The Lofoten chain of islands, part of the county of Nordland and separated from the mainland by the Vestfjord, is actually a submerged mountain range. The islands have been popular with visitors to Norway since the 19th century. Austvågøy is the largest island and has the highest summits in the Higravtinden (1,161 m/3,809 ft). The island chain protrudes out into the North Sea for 250 km (155 mi) like a jagged wall of rock topped with snow-covered peaks.

Moskenesøy Island is known for the village of Sakrisøy, with its houses built on stilts; some of these are nearly 100 years old.

NORTH CAPE

Location: Northern Norway
Best time to travel: June–August
www.nordkapp.no

The rocky promontory to the north of Magerøya Island, also known as North Cape, has for centuries wrongly been regarded as mainland Europe's northernmost point. Admittedly, the actual northernmost point is not far away: the next rocky spit of land, Knivskjellodden (above). Jutting about 1.5 km (0.9 mi) further northward into the sea, it is comparatively flat and not quite as spectacular as its more famous neighbor, a tall headland protruding 307 m (1,000 ft) into the Norwegian Sea. It was an Englishman named Richard Chancellor, the chief navigator of a fleet of seven ships undertaking the first journey in search of the North-East Passage between 1553 and 1554, who first spotted this impressive rocky bluff and, believing it to be the northern tip of the continent, named it the "North Cape".

Tens of thousands of people come to the North Cape plateau on Magerøya island to experience the midnight sun at midsummer.

STOCKHOLM

Location: South-east Sweden
Best time to travel: throughout the year
www.stockholm.se

Founded in 1252, Stockholm has been the Swedish capital since 1634 and has a long history as a dynamic and international city. Its wonderful mix of grandiose buildings, parks, waterways, and bridges give the vibrant metropolis a unique ambience. All of the major sights can easily be visited on foot during a stroll through the Old Town (Gamla Stan), and there are roughly one hundred museums. In addition to the Nationalmuseet, which houses the country's most important art collection, and the Moderna Museet, focusing on contemporary art, there are also Skansen, the world's oldest open-air museum, and the Vasamuseet. The latter exhibits the Vasa, King Gustav Adolphus II's flagship, which sank upon its launch in 1628. The Vasa was raised in 1961 after 300 years at the bottom and now has a whole museum of her own.

Top: The photograph shows Riddarholmen Island with the steeple of Riddarholmskyrka church. This ceremonial place of worship is now a museum and the last resting place of the Swedish kings. Bottom: Royal Stockholm. The first Swedish regent to use the castle was King Adolph Frederick in 1754.

DROTTNINGHOLM

Location: South-east Sweden
Best time to travel: throughout the year
www.visitsweden.com

Completed in around 1700, Drottningholm Palace (or Queen Island) is majestically located on Lovön Island in Lake Mälar. It was constructed on the site of an earlier building dating back to the 16th century. Commissioned in 1662, by Hedwig Eleonora, wife of the late King Charles X Gustav, it is the largest baroque palace in Sweden and widely regarded as the architect Nicodemus Tessin's masterpiece. The main façade of the rectangular structure faces the water, and is the finest example of an 18th-century northern European royal residence inspired by the Palace of Versailles. The palace was enlarged after 1750, and numerous rooms were furnished in the lavish style of the rococo. When the palace was increasingly used for state visits, starting in 1777, some of the important rooms were remodeled in an elegant neoclassical design. King Gustav III (1771–92) had the gardens laid out in English landscape fashion. In addition to the splendid rooms from a range of periods, the China Pavilion and the Drottningholm Theater, one of very few rococo theaters still in use, are a great draw for modern visitors.

Set beside Lake Mälar, Drottningholm Castle is a perfect mix of culture and natural beauty, and is still used as a summer residence.

VISBY (GOTLAND)

Location: South-east Sweden
Best time to travel: April–October
www.gotland.info

Evidence suggests that this town on the north-western coast of Gotland Island was settled as early as the Stone Age. In the 12th century, German merchants visited Visby, initially using it as a stopover for the extremely lucrative trade with Novgorod in the Russian interior, and soon after as a base for the expansion of the mighty Hanseatic League into the east. The Baltic cities of Riga, Reval, Gdansk and Dorpat were ultimately assimilated from here. In the 13th century, Visby was probably the only town to vie with Lübeck for the title of most important trading town in northern Europe. The town even minted its own money and became a legislative center for international marine law that held sway across the entire Baltic Sea. Visby's relatively short heyday ended in 1361, however, when Danish King Valdemar IV conquered Gotland. Nonetheless, the powerful town walls, 3.4 km (2 mi) long and in places up to 9 m (30 ft) high, still testify to the city's former prosperity. Visby is one of the best-preserved Hanseatic towns in Europe.

The very impressive city walls total 3.4 km (2 mi) in length and are topped with 38 well-preserved medieval watchtowers.

ÖLAND

Location: South Sweden
Best time to travel:
April–October
www.olandsturist.se

Öland, the second-largest island in Sweden after Gotland, has a unique geological composition that limits agricultural activities. To the east, the land slopes down gently to the sea, but only the south-eastern end with its moraine soil can be cultivated. Elsewhere sandstone, slate, and limestone dominate the island's southern plateau. The now protected Stora Alvet, a 40-km (25-mi) long limestone heath entirely devoid of trees, has been over-grazed and deforested over the centuries so that the bare limestone is now visible in places.

These gigantic stones, possibly marking graves, are signs of prehistoric settlement.

HIGH COAST (HÖGA KUSTEN)

Location: East Sweden
Best time to travel:
April–October
www.hogakusten.com

These island chains in the Gulf of Bothnia, a fascinating skerries landscape, were shaped by glaciers. The Ice Age has left a legacy of rich, chalky soil and many lakes. With these freshwater lakes, the brackish water of the shallow coastal sounds with their off-shore islands, and the open waters of the Baltic Sea, the small High Coast region boasts three water systems of geological and biological significance. The Skuleskogen National Park is located in the middle of the protected area.

Stones that have been worn smooth and round by glaciation are typical finds on the skerries.

COPENHAGEN

Location: East Denmark
Best time to travel: throughout the year
www.visitcopenhagen.com
www.kk.dk

It has become even easier to travel between the two "united kingdoms" since Denmark and Sweden have been connected by the ambitious Öresund Bridge. The much-loved and down-to-earth Queen Margrethe II formulated probably the most accurate travel recommendations for Denmark: "No country is as much like Denmark as Denmark itself". It is certainly an ideal destination for people who love the sea – where else can you find 7,400 km (4,598 mi) of mostly undeveloped and freely accessible coastline, with a choice of the blue, shimmering Kattegat, the mild Baltic, the rough waters of Jutland, or the tidal North Sea? In Copenhagen, which has been the capital of Denmark since 1443, visitors will find history and tradition around virtually every corner. The ambience is at once cosmopolitan and pleasantly tranquil, and most of the sights can be comfortably visited on foot. The city on the Öresund experienced its first period of prosperity as an important trading port back in the late Middle Ages, but a renewed golden age came about in the 16th and 17th centuries, in particular under King Christian IV, who did much to extend and improve the capital. The Nyhavn Canal district is particularly charming with its old wooden sailboats and a slew of cafés.

The famous statue of the Little Mermaid (Lille Havfrue) in Copenhagen bay was created by the sculptor Edvard Eriksen. She is based on the main character in the eponymous fairytale by Danish poet and author Hans Christian Andersen.

HELSINKI

Location: South Finland
Best time to travel: throughout the year
www.visithelsinki.fi

Roughly 500,000 people live in Finland's compact capital, a city originally founded by King Gustav I of Sweden in 1550. After a series of fires, Czar Alexander II commissioned the Berlin architect Carl Ludwig Engel with the reconstruction of Helsinki in a neoclassical style. Twenty of the monumental edifices from the period between 1820 and 1850 still remain today and combine with other famous buildings, in architectural styles that range from art nouveau to modern, to form the unique cityscape of this impressive capital on the Gulf of Finland. Engel's Senate Square, with the cathedral and the statue of Czar Alexander II, the Government Palace, the main university building, and the university library are all worth a visit, as is the impressive Orthodox Uspenski Cathedral, built in 1868, which boasts a lavish interior. Other attractions include the historic market place and buildings on the south side where the ferries dock that take visitors to the island fortress of Suomenlinna and the skerries. Numerous art nouveau buildings line Luotsikatu, one of Helsinki's most elegant streets, and the esplanade, the capital's pedestrian zone, is bordered by parks. Here you will also find Stockmann's flagship department store, the largest of its kind in Scandinavia. The best panoramic view across Helsinki can be enjoyed from the Katajanokka Peninsula.

The 150-year-old cathedral and the statue of Czar Alexander II on Helsinki's Senate Square. A mighty flight of steps leads up to the cathedral, which contains monuments to Agricola, the reformer of Finland, amongst others.

KOLI

Location: East Finland
Best time to travel: throughout the year
www.outdoors.fi

The Koli mountains are the remains of a prehistoric mountain range which was worn away so completely during the Ice Age that only the hardest strata of quartzite were left. These now tower over the surrounding lakes. In addition to Ukko-Koli, there are two other mountain peaks, Akka-Koli (339 m/1,112 ft) and Paha-Koli (334 m/1,096 ft). These mountains were a site of pagan worship in the pre-Christian era and about 30 sq km (12 sq mi) of the region have been conserved as a national park.

There are superb views of Lake Pielinen from the modest summit of Ukko Koli, a 347-m (1,139-ft) granite rise in Karelia.

SAIMAA

Location: South-east Finland
Best time to travel: throughout the year
http://gosaimaa.fi
www.visitsaimaa.fi

Lying about 250 km (155 mi) north-east of Helsinki, Lake Saimaa stretches almost to the Russian border and contains nearly 14,000 islands. Up to 90 m (295 ft) deep in parts, it has a coastline of about 14,000 km (8,700 mi). This body of water covers a vast area of about 1,460 sq km (564 sq mi), not including the islands, and was created when an ice age glacier thawed to form the largest connected lake district in Finland.

The southern half of Finland is made up of a network of between 50,000 and 60,000 lakes and pools. Some 12 percent of the country's total area is composed of lakes.

TALLINN

Location: North Estonia
Best time to travel: throughout the year
www.tourism.tallinn.ee
www.visitestonia.com

Tallinn is the capital and largest city of Estonia. It is situated on the northern coast of the country, on the shores of the Gulf of Finland, 80 km (50 mi) south of Helsinki. After being severely damaged in World War II, the historic center of the Estonian capital was rebuilt in an 18th-century style. Originally called Reval by the Swedish, Danish, and Germans (a Latin reference to the surrounding area), since 1920 the city has been known as Tallinn, a name whose true meaning is still disputed. The Old Town is clustered around Cathedral Hill. Sights worth seeing include St Mary's Cathedral (begun 1230), the Church of the Holy Spirit (12th/13th centuries), St Nicholas' Church (13th to 14th centuries), and St Olaf's Church (13th century) with its 123 m (404-ft) tall steeple which for many years served as a lighthouse. St Mary's Chapel was built between 1512 and 1523. The trade guilds here also commissioned grand buildings for themselves as symbols of civic pride. The Great Guild, for example, which provided the membership of the municipal council, moved into its hall in 1410. The two-storey town hall, built in the early 15th century, is surrounded by well-preserved medieval houses. The baroque Kadriorg Palace was built as a royal summer residence between 1717 and 1725.

There are a multitude of merchants' houses and churches throughout the city to remind visitors of Tallin's heyday. Right: St Olaf's Church with its distinctive steeple (seen here from the cathedral with the city walls in the foreground).

RIGA

Location: Central Lithuania
Best time to travel: throughout the year
www.rigatourism.lv
www.latviatourism.lv

Riga is situated on the Baltic Sea at the mouth of the Daugava River. Of the many important churches in the city, the cathedral, which was begun in the year 1211 but only completed in its present form in 1775, is of particular interest. Another sight worth mentioning is the octagonal wooden steeple of the Lutheran Jesus Church (1819–22). Of the once mighty medieval fortifications, only the 14th-century Powder Tower and the 13th-century Ramer Tower have survived unscathed. The Citadel was begun in 1760, while the area was under Swedish rule, and the Swedish Gate also dates back to this period. The Guildhall is the only remaining medieval administrative building in Riga. The famous "Small Guild", built around the middle of the 14th century and remodeled in 1866, is one of the most prestigious buildings in the city. The Latvian Stock Exchange was built between 1852 and 1855 in the style of a Venetian palazzo with a witty façade. Other architectural delights include splendid patrician houses such as the renowned Reutern House, begun in the year 1683, and some outstanding art nouveau buildings by Mikhail Eisenstein.

The magnificent Blackhead's House stands on Riga's town square. The façade, which has been preserved in a 16th-century Dutch Renaissance style, is beautifully illuminated at night. The unmarried foreign merchants who would congregate here were once known as "blackheads" after St Maurice, their patron saint, who was often depicted as coming from Mauretania. The building is now open to the public.

VILNIUS

Location: South-east Lithuania
Best time to travel: throughout the year
www.vilnius.lt
www.visitlithuania.net

As with many medieval cities, the Old Town of this former trading settlement on the left bank of the Neris River spreads out from the base of its castle. The city experienced its heyday in the 15th and 16th centuries as a link between the cities of the Russian czardom and what were then the strongholds of the Hanseatic League. As a result of its location, the Lithuanian capital features remarkable urban architecture that mirrors the turbulent history of this small nation. Among the older buildings, a number of late-Gothic churches such as St Anne's Church, St Nicholas' Church, and St Bernard's Church, as well as some baroque-era noblemen's palaces, are today of particular historical interest. The 17th-century Church of Saints Peter and Paul is also baroque in style. The heart of the Old Town is largely dominated by St Stanislaus' Cathedral, whose current appearance dates back to construction undertaken between 1783 and 1801. Neoclassical in style, it resembles a Greek temple. The cathedral's bell tower was originally the defensive tower of the Lower Castle, which was built in the 13th century. During the Soviet period, the church was used as a large exhibition space. Vilnius Town Hall was also later remodeled in a neo-classical style. The Gates of Dawn, one of Vilnius' city portals, features a Renaissance gate capital and a chapel housing an icon of the merciful Mother of God. Consecrated in 1901, the Orthodox Church of the Holy Mother is evidence of Vilnius' Russian connections.

Vilnius' cathedral was consecrated in 1801, and its separate bell tower is a typical feature of churches in the Baltic.

LONDON

Location: South-east England
Best time to travel: throughout the year
www.visitlondon.com

The whole world in one city – not just a great advertising slogan but a reality. London is a truly global metropolis, created and defined by people from every country, bringing with them their different cultures to form the unique urban melting pot that is the British capital. A major settlement for two millennia, its very agitated history goes back to its founding by the Romans, who called it Londinium. The Thames is the city's lifeblood, combining old and new, and linking modern buildings with traditional icons such as the Palace of Westminster (or Houses of Parliament and Big Ben with the London Eye and the Royal Festival Hall. Both the Palace of Westminster and Westminster Abbey were built by Edward the Confessor (1003–1066), although the abbey was replaced in the 13th century with a Gothic cathedral where, until 1760, every monarch was buried. William the Conqueror built the Tower of London as a fortified residence. The castle's current appearance dates back to the 13th century. Buckingham Palace, Westminster Abbey, and the Palace of Westminster are just a few of the United Kingdom's most historic and iconic buildings. The political heart of the country beats here in the historic center of the City of Westminster.

Main picture: A view across the Thames taking in the city skyline, with St Paul's Cathedral to the left and the 180-m (591-ft) high Swiss Re Tower; to the right: View of Big Ben from the four lions at the feet of "Nelson Column" on Trafalgar Square (top); the Tower Bridge, built in the Neo-gothic style (middle); the interior of St Paul's Cathedral (bottom).

»JURASSIC COAST«

Location: South-east England (Dorset and Devon)
Best time to travel: March–October
www.jurassiccoast.com
www.southwestcoastpath.com

The Jurassic Coast is a World Heritage Site on the English Channel coast of southern England. The site stretches from Orcombe Point near Exmouth in East Devon to Old Harry Rocks near Swanage in East Dorset, a distance of 153 km (95 mi). This part of the coastline is like an open history book of the Mesozoic period. Strata of the Triassic, Jurassic, and Cretaceous periods allow an uninterrupted view of the three layers of the Earth's middle geological period. The coastline first came to the attention of geomorphologists, scientists who research the formation of the Earth's

EASTBOURNE

Location: South-east England (East Sussex)
Best time to travel: March–October
www.visiteastbourne.com
www.eastbourne.org

Originally built east of a small stream called the Bourne, Eastbourne declared itself the "Sunshine Coast" and began attracting visitors with a promise of more hours of sunshine than anywhere else in England. It wasn't long before grand hotels shot up along the elegant beach promenade to serve holidaymakers from the cities. The best view of the coastline is probably to be had from Eastbourne Pier.

Many resorts along the English coast have Victorian pier pavilions; built in the 1870s, Eastbourne's is one of the most beautiful.

surface, in the year 1810, when Mary Anning, an 11-year-old girl, discovered a "dragon" in the rocks near the fishing village of Lyme Regis. In fact, it was the first complete fossil imprint of an ichthyosaurus, a name meaning "fish lizard", as the fossil seemed to be a cross between a giant fish and a reptile. It was the first of many finds along the coast of Dorset and East Devon. The rocky scenery here is changing at a breathtaking pace due to constant erosion, and a stroll on the beach is a beautiful journey of discovery though the various stages of evolution and geology.

The path along the south-west coast has some fantastic views of Dorset and East Devon. The fossil remains here offer a fascinating insight into 185 million years of the Earth's geological history.

BRIGHTON

Location: South-east England (East Sussex)
Best time to travel: March–October
www.tourism.brighton.co.uk

In the middle of the 18th century, a doctor named Richard Russell wrote a treatise describing the effectiveness of seawater – and in particular the water off the coast of Brighton – in curing certain diseases. His endorsement sparked off a period of unexpected popularity for the fishing village. In 1786, when the Prince of Wales, later George IV, built the faux-Oriental Royal Pavilion, the crowds of visitors turned into hordes. Brighton is still a popular destination for daytrippers, thanks to its proximity to London.

Enlarged by John Nash in 1815, the Royal Pavilion is decorated in a style any Indian Moghul would recognize.

ST MICHAEL'S MOUNT

Location: South-west England (Cornwall)
Best time to travel: April–October
www.stmichaelsmount.co.uk

St Michael's Mount is located in Penzance Bay on the south-western tip of Cornwall. According to legend, a fisherman saw the Archangel Michael appear on the island in the year 495 and since then, it has been known as "Michael's Mount"; a church was built here in the 15th century. A monastery was also built on the island, although this was transformed into a country mansion by subsequent owners.

At low tide the island can be reached on foot via a causeway. Historians assume St Michael's Mount to be the historical island of Ictis, an important center for local trade in tin during the Iron Age.

ISLES OF SCILLY

Location: South-west England (Cornwall)
Best time to travel: March–October
www.scillyonline.co.uk
www.simplyscilly.co.uk

The 140 Isles of Scilly which lie about 40 km (25 mi) off the coast of south-west Cornwall, can easily be reached by ferry from Penzance. Some 2,000 people, who live mostly from tourism and exporting flowers, are spread out over five inhabited islands consisting of steep granite cliffs, white sand beaches and turquoise bays. The mild climate allows palm trees and exotic plants to flourish here. A collection of the exotic plants indigenous to the islands can be seen at the Abbey Garden in Tresco.

The best way to explore the islands is on foot or by bike.

LAND'S END

Location: South-west England (Cornwall)
Best time to travel: April–October
www.visitcornwall.com
www.cornishlight.co.uk

The westernmost point in England features a number of archeological sites. These include tombs from the Iron and Bronze Ages, stone circles, Celtic crosses, and entire villages from the time before the birth of Christ; all of which are witness to thousands of years of settlement. The overland journey from Land's End to John O'-Groats in northern Scotland is 1,406 km (900 mi) – the furthest distance between any two points in the United Kingdom.

The waves of the Atlantic crash incessantly against the peninsula. The Romans named it "Belerion", or "sea of storms".

DARTMOOR

Location: South-west England (Devon)
Best time to travel: March–October
www.dartmoor-npa.gov.uk
www.discoverdartmoor.co.uk

Dartmoor is famous for being where Sir Arthur Conan Doyle's Sherlock Holmes encounters the Hound of the Baskervilles. The landscape is virtually untouched and can be very romantic as well as a bit spooky, especially when it is cloaked in the typically dense fog. The Dartmoor National Park, founded in 1951, covers more than 950 sq km (367 sq mi) and is noted for its vast meadow and moor landscapes. Much of the land belongs to the Duchy of Cornwall, currently run by Prince Charles' estate.

Grantie "tors" (towers) that have managed to withstand the forces of erosion, are typical of the area.

STONEHENGE

Location: Southern England (Wiltshire)
Best time to travel: March–October
www.stonehenge.co.uk

Stonehenge, an inspiring arrangement of megaliths dating back to around 2000 BC, is still a mystery. How were these stones transported hundreds of miles from their origin, and what was the true purpose of the site? The stones each weigh in at several tons and tower to heights of up to 7 m (23 ft) while an impressive trench 114 m (374 ft) wide surrounds the entire complex. The stones were apparently oriented toward certain heavenly bodies, giving rise to the theory that the complex may have served both religious and astronomical purposes.

M egaliths, arranged as a circle of pillars with horizontal capstones

AVEBURY

Location: Southern England (Wiltshire)
Best time to travel: March–October
www.avebury-web.co.uk

Avebury, to the east of Bath, is the site of an ancient monument consisting of a large henge, several stone circles, stone avenues, and barrows. It is one of the finest and largest Neolithic monuments in Europe. It has the same orientation as Stonehenge and was built between 2600 and 2500 BC. According to an 18th-century British scholar, this Neolithic sanctuary and druid temple was destroyed during the 1300s on orders from the Church.

Only 36 of the original 154 stones remain at Avebury. Of these, 27 are part of the large outer circle of stones (left). Each stone has been dug into the earth to a depth of 15–60 cm (6–24 in).

YORK, YORKSHIRE COAST

Location: Northern England (Yorkshire)
Best time to travel: March–October
www.yorkshire-coast.com
www.discoveryorkshirecoast.com

One of Yorkshire's greatest attractions is its natural beauty, which can be enjoyed along the coast in a variety of forms, whether in villages such as Staithes or picturesque coves like Saltwick Bay and Robin Hood's Bay. There is also a magnificent view from Sutton Bank. The best way to explore this beautiful coastline is to walk the North Yorkshire Coast Path (86 km, 53 mi). A rugged coastline with a backdrop of the North York Moors National Park is the setting for the Yorkshire Coast's resorts and fishing villages. Steps and narrow alleyways wind through picturesque Robin Hoods Bay down to the slipway at the bottom of a steep ravine.

Top left and middle: York Minster is the biggest Ghotic church north of the Alps; rightmost: Typical of the town are the narrow alleyways lined with timbered houses.
Bottom: The enchanting Robin Hood's Bay is located between Whitby and Scarborough.

LAKE DISTRICT

Location: North-west England (Cumbria)
Best time to travel: March–October
www.lakedistrict.gov.uk
www.lake-district.com

The Lake District, one of the most popular tourist destinations in Great Britain, has been run as a national park since 1951, but it was more than 200 years ago that the "Lake Poets", part of the Romantic movement whose greatest exponent was Wordsworth, began extolling the beauty of this stunning landscape. Great Langdale valley is one of the most beautiful dales in the area, and the summits of the two Langdale Pikes can be reached on a trail that is just under 10 km (6 mi) long, which leads up to 730 m (2,395 ft). A road will take you to the remains of a Roman fort at the Hardknott Pass, from which there are superb views of the Eskdale Valley.

Hiking, climbing, sailing, or windsurfing enthusiasts are well served in this varied park comprising twelve large lakes and numerous small ones such as Lake Buttermere (above), or you may just prefer to enjoy the beautiful scenery and breathe in fresh air.

CONWY, HARLECH, CAERNARFON

Location: North Wales
Best time to travel: throughout the year
www.visitconwytown.co.uk
www.harlech.com
www.caernarfon.com

Gwynnedd, a rugged region of north Wales, was ruled for centuries by the minor aristocracy until being conquered by Edward I (1239–1307). After his victorious campaign in Wales in the year 1284, Edward secured his position in the area with the construction of three strongholds on the English border. Conwy Castle was intended as a monument to English rule and a staging post in the systematic settlement of Wales by the English. Begun in 1283 and completed in the incredibly short time of just four and a half years, the castle is considered a masterpiece of medieval military architecture. It was built by James of St George, a leading fortifications architect who also supervised work on the castles at Harlech and Caernarfon, both of which were started in the same year. Together with the castles of Aberystwith, Beaumaris and Flint, they formed a chain of fortresses along the coast of North Wales.

Three of the nine castles, built by victorious King Edward I in the 13th century: Caernarfon Castle (top), Conwy Castle (middle) and Harlech Castle (bottom).

SNOWDONIA

Location: North Wales
Best time to travel: April–October
www.eryri-npa.gov.uk
www.snowdonia-society.org.uk

Densely wooded valleys, mountain lakes, expansive moors and picturesque ocean inlets, all juxtaposed with a fascinating succession of ragged peaks – just some of the delights of the Snowdonia National Park. Founded in 1951, it was the first Welsh national park and is still the largest of three (the Pembrokeshire Coast National Park was founded a year later, and the Brecon Beacons National Park in 1957). Snowdonia extends from Conwy in the north to the peaks of Machynlleth in the south. Its highest point is Mount Snowdon at 1,085 m (3,560 ft), which is also the highest mountain in Wales. The Park's entire coastline is a Special Area of Conservation, which runs from the Llyn Peninsula down the mid-Wales coast, the latter containing valuable sand dune systems. The many hills and mountains in the national park (2,180 sq km/840 sq mi) are often draped in clouds and mist, lending the scenery an almost mystic air. It is a paradise for ramblers and rock climbers, and there are any number of rare plants and animals to discover in this excitingly diverse area.

The dramatic scenery of the Snowdonia National Park is the result of millions of years of erosion.

EDINBURGH

Location: South-east Scotland
Best time to travel: throughout the year
www.edinburgh.org

Edinburgh, the capital of Scotland, features a fascinating architectural contrast between the sprawling medieval Old Town and the carefully planned Georgian New Town. Dominating the Old Town, the fortifications of Edinburgh Castle date back to the 11th century. The Royal Mile, which is formed by Lawnmarket, Canongate, and the High Street, is the main thoroughfare of the Old Town and descends from Castle Rock to the numerous lanes and inner courtyards surrounding such elegant mansions as Gladstone's Land, and a host of religious buildings such as the late-Gothic St Giles' Cathedral. At the eastern end of the Royal Mile there is the Palace of Holyrood House, built in 1128 as an Augustinian monastery and later used as the residence of the Scottish kings. Opposite the Palace is the modern building of the new Scottish Parliament. Despite its declining political importance after Scotland's union with England in 1707, Edinburgh remained an important cultural center. The annual Edinburgh Festival, which takes places in August, is a one-of-a-kind experience; the background music is provided by bagpipes, of course.

Balmoral Hotel and Edinburgh Castle dominate the skyline.

DUNNOTTAR, SLAINS, CRATHES

Location: East Scotland
Best time to travel: throughout the year
www.dunnottarcastle.co.uk-
www.undiscoveredscotland.co.uk

A trip through Scotland is also a journey through history. The earliest evidence of hunter-gatherers in the far north dates back to about 7000 BC. Later, when the clan system had taken hold, Scottish chiefs continued their struggle to control this rugged, expansive landscape. In the Highlands alone there were roughly 180 clans. They allowed farmers to cultivate the land, made pacts with royal houses and built castles and palaces as a symbol of their power by erecting these impressive structures in the heart of breathtaking scenery; the castles are inextricably interwoven into local culture and have become icons of Scotland. Dunnottar Castle, near the small port of Stonehaven, enjoys a panoramic backdrop of majestic rocky cliffs and is so impossibly picturesque that it could be the creation of a set designer. Slaines Castle, north of Aberdeen, is the property of the 19th Earl of Errol and inspired Bram Stoker to pen his world famous novel *Dracula* in 1895. Crathes Castle, situated to the east of Banchory just beyond Aberdeen, is famous for its beautiful gardens.

The castles of Dunnottar, Slains, and Crathes (top to bottom)

HIGHLANDS

Location: West Scotland
Best time to travel: Mid-May to mid-September
www.visithighlands.com
www.visitscotland.org

There is no more iconic landscape in Scotland that the Highlands. Largely escaping English influence, this area of astounding natural beauty was ruled by the Scottish clans for centuries. Scenery comprising majestic mountains, glens, and lakes with breathtaking sea views is a paradise both for hikers and for those wishing to explore the local animal and plant life. Before the 19th century the Highlands was home to a much larger population, but due to a combination of factors including the outlawing of the traditional Highland way of life following the Jacobite Rising of 1745, the infamous Highland Clearances, and migration to urban areas during the Industrial Revolution, the area is now one of the most sparsely populated in Europe. A tectonic fault known as the Great Glen or *Gleann Mór* divides the North-West Highlands to the north from the Grampian Mountains to the south. Ben Nevis, the highest mountain in the British Isles, rises majestically from the Grampian Mountains to a height of 1,344 m (4,410 ft). It is one of 284 "munros", a name given in Scotland to mountains of more than 915 m (3,000 ft) whose summits stand out noticeably from others. While the mountain's north-west slopes are relatively easy for hikers to climb, the 460-m (1,509-ft) rock face of the steeper north-east approach is a challenge even for experienced climbers. Glencoe is a beautiful and wildly romantic valley. Rannoch Moor is the largest expanse of moorland in Great Britain and one of the last virtually untouched natural habitats in Europe.

Storm clouds gather round Ben Nevis and Loch Eil at dusk.

DUBLIN

Location: East of Ireland
Best time to travel: throughout the year
www.visitdublin.com

The first to settle here were the Vikings, who named the area "Dyfflin", meaning "Black Puddle". A bad omen, perhaps, and more than 1,000 years of Dublin's history have largely been shaped by external powers, primarily the English, who took Ireland as their first "colony". Dublin eventually became the flagship of the Anglo-Irish administration and yet, at heart, it was never really British at all. Gaelic traditions, music, poetry, storytelling, and playful banter were nurtured throughout the occupation until the battle for Irish independence began with the Easter Uprising in Dublin in 1916. Dublin experienced a dramatic boom in the 1990s, with the Irish economy growing more quickly than any other in the European Union, and the old charm of the city, such as the the beautiful 18th-century Georgian architecture, was enriched

with some new features. Distinctly modern urban lifestyles and attitudes are particularly apparent in Temple Bar, with its up-market galleries, lively bars, and fancy restaurants. Some of the main sights include St Patrick's Cathedral, built in the Early English style, and Trinity College with its Old Library. The city has a world-famous literary history, having produced many prominent literary figures, including William Butler Yeats, George Bernard Shaw, Samuel Beckett, Oscar Wilde, Jonathan Swift and the creator of Dracula, Bram Stoker. It is arguably most famous, however, as the location of the greatest works of James Joyce. His most celebrated work, *Ulysses*, is set in Dublin and full of topical detail which brings history alive.

The pedestrian bridge connecting Temple Bar with Liffey Street was built in 1816 and is officially called Wellington Bridge; users were required to pay a halfpenny toll and it soon became known as the Halfpenny Bridge.

DONEGAL

Location: North Ireland
Best time to travel: April–October
www.donegal.ie

The town of Donegal, which achieved renown as the family seat of the mighty O'Donnell clan, also gave its name to Ireland's northernmost county. The Irish name *Dún na nGall* means "Strangers' Fort" and refers to a 9th century Viking stronghold. The north coast of Donegal is a sparsely populated, lonely stretch of land. The cliffs of Slieve League, which fall a dramatic 601 m (1,972 ft) into the sea, are among Europe's highest. The Fanad Peninsula offers visitors a variety of scenery, featuring a coastline with beautiful sandy beaches, wooded areas and truly amazing rock formations. In 1607, an event took place in the nearby Carmelite Friary at Rathmullan that was to be a turning point in Irish history: the flight of the

CONNEMARA

Location: West of Ireland (Galway)
Best time to travel: April–October
www.connemara.ie
www.clifdenchamber.ie

Connemara, in the western part of County Galway, is a mountainous region of lakes and moors possessed of an almost mythical beauty. Peat bogs extending between two mountain ranges, the Twelve Bens and the Maumturks, are surrounded on three sides by a coastline of tiny bays dotted with countless little islands. A region of approximately 20 sq km (8 sq mi) on the north-western slopes of the Twelve Bens was declared a nature reserve, and Connemara National Park, which is open all year round, can be explored on two sign-posted tracks starting from the visitors center. The inhabitants of Connemara have traditionally been quite poor. After the Famine of the

Earls O'Neill and O'Donnel in the face of the superior numbers of the English Army cleared the way for Northern Ireland to be settled by Scottish Protestants. The broad expanse of Lough Beagh lies at the heart of the Glenveagh National Park. At some point in the 19th century, a speculator named John George Adair bought this piece of land and evicted the peasants who lived there; breeding sheep, he had figured out, was more profitable than rental income. Henry P McIlhenny, an American of Irish descent, bought the land in the 20th century and donated it to the state; it is now a national park once again open to the public. At its heart is Glenveagh Castle, a beautiful late Victorian summer residence.

The spectacular lighthouse at the tip of the Fanad Peninsula was built after the frigate Saldana foundered near the previously unmarked rocks in 1812.

1840s, when the potato blight deprived almost the entire population of its staple food, many gave up the battle to make a living from the poor soil here and emigrated to the United States. Fresh Atlantic air, a magnificent location above the mouth of the river Owenglin, and the nearby Twelve Bens Mountains combine to make the city of Clifden the most popular place on the west coast of Connemara. The area around the town is rich with megalithic tombs.

The Connemara National Park owes its geological history to sediments from an ancient warm sea which once covered the area. Although the sparsely populated valleys were soon covered in bogs and moors such as those surrounding the Owenmore River, the Twelve Bens and the Maumturk Mountains remained barren.

AMSTERDAM

Location: Western Netherlands
Best time to travel: throughout the year
www.iamsterdam.com
www.amsterdam.info

Amsterdam, the fourth-largest city in 17th-century Europe after Paris, London, and Naples, grew up around the delta at the mouth of the Amstel. The city owed its riches to the river, which facilitated importing and processing of commodities from the former colonies, and trading in spices and slaves. While controlling the seven seas beyond the city, Amsterdam's rich merchants concentrated on promoting the arts at home, building imposing townhouses which still dominate the skyline. Tree trunks were rammed as much as 30 m (98 ft) deep into the peaty ground to form the foundations of Amsterdam's Old Town, creating not only seventy islands on stilts, but also the romantic ambience of a town on the water – unsurprisingly Amsterdam was known as the "Venice of the North". There are 400 bridges in the city's historic center alone and the water level is kept constant with the help of a system of locks and pumps. Commercial cargo is still transported on the city's canals. Hundreds of houseboats lie at anchor on the quays of Amsterdam's 160 waterways as well. They have become an iconic element of city life, just like the bicycles and the flower stalls selling "tulips from Amsterdam". Although Amsterdam is the capital of the Netherlands and the most important center of education and culture, the government has its seat in The Hague to the south-west.

Construction of the crescent-shaped "Three Canal Belt" (the Keizersgracht canal) began at the height of the "Golden 17th Century".

KINDERDIJK

Location: South Netherlands
Best time to travel:
throughout the year
www.kinderdijk.nl
www.kinderdijk.com

The scenery of Kinderdijk-Elshout near Rotterdam is evidence of the Dutch mastery of drainage, being a typical mixture of reservoirs, dykes, pumping stations, monitoring buildings, and beautifully preserved wooden windmills. Simon Stevin refined a technique for draining the *polders* in the early 17th century: the water was "milled" away in two stages. First, water was transported from a lower to a higher canal, then removed by a system of locks.

The 19 windmills lining the canals between Kinderdijk and Ablasserdam are best-preserved collection of historic mills in the country.

KEUKENHOF

Location: Western Netherlands
Best time to travel:
March–September
www.keukenhof.nl

Visitors to the Bollenstreek, or "bulb area" situated between Haarlem and Leiden can enjoy a drive through a veritable sea of flowers. The fields of around 8,000 nurseries specializing exclusively in the wholesale flower trade of are all on display here. The Tulip Route, as it is also known, will take you to the most important locations in the area. One such Mecca for flower-lovers is the Keukenhof, founded in 1949, where more than 700 varieties of tulip are exhibited at the world's largest flower show.

Keukenhof was once the kitchen quarters of a country house belonging to Countess Jacoba of Bavaria (1401–1436).

BRUSSELS

Location: Central Belgium
Best time to travel: throughout the year
www.brussels.org

The Grand Place, a tantalizing mixture of public and private buildings, is one of the most beautiful squares on earth, with Victor Hugo calling it "a true miracle". The square is only 110 m (360 ft) long and 68 m (223 ft) wide, but the densely packed guild palaces squeezed into it make it one of the most outstanding architectural ensembles in Europe.

The square is lined with magnificent houses, such as the baroque guild houses with their sharply defined façades (top). Behind the Italianate façade of the Maison des Ducs de Brabant (bottom), built in 1698, there are six guild houses.

BRUGES

Location: North-west Belgium
Best time to travel: throughout the year
www.brugge.be

The prosperous trade in textiles between medieval England and the European continent was mostly conducted in Bruges, where merchants from 17 countries owned factories. Bruges was transformed into a center of art and culture by Jan van Eyck and Hans Memling (and their generous patrons), reaching its zenith in the 15th century when the dukes of Burgundy, active supporters of late-Gothic court culture, took up residence within its walls. The oval footprint of the town is punctuated by numerous canals and long streets with rows of gabled houses.

The belfry of the Drapers' Hall is an icon of the city's former glory.

GHENT

Location: Northern Belgium
Best time to travel: throughout the year
www.visitgent.be

A center of the textile industry since the Middle Ages, Ghent has managed to remain faithful to its traditions even in modern times. The second most important industry in the city is the cultivation of fruit, vegetables and flowers. The city's most famous sights nestle in the well-preserved historic heart of the city, between the Grafenburg and the 14th-century St Bavo's Cathedral, which can be seen for miles around. Its greatest religious treasure is the famous "Ghent Altar" by the brothers Hubert and Jan van Eyck (15th century).

The capital of East Flanders lies at the confluence of the Schelde and Leie rivers.

ANTWERP

Location: Northern Belgium
Best time to travel: throughout the year
www.antwerpen.be

The lifeblood of Antwerp, Belgium's second-largest city, is its bustling port. An array of car-making and chemical companies are based here, and as one of the busiest ports in the world it has cultivated an atmosphere of openness to the world for centuries – a fact that has contributed significantly to the rise of Antwerp as a world center for diamonds. Antwerp boasts a number of historic monuments and an exceptionally vibrant cultural life. Most of its sights are in the city center.

The north tower of the Cathedral of Our Lady is 123 m (404 ft) high; the church's interior is decorated with works by Peter Paul Rubens.

LUXEMBOURG

Location: South Luxembourg
Best time to travel: throughout the year
www.ont.lu
www.lcto.lu

Luxembourg is a landlocked country, bordered by Belgium, France, and Germany. It has a population of over half a million people in an overall area of approximately 2,586 sq km (999 sq mi). Luxembourg, the largest city and also the capital of the Grand Duchy, boasts a wealth of interesting architecture. Siegfried of Luxembourg founded the fortress of Lützelburg on a steep and strategically important mound called the Bock Fiels some time after 963, and the medieval city grew around its feet. The castle was continually extended until the 14th century, when Henry VII of Luxembourg took the Imperial and German crowns. The Spanish, who conquered Luxembourg in 1555, were the first to leave their mark on modern Luxembourg, building fortifications right across the city and mining tunnels which largely consisted of galleries and casemates blasted out of the rock. Other buildings of interest include the Grand Ducal Palace, the home of the family of the Grand Duke in the Old Town, St Michael's Church, the oldest surviving ecclesiastical building in Luxembourg, and the Cathedral of Our Lady, which is also known as Notre-Dame. This was designed as a church and Jesuit college by Jean de Blocq, a Jesuit priest, at the beginning of the 17th century. The church was completed and dedicated to the Immaculate Conception under Otto Herloy, another of the brotherhood, in 1621.

Grund, the lower town, extends along the banks of the Alzette. The area was once the preserve of handworkers, who needed the river water for their work.

PARIS

Location: Central France
Best time to travel:
throughout the year
www.parisinfo.com
www.paris.fr

No other city has been the subject of more songs, more films, more novels, or more plays – Paris, the city of light, and the city of love. The French capital casts a spell on its visitors, often inspiring love at first sight, whether they are drinking *café crème* or *pastis* in the vibrant Latin Quarter, viewing the breathtaking panoramic view of the the cathedral square at Sacré-Coeur, taking a romantic river trip along the Seine, enjoying a relaxed stroll in the Jardin du Luxembourg, or even inspecting one of the major works of art in the museums – it's just a matter of preference. What is certain is that it is almost impossible to resist the charms of this metropolis. A gigantic city has grown from the seed of a settlement on the Ile de la Cité, but its individual districts can still be explored on foot. Kings and presidents, artists and architects have all left their mark on the city over the centuries: the Roman baths in the Musée de Cluny, Notre-Dame cathedral, the Louvre, the Eiffel Tower, and the Grande Arche de La Défense all prove that Paris has always been a city with a plethora of traditions and yet also well ahead of its time, a place of monumental size and yet seductive in its charm. Paris is a true world metropolis with a wealth of historic architectural gems and cultural highlights. The area surrounding the Pont de Sully and the Pont

d'Iéna is particularly rich in history: it begins at the Île Saint-Louis with its statue of St Geneviève, the patron saint of Paris, and continues to the west to the spiritual heart of the city, the cathedral of Notre-Dame and the Sainte Chapelle, a filigree masterwork of High Gothic style on the Île de la Cité. Next there is the Conciergerie, a former royal palace and prison, and part of the larger complex known as the Palais de Justice, which is still used for judicial purposes. The Louvre opposite houses one of Europe's most important art collections. From the 14th century until 1682, when Louis XIV moved his court to Versailles, the Louvre was actually the Paris residence of the kings of France. After that, the former town palace was transformed into one of the world's most important art museums. On the occasion of its 200th anniversary, the Louvre was remodeled as the "Grand Louvre", the largest museum in the world. Following the Seine downriver we find the Musée d'Orsay, the Grand and Petit Palais, and the National Assembly. Another fascinating destination is the world-famous Eiffel Tower, whose steel frame was revolutionary at the time of its construction.

The Alexandre III Bridge over the Seine was built for the World's Fair in 1900. Its steel frame crosses the river in a single span and guides traffic straight to Les Invalides, a complex of buildings containing museums and monuments, all relating to the military history of France, as well as the burial site for some of France's war heroes, notably Napoleon Bonaparte.

VERSAILLES

Location: Central France
Best time to travel: throughout the year
www.chateauversailles.fr
www.mairie-versailles.fr

In 1661, King Louis XIV began the expansion of his father Louis XIII's hunting lodge, a site that was soon to serve him as the permanent seat of his government. The two leading architects, Louis Le Vau and later Jules Hardouin-Mansart, created a palace complex of roughly 700 rooms with vast manicured gardens – a work of art in themselves with plants, fountains and sculptures – as well as the auxiliary garden palaces of Petit and Grand Trianon. Versailles was the political heart of France for 100 years, with as many as 5,000 people living at court, including a considerable number of French aristocrats and up to 14,000 soldiers who were quartered in the outbuildings and in the actual town of Versailles. Of the many magnificent staterooms in the palace, the Hall of Mirrors has historically been seen as the most important. The room, which bewilders visitors with its sheer size – 73 m (240 ft) long and 11 m (33 ft) wide – is so named for the 17 giant mirrors reflecting the light from the windows opposite; it is here that the German emperor was crowned in 1871 and the Treaty of Versailles was signed in 1919 to put an end to World War I.

Versailles is the prototype of a residence designed for an absolute monarchy. Below: wrought-iron gates separate the Place d'Armes from the château itself. The Hall of Mirrors (bottom left), is part of a series of rooms created in 1678 which run the entire length of the garden façade. Bottom right: this portrait (now in the Louvre) by Hyacinthe Rigaud celebrates the majesty of the monarchy.

FONTAINEBLEAU

Location: Central France
Best time to travel: throughout the year
www.de.fontainebleau-tourisme.com

In the 12th century, King Louis VII commissioned a small hunting lodge in the forest of Fontainebleau, about 60 km (37 mi) south of Paris. After it had lain abandoned for a while, Francis I had it rebuilt in 1528, and only a single tower from the original building was left standing. For the interior design work he hired Italian artists including Rosso Fiorentino and Francesco Primaticcio, both of whom were to become well known for their adaptations of the Mannerist style known as the "Fontainebleau School". The palace was subsequently remodeled on a number of occasions, in particular during the reigns of Henry IV and Napoleon. Today the palace houses some outstanding baroque, rococo and neoclassical works of art from Italy and France. The palace was eventually extended to contain five courtyards, all with differing designs. Among its most impressive rooms are the horseshoe-shaped main stair hall and the luxurious ballroom. The splendid palace gardens are also well worth seeing.

The landscape architect André Le Nôtre – the creator of the park at Versailles – designed the Grand Parterre in the park at Fontainebleau in 1645. As a garden terrace with a few low plants, the area was intended for state occasions.

AMIENS

ocation: Northern France
Best time to travel:
throughout the year
www.visit-amiens.com

Situated about 115 km (71 mi) north of Paris, Amiens is both a university town and a bishop's seat. The cathedral, Notre Dame d'Amiens, is one of the great French High Gothic churches, and its dimensions are awe-inspiring. Covering a total area of 7,700 sq m (82,852 sq ft), it is the largest church in France. Bishop Evrard de Fouilloy laid the foundation stone for the church in 1220 and Robert de Luzarches' plans had been nearly completed by the end of the 13th century.

Archbishops, cardinals, and other religious worthies all lie buried in the Cathedral of Notre-Dame at Amiens.

CHARTRES

Location: Central France
Best time to travel:
throughout the year
www.chartres-tourisme.com

Notre Dame de Chartres is the finest High Gothic cathedral bar none. This triple-aisled basilica with a transept and five-aisled choir is considered to be one of the first purely Gothic structures and was the model for the cathedrals in both Reims and Amiens. Construction began here in the early 12th century and the church was consecrated in 1260. The Crypt of St Fulbert, built in 1024, is the largest Romanesque crypt in France. New construction techniques were employed at Chartres, for example the use of flying buttresses to create such large window spaces.

Chartres boasts a wealth of fully preserved original features.

REIMS

Location: North-eastern France
Best time to travel:
throughout the year
www.reims-tourisme.com
www.ville-reims.fr

Lying in the heart of the Champagne region, Reims can look back on a glorious history. Founded by the Gauls, it became a major city during the period of the Roman Empire. Clovis was anointed first king of the Franks here by St Remigius in around 500, and the archbishop's bones are interred in the 11th-century St Rémi Abbey Church, with its early-Gothic choir adjoining narrow nave and 12th-century windows. Construction of Notre Dame Cathedral, the coronation church of the French kings, was begun 1211 on the site of an earlier church. The building is adorned with expressive stone sculptures and the lovingly restored stained-glass windows (including some by Chagall) are vibrant masterpieces of light and color. French kings traditionally spent the night before their coronation in the archiepiscopal Palais du Tau, built around 1500.

Reims was the starting point for the Christianization of Gaul and, with the Abbey Churchof Saint-Rémi, a bastion of the Catholic Church.

BRITTANY

Location: North-western France
Best time to travel:
June–September
www.bretagne.com

The civilization that grew up in Brittany before the Common Era still puzzles scientists to this day – who were the people of this megalithic culture? Did the menhirs, large stones erected between 5,000 and 2,000 BC, function as solar or lunar calendars? Or were they fertility symbols, religious sites or markers for processional routes? We can't even begin to answer these questions. The veil of mystery only begins to lift after 500 BC, when the Celts arrived and settled in Brittany, a region they fittingly called "Armor": land by the sea. Although they eventually converted to Christianity, many of their pre-Christian customs and legends have survived, as has the Breton language. Certain Celtic characteristics also live on: Bretons are quite imaginative people, and are said to be wilful and proud. Brittany, which covers roughly 27,200 sq km (10,499 sq mi) of north-western France, is dominated by fishing and agriculture – just about every sea bass or monkfish ("loup de mer") that lands on European plates comes from the Breton coast. Other local activities include the export of vegetables and the production of meat and milk. Its 1,200 km (746 mi) of coastline also ranks as one of the country's most popular tourist regions after the Côte d'Azur.

The Atlantic surf breaks constantly over the rocks: the ruins of the old Benedictine Abbey of Notre-Dame-des-Grâces and the village church of St Matthew both lie about 20 km (12 miles) west of Brest. Beside them there are a 36-m (120-ft) high lighthouse and a square signal tower on a 30-m (100-ft) high spit of land.

CHALKSTONE CLIFFS OF NORMANDY

Location: North-western France
Best time to travel: March–October
www.normandy-tourism.org

The countryside stretching along the English Channel coast of north-west France is not exactly delicate, but the wind-battered coast and verdant green hinterland have their own undeniable magic which is impossible to resist. The Atlantic surf, the rugged shoreline, the gleaming white chalkstone cliffs, and the long sandy beaches scattered across hundreds of bays represent a nature full of primordial beauty.

The Alabaster Coast with cliffs over 100 m (330 ft) and its famous eroded arch to the west of Étretat that resembles an elephant's trunk.

MONT-SAINT-MICHEL

Location: North-western France
Best time to travel: throughout the year
www.mont-saint-michel.net

The miraculous history of Mont Saint Michel begins in the 8th century with the Vision of St Aubert: the Archangel Michael appeared to the bishop, and in thanks the bishop had a small prayer hall built for pilgrims. A new structure was built on top of the earlier church of Notre-Dame-sous-Terre in 1022, with the crypt and choir. Due to its shifting sands Mont Saint Michel was difficult to reach even at low tide.

The former Benedictine Abbey, today an icon of the region,occupies an exclusive location on a craggy island about a kilometer (half a mile) off the Normandy coast.

LOIRE VALLEY

Location: Central France
Best time to travel: throughout the year
www.loiret.com

There is a unique concentration of historic monuments along the roughly 200-km (124-mi) stretch of the Loire Valley between Sully-sur-Loire to the east and Chalonnes to the west, a little way downstream from Angers. France's longest river meanders through sensational countryside toward the Atlantic, traversing the historic regions of Orléanais, Blésois, Touraine and Anjou. The growth of the towns along the Loire Valley began between 371 and 397 when St Martin, Bishop of Tours and patron saint of the Franks died, and his tomb in Tours became an important pilgrimage site. In 848, Charles the Bald was crowned in Orléans, and in the 10th and 11th centuries the river valley became the preferred place of residence for the ruling family of France. There are several important Romanesque landmarks on the Loire, among them the abbey churches of St Benoît-sur-Loire with its 11th-century narthex and crypt, Germigny-des-Prés (with a 12th-century mosaic), frescoes in Liget and Tavant, and Notre-Dame de Cunault. Fontevraud Abbey, one of Europe's largest monasteries, was to become the burial place of the Plantagenets. The coronation of Henry Plantagenet as King of England in 1154 created a massive empire whose centers of power were at Angers and Chinon. It was here, in 1429, during the Hundred Years' War, that Joan of Arc met the still uncrowned Charles VII and set off to liberate the town of Orléans, which was besieged by the English. Many beautiful châteaux were rebuilt or remodeled under Francis I.

Chambord (first below), the largest of the castles on the Loire, which Francis I had built as a hunting lodge in 1619. Chenonceaux (below), a castle built in the Renaissance style by Philibert Delorme for Catherine de Medici, distinguishes itself by its extravagant location and its two-storey gallery spanning over the little Cher river. The original castle had already been built between 1513 and1521. A relic of the former structure is the free-standing donjon, the typical residential tower of French fortresses.

STRASBOURG

Location: Eastern France (Bas-Rhin)
Best time to travel: throughout the year
www.strasbourg.eu

Situated on the Grande Île, an island in the River Ill, the medieval city of Strasbourg is a mixture of historic buildings and districts drawing on both French and German influences. Strasbourg's icon is its cathedral, one of the most important sacred buildings of the European Middle Ages. Begun in about 1015, it was originally Romanesque in style, but as it took several centuries to complete, the cathedral also features Gothic elements. The west front, praised for its proportions and ornate portal sculptures, is an especially important element of the structure; it became a way for the citizenry, who took over the financing of the edifice in 1286, to create a monument to this achievement. Further highlights include the magnificent stained-glass windows and its astronomical clock. The cathedral square is lined with half-timbered houses, some of which are up to five stories high, including House Kammerzell and Palais Rohan, built around 1740 in a Louis XV style. The historic cityscape also includes La Petite France, the 16th- and 17th-century tanners' district, the Ponts Couverts (bridges which were once roofed over), and the Vauban Weir.

La Petite France, the old tanners' quarter in the Old Town, begins at the Ponts Couverts (top), The mechanism of the astronomical clock (above left) with its apostle figures in Strasbourg's Minster is a miracle of precision engineering. Middle, the west façade; right, one of the stained-glass windows.

COLMAR

Location: Eastern France (Haut-Rhin)
Best time to travel: throughout the year (September/October: grape harvest)
www.ot-colmar.fr
www.colmar.fr

Colmar's location at the junction of two important valleys in the Vosges, the Vallée de Munster and the Valée de la Fecht, on the Rhine's flood plain allowed it to become the third-largest city in Alsace after Strasbourg and Mulhouse. It is an ideal base from which to explore the Vosges or head south along the Route du Vin. The capital of the Haut-Rhin Département, which grew up from a small royal court and, is first documented as *Columbarium* ("dovecote") in 823, combines all of the delights of the region, which is as well-known for its beautiful half-timbered houses as it is for its wine industry. The river Lauch flows through the Old Town, which boasts some very picturesque and romantic sights such as the St Martin Collegiate Church, the tanners' district, and "Little Venice". Art lovers typically head straight for the renowned Unterlinden Museum to see Matthias Grünewald's famed altar piece of the Passion of Christ which was probably finished between 1512 and 1516. The highlight of the nearby Dominican Church is Martin Schongauer's grand *Madonna of the Rosebush* (1473).

At the heart of the museum's collection of medieval art is the altarpiece created by Matthias Grünewald for the monastery of Isenheim near Guebwiller between 1512 and 1516. This powerful masterpiece was intended to end the "fevers of hell", an epidemic sickness.

LUBÉRON

Location: South of France
Best time to travel: March–November
www.parcduluberon.fr

The expansive limestone plateau of the Lubéron, a rocky landscape of lonely oak groves, tiny mountain villages, and stone huts that has lost none of its impressive natural beauty lies to the east of Avignon, halfway between the Alps and the Mediterranean. The mountains reach 1,125 m (3,691 ft) and contain some largely uninhabited stretches of land with more than 1,000 different species of plants. The "Parc Naturel Régional du Lubéron" was founded in 1977 to protect this unique environment. Despite the remoteness of many parts of the Lubéron, people have always lived on the limestone ridge, which was formed in the Tertiary period. The villages huddled in the hollows and valleys here date back to the Middle Ages. The houses have thick walls and churches served as both places of worship and refuge. The inhabitants of the Lubéron generally scraped a living as farmers – when the harvests began to fail, the villages on the north side were abandoned.

Blooming fields of lavender are iconic images of Provence. The peak period is from mid June to mid July.

AIX-EN-PROVENCE

Location: South of France (Bouches-du-Rhône)
Best time to travel: throughout the year
www.aixenprovencetourism.com
www.aix-en-provence.com

The spa and university town of Aix-en-Provence has been the capital of Provence for centuries: the Romans founded the spa colony of Aquae Sextiae Saluviorum on the ruins of the Celto-Liguric settlement of Entremont in 122 BC. Aix first became an important center for the arts and learning at the turn of the 13th century. The Old Town extends from the Cours Mirabeau, an avenue of plane trees and beautiful 18th-century city mansions to the Cathedral of St Sauveur, whose baptistery dates back to the Merovingians. Other sights worth seeing include the 17th-century town hall, the Musée des Tapisseries and Paul Cézanne's studio; the subject that the city's most famous son returned to was Mont St Victoire to the east of Aix-en-Provence, and it is certainly worth a detour to discover the landscapes which inspired the painter.

The Cours Mirabeau was laid out on the southern edge of the Old Town in 1651. The bustle of the weekly market is quite an experience.

ORANGE

Location: South of France (Vaucluse)
Best time to travel: throughout the year
www.ville-orange.fr

Orange enjoys a history of more than 2,000 years going back to the Romans, who originally founded the town of Arausio on the site of a conquered Celtic settlement in the Rhône Valley. Completed in about AD 25, the triumphal arch here is the most completely preserved Roman archway in Gaul. The Théâtre Romain was one of the largest in Roman antiquity, with a façade measuring 103 m (330 ft) by 37 m (150 ft) which impressed even King Louis XIV.

The Théâtre Romain (left, a statue of the Emperor Augustus; right, the Arc de Triomphe) in Orange is one of the most important Roman ruins in Europe.

LES BAUX DE PROVENCE

Location: South of France (Bouches-du-Rhône)
Best time to travel: throughout the year
www.lesbauxdeprovence.com

Although now only a ruined castle, medieval Les Baux was the seat of mighty feudal lords who claimed descent from the Three Kings of the East. The Bible story is commemorated in the Feast of the Shepherds, in which local herdsmen congregate in the church every Christmas Eve to bring the new-born Savior a lamb. It has a spectacular position in the Alpilles mountains, set atop a rocky outcrop crowned with a ruined castle overlooking the plains to the south.

The surviving buildings mostly date back to between the 14th and 17th centuries.

PONT DU GARD

Location: near Remoulins, South of France (Gard)
Best time to travel: throughout the year
www.pontdugard.fr

This famous three-tier aqueduct was built between AD 40 and 60 to supply water to the fast-growing ancient town of Nemausus, present-day Nîmes. The bridge, was considered a daring feat of engineering at the time and is still a very impressive sight. The bottom level has six arches, which vary in width from 15 to 24 m (49 to 79 ft). The middle level has a total of 11 arches. The 35 arches on the top level, which is 275 m (900 ft) long, are about 5 m (16 ft) wide and support the actual water duct.

The Pont du Gard was built during the reigns of the emperors Claudius and Nero.

NÎMES

Location: South of France (Gard)
Best time to travel: throughout the year
www.ot-nimes.fr
www.nimes.fr

Nîmes, a town of temples, hot springs, and theaters, was founded by the emperor Augustus as Colonia Augusta Nemausus in the year AD 16. The most impressive Roman structure here is the amphitheater with its oval arena and rising rows of stone seats which can accommodate up to 25,000 spectators. The many bathhouses, temples, and the theater are grouped around the Jardin de la Fontaine.

The Maison Carrée, or "square house", features Corinthian columns and an impressive decorative frieze. It is one of the best-preserved Roman temples in Europe.

CÔTE D'AZUR

Location: South of France (Var, Alpes-Maritimes)
Best time to travel: throughout the year
www.cotedazur-tourisme.com
www.ot-saint-tropez.com
www.nicetourisme.com
www.nice.fr
www.cannesinfo.com

Dense forests of pine, oak and chestnut push their way down to the coastline between Fréjus and Hyères and the hills drop off steeply toward the sea, leaving no room for construction or development along the Corniche des Maures. The coast road is all the more attractive because of it, winding along the wooded hills often half way up the incline and frequently offering superb views across the sea. Tiny old fishing villages huddle together in the numerous coves and bays having lost little of their original charm. One of these, on the southernmost shores of the Gulf of St Tropez at the eastern foot of the Massif des Maures was known to the Greeks as Athenopolis. The Romans called it Heraclea Carcabaris and the present name is said to derive from a Roman legionary who died a Christian martyr's death under Nero. During World War II, on 15 August, 1944, it was the site of a military landing called Operation Dragoon, the Allied invasion of southern France. The motto in Saint-Tropez is "see and be seen", the exclusive village first became famous through the film *And God Created Woman*, which was shot here in 1956 by the director Roger Vadim and featured Brigitte Bardot, his wife of the time. In latter years, it has been a resort for the European and American jet set and the inevitable hordes of tourists in search of a little Provençal authenticity and an occasional celebrity sighting.

Nice, the secret capital of the Côte d'Azur and actual capital of the Département Alpes-Maritimes, enjoys a fantastic location on the Baie des

Anges, surrounded by the foothills of the Alpes Maritimes. Nice is a town of contrasts: while the grand boulevards cling to memories of the Belle Époque, life in parts of Nice's Old Town resembles scenes in a village in Italy. The iconic image of Nice is the Promenade des Anglais, built in the 1830s along the waterfront by wealthy English folk who by the mid-19th century had already recognized the attractions of Nice as a desirable place to retire. The most impressive edifices from that period are the famous Hotel Négresco and the Palais Masséna. The Old Town features narrow, winding alleyways and houses with a distinctly Italian feel and the main square, Cours Saleya, has an attractive farmers' market. From the castle on the hill there are amazingly beautiful views of the Old Town and the Mediterranean.

Magnificent views of the entire bay of Cannes unfold from the viewing platform behind the church, and there is a giant hall on the edge of the Old Town that houses the Forville Market. Cannes is of course also a town of festivals; the month of May is firmly set aside for the Film Festival, when the Palme d'Or is awarded for the best film, and the international advertising industry meets in Cannes in June to select the best cinema and TV advertising spots. TV bosses from around the world gather here in the fall to buy and sell their programs. The venue for all these activities is the Palais du Festival at the western end of the Croisette.

The jet set discovered the once sleepy fishing village of St Tropez in the 1950s (top).
The legendary Négresco hotel lies on the eight-lane and about 5-km (3-mi) long Corniche of Nice, also known as Promenade des Anglais (left). Not a bad address: the luxury Carlton Hotel on the Croisette in Cannes (right).

AVIGNON

Location: South of France (Vaucluse)
Best time to travel: throughout the year
www.ot-avignon.fr

Catholic history was made in the 14th century in this southern French town on the Rhône when the Roman curia sought refuge here from the political turmoil in Rome, going into "Babylonian exile" between 1309 and 1376. The papal residence consists of an Old and a New Palace, with the 12th-century Roman cathedral of Notre Dame-des-Doms adjoining them to the north. Avignon was surrounded by an imposing town wall at the beginning of the 14th century. One of the fortified towers, the Tour du Châtelet controlled access to the world-famous "Pont d'Avignon".

The view of Avignon from the other side of the Rhône.

MARSEILLE

Location: South of France (Bouches-du-Rhône)
Best time to travel: throughout the year
www.marseille-tourisme.com

Marseille, France's third-largest city and most important port, boasts more than 2,500 years of history. Its importance as a major gateway for military campaigns in North Africa is also mirrored in the composition of its population. The town of Massalia was originally founded by Greeks from Asia Minor on the hill where Notre Dame de la Garde now stands. The Frioul archipelago in the Bay of Marseille comprises four islands, one of which, If, is the location of Château d'If, made famous by the Dumas novel The *Count of Monte Cristo.*

La Canebière, the city's main boulevard, begins in the old port.

CAMARGUE

Location: South of France
Best time to travel:
March–November
www.camargue.fr

The delta between the two main arms of the Rhône comprises 140,000 hectares (346,000 acres) of swamps, meadows, and grazing land, as well as dunes and salt marshes – it is one of Europe's largest wetlands. The cultivation of rice is concentrated in the north; salt is harvested in shallow lagoons in the south-east. The Camargue is home to more than 400 species of birds; its ponds provide one of the few European habitats for the greater flamingo.

If Camargue horses can be broken in for saddle and tack at an early age, they make tireless mounts and serve the local cowherds well.

CARCASSONNE

Location: South of France (Aude)
Best time to travel:
throughout the year
www.carcassonne.org

Even before the Romans, the Iberians had settled on the hill above the river Aude along the old trading route linking the Mediterranean and the Atlantic. The Gallo-Roman town of Carcasso fell to the Visigoths in 418, who built the inner town fortifications in 485. The Moors conquered the town in 725, followed by the Franks in 759. Carcassonne fell to the French crown in 1229. The impressive Romanesque basilica of St Nazaire was built between 1096 and 1150 during the course of the town's expansion in the Middle Ages.

Two crenelated curtain walls and a ring of towers surround the fortress town.

CORSICA

Location: North of Sardinia
Best time to travel: March–November
www.corsica.net

With the white limestone near Bonifacio, the red granite rock of the calanche, and the green wilderness of the Castagniccia, it is no surprise that the Greeks once called Corsica "Kalliste", meaning "the beautiful". The island is not just a collection of wide beaches and tiny swimming coves in a beautiful setting, there are 50 peaks higher than 2,000 m (6,600 ft) here, and green forests, preserving a landscape that has remained unspoilt despite the all-pervading influences of civilization. No other Mediterranean island is as green as Corsica, and the heady aromas of ilex, eucalyptus, black pines, and lavender waft through the air. The most beautiful part of the island is the coast, 1,000 km (620 mi) long, with its beaches of pure white sand and blue fjords between steep cliffs and rocks. Tourism is particularly concentrated in the area around Porto

Vecchio and Bonifacio in the south of the island and Calvi in the northwest. Napoleon, Corsica's most famous native son, was born in Ajaccio in 1769, but he left his island home only ten years later, in 1779. After various military victories he assumed power in France and had himself crowned Emperor in 1804, with a view to conquering Europe. After the "great Corsican" was defeated in his Russian campaign of 1812 and the Battle of the Nations at Leipzig in 1813, he was exiled to Elba. He escaped and returned to power a year later, but was defeated again at Waterloo in 1815. He eventually died in exile on the island of St Helena six years later, on 5 May 1821. The mountainous Mediterranean island is a true gem and attracts a lot of tourists.

Bonifacio, the southernmost town on the island of Corsica, was built on a narrow cliff surrounded by water on three sides. The rock has been hollowed out at its base by the action of wind and water over centuries.

MADRID

Location: Central Spain
Best time to travel: throughout the year
www.turismomadrid.es
www.feelmadrid.com

The capital of Spain is not only the geographic heart of the Iberian peninsula, but it was at one point also the center of an empire in which "the sun never set." Over centuries, dynasties such as the Habsburgs and the Bourbons each left their own mark on the city. Accordingly, the cityscape is wildly diverse even in the center. Since the end of the Franco dictatorship in 1975, Madrid has undergone a rapid change and developed from a sleepy administrative town into a pulsating world city. As the capital, Madrid has been a big draw for artists and merchants since the 16th century. Velazquez and Goya were invited as painters to the Spanish royal court, during which time they created some of their famous masterpieces. A comprehensive collection of paintings from them and other artists can now be admired in the Museo del Prado, one of the most famous classical collections in the world. It comprises more than 9,000 works of art including Goya's 1814 piece The shooting of the rebels on May 3, 1808 (above), 5,000 illustrations and 700 sculptures.

Gran Via with the Metropolis Building and Plaza de la Cibeles

EL ESCORIAL

Location: Central Spain (Madrid)
Best time to travel: throughout the year
www.elescorial.es
www.turismomadrid.es

Eager to express his hunger for power and bolstered by his successes in the war against France in 1561, Philip II commissioned the construction of a vast imposing palace in Escorial, some 60 km (37 mi) north-west of Madrid. After the death of Juan Bautista de Toledo, the original architect,the project was taken over by Juan de Herrera in 1567, who supervised construction until near completion in 1584. The rectangular complex covers a vast area of more than 30,000 sq m (7 acres) and provides space for sixteen courtyards. It also contained nine towers, 400 rooms, 15 cloisters, and a basilica built in 1576. The composition of the buildings was inspired by the Temple of Jerusalem, and thanks to its perfect symmetry it remained for a long time the prototype for many other extravagant palaces across Europe. The magnificently furnished royal mausoleum has housed the mortal remains of all Spanish monarchs since Philip II.

Besides the countless private and state rooms of the royal family, the comprehensive library contains about 42,000 priceless volumes.

BILBAO

Location: Northern Spain
Best time to travel: throughout the year
www.leon.es

A unique program of urban renewal in which famous architects were asked to develop a new look for the city has transformed Bilbao into one of the world's greatest cities of art and architecture. The most beautiful old buildings are in the Old Town's Siete Calles. The most important new contributions include the Puente del Campo Volantin pedestrian bridge and the futuristic airport, both designed by Santiago Calatrava, and Sir Norman Foster's metro stations. Bilbao's main attraction is however Frank O. Ghery's Guggenheim Museum, known as the "metallic flower".

The Guggenheim museum is one of the main attractios of the region.

ALTAMIRA

Location: Northern Spain (Cantabria), UNESCO World Heritage
Best time to travel: throughout the year
www.spain.info

The Cave of Altamira located in the hills above Santillana del Mar was rediscovered in 1879. At first, the paintings found here were believed to be fakes – it was hard to believe that Stone Age man would have possessed such advanced artistic skills. Only further research and the discovery of additional caves whose paintings were easier to date finally proved beyond doubt that they were genuine. The herd of bison, a ceiling painting, is especially famous.

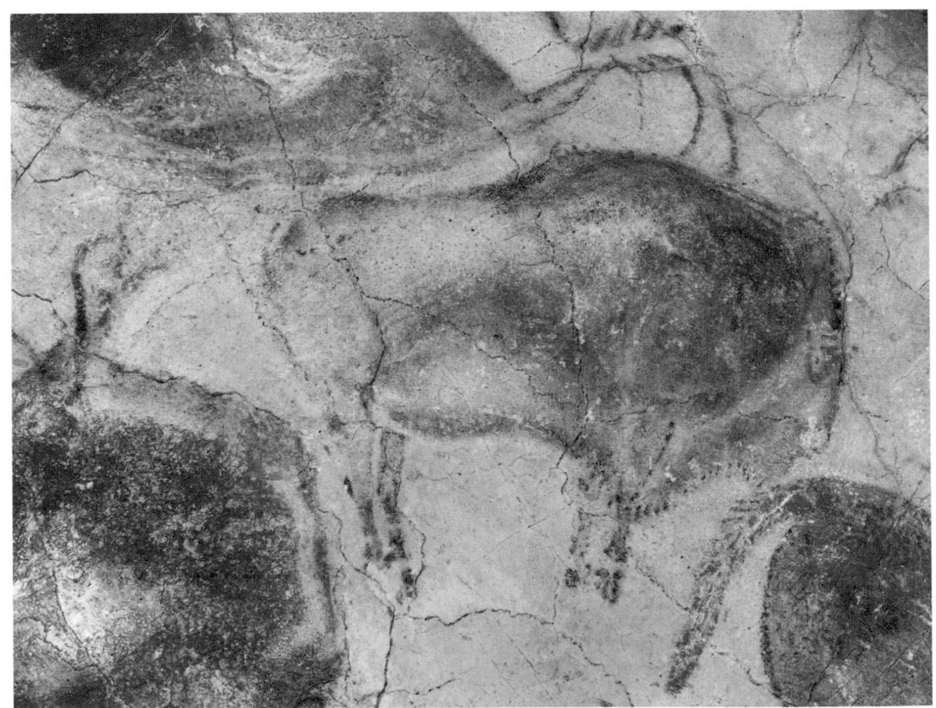

The paintings in the Cave of Altamira are evidence of the acute observation and artistic excellence.

SANTIAGO DE COMPOSTELA

LLocation: North-western Spain (Galicia)
Best time to travel: throughout the year
www.galiciaguide.com

Legend has it that pious 8th-century Christians rescued the bones of the apostle St James the Greater from the Saracens in St Catherine's Monastery on Mount Sinai and brought them to Galicia, where the relics were buried in a purpose-built church. The town of Santiago (derived from Sanctus Jacobus) de Compostela grew up around the church. James became the patron saint of the Spanish Christians in their victorious struggle against the Moors.

The cathedral was consecrated in 1211 and later extended to include further chapels and a dome.

COSTA BRAVA

Location: North-eastern Spain (Catalunya)
Best time to travel: April–October
www.tossademar.com

For most visitors, a visit to the Costa Brava means relaxing on golden beaches with clear waters, picturesque fishing villages, small towns, and excursions into the mountainous hinterland. With its mild climate and low rainfall, this coast was an early discovery for tourists, and here they found the little village of Cadaqués, tucked into a charming bay. Artists such as René Magritte, Pablo Picasso and Henri Matisse all made short stays here, and Salvador Dalí bought a house.

Surrounded by the round towers of the city walls, the Old Town of Vila Vella overlooks the bay of Tossa de Mar.

BARCELONA

Location: North-eastern Spain (Catalunya)
Best time to travel: throughout the year
www.barcelonaturisme.com
www.bcn.es

The city has a lively history: said to have originally been founded by Hannibal's father, it eventually became an important Roman stronghold. During the Middle Ages, it was in the hands of the caliph of Córdoba before becoming the residence of the kings of Aragón. Modern Barcelona is a city of culture, industry and trade. Artists such as Joan Miró, Salvador Dalí, Antoni Gaudí, and Pablo Picasso have lived here and left their mark. The 1992 Olympic Games bequeathed the town Port Olimpico, and the Olympic Quarter, whose restaurants enjoy an unrivalled view of the marina at Barcelona. Port, Vell, the Old Port, lies at the bottom of the Ramblas beside the Custom House (1902) at the Portal del Pau, Barcelona's old port entrance. The five distinct sections of the magnificent Ramblas connecting Plaça de Catalunya with the port are always pulsing with life in the evenings and at weekends. The Barri Gòtic, the Gothic Old Town, is the heart of the city; it extends from the port to the old cathedral and marks the spot where the Romans first established their settlement under Augustus. Construction of the cathedral in the Barri Gòtic began in 1298 but was not completed until the end of the 19th century. The magnificent La Boqueria market is one of the most beautiful in Europe. The medieval Plaça del Rei is the site of the palace of Catalan and Castilian kings. The Palau de la Música Catalana (Palace of Catalan Music) is the most important concert hall in Barcelona. Designed by Domènech i Montaner in 1908 for the "Orfeo Catalá" chorus, the steel frame of this *art nouveau* building is clad in shiny, colorful materials, including ceramics and stained

glass. Some famous artists of the Catalan *art nouveau* style joined in the design of the interior as well, making the harmonious combination of light and space a particularly impressive element. Also noticeable are the lavish flowers and climbers ornamenting the ceiling. Architect Antoni Gaudí i Cornet is considered an outstanding representative of Modernism, or Catalan *Art Nouveau*. He created some of his most magnificent buildings in Barcelona, such as the Sagrada Familia, a church originally designed in the neo-Catalan style in 1882 which has still not been completed. Gaudí designed an idiosyncratic city mansion, the Palau Güell, for Eusebi Güell, and this was completed in 1889. Typically for the artist, ornamentation and organic forms dominate here. The Parc Güell was conceived as a small garden city. Although the park was created according to detailed plans from 1900 to 1914, it seems to have grown naturally. The Casa Milà, built between 1905 and 1911, is a multi-storey apartment block whose bizarre design makes it hard to distinguish between architecture and sculpture. The Casa Batlló is a magnificent city mansion with a roof adorned with mosaic chimneys, designed by Gaudí to represent a large dragon. For the interior design of the Casa Vicens, Gaudí adapted some ideas from Mudéjar architecture. He was only able to complete the crypt of the Colonia Güell Church, but an existing drawing by the master gives an idea of how the structure was supposed to have looked in its final form.

Scenes fromBarcelona. Opposite: bottom, Plaça del Rei (King's Square), is the most noble part of the old Barcelona; top, the proscenium arch of the Palau de la Musica Catalana features Catalan *art nouveau* mosaics of the muses. Page right: Gaudí's buildings in Barcelona (top, the Sagrada Familia, bottom, the Casa Milà) are stunning examples of the age of Moderism.

SEGOVIA

Location: Central Spain (Castile and León)
Best time to travel: throughout the year
www.turismodesegovia.com
www.segoviaturismo.es

Straddling a mountain ridge almost 100 m (330 ft) above the Eresma and Clamores rivers, the medieval Old Town of Segovia boasts a rich architectural heritage that includes more than twenty Romanesque churches. The Old Town is a distillation of everything that is plesant about a trip to Castile – picturesque houses and lanes, beautiful churches, and an impressive castle. In order to channel fresh water from the Río Frío to Segovia over a distance of 18 km (11 mi), the Romans built an impressive aqueduct with a total length of 730 m (2,395 ft). The bridge, erected in the 2nd century AD, rests on 118 arches

SALAMANCA

Location: Eastern Spain (Castile and León)
Best time to travel: throughout the year
www.salamanca.es
www.aboutsalamanca.com

Salamanca was conquered by the Romans in the 3rd century BC and named "Salamantica" before being sacked on several later occasions by the Moors. It achieved great importance after 1085, when it was reconquered by King Alfonso VI of Spain. The university, founded in 1218 by Alfonso IX, was regarded as one of the four most important universities in the West along with Oxford, Paris and Bologna. Its façade is a masterpiece of the Plateresque Renaissance style. Situated on the right bank of the Río Tormes, Salamanca is also rich in Romanesque and Gothic buildings. The 12th-century Old Cathedral is one of

and was built from specially designed granite blocks without the use of mortar. After rule by the Visigoths and the Arabs, the Counts of Castile established a new settlement here and Segovia was the residence of choice for Castilian monarchs for many years. The city's many Romanesque churches are remarkable for their characteristic ambulatories, which served as meeting places for guilds and fraternities. Work on Segovia's late-Gothic cathedral was begun in 1525 on the site of an earlier structure that had been destroyed by fire. After the death of Henry IV in 1474, the coronation of Isabella of Castile took place in the Alcázar fort, which stands high above the town on a rock.

Silhouetted against the Sierra de Guadarrama, two striking buildings overlook Segovia's Old Town: the Gothic cathedral and the Alcázar.

few surviving churches to show Romanesque- Byzantine influences. The church was eventually incorporated into the complex of the New Cathedral, which was begun in 1513 and features late-Gothic, Plateresque and baroque elements. Thanks to its Renaissance sandstone buildings, Salamanca received the nickname La Ciudad Dorada ("The golden city"). Its golden glow is unique in Spain.

Laid out between 1729 and 1755, the Plaza Mayor in the middle of Salamanca was built to designs by Alberto Churriguera to form a courtyard enclosed by four arcades. The buildings are several storeys in height and topped with a balustrade. The bell tower of the Town Hall (in the middle of the image) is a later addition. Bullfights were held here in the "municipal arena" until well into the 19th century.

ÁVILA

Location: Central Spain (Castile and León)
Best time to travel: throughout the year
www.avila.com

Ávila is perhaps the most attractive example of a medieval town in all of Spain. It is built on the flat summit of a rocky hill, which rises abruptly in the midst of a veritable wilderness: an arid table-land, strewn with immense grey boulders, shut in by lofty mountains. Ávila's Gothic cathedral rises like a bastion above the battlements of the perfectly preserved fortifications. The walls date back to 1090, but it was not until the 12th century that they received their present rectangular appearance.

The mighty cathedral of Ávila has been incorporated into the eastern fortifications of the city.

TOLEDO

Location: Central Spain (Castile-La Mancha)
Best time to travel: throughout the year
www.toledo-turismo.com

The Middle Ages still seem to live on wherever you go in this city above the Tagus. The panoramic view from the opposite bank of the river gives you some insight into Toledo's architectural gems: the cathedral, the Alcázar (from the Arabic fort), and a number of medieval structures combine to form a wonderful ensemble, and narrow alleyways typify the Old Town, which is surrounded by a wall with towers. The town's icon is the Cathedral and an old Moorish mosque.

Toledo's Old Town stands on a gentle cliff surrounded on three sides by Tagus river.

LA MANCHA

Location: Central Spain (Castile-La Mancha)
Best time to travel: April–October
www.turismocastilla lamancha.com

"In a place in La Mancha, whose name I don't wish to remember..." – thus begins the first chapter of a novel which, among other things, tells "of the good fortune" which "the valiant Don Quixote had in the terrible and undreamed-of tilting at the windmills..." Where exactly this all happened will probably remain a mystery for all times, but there is something to be said for the idea that it might well have been here in Consuegra.

Eleven windmills and a restored castle still sit enthroned on a hill in Consuegra.

CUENCA

Location: Central Spain (Castile-La Mancha)
Best time to travel: throughout the year
www.turismocuenca.com
www.vercuenca.com

The Old Town of Cuenca was laid out beside a steep cliff which falls away on both sides to the valleys of the Río Júcar and the Río Huécar. The town is most famous for its *casas colgadas*, the "hanging houses", and the Museo de Arte Abstracto Español has been established in one of these to accommodate one of the largest collections of modern Spanish abstract art. The highest point on the plateau is occupied by the Torre de Mangana, once the castle watchtower.

Flanked by two rivers, the Old Town lies on the edge of a sheer cliff.

SEVILLE

Location: Southern Spain (Andalusia)
Best time to travel: throughout the year (Easter Week: Semana Santa)
www.sevillaonline.es

Seville is one of the most beautiful cities in Spain, a great Andalusian beauty with an Arabic past. Moorish invaders from North Africa built the Great Mosque after their initial conquest of Seville in 712, but it was ultimately destroyed during the Reconquest in the year 1248. The chapels of the cathedral house important paintings by Murillo, Velázquez and Zurbarán. The mighty Alcázar with its ornaments and courtyards is a clear survivor from Moorish times.

The Casa Lonja was once the main market and exchange for goods imported from the colonies; it was converted into the Archivo General de las Indias in 1785.

CÓRDOBA

Location: Southern Spain (Andalusia)
Best time to travel: throughout the year (Easter Week: Semana Santa)
www.turismodecordoba.org

Córdoba was an important center of politics and culture even in Roman times. One of Córdoba's most important sons was the Roman philosopher Seneca. In the year 929, the Caliphate of Córdoba rose as the shining star of Al-Andalus and thus competed for fame with Baghdad, also a major world city. As in many cities at the time, Jewish, Arabic and Christian cultures lived peacefully together here while science and philosophy flourished.

The splendid Moorish ornamentation and the mysterious light between the columns make any visit to the Mezquita an unforgettable one.

GRANADA

Location: Southern Spain (Andalusia)
Best time to travel:
throughout the year
www.turgranada.es
www.andalucia.com

The south of Spain remained under Moorish rule even after the so-called Caliphate of Córdoba had ended in 1031. In 1238, for example, Granada became an independent Islamic kingdom, and its rulers built the magnificent complex of the Alhambra. In 1492, the town was the last Moorish possession to be "reconquered" by Christian Spanish rulers. Probably the most famous part of the Alhambra is the Patio de los Leónes, the Court of the Lions. In the middle of the patio, surrounded by richly decorated arcades, is a fountain supported by 12 lion sculptures the likes of which are extremely rare in Islamic art outside of the Iberian Peninsula. They endow the ensemble with a very special character. After the 16th century, the fortress palace of Alhambra grew more and more dilapidated until a large part was lavishly restored in the 19th century. The cathedral, which was built after the end of Moorish rule, contains the graves of the Spanish kings. In the Alhambra district stands the uncompleted palace of Charles V, which was begun in 1526, with total disregard for the existing Moorish structure. The most beautiful declaration of love for Granada was probably that made by the writer Federico Garcia Lorca, who not only said that the city was made for "dreams and dreaming", but that it was the place where a lover "could better write the name of his love in the sand than anywhere else on earth".

Overlooked by the snow-capped peaks of the Sierra Nevada, Granada (left) is bounded to the west by a plateau and to the south by the banks of the Rio Genil. The most famous part of the Alhambra is the Court of the Lions (bottom). In the middle of the patio, surrounded by richly decorated arcades (below), is a fountain with 12 lion sculptures.

BALEARIC ISLANDS

Location: Eastern Spain
Best time to travel: April–October
www.mallorca.com
www.visitbalears.com

"If you like Paradise," wrote Gertrude Stein, "Majorca is paradise". Every year, this Mediterranean island is visited by millions of tourists, and yet it still has some quiet bays and breathtaking landscapes. Majorca is an island like an entire continent, with wilderness and surprisingly high mountains in the north, vast almond plantations and cornfields in the interior, and miles and miles of beaches and coves in the south. A holiday paradise with an area of 3,640 sq km (1,405 sq mi), surrounded by turquoise seas, its capital Palma (right center) with the La Seu Cathedral (right bottom) towering high above the port is the most prosperous town in Spain by gross national product. Those who wish to escape the bustle of the coastal resorts between Andratx and Arenal, and discover the beauty of nature and meet the people in the small villages, only have to go a short way inland. The mountain village Valldemossa, for example, boasts a charterhouse whose monks' cells were converted into small apartments in the 19th century. In 1838/39, Frédéric Chopin and George Sand lived there, a fact that has attracted music lovers from around the world ever since. Near the Port de Valldemossa is the majestic Son Marroig, former summer residence of the Austrian Archduke Ludwig Salvator. Covering an area of 716 sq km (276 sq mi), Menorca is only about one fifth the size of Majorca.

Cap de Formentor (opposite), Majorca's northernmost point; right, from top to bottom: Cala Macarelleta on Menorca; Formenteron Ibiza; La Seu Cathedral in Palma de Majorca

CANARY ISLANDS

Location: Eastern Central Atlantic
Best time to travel: April–October
www.turismodecanarias.com
www.visitenerife.com
www.grancanaria.com
www.turismolanzarote.com
www.gomera-island.com
www.lapalmaturismo.com
ww.fuerteventura.com
www.elhierro.es

Gran Canaria is an island of contrasts. The Tamadaba Nature Park on the west coast of the island is a superb adventure. The subtropical north with its lush vegetation is contrasted by the desert landscape of Maspalomas in the south. The landscapes of Tenerife are as varied as its climate zones, and range from verdant green in the north to rugged mountains and desert-like expanses in the south. San Cristóbal de La Laguna is a lively university town and the cultural capital of the island. In the more isolated mountain villages, people still lead more traditional lives. Thanks to its species-rich vegetation, many visitors regard Tenerife as the most beautiful of the Canary Islands. The Teide National Park, for example, is not only home to Spain's highest mountain, Pico del Teide (opposite) at 3,718 m (12,199 ft), but also to a fascinating volcanic landscape with a rich flora and fauna.

Main picture: Column cactuses on the rocky coast of Los Gigantes, Tenerife, with Pico de Teide in the backdrop. Right: More than a fifth of Lanzarote's surface area is covered with a layer of lava and ash (top); the slopes of the Alta de Garajonay on Gomera with dense ancient forest: The last remnants of subtropical rainforest in southern Europe also contain a forest of laurels dating back to the Tertiary period (middle). This finger of rock (bottom) is known as the Dedo de Dias, the "finger of God".

LISBON

Location: West Portugal
Best time to travel: throughout the year
www.visitlisboa.com
www.lisboa-cidade.com

A sea of houses climbs from the wide estuary of the river Tagus up the steep hills of the "white city". Lisbon, the capital of Portugal, has a superb location that attracts visitors from around the world. Particularly worth seeing is the Alfama, Lisbon's oldest and most picturesque neighborhood, a labyrinthine Old Town on Castle Hill, which is crowned by the ruins of the Castelo de São Jorge. Between the castle ruins and the medieval Sé Cathedral are two of many miradouros, attractive viewing platforms that Lisbon is famous for and from which you can enjoy spectacular views across the city. Author Fernando Pessoa, a native of Lisbon, said of his city there exists "no flowers that can match the endlessly varied colors of Lisbon in the sunlight". Lisbon is divided into an upper town (the bairro alto) – the entertainment quarter with its lively pubs, traditional restaurants and fado bars – and a lower town (the baixa), which was rebuilt after the devastating earthquake of 1755 according to the city's original plans and is today the banking and shopping district. The best view of the baixa can be enjoyed from the Elevador de Santa Justa.

Built in 1901, the Elevador de Santa Justa (left), a wrought-iron elevator between the upper and lower towns, has the best views of the Baixa. Opposite: a good way to explore the "white city" on the banks of the Tagus is to take a trip on one of the old Eléctricos, the old trams which make their bumpy, creaking way through the narrow lanes of Lisbon.

PORTO, ALTO DOURO

Location: North-western Portugal
Best time to travel: throughout the year
www.portoturismo.pt
www.cm-porto.pt
www.visitportugal.com

This port city on the Rio Douro estuary on the Atlantic has much to offer its visitors. Five bridges link Porto with Vila Nova de Gaia, its sister city on the opposite banks and home to most of the port wine cellars. The Ponte de Dom Luís I railway bridge was designed in the offices of Gustave Eiffel. The streets and houses of Porto's Old Town cling tightly to the steep granite rocks beneath it. In the heart of the town, at the bottom end of the Avenida dos Aliados, is the Praça Liberdade with the Torre dos Clerigos, the highest church steeple in Portugal at 75 m (246 ft). At the top of the hill is the town hall with its 70-m (230-ft) bell tower. At the São Bento station, the giant azulejo murals are especially worth seeing. The name of these brightly hand-painted and glazed floor and wall tiles, which decorate all types of buildings in Porto including the Capela das Almas, is probably derived from the Arabic word "al-zulayi", meaning small polished stone, or possibly from the word "azul", meaning blue. On the way to the Ponte de Dom Luis I you come to the cathedral with its superb silver altarpiece. From there you can descend into the Bairro da Sé quarter, Porto's oldest district. The Praça da Ribeiro and the Praça Infante Dom Henriques are the center of the Ribeira district, here rich and poor clash harshly – the stock exchange sits among narrow dingy alleyways.

The Ponte de Dom Luis I (top) was designed by Gustav Eiffel's architecture practice. Bottom, *azulejos* on the Capela das Almas.

ALGARVE

Location: Southern Portugal
Best time to travel: throughout the year
www.visitalgarve.pt

The south of Portugal is a popular destination for many holidaymakers with its superb white sand beaches, crystal clear water, and charming little coves. The fascinating sandstone formations at the Praia de Dona Ana beach and the rocky cliffs on the Ponta da Piedade about 2 km (1.3 mi) south of there are typical of the Algarve. The town of Lagos was once a major staging point for Portuguese explorers setting sail for the New World, and since the days of Henry the Navigator (1394–1460) it has been a center of shipbuilding. The darker side in its history involved the transshipment of captured African slaves. The first recorded auctions took place here on the Praça da República in 1443. Sagres was once the location of Henry the Navigator's legendary nautical school, commemorated by a giant stone compass with a diameter of 43 m (141 ft), on the rocky Ponta de Sagres, not far from the Fortaleza de Sagres. Cabo de São Vicente is almost visible from Sagres jutting out to sea with its 24-m (79-ft) high lighthouse. It is Europe's south-westernmost point. The cliffs, which are up to 60 m (197 ft) high, were still thought of as the "end of the world" in the days of Christopher Columbus.

The magnificent beaches, picturesque rock formations, and turquoise waters of the Algarve are especially attractive in spring, drawing Europeans who are sick of winter to the coast. With some 3,000 hours of sunshine a year, it is no surprise that the Algarve has become one of the most popular tourist destinations in Europe. It is also very much appreciated by passionate golfers thanks to wonderful views over the sea.

MADEIRA

Location: island off North-west Africa
Best time to travel: April–October
www.madeira-web.com

Green banana plantations, bright flowers in the gardens, lovely parks, giant exotic trees, and dense laurel woods – Madeira simply radiates fertility. Funchal, the capital of Madeira boasts grand avenues ranked on both sides by fragrant jacaranda trees. The heart of Funchal is the Sé Cathedral, the interior of which was dedicated in 1514, and features an astonishing, finely carved wooden ceiling with ivory marquetry. In stark contrast to the cathedral stands the Zona Velha, the former fishing district, where low houses fringe the narrow alleyways, and elegant restaurants welcome visitors in the former harbor dives.

Funchal marina at dawn

THE AZORES

Location: Island chain in the Atlantic
Best time to travel: May–September
www.visit-azores.com

Created many years ago by powerful forces in the earth's interior, the island chain of the Azores is located in the middle of the Atlantic Ocean, 1,500 km (930 mi) west of Lisbon, the capital of Portugal, and 3,600 km (2,200 mi) east of North America. There are nine populated islands and a few uninhabited islets with a total surface area of more than 2,300 sq km (888 sq mi). These are arranged in three groups running from the north-west to the east. Much like Madeira, the Azores became an autonomous region as a result of the "Carnation Revolution".

Lagoa do Fogo on São Miguel

BERLIN

Location: Eastern Germany
Best time to travel: throughout the year
www.berlin.de
www.visitberlin.de

"Great Berlin, the open city – it should not be just a German city," wrote Mexican author Carlos Fuentes, before adding, "It is our city, a city of the whole world". History has been made in this city on the river Spree and is still being made today, combining the past with the present to construct the immediate future. This old and new capital has changed radically since the fall of the Wall. The Bundestag and Senate now sit here, making it the center of political power in Germany, and its museums, theaters, and architectural highlights bring it to the cultural avant-garde of the German republic. The city is recognized for its festivals, diverse architecture, nightlife, contemporary arts, public transportation networks and a high quality of living. Berlin has evolved into a global focal point for young individuals and artists attracted by a liberal lifestyle and modern *zeitgeist.*

Tradition and modernism in peaceful harmony: the Band des Bundes ("Federal Strip") on both banks of the Spree (top right) is an attempt by the architects Axel Schultes and Charlotte Frank to unite east and west. A strip 100 m (330 ft) wide and a kilometer (half a mile) wide on both sides of the river is dedicated to governmental and parliamentary buildings. The history of the Brandenburg Gate (right) is a reflection of German history; badly damaged during World War II – the Quadriga was almost completely destroyed – it was isolated behind the wall after 13 August 1961. The gate has since been restored to its former glory.

HELGOLAND, AMRUM, SYLT

Location: German Bight, North Friesian Islands (Schleswig-Holstein)
Best time to travel: May–September
www.helgoland.de, www.amrum.de, www.sylt.de

You have to catch a boat if you want to visit Heligoland, with its famous red sandstone formations and breeding grounds for guillemots and kittiwakes. Germany's only solid rock, high-seas island was actually in British hands for many years before becoming German In 1890, when it was swapped for the island of Zanzibar. South-west of Föhr lies the quiet island of Amrum, about 20 sq km (8 sq mi) in size and featuring dunes up to 30 m (98 ft) high. Amrum also has a sandy beach that is up to 2 m (1.3 mi) wide and 15 km (9 mi) long – the famous Kniepsand beach. The small island has a population of roughly 2,200 people living in five villages, of which the Friesian village of Nebel is the best known and most popular. Sylt is the northernmost point in Germany and little village of List the northernmost community. The island was separated from the mainland by a flood about 8,000 years ago but was reconnected by the Hindenburg causeway in 1927.

Top to bottom: Heligoland's famous sandstone rocks, dunes on Armun, and the lighthouse on the Ellenbogen peninsula, on the island of Sylt.

SCHLESWIG-HOLSTEIN – WADDEN SEA

Location: North-west coast of Germany
Best time to travel: May–September
www.wattenmeer-nationalpark.de
www.nordwest.net

The Wadden Sea is an annual stopover for more than two million migratory birds as well as a summer retreat for about 100,000 breeding shelducks, eider ducks, seagulls and swallows. In addition, the tidal area is a breeding ground for herring, sole and plaice as well as a habitat for gray seals, harbor seals and harbor porpoises. In an area covering more than 4,000 sq km (1,544 sq mi), from the Danish border to the estuary of the river Elbe, Wadden Sea National Park provides more than 3,000 different animal and plant species with an ideal environment. Schleswig-Holstein was the first German state to place the northern stretches of the Wadden Sea under protection, declaring it a national park in 1985, and then a biosphere reserve in 1990. The Wadden Sea is a perfect ecosystem that is rich in nutrients, and many animal and plant species have even found a habitat on the salt flats.

Schleswig-Holstein (seen here, the Westerhever lighthouse) was the first province to place the northern reaches of the Wadden Sea under protection.

HAMBURG

Location: North Germany
Best time to travel: throughout the year
www.hamburg-tourism.de

Think of Hamburg and you will think of the port, the Elbe, and the Alster. Michel, the famous fish market, might get a look-in, or perhaps HSV and FC St Pauli, Hamburg's soccer teams, or the magnificent Elbe boulevards and the legendary Reeperbahn. But the city is much more than all this: it is a throbbing commercial metropolis, a center of international trade, and a diverse city of media and culture. The "Gateway to the World" has not been spared from hard knocks in its more than 1,000 years of history, yet despite its eternal flux it has remained true to its Hanseatic traditions. The view from the Lombard Bridge across the Inner Alster to the Jungfernstieg with its warehouses, townhouses, and the Alster Pavilion is one of the most beautiful panoramas on earth. The people of Hamburg have the emperor Frederick Barbarossa to thank for their port – on 7 May 1189 they received a royal warrant granting them immunity from taxation on the lower course of the Elbe.

Enterprising 19th-century Hamburg merchants built the *Speicherstadt*, an imposing warehouse complex on the Elbe, to store fresh fruit, coffee, tobacco, tea, carpets, and rum.

BREMEN

Location: North Germany
Best time to travel: throughout the year
www.bremen.de
www.bremen-tourismus.de

Bremen is the capital of a province of the same name (which also includes Bremerhaven) and is not only the largest car exporter and fishing port in Europe, but also the home of the Alfred Wegener Institute for Polar and Oceanic Exploration. Many of the sights in Bremen are found in the Altstadt (Old Town), an oval area surrounded by the Weser River, to the southwest, and the Wallgraben, the former moats of the medieval city walls, to the northeast. The oldest buildings and most famous statues in the city are all to be found on the market square. Here Gerhard Marck's Bremen "town musicians" are silhouetted against the 17th-century façade of the 15th-century Town Hall, and nearby there is the "Roland", created in 1404 as a symbol of the city's independence and jurisdiction. St Peter's Cathedral dates back to the 11th century. The gabled houses on the Böttcherstrasse and the *Schoorviertel*, the oldest residential area with its artists' colony, are both worth a look.

Two of Bremen's sights face one another across the market square: the Gothic brick building of the Town Hall and the 10-m (33-ft) high *Roland* as an emblem of former city liberties.

LÜBECK

Location: North Germany (Schleswig-Holstein)
Best time to travel: throughout the year
www.luebeck.de
www.luebeck-tourismus.de

This famous trading town was founded in 1143 by Count Adolf II von Holstein. Lübeck's most famous icon is the Holstentor gatehouse, built in 1478 and one of only two remaining city gates (the other one is the Burgtor). Visitors to Lübeck's Old Town will enjoy a journey back in time to the Middle Ages through a maze of alleyways from Holstentor to Burgtor and the cathedral district.

The brick buildings of Lübeck's Old Town are surrounded by water (seen here with the towers of the Church of St Mary in the background).

SCHWERIN

Location: North-east Germany (Mecklenburg-Vorpommern)
Best time to travel: throughout the year
www.schwerin.de
www.schwerin.com

After the fall of the Berlin Wall, the state of Mecklenburg-West Pomerania needed to designate a new capital for itself. As a result, the small town of Schwerin was chosen despite Rostock's greater size. Schwerin was and still is a ducal residence and with a picturesque location amid charming lakes, a largely restored Old Town, and a fairy-tale palace on the Schlossinsel island. The provincial theater, art gallery of the provincial museum, and the castle festival in the summer have made it a cultural hotspot.

The castle became the seat of the provincial parliament in 1990.

ROSTOCK

Location: North-east Germany (Mecklenburg-Vorpommern)
Best time to travel: throughout the year
www.rostock.de

Rostock has an obsession with the number seven. The "Rostocker Kennewohrn", or the seven symbols of Rostock, is a poem from 1596 that extolls the seven icons that define the cityscape, each of those in turn having seven tell-tale features. After Danish King Valdemar destroyed it in 1161, this former village was given its town charters in 1218. Soon after, in 1229, it became the main principality in the Mecklenburg Duchy of Rostock and by the 14th century had become the most powerful member of the Hanse.

Seen from the Warnow, Rostock's silhouette is a mixture of imposing warehouses and high towers.

WISMAR

Location: North-east Germany (Mecklenburg-Vorpommern)
Best time to travel: throughout the year
www.wismar.de

Wismar is a town that resembles an open-air museum of the Hanseatic League. Many of its churches, burghers' mansions and the market square date back to this period, as do the harbor basin and the "Grube," an artificial waterway to Schwerin lake. After the Hanseatic League came the Swedes who ruled Wismar for 250 years. The high spires of the town churches of St Mary and St Nicholas are evidence of the town's close connections with sea, and were used as navigation features by sailors.

The well in the Old Town was replaced with the "Wasserkunst", an ornamental fountain, in 1602.

RÜGEN

Location: Island off coast of northeast Germany (Mecklenburg-Vorpommern)
Best time to travel: May–September
www.ruegen.de

Rügen, Germany's largest island, has an area of 976 sq km (377 sq mi), and actually comprises five islands that have grown together over the course of centuries. Jasmund, isolated between sea and shallower coastal waters is only reachable via two spits of land. The forested northern half of Rügen is home to the Jasmund National Park (1990). At only 30 sq km (12 sq mi) it is Germany's smallest.

The Selliner Pier (bottom) was destroyed in 1941 by drift ice and only rebuilt in 1998. Right: the romantic chalk cliffs of Rügen were painted by Caspar David Friedrich.

HIDDENSEE

Location: Island off coast of north-east Germany (Mecklenburg-Vorpommern)
Best time to travel: May–September
www.hiddensee.de

Dat söte Länneken, is how this small island is lovingly described in Low German, and a "sweet little land" it is indeed. Hiddensee and its four villages, Grieben, Kloster, Neuendorf and Vitte, is a miniature world of its own without cars, spa resorts or even a pier. Just under 1,100 people live here in what some would consider self-imposed isolation. Many outsiders like it here as well, however, and visit the island to find peace and tranquility.

Island life on Hiddensee: the very picturesque historic "Thornbush" lighthouse (1888).

VORPOMMERN LAGOON AREA NATIONAL PARK

Location: North-east Germany
Best time to travel: May–September
www.nationalpark-vorpommersche-boddenlandschaft.de

The area between Darsswald and the Bug peninsula, part of Rügen, was protected as a nature reserve shortly after Germany's reunification. Much of the area is covered in water, although this is only knee-deep. The Low German word *Bodden* refers to such shallow coastal waters, and these provide a unique habitat for many animal species such as storks.

More than 60,000 storks to rest in the national park every year.

SANSSOUCI

Location: Potsdam, East Germany (Brandenburg)
Best time to travel: throughout the year
www.potsdam.de

"Sanssouci" ("without worries") – that is how Frederick the Great wished to live in his summer palace in Potsdam. With that goal in mind, he had Georg Wenzeslaus von Knobelsdorff build him a graceful retreat among the vineyard terraces in 1747, partly according to his own designs. A single-storey structure, it is considered a masterpiece of German rococo and the most important sight in Potsdam. Adorned with ornate sculptures and rich furnishings, the palace also bears witness to its occupant's lively interest in the arts: in his music room the king liked to play his flute; in his magnificent library he would hold debates with Voltaire, the French philosopher of the Enlightenment. More buildings were added later such as the New Chambers and the New Palace. In 1816, landscape architect Peter Joseph Lenné began the elaborate transformation of the spacious park, which extends all the way up to the Pfaueninsel (Peacock Island) and the green parks of Glienicke and Babelsberg.

The annual Potsdam Castle Festival requires the participation of hundreds; actors entertain the audience against a romantic backdrop.

DRESDEN

Location: East Germany (Saxony)
Best time to travel: throughout the year
www.dresden.de

"The Venice of the East", "Saxon Serenissima", "Florence on the Elbe", "Pearl of the Baroque" – the epithets that have been used to describe the capital of the Free State of Saxony over the centuries are as numerous as they are effusive. And with good reason, for the former seat of the Great Elector is without doubt one of the great European centers of culture. Seat of the Albertiner government from 1485, it developed into one of the most magnificent baroque centers of power in the German states under Elector Augustus the Strong. In the late 18th and early 19th centuries, intellectuals made Dresden a center of German Romanticism. However, the devastating bombing raids of World War II brought the glorious city to her knees and the Old Town was destroyed. Thankfully, many buildings have been lavishly rebuilt including the city's most famous icon, the Frauenkirche (Church of Our Lady), the Zwinger, the Semper Opera House, the Residenz (Dresden Palace), the Hofkirche (St Trinitatis Cathedral), and the Brühlsche Terrasse.

The view of the city from the Elbe (top and middle). The grounds of the Zwinger are surrounded in turn by galleries and pavilions housing museums (bottom).

COLOGNE

Location: West Germany (North Rhine-Westphalia)
Best time to travel: throughout the year
www.koeln.de

Three words sum up Germany's westernmost metropolis: churches, art and kölsch (the local beer). A Roman settlement was the original nucleus of this cosmopolitan city on the Rhine. During the reign of Charlemagne, Cologne became an archbishopric, and by the early Middle Ages it had become one of Germany's leading cities. Romanesque and Gothic churches still bear witness to the former spiritual and intellectual importance of Cologne, most important of all, of course, the famous Kölner Dom (Cologne Cathedral). Art also seems more present here than anywhere else in Germany. Its important galleries and museums are numerous and include the Museum Ludwig and the Wallraf Richartz Museum. The local *joie de vivre* is legendary all year round, not just during the Rose Monday (Carnival) celebrations. People from Cologne often sum up their philosophy of life with two sentences: "Et kütt, wie et kütt." and "Et hätt noch immer jot jejange" ("Things happen the way they do" and "In the end things have always turned out all right"). People take things the way they come in Cologne because they are convinced that in the end all will turn out just fine. If you reflect on 2,000 years of history, you can understand such equanimity. After all, the locals have outlasted the ancient Romans as well as the occupation by the French in the 19th century.

Cologne's main artery is the Rhine and its heart the cathedral. This panorama has a special charm at night, shown here the view from the Deutz Bridge past Great St Martin's to the cathedral, one of the finest church buildings in the Christian world.

FRANKFURT

Location: Western Germany (Hessen)
Best time to travel: throughout the year
www.frankfurt.de
www.frankfurt-tourismus.de

Known as "Mainhattan" for its skyline, Frankfurt am Main looks more the part of a stylish international metropolis than any other city in Germany. One skyscraper after another heaves into view as you approach, and the building boom of the last 20 years has completely altered the appearance of a city with a thousand years of history. The skyline is dominated by the Main tower, the Messe tower, and DZ Bank's Kronenhochhaus, not to mention the offices of the Deutsche, Dresdener, and Commerz banks. Historic Frankfurt (Charlemagne first mentions Franconofurd in 794) has held its own in the shadow of the skyscrapers, however, and at the heart of old the city is the 13th century cathedral, where German kings and emperors were elected and crowned, and the Römer, a row of townhouses which includes the Old Town Hall. The first German national assembly met in nearby St Paul's Church in 1848–9. St Leonhard's church and the Alte Nicolaikirche (Old Church of St Nicholas) are excellent examples of ecclesiastical architecture, as is the Liebfrauenkirche (Church of Our Lady) with its adjoining Capuchin monastery. Goethe's painstakingly reconstructed birth house is a must for fans of the famous writer. The archeological garden between the cathedral, the Schirn exhibition hall, and the Town Planning Office is a display of the ruins of a Roman military camp with its hot spas, and the Carolingian imperial palace.

The cathedral of St Bartholomew stands out proudly against the modern Frankfurt skyline.

MOSELLE VALLEY, TRIER

Location: West Germany
Best time to travel: April–October (September/October: grape harvest)
www.mosel.com
www.trier.de

The Mosel is one of Germany's most capricious rivers, despite the fact that it rises in France, where it is called the Moselle. With its source in the heart of the Vosges Mountains, the Mosel snakes past Metz before reaching Luxembourg and finally enters German territory for the last 243 km (151 mi) of its 544-km (338-mi) total length. More than 2,000 years ago, the river was part of the Roman realm and called the Mosella. Indeed, the Mosel probably has a longer history than any other "German" river. After all, Germany's oldest town, Trier, was founded on its banks. The Mosel is a meandering river that flows past famously steep vineyards and numerous castles such as Cochem, originally built in 1100, destroyed by French soldiers in 1688, and rebuilt in its present neo-Gothic style in the 19th century. It sits perched above the town of the same name. Records document that Trier was founded in the year 16 BC by the Romans during the reign of Emperor Augustus, and subsequently named "Augusta Treverorum", the town of the Treveri. Trier was initially the capital of the Roman province of Belgica before becoming the capital of the divided Western Roman Empire.

The almost fairytale mountain medieval castle Burg Eltz (opposite) in one of the valleys adjoining the Moselle.
This page: Cochem Castle overlooks the town of the same name on the Moselle (top). A bend in the Moselle at Bremm (middle). The Porta Nigra in Trier, the best-preserved Roman city gate north of the Alps (bottom).

BAMBERG

Location: South Germany (Bavaria)
Best time to travel:
throughout the year
www.bamberg.info

This town of emperors and bishops is more than 1,000 years old and cozily situated on seven hills in the valley of the river Regnitz. Unlike Nuremberg or Würzburg, the former "caput orbis" (head of the world) was only lightly damaged in World War II. There are many other sights to see, including the "little Venice" fishermen's quarter, and the late-Gothic cathedral with the Bamberg Horseman. The Emperor's Tomb inside the cathedral was created by Tilman Riemenschneide, and contains the only papal grave in Germany, that of Clement II.

Bamberg's Town Hall was built in the middle of the Regnitz.

WÜRZBURG

Location: South Germany (Bavaria)
Best time to travel:
throughout the year
www.wuerzburg.de

In a beautiful location at the foot of Fortress Marienberg and the picturesque municipal vineyards, Würzburg extends around the market square with its late-Gothic St Mary's Chapel and the House of the Falcon with its rich rococo stucco work. Many of its treasures are hidden, for example, the small Lusam Garden behind the baroque Neumünster. The Residence (1720) is a masterpiece of the baroque built by Lukas von Hildebrandt and Johann Balthasar Neumann.

The magnificent painted ceilings above the staircase in the Residence at Würzburg are the work of Giambattista Tiepolo.

BAYREUTH

Location: South-east Germany (Bavaria, Franconia)
Best time to travel: throughout the year (July/August: Festival)
www.bayreuth.de
www.bayreuther-festspiele.de

The famous Wilhelmine von Bayreuth (1709–1758) was an enlightened margravine, an architect, philosopher, a composer and writer, as well as the favorite sister of Frederick the Great. From her privileged position she was able to influence the look of her namesake town, Bayreuth, with her style of choice, rococo. From 1736, she enlarged the Hermitage, the Old and the New Palaces and splendid palace gardens, and decided to build the beautiful baroque Opera House.

The Margraves' Opera House (1748) whose magnificence attracted Richard Wagner to Bayreuth.

ROTHENBURG OB DER TAUBER

Location: South-east Germany (Bavaria)
Best time to travel: throughout the year
www.rothenburg.de

This small town is the absolute epitome of German Romanticism, and inspired the painter Ludwig Richter to call it a "fairytale of a town". Rothenburg's unique appearance, with its red tile roofs, towers and turrets, the town hall (left), large market square with fountain, town gates, churches, half-timbered houses, and a 2-km (1.5 mi) town wall simply transports you back to another time.

Left: the fork in the road at the Untere Schmiedgasse, with the Siebers Tower in the background, which was once part of the town's fortifications.

NEUSCHWAN-STEIN

Location: near Füssen, South Germany (Bavaria)
Best time to travel: throughout the year
www.neuschwanstein.de

In 1860, Ludwig II commissioned Neuschwanstein Castle. It was built in a neo-Romanesque style according to plans by theater set designer Christian Jank, to replace the ancient ruins of Vorder-Hohenschwangau. Its model was the Wartburg in Thuringia – the setting for the famous Wagner opera "Tannhäuser". Ultimately, Ludwig would only spend a few days at the castle before being arrested and deposed, partly because of the high construction costs of the castle and the resulting debts of the state.

Neuschwanstein is now one of the most visited castles in the world.

HERREN-CHIEMSEE

Location: island in Lake Chiemsee, South Germany (Upper Bavaria)
Best time to travel: April–October
www.herren-chiemsee.de
www.chiemsee.de

The Federal Republic of Germany's legal code was finalized in the "Old Castle" on the lake at Herrenchiemsee in 1948. The much more famous "New Castle" was built by a fairy-tale king: Ludwig II laid the foundation stone of the building in 1878, and the façade overlooking the garden is almost identical with its model in Versailles. The project was to remain unfinished for financial reasons.

Only 20 of the planned 70 rooms could be completed, including the impressive Hall of Mirrors (right).

LINDERHOF

Location: near Oberammergau, South Germany (Bavaria)
Best time to travel: April–October
www.schlosslinderhof.de

Linderhof was an agricultural estate near Ettal that King Ludwig II knew from hunting trips with his father Maximilian II. He wished to build a copy of the palace and gardens at Versailles here, but his plans proved far too ambitious for the narrow valley where Linderhof is situated. As a result, in 1869, construction began on his father's former hunting lodge, which at the time stood on what is now the palace forecourt.

Linderhof Palace (left, the "Grotto of Venus") is the smallest of the three palaces built by King Ludwig II of Bavaria and the only one of which he lived to see completion.

WIESKIRCHE

Location: Steingaden, South Germany (Bavaria)
Best time to travel: throughout the year
www.wieskirche.de

In 1730, monks from nearby Steingaden Abbey produced an image of Christ for the Good Friday procession near Wies. Then, on June 14, 1738, the statue suddenly began to shed tears, a miracle that prompted a pilgrimage rush to see the sculpture. A cult soon developed around the Scourged Savior of Wies, resulting in the commissioning of perhaps the most exuberant rococo church in Germany. The architects were the brothers Dominikus and Johann Baptist Zimmermann.

Beautiful stucco work and ceiling frescos adorn the interior of the Wieskirche (1745–54).

MUNICH

Location: South Germany (Bavaria)
Best time to travel: throughout the year (late September: Oktoberfest)
www.muenchen.de
www.oktoberfest.de

The Residenz is the historical seat of power in Munich and it is from here that Bavaria's counts, electors and kings ruled. It was built in the 16th century to replace the Neuveste Castle, which had in turn replaced the Old Court as the ducal seat. Between 1568 to 1619, a Renaissance complex was built that was later expanded to include baroque, rococo and neoclassical styles. The Residenz now comprises ten courtyards and 130 rooms. The Court Church of All Saints as well as the former Residenz Theater (now the Cuvilliés Theater), a splendid, newly restored rococo building, are also part of the complex. The Residenz still plays an important role in Munich. It houses museums (including the Porcelain, Silver and Treasure Chambers in the Königsbau, the Cabinet of Miniatures, State Collection of Coins, and Collection of Egyptian Art) and is a prestigious venue for festive occasions and receptions. Munich's urban center is framed by the neo-Gothic New Town Hall from 1909 with its famous *Glockenspiel*, as well as the Old Town Hall from 1480. When Ludwig the Bavarian granted the market charter to Munich in 1315, he stipulated that the Marktplatz remain "free of buildings for all eternity". In 1638, Elector Maximilian I had the Marian Column erected there in gratitude for the city being spared during Swedish occupation in the Thirty Years' War. Since 1854, the center of Munich has been known as Marienplatz.

The Field Marshals' hall, inspired by the famous Loggia dei Lanzi of Florence, and Theatiner Church.

SCHAFFHAUSEN

Location: Northern Switzerland (Canton of Schaffhausen)
Best time to travel: April–October
www.schaffhauserland.ch

The Rhine Falls are Europe's largest waterfall in terms of water volume – although the drop in height is only 25 m (82 ft). Without the falls, Schaffhausen would not have developed into a town as it did early in the Middle Ages when the goods transported along the Rhine were offloaded onto wagons here for a few miles. This was a practice from which the waggoners, merchants, aldermen, and toll keepers all profited. The large cathedral is testimony to the town's former wealth and, dating from the 11th/12th centuries, it is a fine example of a very pure form of the Romanesque style. The former Benedictine All Saints Monastery, which now houses the comprehensive All Saints Cultural History Museum, was added later to the cathedral. The town's landmark is the Munot fortress dating from the 16th century.

Dominated by the castle at Laufen on the south bank of the river, the Rhine Falls at Neuhausen are spectacular at any time of the year, but especially in early summer, when the river is in spate.

STEIN AM RHEIN

Location: Northern Switzerland (Canton of Schaffhausen)
Best time to travel: April–October
www.steinamrhein.ch

Stein am Rhein is situated where the Rhine exits the lower section of Lake Constance. Its main gem is the town hall from 1539, which boasts a variety of painted motifs depicting the history of the region. Stein's appeal comes from its meticulously maintained medieval houses. Opposite the town hall, for instance, is the late Gothic Weisser Adler (White Eagle) with its painted Renaissance façade, and the old Benedictine monastery of St George, whose buildings are now used as a museum.

Stein am Rhein rivals the town of Murten for the title of best-preserved medieval town in Switzerland.

ST GALLEN

Location: North-eastern Switzerland (Canton of St Gallen)
Best time to travel: throughout the year
www.st.gallen-bodensee.ch

St Gallen has been an important center in the Lake Constance region since the early Middle Ages. The collegiate church and monastery were rebuilt in the mid-18th century in late baroque style – only in the crypt can remains of the 10th-century building still be seen. The monastery was founded by Abbot Otmar in the 8th century after the Irish missionary and monk Gallus had settled here as a hermit in 612. The library's inventory has been expanded continuously since the early Middle Ages.

A fitting setting for such rare and valuable works: the main hall of the monastery library.

ZÜRICH

Location: North Switzerland (Canton of Zurich)
Best time to travel: throughout the year
www.stadt-zuerich.ch
www.zuerich.com

It is a cliché, and an incorrect one at that, to assume that the country's economic metropolis on Lake Zurich, with its numerous banking headquarters, is just a boring, old-fashioned financial center. Declared a free city in 1218, the city had a monopoly on wool, silk, and leather production throughout the Middle Ages and soon became wealthy. This led to the creation of numerous architectural gems such as the mighty guild halls in the Old Town lining both banks of the Limmat. Zurich is certainly rich – it is the largest city in Switzerland (pop. 380,000) and it has both the largest gold market and

BERN

Location: Western Switzerland (Canton of Bern)
Best time to travel: throughout the year
www.bern.ch
www.bern-incoming.ch

Once the largest city-state north of the Alps, Bern's historic center clearly reflects the chronological order of its different periods of expansion. The stately guild and townhouses with arcades extending for a total of 6 km (4 mi) are characteristic of the city center. Construction of the late Gothic St Vincent Cathedral began in 1421 and was only completed in 1573; the magnificent main portal was designed by Erhard Küng. The late-Gothic Town Hall was erected between 1406 and 1417 and subsequently renovated in 1942. The Heiliggeistkirche (Church of the Holy Spirit), from 1729, is one of the coun-

the fourth-largest stock exchange in the world. Its wealth is obvious from the "shopping de luxe" of the Bahnhofstrasse, where it is easy to spend more on a watch than most people earn in a year. Other architectural features include the Fraumünster church in the Old Town west of the river Limmat , which has a set of five windows by Marc Chagall, and next door, the 13th-century parish church of St Peter, with Europe's largest clock face. The Grossmünster on the other side of the river, its neo-Gothic tower cupolas dominating the cityscape, entered the annals of church history as the domain of the reformer Huldrych Zwingli (1484–1531).

The twin towers of Zurich's Great Minster dominate the skyline of the "smallest metropolis on earth", which is divided by the Limmat river near the northern end of Lake Zurich.

try's most important examples of Protestant baroque architecture. Bern's landmark, however, is the Zytgloggeturm (Clock Tower) city gate. The ensemble of lovely historic residential buildings in the Gerechtigkeitsgasse stands out from the multitude of beautiful buildings in Bern, and some of them date back to the 16th century. Bern's Renaissance fountains with their lovely expressive figures are also worth seeing, three of them having been created by the Freiburg sculptor Hans Gieng.

The Old Town of Bern is a mixture of mighty city gates and arcades. Shown here are the views along the Kramgasse and the Marktgasse, with the Käfigturm und Zytgloggeturm towers in the distance (page left and right respectively). The old town boasts one of the longest covered shopping promenades in Europe.

THE BERNESE OBERLAND

Location: Western Switzerland (Canton of Bern)
Best time to travel: throughout the year (October–April: Ski season)
www.berneroberland.ch

The Bernese Oberland is the cradle of Swiss tourism. Its popularity was instigated by three famous figures: Rousseau, Haller and Goethe. They sparked an enthusiasm for nature that became a trend among high society types to escape to the mountains. The first official "Unspunnenspiele" (a festival uniting town and country) took place near Interlaken in 1805, a huge open-air event with yodelers, Fahnenschwingen (flag throwing), Steinstossen (stone throwing), and traditional costume. Visitors arrived via Lake Thun, some – like the Rothschilds for instance – with their own boats. This is still a nice way to view the spectacular scenery. The perfect way to explore the region is making a day trip by train, bus and gondola.

The legendary trio of the Eiger (3,970 m/13,025 ft), Mönch (4,099 m/13,448 ft), and Jungfrau (4,158 m/13,642 ft), shown here from left to right with the "little" 2,345-m (7,694-ft) Männlicher in the foreground, have made the Jungfrau region the premier Alpine climbing area in the Bernese Oberland.

ENGADIN

Location: South-eastern Switzerland (Canton of Graubünden)
Best time to travel: throughout the year (Ski season: October–April)
www.engadin.stmoritz.ch
www.stmoritz.ch

"The Upper Engadin is the nicest place on earth. I don't readily talk of happiness, but I almost think I am happy here" (Thomas Mann). The scenery of the upper Inn valley is almost without compare: there is nothing cramped or oppressive up by the treeline in the mountains, just a broad, open horizon. The lakes of the Upper Engadin, each as beautiful as the next, lie in the middle of the valley, and the pine forests, illuminated in the golden sunshine of the fall, and the white, snow-capped peaks silhouetted against a deep azure sky make for the sort of Alpine picture that has been attracting nature enthusiasts here since the days of post coaches. The Lower Engadin between the Scharl and Trupchun valleys is the site of the Swiss National Park, opened on 1 August 1914, the oldest national park in Europe. The Morteratsch Glacier is the mightiest glacier in the Bernina Group.

St Mortiz cleverly markets itself as being on "top of the world".

THE ALETSCH GLACIER

Location: Bernese Alps, Southern Switzerland (Canton of Valais)
Best time to travel: throughout the year (Ski season: October–April)
www.jungfraualetsch.ch

The mighty flow of ice extending to the north-east between Konkordiaplatz (2,850 m/9,351 ft) near the Jungfraujoch and Riederalp (1,919 m/6,296 ft) reaches up to 1,800 m (1,968 yards) in width. What has been evident for a long while, however, is also to be seen at the Aletsch Glacier: reduction of mass, a visible sign of climate change. While the glaciers lost about one-third of their surface area and almost half of their total volume between the mid-19th-century and 1975, they have forfeited a further 25 per cent of their mass in the last 30 years. If the trend continues, then more than 75 per cent of the glaciers in the Alps will be gone by 2050. The ice does not only melt, it also migrates. The compacted ice moves down from the peaks and passes into the valleys, out of the so-called feeding areas and into the wear areas; a maximum of 1.5 m (5 ft) per day. A snowflake falling up on the Jungfraujoch onto the Aletsch Glacier will therefore become a drop of water again down below at the entrance to the Massa canyon after a journey probably lasting some 500 years.

The "Top of Europe", the upper end of Europe's highest rack and pinion railway on the Jungfraujoch (3,454 m/11,332 ft), has a superb view of the Great Aletsch Glacier, whose length of 24 km (15 mi) and area of some 118 sq km (46 sq mi) makes it Switzerland's largest. The whole area is part of the Jungfrau-Aletsch Protected Area, which was declared a UNESCO World Heritage site in 2001.

THE MATTERHORN

Location: Valais Alps, Southern Switzerland (Canton of Valais)
Best time to travel: throughout the year (Ski season: October–April)
www.zermatt.ch
www.ski-zermatt.com

What hasn't already been written about this mountain? Bombarded regularly with superlatives, the Matterhorn's incomparable shape is much vaunted, having been referred to as the "advertising mountain" due to its use in promoting just about everything. The Matterhorn adorns not only Swiss yoghurt containers and Belgian beer bottles, it has also found itself on wine labels and on Japanese confectionery, on a cigarette carton from Jamaica and even on a poster for a Rolling Stones European tour in 1976. Luis Trenker made an emotional film out of the tragic first ascent of the mountain (1865) by Edward Whymper, in which the four-man crew lost their lives, and in Zermatt the souvenir shops are full of Matterhorn kitsch. A mythical mountain and yet so much more than just pyramid-shaped rock, "Horu" (as it is called by locals) has brought great prosperity to the country village of Zermatt (1,616 m/5,302 ft). The hotel pioneer Alexander Seiler was the first to recognize the huge significance of this unique mountain backdrop for his tiny village. And indeed, the "mountain of mountains" has been captivating visitors since Whymper's time. They come from all over the world to marvel at this magnificent monument to Alpine altitudes, and some even come to climb it.

The Matterhorn with Riffel Lake in the foreground is a particularly beautiful sight. The normal route to the 4,478-m (14,692-ft) summit involves an ascent of the striking Hörnli Ridge.

AROUND LAKE GENEVA

Location: Western Switzerland (Canton of Geneva, Canton of Waadt)
Best time to travel: throughout the year (September/October: grape harvest on the Lavaux vineyard terraces)
www.geneve.ch
www.montreux-vevey.com
www.swissworld.org
www.lausanne.ch
www.chillon.ch

Geneva (Genève), with its Fontaine des Jet d'Eau shooting water 145 m (475 ft) into the air, lies along the banks of Lake Geneva between the Jura and the Savoy Alps. "Protestant Rome", where John Calvin propagated his rigorous notions of reform and Henri Dunant founded the Red Cross in 1864, is now a truly international city – a third of the population are foreign nationals, and more than 200 international organisations are based here, including the United Nations (UN) and the World Health Organisation (WHO). Apart from the diplomats, expensive watches, and cigars, Geneva has a number of attractions in stone: St Peter's Cathedral with its archeological sites and the adjacent Place du Bourg-de-Four, the well-stocked Museum of Art and History, the Palais des Nations, now the headquarters of the UN, and a monument to Jean-Jacques Rousseau, who was born here. Geneva is a traditional Alpine town as well, as featured in Konrad Witz's altar of St Peter of 1444, which is now in the Museum of Art. Peter's miraculous catch of fish is shown on Lake Geneva, with Mont Blanc in the background. Lausanne, the metropolis of the Waadtland area, lies on the northern shore, with its center surrounded by a series of hills covered in villas. The Cité, the Old Town, with its eye-catching Gothic

cathedral, can also be reached by funicular railway from the port area of Ouchy. Consecrated in 1275, the cathedral is considered the most beautiful of its time in Switzerland. The northern shore of Lake Geneva between Lausanne's eastern city limits and the Château de Chillon (immortalized by Byron in his ballad *The Prisoner of Chillon*) is a 30-km (19-mi) stretch of perhaps the finest scenery in Switzerland. Wine has been cultivated on the terraces of Lavaux for at least a millennium, and the locals maintain that three heat sources warm the grapes: the warmth of the sun, the reflection of the sunbeams from the surface of the lake, and the stored heat in the dry stone walls, which release their energy at night. The Gutedel grape grown on the shores of Lake Geneva is known locally as *Chasselas* or *Fendant*, and the modern terraces were first laid out by Benedictine and Cistercian monks in the 11th and 12th centuries. Mont Blanc can be seen from Geneva and is only an hour's drive from the city centre.

Famed for its location on a rock overlooking Lake Geneva, the Château de Chillon (opposite) is one of the most popular historic buildings in Switzerland.

Geneva (top), which lies on Lake Geneva at the mouth of the Rhône, is the second-largest city in Switzerland after Zurich.

The Château de Chillon (middle), the epitome of a romantic lakeside castle, lies about 5 km (3 mi) south-east of Montreux, a cosmopolitan resort on the north-east shore famed for its Jazz Festival and immortalized in Deep Purple's *Smoke on the Water.*
Lausanne (below), similarly located on the northern shores of Lake Geneva, is the seat of the Federal Court and the International Olympic Committee.

TICINO

Location: Southern Switzerland (Canton of Ticino)
Best time to travel: throughout the year
www.bellinzona.ch
www.ascona-locarno.com
www.lagomaggiore.net
www.lugano.ch

Ticino is a popular holiday region, and some may ask themselves whether this is in fact the southern part of Switzerland or the northern part of Italy. At any rate, the Alpine world here already exudes an air of Mediterranean promise. Hermann Hesse described Ticino, his adopted home, as "wonderfully rich and beautiful", and it is surely the diversity of the region that still fascinates visitors even today. The heart of Ticino beats on the Swiss side of Lake Maggiore. One of the most beautiful towns on the north shore of the lake is Locarno, not far from where the Maggia River flows into the lake from its high mountain source. Locarno has been famous since 1946 for its annual film festival. With approximately 2,300 hours of sunshine a year, the people of Locarno enjoy the mildest climate in Switzerland. The historic center of the town, first documented around the year 789, was originally directly on the lake, but over the course of the centuries, the Maggia has deposited immense amounts of sediment between Locarno and Ascona that today occupies about half the former width of the lake. In around 1900, Ascona was still a peaceful, sleepy fishing village. But then two foreigners settled here, disgruntled with their hectic lives in the city – Belgian Henri Oedenkoven, son of an industrialist, and his partner, German pianist Ida Hofmann. They called Ascona's local mountain the "Monte Verità", or "the mountain of truth", and founded a "vegetabilist cooperative" to help in their individual quests for happiness. Light, air, and love

played an important role in their mission along with nudism, theosophy, emancipation, and loads of raw foods. The days of the cooperative are long gone, but Locarno's much smaller western neighbor clearly still enjoys something of a reputation as a mecca for the avantgarde – and for art. It is also still a very good place to pursue happiness: the mountains, wonderful light and fresh air at least are guaranteed. Etruscans and Gauls had already settled on Lake Lugano long before the Romans came. The lake is around 35 km (22 mi) long, up to 3 km (2 mi) wide, and up to 288 m (945 ft) deep. A view of the lake from one of Lugano's two mountains – Monte Bré at 925 m (3,035 ft) or Monte San Salvatore at 912 m (2,992 ft), which rises like a sugarloaf out of the water – is spectacular. The largest part of the lake, which is 217 m (712 ft) above sea level, belongs to the Swiss canton of Ticino while the smaller part belongs to the Italian provinces of Como and Varese.

The Castello Grande (top), the largest of the three castles at Bellinzona, was built on the hill within the city in the 13th century and extended by the Milanese Duke of Sforza between 1486 and 1489, to keep the Confederacy in check.

Bottom: the pilgrimage church of Madonna del Sasso (left) on the wooded Belvedere hills has become a symbol of Locarno; Lugano (middle) alternated with Locarno and Bellinzona as the capital of Ticnino for six years at a time between 1803 and 1878. It is now considered the capitale morale, the "true" capital of Ticino, and the region around Lake Lugano with its rolling hills and cypress trees is known as "the Tuscany of Switzerland".

Ascona (right), Locarno's neighbor to the west, was still a sleepy fishing village as recently as 1900.

VIENNA

Location: Eastern Austria
Best time to travel: throughout the year
www.wien.info
www.wien.gv.at

ST CHARLES' CHURCH
St Charles' Church is the symbolic building of those euphoric centuries after the second Turkish Siege in 1683, when Vienna was transformed into the elegant metropolis that it is today. It was commissioned in 1713 by the emperor of the same name, Charles VI, at the end of a plague epidemic. Its creators, Fischer von Erlach Sr and Jr, combined the classic forms of Greek, Roman and Byzantine architecture to construct the church. A temple portico rises up under the patina-green dome, while triumphal pillars decorated with spiral reliefs and a bell tower soar up on both sides. A magnificent dome fresco by J. M. Rottmayr adorns the oval interior.

ST STEPHEN'S CATHEDRAL
St Stephen's Cathedral, Vienna's most important religious building and the city's emblem, is visible from afar and affectionately known by locals as "Steffl". It is a masterpiece of stonemasonry made from 20,000 cu m (706,293 cu ft) of sandstone. It dates back a good 750 years. Its west front still originates from the previous Romanesque building; the rest is High Gothic. The southern spire, the third-highest in

Europe, measures 137 m (449 ft) and soars gloriously towards the heavens. From its viewing deck, which is reached by climbing 343 steps, you get a panoramic view of the city.

IMPERIAL CRYPT

From the early 17th century, the Habsburg rulers and their next of kin were buried in a total of 138 metal caskets in the deep vaults here, traditionally guarded by Capuchin friars, at the foot of the rather unimposing Ordenskirche. Maria Theresa and her husband Francis Stephen of Lorraine were laid to rest here – in a double sarcophagus that was lavishly adorned with life-size figures in rococo style. Next to them lies the reformist Emperor Joseph II in a simple copper casket much more in keeping with his humble character. Emperor Franz Joseph I also has his final resting place here, as do his wife Elisabeth of Bavaria (known more commonly as "Sissi"), his son Rudolf, his brother Maximilian, who was murdered in Mexico, and, from 1989, Austria's last empress: Zita.

St Stephen's Cathedral (top left) stands proudly in the heart of the city. The Hofburg (top right) is a remnant of the magnificence brought to the city by the emperors of the Hapsburg dynasty. The *Gloriette* in the grounds of Schönbrunn Palace gives a good idea of the size of the "Austrian Versailles".

SALZBURG

Location: Northern Austria
Best time to travel: throughout the year
www.salzburg.info
www.salzburgerland.com

Hugo von Hofmannsthal called the Salzburg state capital the "heart of the heart of Europe". This city not only produced Wolfgang Amadeus Mozart, but has also inspired artists from all over the world for centuries. The Hohensalzburg Fortress, Cathedral, Collegiate Church, residence, St Peter's and Mirabell Palace – all urban works of art on the Salzach between the hills of the Kapuzinerberg, Mönchsberg and Festungsberg, dazzle the senses with their intense baroque atmosphere. The urban gem that is the Getreidegasse largely has Archbishop Wolf Dietrich von Raitenau to thank for its present-day appearance. Around 1600, the Archbishop had half of the city's medieval center demolished and the expansive central open spaces laid out. His successor, who was just as extravagantly minded, subsequently completed the unique architectural ensemble.

The Hohensalzburg fortress stands serenely on the Mönchsberg as the Old Town of Salzburg huddles at its feet.

LAKE ATTER

Location: Northern Austria (Upper Austria)
Best time to travel: April–October
www.attersee.at
www.salzkammergut.at

Lake Atter is about 20 km (12 mi) long, up to 3 km (2 mi) wide and about 170 m (560 ft) deep, making it the largest lake in both the Salzkammergut and the Austrian Alps. The town of the same name was an imperial residence in the 9th century, and a castle was built here for the Archbishop of Salzburg 400 years later.

Only a narrow strip of forest separates Lake Atter from Lake Mond. The fantastic panorama visible from the 1,782-m (5,846-ft) summit of the Schafberg includes both lakes and the magnificent 3,000-m (9,800-ft) peaks of the Alps.

HALLSTATT

Location: Northern Austria (Upper Austria)
Best time to travel: throughout the year (Ski season: October–April)
www.hallstatt.net

When Johann Georg Ramsauer commenced the first excavations on the pre-history of Central Europe in the shadow of the Dachstein Mountains in 1846, he and his team unearthed upwards of ten thousand priceless discoveries documenting the transition from the European Bronze Age to the early Ice Age.

The pretty little town of Hallstatt (left) on the south-western shores of the Hallstätter See has lent its name to an entire culture; excavations between 1846 and 1849 uncovered a burial site of considerable size dating back to the Iron Age (800–500 BC).

HOHE TAUERN

iLocation: Central Austria
Best time to travel: throughout the year (Ski season: October–April)
www.nationalpark-hohetauern.at

There are six national parks in Austria. The one in the Hohe Tauern is by far the largest (1,836 sq km/709 sq mi) and also the highest. This region supplies the headstream of the Salzach (which flows through Salzburg) and the Isel, as well as two of the mightiest waterfalls in Europe: the 380-m (1,247-ft) high Krimmler Falls in Upper Pinzgau, and the Umbal Falls in the gorgeous Virgental valley. Some 150 years ago, mountaineering pioneer Ignaz von Kürsinger described the Hohe Tauern as a "magical world" of mountain pastures, rock and ice, "full of great, wild natural scenery and beautiful flowers".

Lying at an elevation of 2,464 m (8,084 ft) the Wangenitzsee lake (top right) provides a habitat for ibexes, marmots (top left), bearded vultures, mountain goats, and golden eagles (bottom right). Bottom left: Campion makes the park more beautiful still.

GROSSGLOCKNER

Location: Hohe Tauern, Central Austria
Best time to travel: throughout the year (Ski season: October–April)
www.grossglockner.at

The Grossglockner, Austria's highest peak, is a mighty 3,798 m (12,461 ft) and best admired from the lookout on Kaiser Franz Josefs Höhe. The high alpine road named after it, which leads into the Salzburg Fusch Valley from Heiligenblut, winds its way through 26 hairpin turns and over 60 bridges to an altitude of 2,500 m (8,203 ft). Built in the 1930s, it has brought more than fifty million visitors closer to these exhilarating mountains since its opening in 1935. The 50-km (31-mi) stretch of road is only open from April to November, depending on the snow conditions, and features a number of museums, educational tracks and signposted viewing points.

The Pasterze (bottom), the largest glacier in the Eastern Alps, lies at the feet of the Grossglockner (top) on the border between Carinthia and the East Tyrol.

MELK

Location: Central Austria (Lower Austria)
Best time to travel: throughout the year
www.stiftmelk.at

After the tribulations of the Reformation, the Thirty Years' War, and skirmishes with the Turks and the Bohemians, Melk Abbey still stands serenely at the farthest western end of the Wachau valley, an incomparable guardian of the Danube, a masterpiece of baroque architecture, and the true epitome of monastic majesty. Its great importance is due not only to its imposing exterior (the southern façade is 362 m/1,188 ft long) but also its more than 900 years of history. Initially just a base camp for the exploration of the lands further along the Danube, in the Middle Ages the abbey attracted leading

WACHAU

Location: Central Austria (Lower Austria)
Best time to travel: April–October (September/Oktober: grape harvest)
www.wachau.at
www.niederoesterreich.at

The steep, narrow valley road that leads through Wachau begins in the west with the grandiose, baroque monastic residence of Melk which, with its imposing twin-spired domed church, is the "crown jewel" of this area. A number of castles, castle ruins, palaces and churches adorn the river valley between the pretty villages of Obstbauerndorf and Winzerdorf. This area is also home to the small township of Willendorf, made famous by what was the most important discovery from the Old Stone Age – the Venus of Willendorf. After the wine-growing towns of Spitz and Weissenkirchen you reach Dürnstein,

scholars and philosophers who published seminal theological and scientific tracts here. Modern visitors will be bowled over by the the baroque magnificence of the abbey chapel and the library, or the imperial apartments and the Marble Room. The guided tour through the museum-like rooms of the monastery will also bring the history of the Order to life. However, Melk Abbey is not just a museum – some 30 Benedictine monks still live, work, and pray here. Over the course of the years, Melk Abbey has traditionally been associated with two tasks – one is teaching and education, and the other parochial care. The two schools here are open to pupils of all faiths.

The Benedictine abbey at Melk is an outstanding guardian of the Danube valley (right, the monastery library with countless medieval manuscripts).

where a hike up to the monastery beneath the castle ruins is worth the effort. The slender late-baroque tower of the monastery is one of the most elegant of its kind. The valley widens after Dürnstein, and provides a clear view as far as Krems, the medieval town with the Gothic buildings of the Gozzo-Burg, the Dominican Church and the Church of the Piarist Order. The Göttweig monastery perched ceremoniously on a hilltop marks the end of the Wachau Valley.

Dürnstein (left), with its ruined castle, Renaissance palace, baroque collegiate church, and former Poor Clares convent, has become an iconic symbol of the Wachau valley.
The wine-growing town of Weissenkirchen (right) with its imposing 14th-century fortified church lies only a short distance from Dürnstein.

ROME

Location: Central Italy (Lazio)
Best time to travel: throughout the year
http://en.turismoroma.it

The center of the present-day metropolis of Rome – located at a bend in the Tiber River – was first settled around 3,000 years ago. The people who settled here left traces of their civilizations from the very start, providing Rome with tremendous appeal for anyone interested in art, architectural and cultural history. The presence of the city's mythical founders, Romulus and Remus, can be felt during a walk through its fascinatig streets just as much as that of the other well-known Roman emperors and popes who resided in this, the capital city of Christianity, during the Renaissance and baroque periods. More than any other city, Rome is testimony to the advanced development of European culture and it is here that some of the deepest roots of western civilization are to be found. In ancient times, there was a temple on the Capitoline Hill that was dedicated to Jupiter, king of the gods. It was reached by a winding path leading south-east from the Forum. Today you climb the hill from the west on a flight of stairs designed by Michelangelo. At the top is a piazza, also designed by Michelangelo, and which is paved with a geometric pattern. The bronze equestrian sculpture of Marcus Aurelius in the

center of the square is the only one of its kind to have escaped being melted down in the Middle Ages because the rider was thought to be Constantine I, defender of Christianity. The Palazzo Senatorio on the piazza is the seat of the mayor of Rome. Located between the Palatine Hill and the Capitoline Hill, the Roman Forum and the other buildings dating from the 6th century BC were the site of religious ceremonies and political gatherings. The fall of the Roman Empire saw the deterioration of Forum buildings such as the triumphal arch of Septimius Severus, the Temple of Saturn, and the Temple of Vespasian in front of the baroque Santi Luca e Martina Church, which then fell into disuse.

Protection of the historic legacy of the city of Rome (opposite: the Via Appia Antika, commonly said to be the "queen of the long roads", which once connected Rome to Brindisi, Apulia in southeast Italy, and, below, the famous Colosseum of Rome. This page, main picture: the Forum Romanorum, located between the Palatine Hill and the Capitoline Hill and the Pantheon (bottom, left), and the Spanish Steps (right) was a matter of concern even in late antiquity. The Western Roman emperor Majorian decreed in 458 that "everything contributing to the glory of the city should be kept in good order through the diligence of the citizenry".

THE VATICAN

Location: Rome, Central Italy
Best time to travel: throughout the year
www.vatican.va
www.vaticanstate.va

Laid out in 1937, the Via della Conciliazione is not just a literal connection between Rome and the Vatican, it is also a symbol that the Papacy, which had had to relinquish its position as a secular ruler after the unification of Italy in 1870, had, with the Lateran Pacts of 1929, agreed to a reconciliation (conciliazione) between state and church. The head of the Church at least managed to retain the title of the "Sovereign of the State of the Vatican City". Facing St Peter's Square is the mighty façade of St Peter's Basilica, officially known as San Pietro in Vaticano which was built in the 16th century. The present-day building is some 45 m (148 ft) high and 115 m (377 ft) wide. The height of the lantern crowning the dome is 132 m (433 ft) and the interior covers an area of 15,000 sq m (16,145 sq ft). It can accommodate around 60,000 worshippers, and with this building the Papacy sought to provide a foundation for its claim to be the one true representative of God on earth. The square in front of the church was designed by Bernini and built between 1656 and 1667, the elliptical area is 240 m (790 ft) long and surrounded by a 17-m (56-ft) wide colonnade of 284 pillars topped with the statues of 140 saints. The most famous artists of the age were involved in its construction: architects Bramante and Sangallo, sculptors Bernini and Maderno, and master painters Michelangelo and Raphael. St Peter's grave is said to be located in the so-called "grotto" beneath the church.

The Sistine Chapel, commissioned in 1477 by Pope Sixtus IV, was not just a place of worship but also a fortress with walls that are 3 m (10 ft) thick. It continues to serve as the venue for the papal conclave, in which the College of Cardinals elects a new pope. Upon the completion of construction work in 1480, Lorenzo de' Medici, the "ruler" of Florence, sent a number of his city's leading artists to Rome to decorate the interior of the chapel with frescoes. The artists included Pietro Perugino, Sandro Botticelli and Domenico Ghirlandaio. The walls were decorated with scenes from the lives of Jesus and Moses, while the ceiling of the dome was transformed into a blue sky with golden stars. It was only later (from 1508 to 1512) that it was painted over by Michelangelo to include his famous frescos of the Creation and the Fall of Man.

St Peter's Square and Basilica compete with the Sistine Chapel and its frescos by Michelangelo. The latter is famous for its architecture, evocative of Solomon's Temple of the Old Testament. The Vatican is watched over by the Papal Swiss Guard.

LAKE GARDA

Location: Northern Italy
Best time to travel:
April–September
www.lagodigarda.it
www.gardatrentino.it

The Upper Italian lakes, include Lake Garda, Lake Como, much of Lake Maggiore, Lake Orta, and a few others. Lake Garda was known as *Lacus benacus* in antiquity, after the Neptune-like divinity Benacus. The lake, 54 km (33 mi) long and up to 346 m (1,135 ft) deep, is fed by the Sarca, Ponale and Campione rivers. It has long been a popular holiday destination and is particularly popular among windsurfers.

A place to yearn for: Gardone on Lake Garda. The tower of the Grand Hotel Gardone, which was built on the lake shore in 1884, can be seen in the middle of the image.

LAKE COMO

Location: Northern Italy
Best time to travel:
April–September
www.lagodicomo.com
www.turismo.como.it

Lake Como is 51 km (32 mi) long and 4 km (2.5 mi) at its widest point and is situated between the Lugarno and Bergamo Alps. The lake is also known as Lario in Italian. Bellagio is the loveliest town on this stunning body of water, carved into the narrow valley by the Adda glacier and still fed by the Adda River. Comer divides into the Como and Lecco arms to the south. The resort town of Varenna lies on the widest section of the lake, and from here there is a ferry connection to Bellagio and Menaggio.

The picturesque town of Bellagio is known as the "Pearl of Lake Lario".

THE DOLOMITES

Location: Southern Alps, Northern Italy
Best time to travel: throughout the year (Ski season: October–April)
www.infodolomiti.it
dolomiti.discover-eu.com

The Tethys Ocean is said to have once covered the area where the towering Dolomites now stand. The Dolomites have a total area of about 1,419 sq km (548 sq mi) and the Marmolada (3,343 m/10,968 ft) is the highest peak. The "Three Peaks" or the Rosengartenspitze are probably best known for their charming appearance, although the Kesselkogel, the highest peak in the Rosengarten group, is 3,004 m (9,812 ft) high. The Dolomites is a region of opposites, with lush Alpine meadows alternating with jagged rocky peaks, and plains filled with moraine. Such variation is explained by the different ways these local landscapes were created: some are fossilized and elevated coral reefs, others are volcanic rock. There are plenty of glaciated surfaces to be found in the Dolomites as well as the *karst* scenery typical of limestone areas, and the Dolomites are an excellent example of a landscape whose genesis can be documented by the geology and the fossil record. This genesis is still ongoing and evident in every flood, mud slide, rockfall, and avalanche which re-shapes the surface.

Top: the most famous peaks in the Dolomites lie in the far eastern reaches of the chain. Although they are known as the "Three Peaks" there are actually five of them. Bottom: "The most beautiful mountain range in the world? The Dolomites!" – according to Le Corbusier. The area enclosed by the Eisack, Marmolada, the Puster Valley and Feltre is full of beautiful natural spectacles.

VENICE

Location: North-eastern Italy (Veneto)
Best time to travel: throughout the year (February: Carnival)
www.turismovenezia.it
www.comune.venezia.it

Make way for a city about which the writer Harold Brodkey said it is "a country in itself ... a city of independent will". Two pillars – a third collapsed into the sea as it was being erected – form a monumental entrance to the Piazzetta opening onto the lagoon. Originally looted from the Phoenician city of Tyre, they were installed in the first year of his reign by the Doge Sebastiano Ziani, a diplomat and merchant who had become rich by assiduously collecting interest payments. From the Piazzetta at the Doge's Palace it is easy to see the San Giorgio Maggiore Church situated on a small island in the Canale della Giudecca – one of more than 100 islands in Venice. The relics of St Stephanus of Constantinople are said to have been brought here in 1109, the result being that the church and monastery adjacent to the grave of the apostle Mark subsequently became an important pilgrimage site in the lagoon city. In 1223, the monastery was destroyed by an earthquake, but its buildings were rebuilt between the 15th and 17th centuries and those are what you see today. St Mark's cathedral features five mosaic portal niches that form the eastern end of St Mark's

Square. The square is the site of a number of the principal tourist attractions in the city, including the Palazzo Ducale, the campanile, the Torre dell'Orologico (clock tower), and the Quadri and Florian cafés. The close connections with the Byzantine Empire meant that Venice's main church, built between 976 and 1094, had the stylistic influences of that region. Starting in 9th century, the Doge's Palace was the residence of the Venetian head of state and the seat of the Venetian government. The present day appearance of this marble and stone masterpiece dates from the 14th and 15th centuries. The Canale Grande is roughly 4 km (2.4 mi) long and lined with magnificent palaces built and owned by nearly five centuries of merchants and nobility. It is the main traffic artery in Venice upon which a throng of gondolas and *vaporetti* make their way. The end of the canal is marked on the right bank by the baroque Santa Maria della Salute Church with its wonderful dome. The roofed Rialto Bridge (above) spans the canal at about its halfway point. Originally a wooden bridge, between 1588 and 1592 it was built of stone with its present design.

Opposite, from top: looking between the gondolas towards the Giudecca San Giorgio Maggiore, the Piazzetta (middle), and the Rialto Bridge (bottom). This page: the Basilica di San Marco.

MILAN

Location: Northern Italy (Lombardy)
Best time to travel: throughout the year
www.turismo.milano.it

During Late antiquity the Roman Empire was at times ruled from Milan, and the city became one of the focal points of the new Italy in the Middle Ages. Its greatest sightseeing attraction is the cathedral (left), a masterpiece of Italian Gothic 157 m (515 ft) in length and 92 m (302 ft) wide. It is one of the world's largest Gothic churches and the marble façade is decorated with no less than 2,245 statues. The Piazza del Duomo forms the heart of Milan and is linked to the Piazza della Scala by the Galleria Vittorio Emanuele II, which has been an exemplary model for many modern shopping centers.

The majestic cathedral of Milan

FERRARA

Location: Northern Italy (Emilia-Romagna)
Best time to travel: throughout the year
www.ferraraterraeacqua.it
www.ferraraturismo.it

The Este, one of the oldest aristocratic families in Italy, ruled Ferrara from the 13th to the 16th century, and under them, Ferrara attracted such leading artists as Antonio Pisanello. The Palazzo Comunale opposite the cathedral (built 1135–1485) is connected to the Castello Estense by a gallery whose rooms are adorned with precious frescos. *Maestri* from the Ferrara school created an exceptional cycle of frescos in the Palazzo Schifanoia, one of the Este's town houses.

Ferrara's cathedral of San Giorgio has an impressive marble façade.

CINQUE TERRE

Location: North-western Italy (Liguria)
Best time to travel: April–October
www.cinqueterre.com

The five villages (Cinque Terre) of Monterosso, Vernazza, Corniglia, Manarola, and Riomaggiore are simply striking, clinging to the cliffs and bays of the steep Ligurian coast between Levanto and Portovenere. Though hard to believe, there is still no direct road along the coast that connects the five sleepy hamlets – but perhaps it is for the better.

Adjoining the port in Vernazza there is a small piazza with brightly painted houses and the Romanesque church of Santa Maria di Antiochia (1318). Parts of the Genoese fortifications have survived to the present day.

RAVENNA

Location: North-eastern Italy (Emilia-Romagna)
Best time to travel: throughout the year
www.turismo.ra.it
www.turismo.ravenna.it

Ravenna was once the capital of the Western Roman Empire, later becoming the center of power of the Goths, before developing into the focus of the Byzantine part of Italy until it was conquered by the Lombards in 751. Several buildings from that era survive in nearly original form, and feature fascinating mosaics. They are among the most important remnants of early Christianity.

San Vitale Church was built close to the old city wall between 525 and 547 and closely modeled on the Hagia Sophia in Constantinople (now Istanbul).

PISA

Location: North-western Italy (Tuscany)
Best time to travel: throughout the year
www.comune.pisa.it
www.pisaunicaterra.it

In 1063, a site just beyond the city walls of the time saw work begin on a cathedral that had been designed by the architect Buscheto. Its magnificent, 35-m (116-ft) long façade was designed by Rainaldo and the bronze doors of the Porta di San Ranieri were created by Bonanno Pisano in 1180. The ornately decorated coffered ceiling in the vaulting of the nave dates back to the 16th century and the free-standing, cylindrical *campanile* was begun by Bonanno in 1174 but began to lean in 1185, at which point only the first three floors had been completed. One hundred years would pass before any efforts were made to counter the leaning by creating a significant slant in the opposite direction, and it was feared for many centuries that the tower would collapse. It has since been underpinned with new foundations. The decoration of the baptistery (1152–1358) is a good example of the transition phase between the Romanesque and the Gothic periods. The cathedral features the characteristic light and dark stone stripes of the Pisan style. The most eye-catching feature of the interior is the mosaic by Francesco di Simone and Cimabue in the apse depicting the seated Christ, flanked by Mary and John. The use of white Carrara marble and the common architectonic elements (such as arcades and colonnades) allow all the buildings on the cathedral square to blend together in a cohesive whole.

Right: the cathedral, the Leaning Tower, and the Fontana dei Putti. Above top, the Piazza by night; bottom, a view of the nave.

FLORENCE

Location: Northern Italy (Tuscany)
Best time to travel:
throughout the year
www.firenzeturismo.it
www.firenze-tourism.com

The Tuscan capital on the Arno River is considered to be the birthplace of the Renaissance and of humanism, which began around 600 years ago and is of paramount importance for the history of European art. The elevated Piazzale Michelangelo provides a stunning view of the city including the mighty red dome of Santa Maria del Fiore built by Filippo Brunelleschi between 1420 and 1436. Upon seeing the baptistery Michelangelo is purported to have said that, "only the gates of paradise could be so wonderful". The church, which dates back to the 4th century and is the location of Dante's baptism, is among the oldest buildings in the city. Magnificent 13th-century mosaics adorn the cupola above the baptismal font. The baptistery is also renowned for its splendid portals depicting scenes from the Old and New Testaments. Construction of the Santa Maria del Fiore Cathedral began in 1296. Consecrated in 1436, Florence's most famous landmark is 153 m (502 ft) long, 90 m (295 ft) wide in the transept and, with the lantern on the octagonal dome, 116 m (381 ft) high, making it the fourth largest church in the Occident after the cathedrals in Rome, London and Milan. Construction of the free-standing bell tower, almost 85 m (279 ft) in height and clad in marble of different hues, was begun by Giotto in 1334. The secular center of Florence is the Piazza della Signoria, home to the Loggia dei Lanzi, with its priceless sculptures, and the Palazzo Vecchio, the seat of the mighty Medici government, which was completed in 1322. The Medici family determined the city's fate for generations. Their rise began with

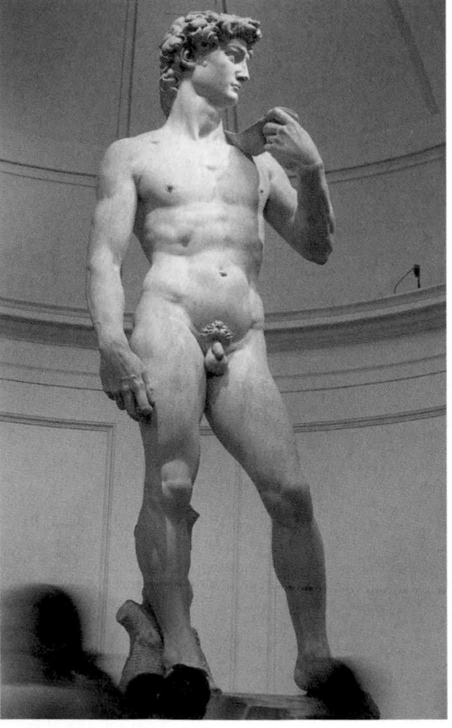

Giovanni (1360–1429), who was able to increase his fortune through banking, the Pope being his best customer. The Uffizi, begun in 1560, was initially used as administrative buildings for the Medicis. Only goldsmiths used to be permitted to ply their trade on this world-famous bridge with its tiny shops. In Roman times a wooden bridge spanned the Arno here. The Palazzo Pitti was begun in 1457 for the banker Luca Pitti and completed in 1819. It combines several styles due to its centuries of building phases. In 1550, the Medicis made the palace their main residence. The adjacent Boboli Garden from 1590 is a gem of Italian garden design. Today the palace and garden are home to seven museums and galleries, including the world famous Galleria Palatina. This Dominican church was built in the 13th century and is famous for the many frescos in its choir chapel. San Lorenzo is one of the oldest churches in Florence. The first structure was consecrated in 393; the second was built in 1059; and Brunelleschi renovated the church in 1419. This imposing complex is the final resting place of the many members of the Medici family. It includes the Cappella dei Principi, designed in 1604, and its crypt, as well as the Sagrestia Nuova, the new sacristy.

There is a magnificent view of Florence from the Piazzale Michelangelo. The city skyline includes the giant dome of the cathedral, the Palazzo Vecchio and their respective bell towers.

Below from left: the original of Michelangelo's monumental sculpture of David can now be admired in the Galleria dell'Accademia. The Hall of Five Hundred on the first floor of the Palazzo Vecchio is adorned with city views and battle scenes by Vasari and his pupils.

VOLTERRA

Location: North-western Italy (Tuscany)
Best time to travel: throughout the year
www.comune.volterra.pi.it
www.volterratur.it

The former Etruscan town of Volterra is situated about 45 km (30 mi) from the coast on a cliff amidst the Tuscan hills. Excavations indicate that the town was extremely prosperous during the 4th century BC. A 7-km (4-mi) long wall encompassing fields and pastures surrounded Volterra at the time, meaning the residents were able to fend for themselves when under siege.

Volterra has a magnificent location overlooking the Cecina Valley. The picturesque *balze* – rocky clefts and scree slopes – are the result of centuries of erosion.

SAN GIMIGNANO

Location: Northern Italy (Tuscany)
Best time to travel: throughout the year
www.sangimignano.com
www.turismo.intoscana.it

Seen from afar, San Gimignano looks like a hedgehog and you could be forgiven for assuming that the many fortifications were intended to deter outside enemies. In fact, they are much more related to the internal rivalries between aristocratic dynasties; these families built the tower houses in order to outdo one another.

Only 15 of San Gimignano's 72 original towers are still standing. They stand guard over the Piazza della Cisterna in the center of the Old Town, giving San Gimignano its characteristic skyline.

SIENA

Location: Northern Italy (Tuscany)
Best time to travel: throughout the year (July/August: Palio di Siena)
www.terresiena.it

Siena was originally an Etruscan settlement, later became a Roman colony (Saena Iulia), and eventually sided with the Ghibellines in the Middle Ages, thus becoming Florence's arch rival. The city reached the height of its political power in the 13th century, after which it was ruled by a council of nine merchants between 1287 and 1355. Siena was conquered by the Spanish in 1555, who then ceded it to the Grand Duchy of Tuscany. The historic city, which has survived almost entirely intact, is dominated by the Gothic cathedral.

The Piazza del Campo with its Palazzo Pubblico und Torre del Mangia is the heart of the city.

LUCCA

Location: North-western Italy (Tuscany)
Best time to travel: throughout the year
www.luccatourist.it
www.luccaportal.it

Lucca originally developed on a tiny island in the marshes of Serchio. Situated on the Via Francigena, Lucca enjoyed economic importance even as a Roman colony. The fortifications of the town began in 1544, and anyone wanting to reach the city center today has to pass through one of the 11 fortified gates. The city wall, which is 4 km (2.4 mi) in length and up to 30 m (98 ft) thick, has trees growing on it.

The buildings surrounding the Piazza del Mercato were constructed around the site of the former Roman amphitheater.

CHIANTI, MAREMMA, MASSA MARITTIMA

Location: Northern Italy (Tuscany)
Best time to travel: April–October (September/October: grape harvest)
www.chiantiturismo.it
www.maremmaturismo.com
www.massamarittima.info

CHIANTI
The center of the Chianti region lies north of Siena. Extensive vineyards, wine estates and attractive cypress and pine alleys characterize the scenery. And yes, Chianti Classico wine estates with their Gallo Nero – black cockerel – emblem as a quality guarantee are everywhere, tucked into misty valleys down narrow country roads. The turning point for the region came in 1841, when Bettino Ricasoli developed his idea of an "original" chianti at Brolio Castle, and it was he who established the best blend of grapes.

MAREMMA, MASSA MARITTIMA
Maremma, the coastal region between Livorno and Monte Argentario, has been settled since Etruscan times. The Romans were also able to cultivate the area, although their drainage systems later fell into disrepair and were forgotten.

The rolling hills of typical Chianti scenery in the morning light at sunrise (top). Massa Marittima (bottom) became a bishop's see in the 12th or 13th century, and a few medieval buildings are still standing here.

CRETE, VAL D'ORCIA, MONTEPULCIANO

Location: Northern Italy (Tuscany)
Best time to travel: April–October (September/October: grape harvest)
www.turismo.intoscana.it
www.valdorcia.it
www.montepulciano.com

CRETE
"Crete" , not to be confused with the island, is an area to the south-east of Siena, between Vescona and Asciano. It lures with its unique and at times lunar landscape, known as the Crete Senesi. The grey and yellow boulders, a result of erosion, are still a beautiful feature of this surrealist lunar landscape. Here – and a little further south in the Val d'Orcia in particular – was where the first landscape artists found inspiration for their frescoes.

VAL D'ORCIA
The Val d'Orcia – roughly 50 km (31 mi) south of Siena – embodies a Renaissance landscape. Over the centuries, graphic depictions of this area had a major influence in the history of European art.

MONTEPULCIANO
Situated on top of a picturesque hill between Valdichiana and the Val d'Orcia, Montepulciano at 605 m (1,985 ft) is one of the highest towns in Tuscany.

Cypresses, lonely farmhouses, and a little church on a hill add up to typical Tuscan scenery (top, Crete; middle, Val d'Orcia). San Biagio (bottom) near Montepulciano.

URBINO

Location: Central eastern Italy (Marche)
Best time to travel: throughout the year
www.turismo.pesarourbino.it
www.isairon.it

Perched upon two hills in the Marche, Urbino enjoyed its heyday back in the 15th century, when important Renaissance artists and scholars made it Italy's center of culture and science. Under the Montefeltro dynasty the artists of the age created an architectural ensemble of Renaissance buildings, the homogeneity of which is unique.

The town's major building is the Palazzo Ducale (now in use as an art gallery), which was transformed from an old fortress into a extensive Renaissance palace starting in 1444.

ORVIETO

Location: Central Italy (Umbria)
Best time to travel: throughout the year
www.orvietoturismo.com

Orvieto's origins go back to Etruscan times when the town was settled above the Paglia Valley. During the course of some 3,000 years of human activity here, a labyrinth of caves both large and small has developed within the depths of the underlying mountain, interconnected via stairs and passages. The town's inhabitants also dug into the soft rock to remove "pozzolan", which can be mixed with water to make a cement-like material.

Orvieto cathedral is considered one of the most beautiful in Italy. It took 500 years to build and was not completed until the end of the 17th century.

ASSISI

Location: Central Italy (Umbria)
Best time to travel: throughout the year
www.assisionline.com
www.bellaumbria.net

St Francis of Assisi was born here in 1182 and founded the mendicant Franciscan order in 1210. He was canonized in 1228, two years after his death, the same year that work began on the construction of the Basilica di San Francesco where he was buried in 1230. The church, which consists of an upper and lower basilica, is decorated with magnificent frescoes – it is considered to be Italy's largest church of artworks.

Situated on a rocky promontory beneath the summit of Monte Subasio, Assisi, Italy's principal pilgrimage site, can be seen from all around.

PERUGIA

Location: Central Italy (Umbria)
Best time to travel: throughout the year
turismo.comune.perugia.it
www.bellaumbria.net

Perugia, the capital of Umbria, is situated on a range of hills between the Tiber Valley and Lake Trasimeno. It was an important town even in Etruscan times and remains so today, a fact evidenced by its university and the historical buildings that give Perugia's Old Town its very special atmosphere, with narrow, often covered alleyways, and splendid squares.

The Piazza IV Novembre and the Palazzo dei Priori lie at the heart of the Old Town. The Fontana Maggiore was built in 1278, and the fountain is still fed with water from the hills around the town.

NAPLES

Location: South-western Italy (Campania)
Best time to travel: throughout the year
www.inaples.it
www.comune.napoli.it

The historic center of Naples, capital of the province of the same name, dates back to the Greek settlement of Partenope, whose Old Town was eventually expanded with a new town ("Neapolis"). Numerous Mediterranean cultures – from the Greeks to the Normans and the Spanish Bourbons – have all made their mark here. Time seems to have stood still in some parts of the city, and the fact that it dates back to a Greek settlement from the 5th century BC can be seen in the remains of a market from ancient Neapolis, the ruins of which were found under the Gothic San Lorenzo Maggiore Church. Next to the Chapel of St Januarius is the 6th-century Santa Restituta Basilica, a proud testament to the early prevalence of paleo-Christianity belief in the region. Located inside the San Gennaro Church, the basilica features ancient columns and a baptistry from the 4th century. San Gennaro also has important catacombs. The Castel Nuovo, residence of the Neapolitan kings and viceroys, dates back to the 13th century. The city councilors today meet in the castle's Sala dei Baroni, with its ornate star vault. The Palazzo Reale was built between 1600 and 1602 based on designs by Domenico Fontana.

"Old Naples" is to be found down by the port, with busy sellers racing through the narrow lanes on mopeds and storekeepers displaying a variety of wares. The crib scenes, presepi in Italian, from the stores on the Via San Gregorio Armeno are extremely popular.

POMPEII

Location: South-western Italy (Campania)
Best time to travel: throughout the year
www.pompeiturismo.it

Vesuvius erupted on August 24 of the year AD 79, completely covering the Roman town of Pompeii under a layer of ash within roughly six hours. The neighboring town of Herculaneum was also smothered under glowing lava. After the eruption, the towns were not rebuilt and were eventually forgotten. However, Pliny the Younger (ca. AD 61–113), whose uncle and adopted father were killed by the eruption, had described the event, which pointed archaeologists in the right direction. The first excavations began in 1748, and today the resulting finds provide an invaluable impression of life in antiquity. The remains of shops and the painted walls of splendid villas were still left standing; even petrified bread was found in the bakeries. Other discoveries included a mill, a latrine, and some "graffiti" on the walls. The stepping stones that enabled passers-by to cross the street without getting their feet wet are even still visible. The dead are the most impressive, however, their bodies forming hollows of volcanic ash. Filled with plaster, the human figures are now visible again as sadly authentic and silent witnesses of the eruption.

Vesuvius (top), the only remaining active volcano in mainland Europe, lies only 15 km (9 mi) from Pompeii. Excavations in the layer of lava and ash have been unearthing finds from the settlement since the 18h century (below, middle).
This representation of two gods (far left) or the double portrait of Paquius Proculus and his wife (left) are just two of the treasures which have been discovered.

AMALFI COAST, CAPRI

Location: South-western Italy (Campania)
Best time to travel: throughout the year
www.amalfitouristoffice.it
www.aziendaturismopositano.it
www.turismoinsalerno.it
www.capritourism.com
www.capri.it

The small town of Amalfi on the Gulf of Salerno was once one of Italy's leading seafaring republics. Today the name is associated with one of the loveliest stretches of Mediterranean coastline. Cut straight into the cliffs in places, the Amalfitana coastal road connects the villages between Nerano and Salerno. It follows winding stretches of the shoreline for around 45 km (30 mi), continually providing spectacular views of the azure-blue ocean and the Costiera Amalfitana. The view from the garden of the Villa Cimbrone is especially lovely, as is that from the Villa Rufulo, both in Ravello. The villages are strung together like pearls with lemon groves and vineyards scattered between them. The world's oldest maritime law – the Tavole Amalfitane – has its origins in Amalfi, the most important town along this stretch of coast. The 9th-century cathedral, which can be reached by a magnificent flight of steps from the Piazza Duomo, is a source of local pride. "I have the feeling", wrote John Steinbeck of this town founded in the Middle Ages, "that the world is vertical in Positano. An unimaginably blue and green ocean washes up on the fine pebble beach in the bay". There are crossings to the island of Capri from this splendid town.

Amalfi (right) is the largest town along the coast here. Far right from top: the view from Ravello is particularly beautiful. Cosmopolitan Positano and Capri.

SICILY

Location: South Italy (Sicily)
Best time to travel: all year
www.sicilytourist.net

"Without Sicily, Italy leaves no image in the soul. Sicily is the key to everything", thus wrote Goethe in his Italian Journey on April 13, 1787, about the largest island in the Mediterranean. Separated from the tip of the Italian "boot" by an only 3-km-wide (10-mi) strait, at the crossroads between Europe and Africa, it rests – according to legend – on top of three pillars that are deeply anchored in the sea, reflecting its Greek, Arabic and Roman roots. The geological continuation of the Apennine peninsula, the island is traversed from east to west by three mountain ranges – the Peloritani, Nebrodi and Madonie mountains. Sicily's east is strongly characterized by volcanic activity. Here rises Mount Etna, the largest and most active volcano in Europe and also the highest peak in Italy south of the Alps. An earthly paradise with almond and orange tree plantations thrives on its fertile volcanic soil. In 1693, the entire south-east of the island was shaken by an earthquake that was to claim the lives of about 60,000 people. The baroque cities and churches for which Sicily is still famous today, were built as part of the reconstruction projects. The vibrant metropolis of Catánia and the tourist resort of Taormina are located within the sphere of influence of Mount Etna, whose silhouette dominates the entire east coast.

Palermo was the main base for the Carthaginian fleet in the First Punic War and went on to enjoy exceptional periods of prosperity under the Moors, Normans and the Hohenstaufens of Germany. Thankfully, a tremendous number of historic buildings have survived from all of these epochs. In the Old Town, Byzantine churches stand next to

Moorish mosques, and baroque and Catalan palaces are juxtaposed with classical barracks and Arabian-style pleasure palaces. Highlights here include the splendid cathedral; the Norman Palace with the mosaic-embellished Cappella Palatina, and the 16th-century Piazza Pretoria with the mannerism-style Fontana Pretoria. The San Cataldo, La Martorana and San Giovanni degli Eremiti churches, the La Zisa Palace, the Teatro Massimo, the catacombs of the Capuchin monastery, the National Gallery, and the Archaeological Museum are all worth seeing as well. The lively Vucciria market on the Piazza Caracciolo is nicknamed the "belly of Palermo". The kiosks and shops selling fish, meat, fruits, and vegetables are all strung together like an oriental souk. Situated around 8 km (5 mi) from Palermo is the small episcopal town of Monreale. Monte Caputo provides fabulous views of the Sicilian capital.

Greeks have begun arriving in Sicily from the middle of the eighth century BC, and cities founded by the Greek immigrants on Sicily included for example Naxos, Messina, Catania, Syracuse, Gela and Agrigentum. Thus the island became a western center of Greek culture. Located not far from the present-day city of Agrigento on Sicily's south coast is the Valle dei Templi, the impressive remains of Akragas, one of the most important Greek colonies and trading cities in the Mediterranean region.

Sicily's entire east coast is dominated by Mount Etna. A veritable phalanx of Doric temple ruins attests to the heyday of the Greek colony of Akragas in the Valle dei Templi. The Elephant Fountain on the Piazza del Duomo is the emblem of Catania. Palermo's lively Vucciria Market is also known as "the belly of Palermo". Covering an area of about 6,300 sq m (67,800 sq ft), the mosaics in the cathedral of Monreale retell the stories of the Bible.

SARDINIA

Location: Island off western Italy
Best time to travel:
April–October
www.sardegnaturismo.it
www.marenostrum.it

Sardinia is the second-largest island in the Mediterranean after Sicily and has a tremendous cultural heritage to match its magnificent natural splendor. Over thousands of years, the Phoenicians, Romans, Vandals, Byzantines, Moors, Pisans, Genoese, Aragonese, Spanish, and mainland Italians have all left their mark here. Nevertheless, Sardinia was able to maintain its own language and culture. The north is the most popular region with magnificent diving, various watersports, and sailing. It features quaint villages with ancient, labyrinthine town centers, good infrastructure, and a romantic landscape with granite cliffs and dark maquis shrub land in the interior. The "Costa Smeralda", the Emerald Coast where the Aga Khan created an exclusive holiday resort in the early 1960s, is of course legendary. Archaeological sites include the Li Muri "Tomba dei Giganti" (Giants' Grave). The Capo d'Orso rock formations are one of the landmarks of the Costa Smeralda, with its clear blue bays and idyllic landscape. Just a few miles wide, the Bocca di Bonifacio separates the Capo Testa from the bizarre rock formations of the island of Corsica to the north. This group of tiny islands belong to the Parco Nazionale dell'Arcipélago de la Maddalena to the north-east of Sardinia. There are 62 in total. The Capo Caccia is Sardinia's westernmost point. The Grotta di Nettuno can be reached via the Escala del Cabirol with its 656 steps.

Capo Caccia is the westernmost point of Sardinia (top). The bizarre rock formations of Capo d'Orso (bottom, right) count among the icons of the Emerald Coast with its crystal clear bays and turquoise waters, and spellbound landscapes (bottom, left).

VALLETTA, MEGALITHIC TEMPLES, HYPOGÄUM HAL SAFLIENI

Location: Malta
Best time to travel: April–October
www.visitmalta.com

Surrounded by the sea on three sides, Valletta is situated on a 60-m (200-ft) high cliff on the northern coast of Malta. Control over the town of Valletta changed hands many times over the centuries starting with the Phoenicians and moving on to the Greeks, the Carthaginians, the Romans, Byzantium, and the Moors until it was finally handed over to the Order of St John following the Turkish siege of 1565. Their leader Jean Parisot de la Vallette founded the town anew after the siege was lifted and Valletta was named after him. It then grew into a fortified town, characteristic of the 16th century, and was extended between 1566 and 1571 to designs by the architects Girolamo Casar and Francesco Laparelli, one of the Medici's military designers and a pupil of Michelangelo. The Order of St John proceeded to construct a series of Renaissance and baroque palaces, churches and hospices within its walls, the Order's newly-found confidence and wealth being expressed in the magnificent décor of the Grand Master's palace and its two courtyards. The baroque church of Our Lady of Victory was built as a sign of gratitude for having survived the siege of 1567. St. John's Co-Cathedral, built between 1573 and 1578 as a burial place for the knights of the Order, was decorated with ceiling frescoes and magnificent side chapels. The library founded by the order in 1555 houses valuable manuscripts. The Manoel Theatre dating from 1731 can be found within the labyrinth of alleys and steps and is one of the oldest stages in Europe. Stage productions are in English and Maltese.

The principal church in the Maltese capital of Valletta is the imposing St John's Co-Cathedral, with its ornate interior and side chapels (left; right, a rather lovely depiction of the Madonna).

WARSAW

Location: Central Poland
Best time to travel: throughout the year
www.e-warsaw.pl
www.warsaw-hotel-guide.net

Rise, occupation, and reconstruction – the changing fortunes of the Polish capital reflect the turbulent history of the the whole country: the first phase of prosperity was ushered in when King Sigismund III moved his court from Krakow to Warsaw in 1600, but this was swiftly followed by the depredations of the Swedes and then a Renaissance at the hands of the Wettins, a dynasty of princes from Saxony. The Russians gained control of the city after the division of Poland in 1815, and it was completely destroyed by the Germans during World War II. It took the Communists less than ten years to rebuild the city completely – reconstructing the Old Town using the original plans, although the rest of the city was rebuilt according to the precepts of Socialist Functionalism. The city's skyline is still dominated by the 230-m (755-ft) high Palace of Culture (top) which was built between 1952 and 1955.

According to legend, Warsaw was founded by Wars and his sister Zawa at the command of a water sprite, a myth commemorated by the statue of the naiad Syrenka on the market place (above right; left, the Knights' Hall in the castle.

GDANSK

Location: Northern Poland
Best time to travel: throughout the year
www.gdansk.pl
www.en.gdansk.gda.pl

Gdansk has a history going back more than 1,000 years. It maintained close trade relations with Flanders, Russia and Byzantium, and this continued well into the 12th and 13th centuries. Danzig, as it was known, was a member of the Hanseatic League from 1361 and was assigned to the Polish crown in 1466. With ninety-five percent of the city in ruins at the end of World War II, Gdansk has since become a model of reconstruction work. The most important attractions are naturally in the city center. St Mary's Church, for example, is the largest medieval brick church in Europe, its most striking feature being the 82-m (269-ft) high bell tower. The city's Old Town comprises Long Street and the streets adjoining it. Influential patricians built magnificent palaces for themselves in the heart of the Old Town. The 15th-century Arthur's Court is among the finest examples of late-Gothic architecture in Northern Europe; the town hall, the Golden House and the Torture House are also worth seeing.

The Crane Gate on the Motlawa in Gdansk was a city gate during the Middle Ages and was later converted for use as a loading crane.

MALBORK

Location: Northern Poland
Best time to travel:
throughout the year
www.polish-online.com
www.visitmalbork.pl

A white cloak with a black cross was the uniform of the Teutonic Knights, an order of knights that formed in the Holy Land during the Third Crusade (1189–1192). The knights turned their attention to Europe just a few decades later and Prussia, along with Livonia and Courland, were subordinated and Christianized in the name of the black cross. Given sovereign powers as landlords by the emperor, the order founded towns, built castles, brought in German farmers as colonists, and promoted the arts and science. At the head of the order was the Grand Master, who was elected for life and whose seat and main fortress after 1309 was here in Mal-

FROMBORK

Location: Northern Poland
Best time to travel:
throughout the year
www.frombork.pl
www.frombork.art.pl

The small town of Frombork in Warmia is culturally the most interesting town in the region with its historic complex located on the cathedral hill. The museum next to the cathedral is dedicated to the important work of the astronomer Nicolaus Copernicus. He developed his theory of a heliocentric solar system, which displaced the Earth from the center of the universe, here in the 16th century. The water tower provides lovely views of the Vistula Lagoon and the port.

Nicolaus Copernicus, the dean of Frauenburg Cathedral (14th century).

bork Castle on the Nogat River. It was here that all of the threads of the order's states came together, its territories extending far into the Baltic States as well as into southern and central Germany. The costly Battle of Tannenberg in 1410 against the more superior Poles and Lithuanians is seen to represent the beginning of their decline. Held with some effort until 1457, Malbork Castle finally fell into Polish hands in 1466 with the Peace of Torun. The story of the holy state came to a definitive end in 1525 when it became the secular Duchy of Prussia with Albrecht von Brandenburg-Ansbach as its first duke. It later became a hereditary duchy under Polish sovereignty during the Reformation.

The castle precincts of Malbork, the official residence of the leader of the Teutonic Knights between 1309 and 1457, are surrounded by mighty walls and towers.

TORUN

Location: Northern Poland
Best time to travel: throughout the year
www.torun.pl

The knights of the Teutonic Order built a castle here, and a commercial center developed around it in the 14th century. The town even maintained its own merchant fleet for the purposes of trading with the Netherlands. The First and the Second Peace of Torun were concluded here in 1411 and 1466 between the Teutonic Order and Poland. In 1454 the Teutonic Order castle was burnt down by the citizens of Torun (only remnants survive to this day) and the town became an independent city-state under the sovereignty of the Polish king.

The 14th-century Church of St Mary's is just one of the imposing churches in the city.

KRAKÓW

Location: Southern Poland
Best time to travel: throughout the year
www.krakow-poland.com

Krakow was the capital of the Polish kings until 1596, and their coronation venue from the 11th to the 18th centuries. Wawel Hill with its royal castle and cathedral remains a striking testimony to this bygone era. The Old Town here was designed by master builders and artists from throughout Europe, from the 12th to the 17th centuries. The market square, one of Europe's largest medieval town squares, is the site of the textile halls and the Gothic St Mary's Church, converted in the 14th century. The famous high altar by Veit Stoss who created his most important works in Krakow between 1477 and 1496, can be found here. Pivotal medieval intellectuals taught at the university, founded in the 14th century. A number of Gothic, Renaissance and baroque buildings also demonstrate the city's rich history. The Kazimierz Quarter was once home to a thriving Jewish community where the Old Synagogue is worthy of special mention.

The Drapers' Halls in the middle of the market square (Rynek) were built in the 13th century.

THE MASURIAN LAKE DISTRICT

Location: Northern Poland
Best time to travel: April–October
www.visitpoland.org

Hikers, cyclists, and canoeists alike can all enjoy the thoroughly fascinating water landscape here. More than 3,000 lakes are linked via rivers and canals, all mingling with wonderful forests. Gnarled trees shade cobblestone alleys that are still traveled by horsedrawn carts, while storks build their nests in the tops of the steeples. A visit to Masuria is like taking a journey back in time to the early 20th century. Olsztyn is the main center of the Masuria region as well as the perfect starting point for excursions.

The natural paradise of the Masurian Lakes: more than 350 species of bird have found a habitat here.

BIAŁOWIEŻA

Location: North-eastern Poland
Best time to travel: April–Oktober
www.bpn.com.pl
www.bialowieza-info.eu

Despite the extreme temperatures here, which often sink well below freezing point in winter, this cross-border national park possesses an astounding level of biodiversity. There are some 3,000 types of mushrooms and more than a dozen species of orchids. The protected central zone of the park is home to the highest trees in all of Europe: 55-m (180-ft) high spruces and 40-m (131-ft) high ash trees. The Polish government began using zoo animals to breed European bison in the 1920s to reintroduce them step by step into the wild by 1952.

Bison have been released into the wild to live in the national park.

ZAMOŚĆ

Location: South-east Poland
Best time to travel: throughout the year
www.zamosc.pl

Every aspect of life was thought of during the planning of the town of Zamość in the province of Lublin: two market squares form the heart of a city which was to be settled by Armenians, Jews, Greeks, Italians, and Germans, creating a vibrant multi-national community. The town houses built around the squares are decorated with impressive arcades and ornate façades. The Town Hall was built between 1639 and 1651, although the monumental baroque steps are an 18th-century addition.

The Town Hall with a 52-m (170-ft) octagonal tower, and surrounded by Renaissance houses where once occupied by Armenian merchants.

WOODEN CHURCHES

Location: South Poland
Best time to travel: April–October
www.wrotamalopolski.pl

The wooden churches of Małopolska are log buildings constructed from horizontally placed tree trunks. A widely used method of building in eastern Europe, it was less commonly applied to Roman Catholic churches. Aristocratic families commissioned wooden churches for the villages of Binarowa, Blizne, Dębno, Haczów, Lachowice, Lipnica Murowana, Orawka, Sękowa and Szalowa in southern Małopolska. With one exception, they all date from the late 15th and the 16th centuries.

The churches, although rather modest in appearance from the outside, like this one in Haczów, feature lovingly furnished interiors.

SPIŠ CASTLE

Location: North-eastern Slovakia
Best time to travel: May–September
www.spisskyhrad.com

Medieval Spis Castle, one of the largest of its kind in Central Europe, was built on the site of an earlier Slavic fortress in Spis, a scenic region and historic administrative district in the foothills of the High Tatras. Following its sudden collapse, the 13th century tower house was subsequently replaced by a two-storey Romanesque palace with a new round tower. The castle chapel also dates back to the 13th century, when the castle survived an attack from the Mongolians almost without damage.

After a fire in 1780, the castle lay in ruins for several centuries before being partially rebuilt in the 20th century.

CARPATHIANS

Location: North-eastern Slovakia and several other states
Best time to travel: throughout the year (Ski season: October–April)
www.carpathianparks.org

The Primeval Beech Forests of the Carpathians (a UNESCO world heritage site), are an outstanding example of undisturbed, complex temperate forests. They contain an invaluable genetic reservoir of beech and many species associated with, and dependent on, these forest habitats. They are also an outstanding example of the recolonization and development of terrestrial ecosystems and communities after the last Ice Age, a process which is still ongoing.

Pure beech woods and forests which are found in the Ukrainian and Slovakian Carpathians.

PRAGUE

Location: Central Czech Republic
Best time to travel: throughout the year
www.prague-tourist.com

The unique beauty of the historic buildings in the "Golden City", combined with centuries as a European intellectual and cultural capital have made Prague a truly wonderful place to visit. Despite having been spared much of the destruction of World War II, the ravages of time have nevertheless left a definite mark on the city. Thankfully, however, renovations have seen this more than 1,000-year-old city on the banks of the Vltava River restored to its former glory. Indeed, the Czechs have every reason to be proud of their lovely capital, which was formerly a grand residence of the Bohemian kings and seat of the Hapsburg emperors. Their former place of residence, the Vysehrad, also provides the best views of this marvel of historical urban development.

Construction of the Charles Bridge (right) in Prague was begun under Charles IV in 1357. The master builder Peter Parler took his inspiration from the stone bridge in Regensburg. Far right: the Old Town Square is about 9,000 sq m (97,000 sq ft) in size. It was originally a central market place for merchants, but was also used as a stopping point for the coronation processions of Bohemian kings, and as a place of execution. The houses of the Golden Lane (middle) were built beside the castle walls in the 16th century to provide accommodation for guards and artisans. Franz Kafka lived in one for a number of years. The Old New Synagogue in Prague (bottom) is the only synagogue of its age on European soil where Jewish services are still held.

Hungary

BUDAPEST

Location: Northern Hungary
Best time to travel: throughout the year
www.budapestinfo.hu
www.budapest.com

Buda, Óbuda (Old Buda) and Pest were all joined in 1872 to form "BudaPest," the new capital of the former Kingdom of Hungary. The royal castle town of Buda has largely retained its medieval character, with numerous Gothic and baroque buildings lining the narrow streets. Trinity Square lies at the center of the castle hill, which has been a municipality since the 17th century, and is dominated by the Church of Our Lady. Originally built in 1250, the church underwent a neo-Gothic conversion in the 19th century. The royal castle, built on the site of a structure that was destroyed in the great siege of 1686, was begun in 1749 and is located just to the south of the castle hill. The excavation sites of the Roman settlement of Aquincum, with its large amphitheater that accommodated some 13,000 spectators, can be found in Óbuda. The monumental, classical-style synagogue was erected in 1820 and is also worth visiting. Pest, which lies on the other side of the Danube, was a commercial hub and a center of intellectual life for the *haute bourgeoisie* of the 19th century. The parliament building, which architecturally has much in common with the Palace of Westminster in London, has a magnificent staircase and was built between 1885 and 1904 to plans by Imre Steidl. The Hungarian parliament has sat here since 1989. Built in the Secessionist (*Art Nouveau*) style and opened in 1918, the Gellért Hotel and the Gellért Baths are the most famous in Budapest. The men's baths, the outdoor pools, and the thermal and steam baths for women are opulent in their design and decorated with lovely mosaics.

The Danube is Budapest's principal artery. Nine bridges (top left, the Elizabeth Bridge in the foreground, with the Chain Bridge behind it) connect the two parts of the city, Buda and Pest. The Fisherman's Bastion (top) was built between 1895 and 1902 on the site of the old fish market at Buda. Bottom, left to right: the golden staircase of the Parliament, the Gellért Baths, very ornate with beautiful mosaic tiles (middle), and the richly decorated auditorium of the Budapest Royal Opera House with frescoes and sculptures.

THE JULIAN AND KAMNIK ALPS

Location: North-western Slovenia/Italy/Austria
Best time to travel: throughout the year (Ski season: October–April)
www.julijske-alpe.com
www.slovenia.info

The arduous journey through the passes on the Carinthian border is suddenly interrupted by the Julian and Steiner Alps. Almost every path here will quite literally lead you away into the wilderness – the Triglav National Park includes almost all of the Julian Alps. Parts of the Steiner Alps (Grintovec, 2,558 m/8,392 ft) to the north of the Slovenian regional capital of Ljubljana have also recently been placed under protection.

The highest peak in the Julian Alps is the Triglav ("Triple-headed"), at 2,865 m (9,400 ft).

BLED

Location: North-western Slovenia
Best time to travel: April–October
www.bled.si
www.slovenia.info

The 8-km (5-mi) long Karawanken Tunnel ensures a comfortable journey from Carinthia into Slovenia. The spa town of Bled on the lake of the same name is definitely worth a visit, and the little island here has been a popular pilgrimage site for more than 1,000 years. Bled's most interesting attraction by far is the castle on its high rock – many sections of its Romanesque walls have survived the centuries unscathed. There is a comprehensive regional museum in the baroque section of the castle.

St Mary's Church on its island has become an iconic symbol of Bled.

ŠKOCJAN

Location: East Slovenia
Best time to travel:
June–September
www.park-skocjanske-jame.si

The waters of the Reka River disappear underground at skocjan, only emerging again eight days later near the Adriatic coast. The intervening stretch of the Reka has carved a series of beautiful *karst* caves with all the typical features left in limestone by thousands of years of erosion: fissures, gorges, chimneys, collapsed funnels, chasms, lakes, waterfalls, narrow crevices, and "chambers". Water levels can rise rapidly here as the snow melts.

The almost 6-km (4-mi) long cave system to the east of Trieste in the Slovenian karst is one of the most important caves in the world.

LJUBLJANA

Location: Central Slovenia
Best time to travel:
throughout the year
www.visitljubljana.si
www.ljubljana-calling.com

Although it has a population of less than 300,000, Slovenia's capital has all the trappings of state sovereignty: embassies, a parliament, a national museum, gallery, and library. It also has a vibrant cultural life, but most of all it has an abundance of grace and charm. Just as in Salzburg, the historic Old Town is dominated by a castle, and from here the viceroy of the emperor in Vienna ruled the dukedom of Krain for centuries.

The view from Ljubljana's western riverbanks towards the Three Bridges and the Old Marketplace is especially atmospheric.

TROGIR

Location: Southern Croatia (Dalmatia)
Best time to travel: April–September
www.trogir.hr
www.trogir-online.com

Trogir's beach promenade and Old Town are dominated by the St Nicholas tower of the Benedictine monastery and the clock tower of the St Laurence Cathedral. The Dalmatian port dates back to a Greek colony founded in 385 BC. The town, built on an island, fell under Byzantine control in the 6th century, after which the Croats, Bosnians, Hungarians, and Venetians disputed its possession, with the Republic of Venice ultimately gaining the upper hand from 1420 to 1797. The Benedictine monastery is home to reliefs and inscriptions dating from the 3rd to 1st centuries BC. The St Laurence Cathe-

POREČ

Location: North-western Croatia (Istria)
Best time to travel: April–September
www.porec.hr
www.istra.hr

There have been Christians in Poreč since the 3rd century, and a chapel was built here in the 4th century to house the relics of St Maurus, the first bishop and a martyr. Little was left of him, and still less remains of the chapel today. The first large basilica was erected here in the 5th century, and was given its present appearance under Bishop Euphrasios in the 6th century.

The marble columns lining the interior of the Euphrasian Basilica, came from the island of Prokonnesos near ancient Constantinople (Istanbul).

dral, a Romanesque-Gothic work, houses masterpieces of medieval painting and its West portal, built in around 1240 by master builder Radovan from Trogir, is one of the most important stone works in Croatia. The town hall and the loggia with the clock tower date from the 15th century. Camerlengo Castle and the Markus Tower are part of the Venetian fortifications from the 15th and 16th centuries. Numerous Late Gothic as well as Renaissance and Baroque palaces and town houses have also been preserved. The main street running north-south in the center of town has been named the *Ulica Kohl-Genschera* in honor of the German chancellor and minister who campaigned for Croatian independence.

The spire of St Nicholas' Church and the bell tower of St Laurence's Cathedral overlook the marina promenade and the Old Town.

THE PLITVICE LAKES

Location: Central Croatia
Best time to travel: throughout the year (Ski season: October–April)
www.tzplitvice.hr

The 16 lakes of Plitvice Lakes National Park, close to the border with Bosnia and Herzegovina, are connected by terraces, cascades, and waterfalls and are testimony to the constantly changing yet pristine natural panorama of Croatian limestone. The chain of lakes extends over about 7 km (4 mi) and owes its existence to calcification and sinkholes. Over several thousand years the limestone sinter has formed barriers and dams with water basins: algae and mosses are the reason for the shimmering blue and green hues of the 12 larger lakes.

Some lakes and caves are only accessible by boat.

KORČULA

Location: Island off southern Croatia (Dalmatia)
Best time to travel: April–September
www.korculainfo.com
www.korcula.ca

The capital of the island of the same name is proud of the fact that it is Marco Polo's birthplace. The late-Gothic St Mark cathedral boasts modern sculptures that contrast with the Gothic tracery. Renaissance and baroque palaces line the alleyways of the Old Town, and Marco Polo House documents the life of the legendary sea voyager.

The beautiful Old Town of Korčula is surrounded by walls, and the streets are arranged in a herringbone pattern allowing free circulation of air but protecting against strong winds.

SPLIT

Location: Southern Croatia (Dalmatia)
Best time to travel: throughout the year
www.visitsplit.com

The Roman Emperor Diocletian had a palace built for the period following his abdication in 305. His retirement home near the Roman town of Salona covers an area of about 215 by 180 m (705 by 591 ft) and was fortified with battlement walls. Following the Avar and Slav incursion (615) some of the residents of Salona fled into the ruins of the ancient Roman palace, the grounds of which came to form the core of what is now Split.

The imperial apartments in the palace are accessed via an anteroom (right). The Riva marina promenade has a Mediterranean atmosphere (opposite).

DUBROVNIK

Location: Southern Croatia (Dalmatia)
Best time to travel: throughout the year
www.dubrovnik-online.com
www.tzdubrovnik.hr

Dubrovnik was one of the most important centers of trade with the Eastern Mediterranean (the Levant) during the Middle Ages. Known at the time as Ragusa – Dubrovnik being its official name only since 1919 – the town successfully fended off claims in the 14th century by the Venetians and the Hungarians. Officially under Turkish rule as of 1525, it determined its own fate as a free republic up until the annexation of Dalmatia by Napoleon in 1809. Its mighty fortresses, with walls up to 6 m (20 ft) thick and 25 m (82 ft) high remain a testimony to its strength. Ragusa was a bastion of Humanism in its time and had a tremendous influence on Slavic literature and painting. It was here that Croatian developed as a literary language between the 15th and 17th centuries. The town was almost entirely destroyed by an earthquake in 1667, but large medieval buildings such as the Rector's Palace and the monastery have been renovated. Most of the structure and some of the interior decor of the cathedral were rebuilt in the baroque style.

With its old port and the fortress of Sveti Ivan, Dubrovnik (top) presents a breathtaking panorama. A stroll through the Old Town is especially atmospheric; left, a view of the pillared portico of the Sponza Palace on St Vlaho; right, lined with cafés, Lula Square is also the site of both the 31-m (103-ft) high clock tower, built in 1444, and the baroque church of St Blasius, Dubrovnik's patron saint, which was built between 1706 and 1715 to a design by Marino Gropelli.

MOSTAR

Location: Bosnia and Herzegovina (Herzegovina)
Best time to travel: throughout the year
www.visitmostar.net

The capital of Herzegovina is an extraordinary example of multi-cultural urban life – but mainly as a result of the conflicts that this can cause. Mostar ("guardian of the bridge") derives its name from an old wooden bridge over the Neretva which was replaced in 1566 by a single-span bridge on the orders of the Sultan. Even today, most of the city's Christians live on the western side and the Muslims live on the eastern side, a division which was only cemented during the war which raged in Bosnia between 1992 and 1995. The Croats and Muslims initially joined forces against the Serbs at the beginning of the 1990s, governing the city jointly for about six months before declaring war on one another (1993–4). Bosnian Croat forces began shelling the bridge, and it collapsed in 1993; many other old buildings on the eastern, Bosnian side of the city were also badly damaged or destroyed. The reconstruction of the city was not to begin for another five years, supported by an huge international aid program which started in 1998.

Christianity and Islam face one another in Mostar in the form of the spire of the Franciscan church in the west and the minaret of a mosque on the eastern banks of the Neretva (top).
The Old Bridge over the Neretva (above) which was destroyed in 1993 was ceremonially reopened on 23 July 2004. It is particularly picturesque when it is illuminated at night.

OHRID

Location: South-western Macedonia
Best time to travel: April–September
www.ohrid.gov.mk

Founded by the Illyrians as Lychnidos, the Romans were also quick to recognize the strategic position of the town that later would be called Ohrid. Situated on the Via Egnatia, the main arterial road between Byzantium and the Adriatic, the town quickly developed into an important staging post. The town became a Greek Orthodox bishop's see at the end of the 10th century as well as the imperial capital of the Bulgarian Czar Samuil for a spell. Subsequent Serbian rule under the auspices of Dushan was ended by the Ottomans in 1394, who then remained in Ohrid until 1913. The Church of St Sophia was built by Archbishop Leo in the 11th century. It was converted to a mosque by the Ottomans and lost its dome, bell tower, and interior galleries. The Church of St Clement houses the region's most valuable collection of icons. The historically protected Old Town boasts numerous Macedonian-style buildings of particular appeal. In 1980, Ohrid and Lake Ohrid were accepted as a World Heritage Site by UNESCO. Ohrid has been referred to as a "Jerusalem".

Lake Ohrid is said to be the oldest and deepest lake of the world. The Church of St John at Kaneo, which dates from the 13th century (below), overlooks the lake. Its octaconal tower can be seen from the lake. The rather unusual fresco in a side cupola of the church in Naum monastery in Ohrid in Macedonia appears to show Jesus as the ruler of the world holding a child in his arms (above).

THE CHURCHES IN MOLDOVA

Location: Northern Romania
Best time to travel: throughout the year
www.romanianmonasteries.org

During the 15th and 16th centuries, Moldovan Prince Stephen III (Stephen the Great, 1457–1504), his successors and other high-ranking dignitaries founded some forty monasteries and churches in the north of the country around the capital Suceava. The exterior walls of the religious buildings in Humor, Voronet, Moldovita, Sucevita, and Arbore were painted up to their overhanging eaves. The tradition came to an end with the ornamental painting in Sucevita in around 1600. The probable intention was to provide an object of worship for the faithful for whom there was no room in the church. The images included legends of the saints, scenes from the Bible such as The Last Judgment, the genealogy of Jesus, and the Hymn to the Mother of God. There are also references to political events such as the siege of Constantinople by the "non-believers". The paintings in the church in Arbore date back to 1541 and are of particular artistic value.

The paintings in the churches (top left, Voronet) brought the Christian content to ordinary people, who may not have understand the official Slavic language of the church.

THE DANUBE DELTA

Location: Eastern Romania
Best time to travel: April–September
www.romaniatourism.com

One of the highlights of a trip to Romania is an excursion through the Danube Delta. This mighty river divides into three main arms close to Tulcea, over 2,800 km (1,740 mi) from its source in Germany and almost 80 km (50 mi) before its estuary on the Black Sea coast. The three broad waterways encompass a wetland of around 4,500 sq km (1,737 sq mi), a unique ecosystem that is home to the world's largest cohesive reed cluster (over 800 sq km/309 sq mi). This vast network of waterways, backwaters, canals, lakes, islands, floodplain forests, and marshes is also home to a huge diversity of animals and plants. The mighty forests of oaks, willows and poplars are overgrown with lianas and creepers, an especially impressive sight. Water lilies and floating reed islands (Plaurs) cover vast expanses of the water. The diversity of the bird life is also particularly striking, with huge flocks of pelicans and cormorants, for example, and fish eagles and egrets – so rare elsewhere. Gliding slowly through the narrow channels in a boat or crossing one of the lakes is a wonderful experience.

The area surrounding the Danube delta as it flows into the Black Sea regularly floods in spring.

RILA

Location: South-western Bulgaria
Best time to travel: throughout the year
www.rilanationalpark.org

It is traditionally thought that the monastery was founded by the hermit St. Ivan of Rila, whose name it bears, during the rule of Tsar Peter I (927–968). The hermit actually lived in a cave without any material possessions not far from the monastery's location, while the complex was built by his students, who came to the mountains to receive their education. Ever since its creation, the Rila Monastery has been supported and respected by the Bulgarian rulers. Large donations were made by almost every tsar of the Second Bulgarian Empire up until the Ottoman Conquest, making the monastery a cultural and spiritual centre of Bulgarian national consciousness that reached its apogee from the 12th to the 14th century. The Rila monastery fell into disrepair following Bulgaria's conquest by the Ottoman Empire. After being restored to its former glory between 1816 and 1862, it again became a cultural center and a "national sanctuary". The multi-storey monastery buildings surround an inner courtyard of 3,000 sq m (32,300 sq ft) and are overlooked by the five-storey Chreljo Tower (1335).

The pride of the complex is the Nativity of the Virgin Church, surrounded by an open arcade.

PIRIN

Location: South-western Bulgaria/Northern Greece
Best time to travel: throughout the year (Ski season: October–April)
www.bulgariaski.com
www.visitbulgaria.net

The craggy landscape of the Pirin Mountains, which boasts 45 peaks above the 2,600 m (8,531 ft) mark, includes the national park of the same name. The park is dominated by Wichren, the third-highest mountain on the Balkan Peninsula at 2,914 m (9,561 ft). Characteristic of this limestone soil region are the approximately seventy glacial lakes – remnants of the last ice age – as well as the many waterfalls and caves. The diverse flora includes coniferous forests and many rare plant species, some of which, such as the Rumelian pine, are endemic. The huge relief diversity of the park is the reason for the variety of plant species on its territory, making it one of the most botanically interesting areas in Bulgaria. This pristine landscape is also home to endangered wolves and rare bird species.

The Pirin National Park has an area of about 270 sq km (104 sq mi) and an impressive variety of scenery. The national park encloses a number of different vegetation zones from beech forests to treeless meadows. The European brown bear has also found a habitat in this unspoilt landscape.

ATHENS

Location: South-eastern Greece (Attica)
Best time to travel: throughout the year
www.cityofathens.gr
www.athensguide.org

Settlement on the fortress hill in Athens can be traced back to the New Stone Age. The former royal fort was converted into a religious site as far back as the 6th century BC. After being destroyed by the Persians, the sanctuaries were quickly rebuilt in the second half of the 5th century BC. The image of Athens' Acropolis is now dominated by the Parthenon. This temple, built between 447 and 422 BC, was dedicated to the goddess of the city, Pallas Athene. The structure is flanked by a series of mighty columns with eight across the ends and 17 along the sides. The cult image of Athena once adorned the interior of the temple, the so-called Cella. The inside and outside of the building were decorated with elaborate, three-dimensional marble statues, of which only parts still exist today. The gable reliefs in the west, for example, depict Athena's birth, while those in the east illustrate her epic battle with Poseidon. The Erechtheion, named after the mythical king of Athens, was built between 421 and 406 BC. It is home to several religious sites, which explains the unusual layout of the complex. The structure is surrounded by three large porches; the roof of the Caryatid Porch is supported by columns in the shape of young women. The Propylaea are the monumental gate complexes of the walls surrounding the Acropolis. They are considered the masterpiece of architect Mnesikles and were built between 437 and 432 BC. The variety of column arrangements here are remarkable. While the entire façade is Doric, slender Ionic columns form a con-

trast in the central passage. Kallikrates' temple of Athena Nike was built between 425 and 421 BC, and is one of the oldest remaining buildings in Ionic style. The small but elegant temple has porches on both the eastern and western side. The "Dimotikí Agora" market is over 100 years old and still the best address for fresh meat and fish. Although the products are now displayed in glass freezers and include everything from hen and sheep tongues to cow hearts and lamb cutlets, they are always artistically organized on their various shelves. Cheese, nut and olive dealers have their stalls outside while fruit, vegetable, sausages, and stockfish are traded on the opposite side of the road. Athens' most beautiful historic quarter is the Plaka, right below the Acropolis. You'll find eateries, small hotels and of course a slew of souvenir stores here among the stately neoclassical villas from the 19th century. Folklore is the focus in the music taverns of the steep "Odos Mnisikleous" alleyway. The merchant and handicrafts quarter, Psirrí, has become the hip place to be, but many artisans and merchants still pursue their trade here during the day.

The Parthenon (top) lies at the heart of the Acropolis in Athens and was designed by the famous sculptor Phydias at the command of the Athenian statesman. The main temple of the complex stands on a plateau created out of the piled-up rubble from a demolished Temple of Athene. Far left: The Athenians worshiped a number of gods and heroes in the maze of the Erechtheion. The roof of the Caryatid Porch to the south is supported by six female figures. Left: The market halls of the Dimotikí Agora are open 24 hours a day and have become a hangout for night owls and early risers.

MT ATHOS

Location: North-eastern Greece (Chalkidikí Peninsula)
Best time to travel: throughout the year
www.mountathos.gr
www.inathos.gr

The first monastery was built on Mt Athos in 963, a holy mountain at the southern tip of the Chalcidice Peninsula. The monks' republic proclaimed here was declared autonomous as early as Byzantine times. Men under the age of 21 and women are still forbidden from entering. The monastery's quarters are currently inhabited by some 1,400 monks. Athos has been an important center of Orthodox Christianity since 1054. Over the centuries, its scope of activities also included some 3,000 farmers working for the monastery in the 14th century; at its height, the republic's estate covered around 20,000 hectares (49,420 acres). The Athos school of icon painting had a significant influence on Orthodox art history, and the typical monastery architecture left its mark in regions as far away as Russia. Each of the 20 main monasteries – 17 Greek, one Russian, one Serbian and one Bulgarian – has a Greek cross plan church in the center of the courtyard, with apses on three arms of the cross. Other buildings as well as the residential cells are located around the courtyard.

The fortress-like monastery of Moní Esfigmenou (opposite) is located on the very edge of the north-eastern coast of the Athos Peninsula. A miraculous icon is kept in the monastery chapel. This page: There are 20 large monasteries (top, Vatopediou, bottom, Hılandarı) and 22 sketes (monastic communities) make up the monastic republic of Athos. The monastery church of the Romanian skete is particularly beautifully painted.

METEORA

Location: Northern Greece (Macedonia)
Best time to travel: April–October
www.meteora-greece.com

The name Meteora means "floating", which is a good description of the location where these monasteries are perched. The seemingly impossible Meteora formations soar out of the glacial valley of the Pinios like bizarre bowling pins. Hermits settled on the pillars in the 11th century, and a monk from Mount Athos founded the first of these rock monasteries in the 14th century. A total of 24 were eventually built. The Megalo Meteoro was founded by St Athanasios, Bishop of Alexandria, around 1360 and is the highest. The other monasteries were subordinate to it after 1490. The walls of the St Nikolas Anapavsas Monastery, founded around 1388, rise up on one of the other high cliffs. The Varlaam Monastery, named after the hermit who had built a church here back in the 14th century, was completed in 1517. The Roussanou Monastery has recently been re-inhabited by nuns and very much looks like a smaller version of Varlaam with its octagonal church. Agia Triada, or Holy Trinity, was established as early as 1438 and is accessed via 130 steps.

At one time, the monasteries could only be reached using rope ladders or pulleys. Toda, steps and bridges make access easier.

SOÚNIO

Location: South-eastern Greece (Attica)
Best time to travel: March–October
www.greeklandscapes.com
www.athensinfoguide.com

The Temple of Poseidon in Sounion, has 16 remaining Doric marble columns which still support the epistyle on which the temple's roof once rested. The location marks the southern border of Attika, which starts in the north near Egosthena at the Corinthian Gulf and Skala Oropou at the Southern Euboean Gulf. In ancient times, Attica was basically the bread basket of Athens' agricultural hinterland. Slaves labored and largely contributed to lay the foundations for Athens' wealth in the silver mines of Lavrio near Sounio. In the Demeter Sanctuary of the present-day industrial city of Elefsina, free citizens demanded better conditions for the afterlife by participating in a mysterious cult. In ancient times, the crews of Athenian war and trading ships thanked the temperamental god of the sea for their safe return at the Temple of Poseidon, which was partly decorated in gaudy colors. People hoped to be healed of illnesses in the Amphiareion, while pregnant women made pilgrimages to Brauron to ask for assistance from the Goddess Artemis.

The Temple of Poseidon built between 444 and 440 BC on Cape Sounion at the tip of the Attic Peninsula can be seen for miles around. Poseidon, Zeus' brother, was god of the sea, but his other siblings were also venerated in the Olympic pantheon: Hades ruled the underworld and the realm of the daed, and sacrifices were made to the earth goddess Demeter to ensure a good harvest.

DELPHI

Location: Central Greece
Best time to travel:
March–October
www.greecetravel.com

Delphi is both an archaeological site and a modern town in Greece on the south-western spur of Mount Parnassus in the valley of Phocis. From the 8th century BC, Delphi was one of the most important shrines of ancient times. In the center of the holy district was a temple for Apollo where Pythia, a divine priestess, presided over the famous Oracle of Delphi. The Pythic Games took place every four years, with the musical and literary competitions held in theater, and the athletic disciplines held in the stadium above the Corinthian Gulf.

Three of the Doric columns in the round temple dedicated to Athena Pronaia have been reconstructed.

MYCENAE

Location:Southern Greece (Peloponnese)
Best time to travel:
March–October
www.gnto.org

The Mycenaean culture (15th to the 12th centuries BC) played an invaluable role in the development of classical Greece. Its name was taken from the Bronze Age fort, Mycenae, in the eastern Peloponnese. The region had been settled since 4,000 BC, but greater development did not start until the late Bronze Age. Most of the ruins of Mycenae uncovered by Heinrich Schliemann date back to the 13th century BC.

The "Lion's Gate" (left) forms the entrance to Mycenae, where the Heinrich Schliemann discovered the death-mask of Agamemnon, the king of Mycenae (far left).

EPIDAUROS

Location: Southern Greece (Peloponnese)
Best time to travel: March–October
www.ediakopto.gr

The complex of Epidaurus, located in a narrow valley in the far eastern expanses of the Peloponnese, spans several levels. It was of key importance to the cult of Asklepios, which spread throughout all of Greece in the 5th century BC. In Greek mythology, the god of medicine was the son of Apollo, whose powers of healing were also channeled through him. Religious Epidaurus was also a health resort at that time.

The seats are arranged around the circular *orchestra*. As is usual for Greek theaters, the open view of the landscape is an integral part of the theater itself.

OLYMPIA

Location: Southern Greece (Peloponnese)
Best time to travel: March–October
www.greecetravel.com

An ancient document registers the name of the first winner of a track race in the Sanctuary of Zeus in Olympia in the year 776 BC, a date that has since been considered the date of the first Olympic Games. They were held every four years for over 1,350 years until a Byzantine emperor forbade them as heathen practices. Near the village of Olimbía, German archaeologists have been excavating the remains of this ancient cult district, including its sporting sites; the Olympic flame is always lit here at the Temple of Hera until today.

There is also the Nike of Paionios to admire.

SANTORINI

Location: Island in the southern Aegean
Best time to travel: March–October
www.santorini.gr
www.santorin.gr

Delicate bell towers and blue church domes are as much a feature of this island's scenery as its windmills and the cats that roam every street. Until some 3,600 years ago, a mighty volcano soared out of the sea here. When it erupted, only the edges of the island remained. The Aegean branched into the resulting crater and eventually people built quaint whitewashed villages on the more than 300-m (984-ft) high crater rim. The hamlets stretch far down the steep lava wall and use all available space for small terraces. Anyone who spends a few days here, or even just enjoys a sunset, will be spending time between heaven and earth. Santorini was already settled before the volcano erupted, and the island was circular and known as Strongili ("the round one"). The first settlers of any influence were the Minoans, who arrived here from Crete and whose civilization reached its climax some time around 2000 to 1600 BC. Merchants and sailors, who had their houses decorated with artistic murals, lived in a city near present-day Akrotiri. In 1967, archaeologists discovered it under a thick layer of ash and lava, and it is thought that the volcanic eruption could well have been responsible for putting an end to Minoan culture. The well preserved ruins are often compared to the spectacular ruins at Pompeii in Italy.

All of Santorini's towns and villages are located on the lip of the crater created by a volcanic eruption about 3,600 years ago. The Aegean flowed into the chasm created to form the archipelago.

DELOS

Location: Cyclades, Aegean Sea
Best time to travel:
March–October
http://you.travel/Cyclades

The island of Delos, near Mykonos, is one of the most important mythological, historical and archaeological sites in Greece. Settled since the 3rd century BC, the island first appeared in historical texts in the 14th century BC. It then became an important cult center and pilgrimage destination in the 7th century BC as the "birthplace" of the god Apollo. In the 5th century BC, the island was the focal point of the First Delian League, and later became an important trading site deemed useful by the Romans in the 2nd century BC. The emergence of new trading centers, pirate raids, and attacks by the soldiers of Mithridates of Pontos in the 1st century BC finally resulted in Delos' collapse. Excavation work since has unearthed the ruins of numerous houses whose inhabitants had laid mosaics in their interior courtyards depicting different images such as dolphins, tigers and a variety of religious idols. The three temples of Apollo, reached via the Holy Road, are probably the simplest of all the sanctuaries dedicated to this god. To the west is the Artemision, the temple to Apollo's sister.

Delos boasts of mythical houses. The House of Dionysus, shown here, is a luxurious 2nd century private house on the island of Delos. This mosaic depicts Dionysus, the Greek god of wine, intoxication, and fertility, riding on a leopard whose collar is adorned with a wreath.

RHODES

Location: Dodecanese island (Eastern Aegean)
Best time to travel: March–October
www.rhodos-info.de
www.rhodos-travel.com

The main island of the Dodecanese group, and Greece's fourth-largest island, has seen many a ruler come and go. The island fell under Macedonian hegemony during the time of Alexander the Great, before a spell of independence, and later rule by Byzantium. From 1310, Rhodes fell under the rule of the Order of St John, and then in 1523 under Ottoman control. The Turkish rule lasted until 1912, when Italy conquered the island and held on to it until 1943. It was not until 1948 that the island became part of Greece.

Rhodes was considered the property of the sun god Helios.

KARPATHOS

Location: Dodecanese island (south-eastern Aegean)
Best time to travel: March–October
www.karpathos.org

The second-largest island of the Dodecanese is still very unspoilt. The whitewashed and pastel-coloured houses, churches, and windmills of what is arguably Greece's most beautiful mountain village are nestled tightly onto a steep slope. The town of Olympos was founded in 1420 by inhabitants of the now orphaned neighbouring island of Saria, and the ancient Vrykos, who sought protection from pirates in the mountains.

From its remote position Karpathos has preserved many peculiarities of dress, customs and dialect, the last resembling those of Crete and Cyprus. Easter is celebrated with much enthusiasm for tradition.

MYKONOS

Location: Cyclades, Aegean Sea
Best time to travel:
March–October
www.mykonos.gr

One hundred years ago, admirers of Greek antiquities stayed on the Cyclades island of Mykonos and visited the sites of Apollo's cult on nearby Delos. They were also drawn here by the attractive hamlet of Chora, with its Old Town quarter. Artists and bohemians soon moved in. For fifty years now, the rich and beautiful of Europe have been frequenting Mykonos and, although the long beaches near town as well as those on the southern and south-eastern coast are often quite crowded, the largely treeless coasts and bays still boast long pristine sections.

Mykonos has become a smart jet set destination.

NÁXOS

Location: Cyclades, Aegean Sea
Best time to travel: March–October
www.naxos.gr

The Portara, a monumental marble gate on the Palateia Peninsula north of the port, is the only remains of a giant temple project that had been planned to honor the god Apollo in the 6th century BC. Also revered in Naxos is a mountain grotto beneath Mt Zas ("Zas" is Modern Greek for Zeus), where Crete-born Zeus is said to have grown up. The Bronze Age culture of the Cyclades in the 3rd millennium BC saw the emergence of a special form of marble idols. The slender, usually female and often abstract figures range in scale from a few centimeters to life-size.

The Portara, which has become the symbol of Naxos, can be seen for miles around.

CRETE

Location: Crete (southern Aegean)
Best time to travel: March–October
www.culture.gr
www.crete-region.gr
www.explorecrete.com

Crete is roughly 260 km (162 mi) long and 60 km (37 mi) wide and situated between the Aegean and the Libyan Sea. Three mighty mountains, each of them over 2,000 m (6,562 ft), cut through the island and represent a continuation of the mountain range of the Peloponnese towards Asia Minor. Surrounded by a large wine-growing area, Heraklion, the vibrant capital, is home to a quarter of the island's population. It has long since expanded beyond the Old Town, whose ancient Venetian and Turkish walls have survived into the modern period; the marina, airport, industrial estates, administrative district, and university here ensure it is the undisputed center of the Cretan economy. German bombing during World War II and random attempts at regeneration have destroyed much of the city's ancient appearance. However, a few lone buildings, such as Venetian churches and fountains, are occasional evidence at least of its long history, and a fortress and some Venetian shipyards have been preserved down by the docks. Nikos Kazantzakis, the author of *Zorba the Greek* and probably Crete's most famous literary son, lies buried in the Martinengo Bastion in the city walls. This was where Europe's first civilization was created 4,000 years ago. The enigmatic Minoans were, for over 500 years, able to pacify the eastern Mediterranean and operate a flourishing trade with Egypt and the kingdoms of the Middle East. From 1900 to 1941, English archaeologist Sir Arthur Evans excavated the economic and religious center of the Minoans some 5 km (3 mi) south-east of the island capital at Knossos: a building complex up to

four stories high with 1,400 rooms and covering 20,000 sq m (215,200 sq ft). Many of the corridors and halls in Knossos were adorned with artistic frescoes. Drinking and sewage problems were solved with clever pipe systems. The Minoans also already had their own writing system. Western Crete is dwarfed by the 2,453-m (8,048-ft) summits of the Lefka Ori, the "White Mountains", which in winter form a snow-capped backdrop for Hania and Rethimno, the second- and third-largest towns on the island. There are four peninsulas here – the two lying furthest to the west are almost uninhabited – enclosing wide bays, with mountain slopes covered with olive groves and vineyards which gradually merge with the chestnut and coniferous forests higher up. The skyline of the Old Town of Rethimno is punctuated with the minarets of several mosques and the narrow streets of Hania radiate from palaces built by the Venetian aristocracy. Beaches that stretch as far as the eye can see can be found either side of Rethimno and to the west of Hania. The sandy shores near Falasarna on the west coast are lined with high dunes and the blue and turquoise hues of the shallow lagoon at Elafonisos are almost reminiscent of the South Pacific. Agios Nikolaos and Sitia in eastern Crete are the counterparts of Rethimno and Hania to the west. The coast further to the east is steep and rocky, and Sitia's only road connection to the west is less than 50 years old. The furthest eastern reaches feature rocky canyons, red sandstone, and the palm-fringed beaches at Vai.

Knossos (left, the north wing of the palace) is considered the most important Minoan burial site. Detailed images of Cretan life in the late Bronze Age are provided on the walls of this palace. It was probably the ceremonial and political centre of the Minoan civilization and culture.

ISTANBUL

Location: North-western Turkey
Best time to travel:
throughout the year
www.istanbul.com
www.istanbulcityguide.com

Its fairy-tale location would be enough to make Istanbul one of the most fascinating cities on earth. Situated on seven hills beside the straits of the Bosphorus, the meeting-place of Europe and Asia, this historic metropolis offers a wealth of sights lying between the Occident and Orient. A city of three names – Byzantium, Constantinople, and Istanbul – it is the legacy of two empires which led the fortunes of the Mediterranean for nigh on 2,000 years: the Eastern Roman or Byzantine Empire and its direct successor, the Ottoman Empire.

The Sultan Ahmed or Blue Mosque (right) has six minarets, an unusual number for a mosque. Legend has it that the minarets were initially intended to be covered with gold, but this would have exceeded the original budget, and so the builders intentionally misheard the Turkish word *alt'n* ("gold") as the number *alt* ("six"). Far right: another legend recalls how the population of Byzantium threw so much treasure into the harbor as they fled from the Ottomans that the water shone gold – and the "Golden Horn" (top, with the Galata Bridge and the Yeni Camii Mosque, completed in 1663) was born. The Hagia Sophia (middle), a masterpiece of Byzantine architecture, is no longer used as a place of worship but serves as a museum. The Hagia Sofia stood as the largest cathedral for more than a thousand years, until the completion of the Cathedral of Seville. The Great Bazaar (bottom) is the largest roofed bazaar in the world.

PERGAMON

Location: Western Turkey
Best time to travel: March-October
www.tourismturkey.org
www.goturkey.com

Pergamon was an ancient Greek city in modern-day Turkey. The cliffs, soaring to heights of over 300 m (984 ft), were used by the rulers of Pergamon for their capital city's acropolis. The awe-inspiring Altar of Zeus is now actually housed in the Pergamon Museum in Berlin, but extensive remains of the royal city can also be seen on the original site and in the modern city of Bergama at the foot of the castle hill. The Temple of Emperor Trajan was completed by the emperor's successor, Hadrian, at the highest point of the ancient royal city.

The columns of the Trajaneum have been reconstructed on the acropolis at Pergamon.

MILETUS

Location: Western Turkey
Best time to travel: March–October
www.kultur.gov.tr

Along with Ephesus and Priene, the ancient city of Miletus owes its wealth to sea trade, but had to be relocated several times due to the threat of silt buildup in the port. A field of ruins, with the mighty theater building, the agora, and the walls of the thermal baths has been preserved. Today, frogs and storks make their home in the compound, which was formerly the largest city in ancient Greece, a region that comprised some eighty daughter cities, where Thales, Anaximander and Anaximenes developed the basics of philosophy and mathematics.

The ancient and beautiful theater could accommodate up to 15,000 spectators.

EPHESUS

Location: Western Turkey
Best time to travel: March–October
www.bodrumpages.com

This ancient city of ruins lies not far from the town of Selcuk. Long before Greek merchants and settlers arrived here, the Carians and Lydians considered it to be a holy place of the Goddess Kybele. In around AD 129, Ephesus became the capital of the Roman province of Asia and was home to an astounding 200,000 inhabitants. Archaeologists have been able to reconstruct more of this ancient city's temples, grand boulevards, baths, and residential dwellings than any other site in Turkey. Only the port has disappeared through centuries of silt deposits.

The majestic columns of the Celsus library.

PRIENE

Location: Western Turkey
Best time to travel: March–October
www.bodrumpages.com

Just like Miletus and Ephesus, the ancient city of Priene, located on the spectacular southern slope of the Mycale Mountain, was also a member of the mighty Ionian League, which was made up of 12 city-states and presumably founded sometime before the year 1000 BC. The city was created around 450 BC by master builder Hippodamus of Miletus. The Temple of Athena, built in the 4th century BC to honor the city's goddess, is considered a masterpiece of Ionian architecture, and Alexander the Great continued to fund the construction after capturing the city.

An authentic example of Hellenist city architecture: the ruins of Priene (left, the Temple of Athene).

PAMUKKALE

Location: South-western Turkey
Best time to travel: March–October
www.pamukkale.net

In addition to the remains of ancient buildings erected here until well into the 4th century, Pamukkale also has a magnificent and unusual natural spectacle to offer: hot springs which rise to a height of roughly 100 m (328 ft) from a ledge in the Cokelez Mountains and flow down into the valley.

Pamukkale means "cotton fortress" or "cotton wool castle" and the name is a fitting description of the natural wonder that the limestone deposits from the hot springs have created here. The geothermally heated and healing water flows from one limestone basin to the next, at each stage giving rise to bizarre formations.

HIERAPOLIS

Location: South-western Turkey
Best time to travel: March–October
www.pamukkale.net

There have been settlements in the hot springs district of Pamukkale for thousands of years. The area was part of the Roman province of Asia in the 2nd century BC, and King Eumenes II of Pergamon had the city of Hierapolis built here in 190 BC. It was mainly planned as a fort complex. Along with the town came the first construction of thermal baths. Residential buildings, temples, a theater, as well as other Hellenic buildings. Some early Christian churches, whose ruins can still be seen today, were built in the area around the baths.

On the hill above today's Pamukkale: the Hadrian's gate

GÖREME

Location: Central Turkey
Best time to travel: March–October
www.goreme.org

The location of Goreme was first settled back in the Roman period. Christianity was then the prevailing religion there, which is evident from many rock churches. This landscape of volcanic tuff rock stretches from the Kizilirmak ("red river") in the north to the underground cities of Kaymakli and Derinkuyu to the south. It seems incomprehensible to modern man that 1,000 years ago, people were able to excavate level after level of passageways and dwellings out of the sort rock here, to a depth of 85 m (280 ft), all to escape the attacking Muslims.

The 11th-century Karanlik Kilise ("dark church", left) is famed for its frescos of Biblical scenes.

KONYA

Location: Central Turkey
Best time to travel: March–October
www.konya.bel.tr

The mosques and madrasas (teaching buildings) of this old Seljuk capital have enough beautiful carvings to satisfy any fan of historic architecture and sculpture. The Mevlana Tekkesi, a monastery of the Dervish order, has been a center of Mevlana worship for many centuries. The Hall of Huzuri Pir ("presence of the divine") is packed with visitors wishing to press their hands and lips to the sarcophagus of Jalal ad-Din Rumi. The founder of the order, who was born in Persia, taught for almost half a century in Konya and died there in 1273.

The Order of Whirling Dervishes was founded in Konya.

KYKKOS

Location: South-western Cyprus
Best time to travel: March–September
www.kykkos-museum.cy.net

Kykkos Monastery is located near the town of Pedoulas. It is the most famous and also the mightiest monastery on Cyprus. It was founded by Alexios Komnenos toward the end of the 11th century, the Byzantine emperor who also donated his most precious treasure to the church: the fascinating and elaborate icon of St Mary painted by the Apostle Luke. Cyprus' first president, Archbishop Marakios III, who is buried in the nearby town of Throni, was a true neophyte in the Kykkos Monastery during his younger years.

Kykkos is the oldest and most powerful monastery on the island.

ASINOU

Location: Northern Cyprus
Best time to travel: March–September
www.visitcyprus.com

The Church of Our Lady of Asinou, or "Panagia Forviotissa", stands alone on a wooded hill near Nikitari. From the outside, it appears to be a simple facility, but inside it is home to what is probably the most amazing and beautiful Byzantine fresco treasure on the island. The *Last Supper*, *Annunciation* and *Nativity*, the *Vita Jesu* and dozens of pictures of martyrs illustrate the complete spectrum of exhilarating imagery from the Orthodox faith. Most of the murals date back to the 11th century.

The beautiful frescos at Asinou have been painstakingly restored and cleaned.

PAPHOS

Location: South-western Cyprus
Best time to travel:
March–September
www.visitpafos.com

This island state in the eastern Mediterranean has been thought of as the island of Aphrodite since she rose fully-formed from the waters here in ancient times, but Cyprus has far more to offer than love, fresh air, and long beaches. There is ancient art and culture in Paphos, or the barn-roofed churches and monasteries in the Troodos Mountains. Near the village of Kuklia to the south-east of the modern city of Paphos you will find the ruins of a town that was probably settled by the Phoenicians in the 12th or 13th century BC. A shrine to Aphrodite grew up here during Mycenean rule in the 12th century, and the ruins of the religious site in Old Paphos take the form of an oriental courtyard shrine constructed of giant blocks of limestone. In the middle of the courtyard there was an oval stone symbolizing the goddess of love, beauty, and sensual desire. New Paphos was founded in the 4th century BC on the site of the modern city and here too there was a shrine to Aphrodite. The ruined city walls, burial sites, and several elaborate mosaics are evidence of the continuing importance of ancient Paphos as a trading center even into Roman times. Early Christianity and Byzantine culture also left major monuments here in the form of catacombs and churches, many of which have beautifully decorated interiors.

The Roman floor mosaic discovered in the House of Aion in 1962 illustrates the climax of the flute-playing competition between Apollo and Marsyas (left) as well as depicting a lyre-playing centaur paying court to a maenad (above). The mosaic floors of these elite villas are among the finest in the Eastern Mediterranean.

MOSCOW

Location: Western Russia
Best time to travel: throughout the year
http://mos.ru
www.moscow-city.ru

Russia's capital lies on the Moskva River, a tributary of the Volga. First mention was made of it in 1147, and by 1325 it had become a grand ducal residence. During the reign of Czar Peter the Great, Moscow lost its capital city status in 1713 to newly founded St Petersburg. It was the Bolsheviks who made Moscow the political center of Russia again in 1918. Over the course of its history the city has been plundered repeatedly as well as suffering devastating fires. At the beginning of the 20th century Moscow boasted 450 churches, 25 monasteries, and 800 charitable institutions. After the disintegration of the USSR, the metropolis still has an impressive cultural complement. For centuries, historical and political events in Russia have been inextricably linked to the Moscow Kremlin, seat of the czars and the metropolitan bishops since the 13th century. Architecturally speaking, the Kremlin had already attained its current size at the time of Grand Prince Ivan IV, known as Ivan the Terrible, who had himself crowned as czar in 1547. First mention of the city's defensive wall was documented in 1147; it was still a wooden construction until the 14th century. Ivan the Terrible gradually had the city walls and the numerous churches almost entirely rebuilt by the leading Italian and Russian master builders of the time, preferring to have more ostentatious and imposing buildings constructed in their place. These grand edifices were continuously expanded and remodeled until well into the 20th century. They now house priceless works of art. The Kremlin is still Russia's seat of government, for which

the term "Kremlin" is synonymous. Within its walls are magnificent palaces, armories, senate buildings, as well as cathedrals and churches with characteristic gilded domes. Red Square is roughly 500 by 150 m (1,640 by 492 ft) and was built at the end of the 15th century as a market and gathering place, in addition to its use as a place of execution. The famous St Basil's Cathedral was built by Ivan the Terrible after his victory over the Mongol Golden Horde. The magnificent cathedral, consecrated in 1561, is considered an outstanding masterpiece of Old Russian construction. The central, steepled church is surrounded by eight chapels on a single foundation and arranged in the shape of a cross. It was the addition of St Basil's Chapel that gave the whole complex its name. Actually, the central building with the pavilion roof is dominated by the nine differently designed chapels. At the time of its completion in 1893, GUM, which was designed as a marketplace and today houses one of the largest department stores in the world, was considered one of the most advanced buildings in Russia with its steel and glass roof. The architect Pomeranzev combined both Renaissance and traditional Russian architectural elements in the building, designing it as a shopping center.

The Kremlin in Moscow is composed of a whole collection of fortresses and church towers (opposite, top, the banks of the Moskva River).

The Church of the Deposition was built by Russian artisans between 1484 and 1485. Its ornate interior includes a beautiful 17th-century iconostasis (middle).

Red Square is surrounded by the Kremlin wall, St Basil's Cathedral (left) the GUM department store, and the Museum of History.

THE GOLDEN RING

Location: Western Russia
Best time to travel: April–September
www.visitrussia.com
www.vladimir-city.ru
www.museum.vladimir.ru
www.city-yar.ru
www.adm.yar.ru

The Golden Ring is the absolute zenith for fans of Old Russian art and architecture. The term Golden Ring, which was first coined in Russia at the start of the 1970s, refers to a ring of enchanting old towns north of Moscow. The main towns are Vladimir, Suzdal, Yaroslavl, Rostov Veliky, Sergiev Posad, Pereslavl-Zalessky and Kostroma. What began in the Middle Ages as fortresses providing protection against the Mongolian hordes from Central Asia, have since developed into a series of Old Russian towns with mighty kremlins, defensive monasteries and quaint churches whose magnificent mosaics, icons, and invaluable treasures stood in stark contrast to the misery of everyday life in these poor rural towns.

The term "golden" refers to the striking, gilded domes of the medieval churches (right, the Church of St Elias in Jaroslawl), and the word "ring" denotes the close cultural and historic ties that bind the individual towns. They stand as mute stone reminders of a bygone era – that of the "Old Russia"that existed up until the October Revolution of 1917, and until that time was a deeply religious nation.

ST PETERSBURG

Location: Western Russia
Best time to travel: throughout the year
http://petersburgcity.com
www.saint-petersburg.com

After Czar Peter the Great had forced the Swedish King Charles XII to part with a strip of coastline along the Gulf of Finland, he finally gained his long-awaited access to the Baltic Sea, and thus to the West. He then built his new capital there, St Petersburg, which was intended to outmatch the splendor of other European cities. A great number of master architects and builders from Western and Central Europe such as Bartolomeo Rastrelli, Domenico Trezzini and Andreas Schlüter were involved in the construction of St Petersburg, a city that is particularly impressive with regard to the harmony created between its baroque and classical styles, grandiose squares, and numerous canals with more than 400 bridges. Nevsky Prospekt, St Petersburg's magnificent promenade, is lined with ostentatious buildings such as the Anitchkov and Stroganov Palaces. The Winter Palace is one of the most significant buildings in Russian baroque style. Begun in 1754 based on plans drawn up by Bartolomeo Rastrelli, it was intended as an imperial residence alongside the Neva River. The Winter Palace is the largest component of the Hermitage complex. The Hermitage is one of the most important art museums in the world. It comprises the Winter Palace, the Small, the New and the Old Hermitage, as well as the Hermitage Theater. The Hermitage art collection, which was started by Catherine the Great, is a museum of superlatives. The more than 1,000 magnificently designed rooms display around 60,000 exhibits, while the archive encompasses three million items. In addition to the archaeological section with ex-

hibits dating back to antiquity, visitors can also enjoy a massive collection of classical European art. The Winter Palace owes its current design to Peter the Great's successor, Empress Elizabeth. In fact, the building where the Emperor died in 1725 – on the site that is now occupied by the Hermitage Theater – was torn down completely to make way for the new palace. The square in front of the Winter Palace with the Alexander Column has been the scene of key historical events. It was here that more than 1,000 demonstrators were murdered by czarist troops in 1905, and it was here that the October Revolution began in 1917, when the Bolsheviks stormed the grounds. The Peterhof residence was built in 1714. It has an ornately designed garden and is indubitably the most elegant of the imperial residences around St Petersburg. Particular attention was paid during its planning to sophisticated water features including decadent fountains for which special wells were built. The suburb of Lomonossov, once referred to as Oranienbaum, is home to an extensive complex of palaces and parks built for Prince Alexander Menshikov in the 18th century by Italian and German architects. It was later converted into a summer residence. The interior of this rococo palace boasts magnificent decor: furniture and parquet flooring of the finest wood, silk wall hangings, embroidery, porcelain vases and lacquer work as well as wall and ceiling paintings.

Left: the Winter Palace is one of the Russian baroque's finest creations. The Cathedral of St Peter and St Paul with its golden spire was built within the grounds of the fortress of the same name between 1712 and 1733. Opposite: middle, the Anichkov Bridge over the Fontanka; below, the Jordan Staircase in the Winter Palace; top, the interior of the Hermitage.

The world's highest mountains, vast shimmering deserts and dense misty rainforests are all hallmarks of Asia, the largest continent on earth. The cultures from the Euphrates and Tigris rivers were the cradle of human civilizations. The empires of the ancient Orient, of Islam, Hinduism, and Buddhism all generated an immeasurably rich cultural heritage. One example are the rice terraces built into steep mountain slopes on Bali, a testament to the skills the local people developed over centuries.

GEGHARD

Location: Central Armenia
Best time to travel: April–September
www.armenica.org

The monastery complex of Geghard, situated some 50 km (31 mi) west of Yerevan, owes its extraordinary character to its cave churches and the tombs that have been painstakingly cut out of the living rock. Even in pre-Christian days pagan cults were said to have been celebrated in the caves at the end of the Azat River Gorge. An indication of this is also found in the earlier name the monastery, which allegedly refers to Gregory the Illuminator (c. 240 to 332): "Ayrivank" means "cave monastery". The present name "Geghard" (meaning "lance") is connected with the legend of the Holy Lance, said to have been brought to Armenia by the Apostle Jude, also known as Thaddeus, according to a chronicle dating from as early as the mid-12th century. The lance is said once to have been hidden here as a sacred relic. In the early 13th century the Geghard Monastery became the property of the Zaqaryan Princes, who also ordered the central Church of the Holy Mother of God to be built in 1215. Only a few centuries later the aristocractic Proshyan Family took over the monastery which they used mainly as their burial site.

Many individual structures, mostly built inside the excavated rock-face, are grouped together in the monastic complex. The central Church of the Holy Mother of God rises on a small plateau outside the rockface, immediately in front of the caves. The adjoining larger building was already hewn from the rock. The picture above shows an Easter mass in the Church of the Holy Mother of God.

DAMASCUS

Location: South-western Syria
Best time to travel: all year
www.esyria.sy
www.damascus-online.com

While the façades of the Sayyida Ruqayya Mosque, the main Shiite mosque in the Old Town of Damascus, are fairly plain, its interior decoration is a superb example of Persian interior architecture. The mosque was completed in 1985 with financial support from Iran, and houses the mausoleum of Ruqayya bint al-Hussein ash-Shaheed bi-Kerbala, a granddaughter-in-law of the Prophet Mohammed and the daughter of the martyr, Hussein of Kerbala. The shrine is decorated with solid gold plates, and the walls are adorned with polychrome mosaics. Mohammed himself is said to have refused to visit the city of Damascus because he did not wish to enter any paradise other than that awaiting him in Heaven. Today the city still does justice to its poetic name, "Diamond of the Desert". The cityscape has been marked by the Muslim faith and its architecture since the eighth century. The Great Mosque was built on the foundations of a Christian church in 705, at the zenith of Omayyad rule. It is one of the oldest Islamic prayer houses and a trend-setter in Islamic sacred architecture.

In the immediate vicinity of the Great Mosque can be found the city's famous markets (souks), including the roofed Souk al-Hamidiyya, as well as other treasures of Islamic architecture including Maristan Nureddin, a hospital built in 1154; the Nureddin Madrassa; the Hammam Nureddin, a men-only bath house; and the mausoleum with Saladin's Tomb dating from the year 1193.

ALEPPO

Location: North-western Syria
Best time to travel: all year
www.visit-syria.com
www.syriatourism.org

Testimonies of the most diverse of cultures have been preserved in this city in the far north-west of present-day Syria, located on the crossroad of ancient trading routes. Excavations on the Citadel Mound indicate that Aleppo (Halab) was populated as early as the third millennium BC, making it one of the oldest continuously settled places in the world. Two historic buildings stand out on the Old City, which is richly endowed with medieval madrassas, palaces, caravanserais and bath houses: the Citadel and the Great Mosque of Aleppo, founded in 715 by the Omayyads and rebuilt by the Zengid Sultan Nur al-Din after a devastating fire in 1190. On Citadel Mound, an Assyrian-Hittite temple complex existed as early as the 10th century BC. After they had refounded the city in the 3rd century BC, the Seljuks built a first fortress on the mountain plateau. In its present form the Citadel dates from the late 13th century. The Omayyad Mosque is adorned by one of the main works of medieval Assyrian architecture: the 48-m-high (157-ft) minaret, dating from the end of the 11th century and richly embellished with carved inscriptions.

An arched entrance bridge (top left in the picture) leads to the Citadel's fortified gateway, built in 1211. The Citadel is sited on a moated mound and dominates Aleppo.

PALMYRA

Location: Central Syria
Best time to travel: all year
www.syriatourism.org

Monumental ruins in the Syrian Desert testify to the former political and economic power of the Roman colony of Palmyra and the subsequent splinter empire under Zenobia, the legendary queen of Syria. Located between Damascus and the Euphrates River, this merchant city was already of great importance in pre-Roman times, acting as a trading hub between East and West. However, the greatest period of prosperity for Palmyra, the present-day city of Tadmur, came at the time when Rome dominated Asia Minor. A crossroads for caravan routes, the oasis city attained its great economic significance when Emperor Caracalla raised it to the status of a Roman colony. Located on the Silk Road, Palmyra quickly accumulated great wealth. Queen Zenobia, who ruled the Palmyrene Empire from 267, expanded the city into a superb royal residence based on Roman models, and in the process mingled the cultures of the Hellenic Orient with those of the Parthians and Romans. The Baal Temple of Palmyra, a columned road, an amphitheater, an agora, the tower graves and the cemeteries in the "Valley of the Tombs" all testify to the sophisticated art of the time.

The columned road, one of ancient Syria's magnificent boulevards, began at the triumphal arch of Palmyra, built in the honor of the Emperor Hadrian. The 16th-century Arab fortress on the hill makes for an atmospheric backdrop.

BAALBEK

Location: Eastern Lebanon
Best time to travel: all year
www.lebanon-tourism.gov.lb

According to the Bible, Adam, the original man, lived near Baalbek. Cain, Noah and Abraham are said to be linked with this place as well. The name Baalbek goes back to the Phoenician period, when the town was founded. It means "Lord of the Bekaa Plain". In the third and second centuries BC, the settlement was known as Heliopolis, the "City of the Sun". Various rock graves are preserved from that time. As is often the case, however, it owes its most important remains to the Romans, who conquered Syria in the year 64 BC and proceeded to construct one of the largest and most interesting temple complexes of the ancient world. In the year AD 14, during the reign of Emperor Augustus, construction began on the enormous Temple of Jupiter, which was built on the ruins of existing Phoenician houses of worship. It took some fifty years to complete.

From the same period are the Temple of Bacchus, a masterpiece of Greco-Roman architecture that is considered the best-preserved ancient temple complex in the entire Middle East. Baalbek is also famous for its giant stone foundation blocks used in constructing the temple town. The "largest building block in the world" weighs 1,500 metric tons.

The 22-m-high (72-ft) columns still give an excellent indication of the once truly gigantic proportions of the Temple of Jupiter.

PETRA

Location: Western Jordan
Best time to travel: all year
www.visitjordan.com

In 169 BC the Nabataeans chose for their capital the bottom of the Wadi Musa valley behind the Siq Gorge, which is only a few meters wide but 200 m (656 ft) deep and thus virtually inaccessible. The most impressive structures of Petra are giant rock graves cut into the rock, their splendid façades presenting an impressive interplay of traditional Arab construction methods and Hellenic architecture featuring mighty columns, cornices and gables. Richly adorned tombs with interesting names make it apparent that the Nabataeans believed in life after death.

Petra, the "Rock City" is also known as the "Treasury of the Pharaohs" among Bedouins.

WADI RUM

Location: Southern Jordan
Best time to travel: April–September
www.wadirum.jo
www.visitjordan.com

People have made use of the favorable conditions here since prehistoric times as is apparent from the countless wells between the bizarre sandstone formations and the much deeper impermeable granite plinth. Less known is the fact that the Wadi Rum is a rich source of phosphate, which is an important source of income for Jordan.

The 50-km-long (31-mi) valley is one of Jordan's great destinations (top) where for centuries Howeitat Bedouins (left) have lived with their camels and goats. Today, many Bedouins work as guides in the valley and the nature reserve.

JERUSALEM

Location: Central Israel
Best time to travel: all year
www.jerusalem.muni.il
www.jerusalemtourist.com

In the city of David und Jesus Christ, the Prophet Mohammed experienced his "Miraj", or "Stairway to Heaven", and Babylonians, Romans, Arabs, Crusaders and Turks also ruled in this city at various times: There are few other places in the world that are as intertwined with world history as Jerusalem.

The city offers a multifaceted journey through time, with the great monuments of Judaism, Christianity and Islam clearly visible to all – and most are located within the Old City of Jerusalem and its fortified walls. The main sites include the Citadel with the Tower of David; the Armenian Quarter with the St James Cathedral; the Jewish Quarter with the Ha'ari and Ramban synagogues; the ruins of the Hurva Synagogue; the "Burnt House"; and the Western Wall, the most important Jewish sanctuary. Nearly one-sixth of the Old City is taken up by the Temple Mount where, according to the Old Testament, Abraham sacrificed his son Isaac.

The Via Dolorosa, the "Road of Pain" along which Jesus carried his crucifix in the New Testament, leads via the fourteen Stations of the Cross up to Calvary with the Church of the Holy Sepulcher on Temple Mount. In the middle of the Temple Mount area stands the Dome of the Rock, which is adorned by mosaics. The original exterior mosaics suffered in the winter weather and were later replaced by tiles by Suleiman the Magnificent in 1545.

The Western Wall, also known as the Wailing Wall, is a 48-m (130-ft) section of a wall dating back to the Second Temple. Built on the site of the Holy Temple, it is one of the most sacred and important sites in

Judaism, a place where visiting pilgrims can place slips of paper containing prayers, wishes and thanks into cracks in the wall.

The neighborhood below the Western Wall has been settled by Jews since the eighth century BC but their presence grew through the 13th century when they began building Talmud Torah schools and synagogues. In 1701, construction of the Hurva Synagogue began under Rabbi Yehuda Hassid. When the Jewish cleric died, however, construction was halted and the synagogue was not completed until 150 years later. It was then destroyed by the Jordanians during the 1948 Arab-Israeli War. The ruins have been preserved as a memorial.

At the end of the seventh century, during the reign of Caliph Abd al-Malik (646–705), Byzantine and Arab architects built the Dome of the Rock on the Temple Mount, the oldest of all sacred Islamic buildings. Stained-glass windows allow soft light to flood the interior of the cupola, which is supported by colonnaded arcades.

Six Christian denominations share the Church of the Holy Sepulcher on Temple Mount: the Eastern Orthodox, Armenian Apostolic, Roman Catholic, Coptic Orthodox, Ethiopian Orthodox and Syriac Orthodox Churches. It marks the location of the Resurrection of Christ, hence it is also known as the Church of the Resurrection. The Roman Catholic Chapel of the Invention of the Holy Cross is said to be on the spot where the True Cross of Christ was found.

"Man is but a fleeting guest on earth, but the Jerusalemite is a fleeting guest in a spot of land that is impregnated with eternity" (Shalom Ben Chorin). Clockwise from top left: a view of the Western Wall; the Dome of the Rock on Temple Mount; the Jewish Quarter; and the Church of the Holy Sepulcher.

MECCA, MEDINA

Location: Western Saudi Arabia
Best time to travel: all year (open only to Muslims)
www.asiarooms.com

As the birthplace of the Prophet Mohammed (c. 570–632), Mecca, situated in western Saudi Arabia, is the holiest and most important sacred site in Islam. Every year millions of worshippers make the pilgrimage to the town, which is closed to non-Muslims. In the courtyard of the central mosque with its seven minarets is the Kaaba where the faithful call, like Mohammed and Abraham before them: "Labbaik Allah humma labbaik!" – "Here I am at Your service O Lord, here I am!" The Kaaba a cube-shaped, windowless building, each year covered by a new black cloth (kiswa). Pilgrims touch the "Black Stone", in the eastern corner of the otherwise bare Kaaba that was venerated by Arab tribes in pre-Islamic days already. According to legend, Abraham, the first of the patriarchs in the Bible and the

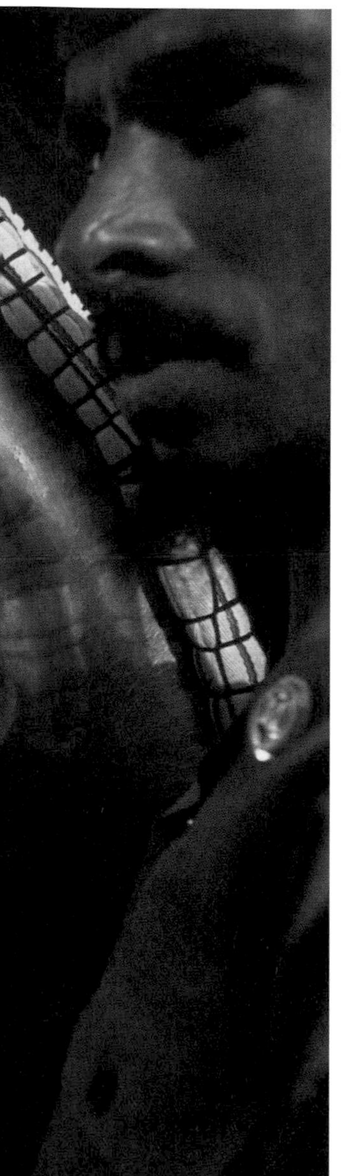

father of the people of Israel, is said to have been gifted the stone by the Archangel Gabriel as a gift from Paradise. The stone, believed by some to be a meteorite, has never been scientifically examined but has spawned many a legend: Thus, it is said to have been white originally and only to have turned black in grief over the sins of mankind.

Medina is the second most important pilgrimage destination in Islam. It was the refuge of Mohammed in the year 622 and became his home. It is also closed to non-Muslims, but the haram, or closed area, is much smaller than that of Mecca.

Every year, some two million faithful set out on the Hajj, the pilgrimage to Mecca. In the courtyard of the main mosque stands the Kaaba, a cube-shaped structure (large picture and top on this page). The Prophet Mohammed and his only daughter, Fatima, are buried in the Great Mosque of Medina (above).

SANAA

Location: Western Yemen
Best time to travel: all year
www.visityemen.com
www.yementourism.com

The town of Sana'a dates back to a fortress from Sabaean days. It prospered under the rule of the Himyarite kings after 520. In 628 present-day Yemen became part of an Islamic caliphate; Mohammed himself is believed to have supervised the building of the first mosque in Sana'a. The Great Mosque from that time is certainly impressive, yet it is undisputedly the Old City of Sana'a which is of the greatest historic significance. Ancient "skyscrapers" up to 1,000 years old dominate the cityscape in Sana'a, some of them boasting up to eight levels in height. The lower floors were built in traditional style using natural stone while the upper floors were constructed from rammed earth or pisé. The façades of these tower houses is especially remarkable. Various decorative elements adorn the houses: the white trim and stucco friezes indicate the height of each floor level and outline the windows. The most common features are the semicircular skylight openings that are framed by stucco carvings with rich floral or geometric designs and decorated all over with beautifully stained glass.

Mud brick tower houses rise tall in the picturesque Old Town of Sana'a, the capital of the Yemen and probably one of the most beautiful places along the Incense Road.

HAJAR

Location: North-eastern Oman
Best time to travel: October–May
www.omantourism.gov.om

From Muscat it is worth taking a detour into the Al Hajar Mountains, which rise to 3,000 m (9,843 ft) and stretch in a gentle S-shape along the coast from the Musandam Peninsula in the north to the south-eastern corner of the Arabian Peninsula. Farmers still irrigate the narrow terraced fields on the slopes here using the ancient falaj tunnel system. About 80 km (50 mi) outside of Muscat is the village of Barka.

South of Barka, at the foot of the Al Hajar Mountains, the eastern end of the Al Batinah Plain extends. Well worth seeing is the village of Nakhl ("palm tree"), which is dominated by one of Oman's largest mud brick fortresses.

MUSCAT

Location: Northern Oman
Best time to travel: October–May
www.omantourism.gov.om

The capital of the Sultanate of Oman is surrounded by the mountains of the Al Hajar range, directly by the sea. The Portuguese conquered the town in the early 16th century but were forced to withdraw 150 years later. The two fortresses Al Mirani and Al Jalali were further enlarged by later rulers. Today, lovingly cared for parks characterize the city, which has long expanded from Old Muscat. The Sultan Qaboos Grand Mosque was completed in 2001. Despite modernization, the "Capital Area" has preserved its unique charm.

Some brightly painted 18th-century merchants' homes still stand in the port area of Mutrah, a former suburb of Muscat.

BAT, AL-KHUTM AND AL-AYN

Location: Central Oman
Best time to travel: October–May
www.omantourism.gov.om

The historic site of Bat and the nearby excavation sites of Al-Khutm and Al-Ayn are deep in the interior of the Sultanate of Oman, near the Bat Oasis. The remains of four towers and a settlement as well as interesting necropolises were found here. In front of the steep walls of the western Al Hajar Range you can see beehive-shaped tomb structures made from the local brownish limestone, which disintegrates into tile-like blocks when cut and which was ritually piled up to 8 m (26 ft) high.

Excavations indicate that this region on the ancient copper trade routes to Mesopotamia was once densely populated.

DUBAI

Location: United Arab Emirates
Best time to travel: October–May
www.dubai.ae

The "Las Vegas on the Gulf" attracted seafarers from Great Britain and India back at the beginning of the 20th century, at a time when the trade in gold was already an important pillar of the economy. Indeed, the rulers of Dubai do not simply rely on oil when planning for the future. Aside from the Jebel Ali Free Zone and the international airport, tourism is adding ever-larger sums to the state's coffers. Luxury hotels are built in neo-Oriental style and new beaches are created using the finest white sand. One of the most impressive examples of making dreams come true are the Palm Islands, the new icon of Dubai next to the Burj Al Arab Hotel, which is shaped like the sail of a dhow, and the 818-m (2,684-ft) Burj Dubai, the world's tallest skyscraper completed in 2009. Next to them, the old houses with their wind towers are quite modest. Divided in two by Dubai Creek (al-Khor), the emirate markets itself is as "the most beautiful shopping paradise in the world" with lively bazaars, or souks, arranged in covered shopping alleys. In the south-west is Bur Dubai with the Dubai Museum in the old Al-Fahidi Fortress and the oldest district, Bastakiah. On the other side of the Creek, in the Deira port district, you can still get an idea of life in the Emirates before the oil boom. This is where the dhows anchor, merchant boats with triangular sails from pre-Islamic days.

A place of superlatives (clockwise from top left): from the giant Palm Islands via the tallest skyscraper in the world to the as yet only 7-star hotel in the world, designed as a stylized sail. Time seems to stand still only in the soukhs.

ISFAHAN

Location: South-western Iran
Best time to travel: all year
www.isfahan.ir

Isfahan, about 350 km (217 mi) south of Tehran in the foothills of the Zagros Mountains, developed as a center of Islamic architecture and scholarship in the 16th and 17th centuries. Shah Abbas I (1587–1629) was obsessed with construction and made extensive changes to his residence. During his reign, Isfahan became one of the most important cities in the Orient as far as culture and art are concerned. His main building project was the vast Naghsh-e Jahan Square (the "Design of the World"), later renamed Meidan-e-Shah ("Royal Square"), and known as Meidan-e Imam (Imam Square) since the revolution. Surrounded by two-story arcades and extending over a length of 500 m (1,600 ft), it is among the largest squares in the world.

The square is framed by four remarkable building complexes: the former royal mosque known as Imam Mosque on the south side; the Sheikh Lotfollah Mosque on the east side; the royal Ali Qapu Palace ("High Gate") on the west side; and the portal to the Royal Qeisarieh Bazaar on the north side. The most important edifice on the grand square is the Imam Mosque with its four tall iwans typical of Iranian-Islamic architecture.

A characteristic style element, muqarnas fill the niche above the main portal of the Imam Mosque with its stalactite-like decoration (top center). The mosque, which has a separate area for women, is resplendent with an abundance of decorative tiles and mosaics.

PERSEPOLIS

Location: Central Iran
Best time to travel: all year
www.irol.com

The Achaemenid King Darius I, the most important ruler of the Achaemenid dynasty, laid the foundation stone for the royal palace of Persepolis in 520 BC. Although he already had two capitals at the time – Pasargadae and Susa – he wished to present the world with a remarkable residence that would reflect the size of his empire. The result was the most magnificent work of Achaemenidic Persian art, built on an artificial terrace covering 125,000 sq m (1,345,000 sq ft). The royal buildings took almost sixty years to complete. A relief in the treasure house of Persepolis depicts King Darius I receiving a delegation of Medeans who had been subjugated by Cyrus II, a predecessor. Darius I himself only lived to see the completion of the palace, the treasury and the colonnaded hall (Apadana) with its thirty-six 20-m (66-ft) columns featuring superb reliefs. It was his son Xerxes who continued with the ambitious plans. Upon arrival, everyone had to be registered in order to be considered for an audience with the king. However, the "Dream of Darius" was laid to waste in 330 BC by Alexander the Great. The last Shah of Iran, Reza Pahlavi, had some parts of the town rebuilt in 1971.

The 70-m (230-ft) relief on the eastern ascent of the colonnaded hall of Persepolis depicts the delegates from twenty-eight countries in the Achaemenid Empire, who had come to pay their tribute. Top left: the "Gate of all Nations", the main entrance to the royal residence.

SAMARKAND

Location: Eastern Uzbekistan
Best time to travel: all year
www.visit-uzbekistan.com

Samarkand was first mentioned in documents in 329 BC when Alexander the Great conquered the former Marakanda. Trade, artisanship and culture flourished in this oasis city in the valley of the Zarafshan River. Once the Silk Route had finally linked China with the Mediterranean in the first century BC, Samarkand became a lively hub of culture and civilization. The prosperous trading town was conquered by a number of empires and dynasties including Chinese, Arabs, Samanids and Seljuks – and was finally destroyed in 1220 by Genghis Khan.
In 1369, Mongol ruler Timur Leng (Tamerlane) made Samarkand the capital of his empire. He commissioned the most eminent artists, architects and scientists of the day to build a city of unsurpassed splendor. His grandson Ulughbek, ruler of the Timurid Dynasty from 1447, continued Timur's work. Ulughbek himself was also known as an outstanding astronomer. His three-story observatory and its brick sextant were excavated in the 20th century. Another masterpiece of medieval Islamic architecture from this period is the Bibi-Khanym Mosque with its 44-m-high (144-ft) domed central building. One of the most splendid squares in all of Central Asia is the Registan. On the city limits is the Shah-i-Zinda necropolis, a pilgrimage destination with many mausoleums from Timur's period.

Top: The magnificent Ulugh Beg, Tilla Kari and Sher Dor madrassas (from left to right) around Registan Square in Samarkand. Below: the Sher Dor Medrasa with its ornamental minarets, the prayer hall of the Tilla Kari Medrasa and the Shah-i-Zinda necropolis.

JAM

Location: Central Afghanistan
Best time to travel: all year
www.afghan-web.com

The second-highest minaret in the world (after the 210-m/689-ft minaret of the Hassan II Mosque in Casablanca) is situated in the narrow Hari Rud Valley, west of Chaghcharan in the desolate mountain landscape of the Hindu Kush. The 65-m (213-ft) Minaret of Jam, built in 1194, is a lavishly decorated brick structure with floral and geometric ornamentation as well as tiled inscriptions. Thanks to its enormous size and the artistic decoration, this slim brick tower marks a highpoint not only of Islamic architecture in the Middle Ages, but also illuminates the period of the Ghorids, who ruled in this region in the 12th and 13th centuries. Their sphere of influence extended all the

BAMIYAN VALLEY

Location: Central Afghanistan
Best time to travel: June–September
www.afghan-web.com

About 2300 years ago, one conqueror left a lasting impression on Afghanistan: Alexander the Great. He arrived with a posse of artisans and artists in his entourage who settled in the newly founded cities and there continued the Hellenic culture. The Bamiyan Valley is located around 200 km (124 mi) north-west of Kabul, at the crossroads of trading and pilgrimage routes from China to the Mediterranean and from India to Central Asia. Kanishka, the great Kushan King who ruled in Bamiyan during the first century BC, converted to Buddhism and laid the foundations for developing the Bamiyan as a Buddhist center and a destination

way to the Indian subcontinent – the Minaret of Jam actually became the model for the Qutb Minar in Delhi, which is actually much better known today.
After the decline of the Ghorid Dynasty, Jam was long forgotten until it was rediscovered during an archaeological expedition in 1957. Less spectacular, but also of great historic interest, are the ruins of a fortress, a palace, a Jewish cemetery and a bazaar as well as a fortification wall near the minaret.

The Minaret of Jam rises from an octagonal base, tapering towards the top. Its outside is decorated with geometric stucco patterns as well as relief tiles and ribbons with an inscription in shiny blue ceramic of the 19th Sura (chapter) of the Qur'an, which chronicles the work of the prophets. Medieval fortresses were secured in the surrounding hills.

for scholars and pilgrimages. A distinctive, strongly Greek-influenced style of Buddhism emerged. Work was soon begun on some 900 cave homes which were hewn into the cliffs and then decorated with religious frescoes and stucco details. Later, probably during the sixth century, two giant Buddha statues were also chiseled out of the rock. These were tragically destroyed in March 2001 by the Taliban, who considered them idolatry, which is prohibited under Sharia Law.

In an impressive mountain landscape south of the HIndu Kush lies the Bamiyan Valley. Many residential caves have been hewn from the rock (left) and two monumental Buddha statues were also chiseled out here. The picture on the page opposite shows the larger of the two, the 55-m (ft) Buddha, with his Greek-like toga before destruction by the Taliban.

KARAKORAM

Location: Central Asia (Pakistan, China, India)
Best time to travel: June–September
http://karakorams.com

Northern Pakistan is dominated by enormous mountain ranges that continue into China to the east. The Karakoram join the Himalayas here in the Hindu Kush and boast some of the highest peaks on earth. In fact, about half of the world's one hundred tallest mountains are in the Karakoram, all within a very small area. The tallest of them all, K2, at 8,614 m (28,263 ft) is also the second-highest on Earth. The Karakoram Highway, a combined project of Pakistan and China completed in 1978, is 1,284 km (798 mi) long and connects Havelian in north-western Pakistan with Kashgar in the western Chinese province of Xinjiang. Snaking its way past 8,000-m (25,000-ft) peaks such as Nanga Parbat, the Karakoram Highway – the highest road in the world – reaches its apex on the 4,733-m (15,529-ft) Khunjerab Pass, which marks the border between Pakistan and China. The architectural style of the 600-year-old Baltit Fort, the former residence of the Hunza commander, also reveals Tibetan influences. In 1979, a German ethnographer discovered some 30,000 rock paintings and inscriptions in the Hunza and Indus valleys, the oldest of which date from the Early Bronze Age.

The section of the Karakorum Highway with the most beautiful landscape is located in the Hunza Valley (right): snow-covered peaks seemingly close enough to touch, with the Rakaposhi (7,788 m/-25,552 ft) towering above all; glaciers extending down to the road as well as isolated villages. Opposite: K 2 is the world's second-highest mountain.

DELHI

Location: Northern India
Best time to travel: all year
www.visitdilli.com
www.delhitourism.com

Old and New Delhis present themselves as a story of contrasts, with historic monuments sprinkled far and wide across both districts of the city, the silent witnesses of a turbulent history. In the late 12th century, Muslims under Qutb-ud-din Aybak conquered northern India and the Rajput fortress of Lal Kot, a settlement that preceded the foundation of Delhi. When they erected their first mosque there, Qutb-ud-din's subjects relied primarily on local architects and traditions, which is why the Quwwat ul-Islam (Might of Islam) Mosque was built in the reddish-yellow sandstone typical of the area on the site of a columned hall characteristic of earlier Jain sanctuaries. Only the decoration and the bands of calligraphic script along the walls and façades are actually traditional Islamic features. From the ruins of the large mosque rises the 72-m-high (236-ft) Qutb Minar, the tallest brick minaret in the world. Its base is around 15 m (49 ft) in diameter while the tip measures just under 3 m (10 ft). Known for its red sandstone fluting, used here for the first time in India as a stylistic feature, the top two floors of Qutb Minar were destroyed by lightning in the 14th century and rebuilt later in white marble.

Shah Jahan (Persian for "King of the World") was the fifth in a notable series of Mughal rulers in India and was an energetic commissioner of buildings, including the Taj Mahal in Agra. Begun in 1639, it took just nine years to complete the Red Fort next to the Salimgarh Fort, which had been built by Islam Shah Suri back in 1546.

Together, these two grand edifices form the complex of the Red Fort in

Old Delhi. This impressive structure, which was plundered twice during its colorful history – once in 1739 by Persian forces and then again in 1857 by British troops –, owes its name to the imposing, 16-m-high (52-ft) sandstone walls that surround the complex. During sunset the red hues of the stone create a dazzling spectacle.

The works of Humayun, the son of Babur, founder of the Mughal dynasty in India, were pivotal in the history of Mughal architecture. Although the security of his empire in India – he ruled between 1531 and 1556 – was initially less than ideal, the result was a boon. The young regent spent fifteen years in exile in Persia before returning, this time not just with a mighty army, but a host of master builders and artisans as well. His decision proved to be of great benefit to the architectural milieu on the Indian subcontinent, which flourished in the flood of new inspiration.

The Persian influence of his court is exemplified by the dome atop the high tambour, the gracefully arched alcoves and the spacious corridors of the tomb. The white marble and red sandstone façade also recalls Persian tradition.

Generous halls with vaults featuring great decorative detail, columns and windows are typical of the buildings in the Red Fort (large picture). The shapes and patterns combine Persian-Central Asian and Indian Hindu architectural elements. Humayun's tomb (left) was built on the orders of his wife, Haji Begum. The Great Mughal, who had died fourteen years earlier, did not find his last resting place in the burial chamber until the year 1570. The famous Qutb Minar (opposite, bottom far left in the picture), the first Islamic structure on Indian soil, clearly demonstrates the fusion of Hindu and Islamic architectural shapes.

TAJ MAHAL

Location: Agra, northern India (Uttar Pradesh)
Best time to travel: October–March
www.taj-mahal-india-travel.com

The name of this famous white-marble architectural gem derives from Mumtaz Mahal, the endearing name of Shah Jahan's beloved wife, Arjumand Banu Begum, who lies buried there. The name means "Diadem Palace", or "Pearl of the Palace", and the edifice represents the zenith of a style that was initially developed in the tomb of Humayun, one of Jahan's predecessors. At the end of long, terraced gardens and surrounded by grand water fountains, the perfectly symmetrical mausoleum rises elegantly from a massive square plinth. The central domed tower sits on a high tambour in the Persian style and is surrounded by other domed pavilions. The wonderful façades, also in the Persian style, are oriented towards the four points of the compass while the four minarets accentuate the four corners of the plinth. The obvious Persian influence is thought to be the work of Isa Afandi, a master builder from Shiraz in the south-west of what is now Iran.

One of the most beautiful structures in Islamic architecture is the Taj Mahal – the tomb Shah Jahan built in Agra for his late beloved wife Mumtaz Mahal in 1631.

RED FORT

Location: Agra, northern India (Uttar Pradesh)
Best time to travel: October–March
www.tourismagra.org

Agra owes its importance to the Mughal emperors, who built the Red Fort here. One of the largest fortresses in the world – although it could more accurately be described as a walled palatial city – it once had more than five hundred separate buildings. Like the Red Fort in Delhi, this fortress in Agra also owes its name to the red sandstone from which it was once constructed, but many of the later buildings in fact used white marble as the main building material.

Begun in 1565 by Mughal Emperor Akbar (which means "the Great" in Arabic), the Red Fort was later enlarged as a vast palace by Akbar's grandson, Shah Jahan. Enclosed by a broad moat and a 2.5-km (1.5-mi) wall, it comprises superb palaces, such as Shah Jahan's Jahangir Palace and Khas Mahal, audience halls and two beautiful mosques.

Agra is situated on the west bank of the Yamuna River, the largest tributary of the Ganga. The Red Fort complex offers stunning views all the way to the Taj Mahal (above left). Typical of Shah Akbar's imperial style is the Amar Singh Gate (top left), which stands in marked contrast with the fairy-tale styles of his successors.

KEOLADEO

Location: North-western India (Rajasthan)
Best time to travel: October–March
www.rajasthantourism.gov.in
www.indiawildliferesorts.com

Keoladeo National Park is a vast, man-made wetland region that was originally created by the maharajas of Bharatpur, who once enjoyed hunting the plentiful duck population. The marshy area was so abundant with the waterfowl they coveted that several thousand birds could be rounded up in a single day. In order to make an even larger marshland area for hunting, the maharajas built artificial canals and dams in the 19th century. This allowed a region to develop that soon became a popular breeding ground for other birds due to the very dry surrounding country.

FATEHPUR SIKRI

Location: Northern India (Uttar Pradesh)
Best time to travel: October–March
www.travelmasti.com

A Sufi saint and advisor to the emperor, Salim Chishti, once lived not far from Agra. When Salim's prophecy came true that the Mughal emperor would be borne three sons, Akbar pledged to build a town near the wise man's camp. The foundation stone was laid in 1569, and after just three years the Royal Mosque with a mausoleum for Sheikh Salim was completed. Inside, followers oft he Sufi faith say their prayers – Salim was an important representative of its teachings.

Emperor Akbar built the Fatehpur Sikri residence, "The City of Victory", to fulfil a vow he had made.

Today, the protected area provides a permanent sanctuary for about 120 bird species. It is also home to one of the largest populations of herons in the world. In the winter months some 240 species of migratory birds make their way to the national park including the rare Siberian crane (or snow crane) and the falcated duck. The Siberian cranes used to be one of Keoladeo's main attractions – more than 100 birds were still coming to spend winter in the swamps in 1976. Now they are unfortunately all but extinct.

The Keoladeo National Park is populated especially after the monsoon rains, when many migratory birds join the indemic water birds. Among those who feel at home in the refuge are the purple heron (opposite; this page from top left: Indian roller, rose-ringed or Alexandrine parakeet, and river kingfisher).

AMBER FORT, JAL MAHAL

Loction: North-western India (Rajasthan)
Best time to travel: October–March
www.rajasthantourism.gov.in

The fortified Palace of Amber was built in 1592 on the remains of a fort from the 12th century. Visitors can ride elephants up the serpentine path to the structure on the ridge, entering through the Suraj Pol, or Sun Gate. On the way to Jaipur, the capital of Rajasthan, you come upon another Mughal landmark, the Jal Mahal "Water Palace", built in the 18th century.

During the monsoon, then the water level rises, the "water palace" in the Man Sagar Lake seems to be floating (below left; above the Amber Fort).

JAIPUR

Location: North-western India (Rajasthan)
Best time to travel: October–March
www.jaipur.nic.in

It was the pink façades of the buildings that gave Jaipur its other name, the "Pink City". The capital of Rajasthan, Jaipur was founded in 1727 by Maharaja Sawai Jai Singh II (1688–1743), a man with a prominent place in his country's history books as a brilliant statesman, scholar and promoter of the arts. The honorary title of Sawai ("One and a Quarter") was bestowed on the maharaja early in his life.

From the bow-fronted windows of the Hawal Mahal ("Palace of the Winds") the ladies of the court were able to observe the streetlife without themselves being seen.

PUSHKAR

Location: North-western India (Rajasthan)
Best time to travel: October–March
ww.pushkar-fair.net

The tiny Pushkar Lake is said to have sprung from a lotus flower-dropped here by Lord Brahma, and the small town of Pushkar is one of the holiest places in India. "Little Varanasi" on the Lake is best visited in the early morning. The Savitri Temple on top of the hill is dedicated to Brahma's wife and affords superb views of the surrounding area. It takes about thirty minutes to reach the shrine on foot.

In October/November, visitors come for the Pushkar Mela, a camel and cattle market that is reminiscent of One Thousand and One Nights – a special experience.

MEHRANGARH FORT

Location: North-western India (Rajasthan)
Best time to travel: October–March
www.mehrangarh.org

Mighty Mehrangarh Fort, towering proudly over the town of Jodhpur, is home to magnificent buildings from the 16th to 19th centuries including the Pearl Palace (Moti Mahal) and the Palace of Flowers (Phool Mahal). Their lavish murals, stained-glass windows and stunning mirrors recall the opulent lifestyle of the maharajas of the Rathore clan.

In 1459, King Rao Jodha selected the nearly 120-m-high (39-ft) promontory as the site for the Mehrangarh Fort. Jodhpur, the city at the foot of the ridge, was also named after him.

JODHPUR

Location: North-western India (Rajasthan)
Best time to travel: October–March
www.jodhpur.biz

Jodhpur, in the south-eastern corner of the "Golden Desert Triangle", is Rajasthan's second-largest city and forms a stark contrast to the rural areas either side of the road that leads there. Hectic traffic and lively trading in the bazaar characterize life in the center. Jodhpur is also known as the "Blue City" after the color of its houses.

Blue is the divine color of Hinduism. Krishna (Sanskrit for "the dark one"), the most popular Hindu god, is typically depicted with blue skin and in the past only members of the Brahmin caste were allowed to paint their houses blue.

VARANASI

Location: North-eastern India (Uttar Pradesh)
Best time to travel: October–March
www.varanasicity.com
http://varanasi.nic.in

Varanasi (formerly called Benares) has been a documented Hindu pilgrimage site since as early as the 7th century. Most of the temples were built between the 16th and the 18th centuries and are dedicated to Shiva. Every day, pilgrims from around the world flock here to take a ritual cleansing bath in the Ganga River (or "Mother Ganga"), trek from temple to temple and pour the water from the Ganga over the lingam, Shiva's phallus symbol. Every Hindu is supposed to make a pilgrimage to Varanasi once in his or her life in order to achieve a better reincarnation or perhaps even the release of the soul from the circle of transmigrations. Life on the ghats is particularly lively in the early morning, when the sun lifts above the horizon. Stone staircases with a hundred steps each lead down to the river, religious tunes can be heard from the temples, and the faithful submerge themselves in the murky waters while muttering prayers and setting adrift sacrificial orange garlands of marigolds and oil lamps on the holy river.

Varanasi is also known as "Kashi" ("City of Light" or "The Shining One") to Indians. In the Hindu faith it is the holiest city for Shiva is said to have risen to heaven here as a glowing column of light, after cleansing himself of his sins. Many faithful come here not only for a cleansing bath in the Ganga River, but also in order to die. The dying, allegedly, can hear the god Shiva whisper into their ears, and whoever dies in Varanasi is said to be assured of redemption.

SANCHI

Location: Central India (Madhya Pradesh)
Best time to travel: October–March
www.buddhanet.net

Legend has it that the complex was originally founded by Ashoka the Great (r. 268–233 BC). Highlights here can be seen in the magnificent masonry works in Stupa 1, dating from the middle of the 3rd century BC. It is said to have been built over the bones of the Buddha himself. The sanctuary is shaped like a semicircle and surrounded by a palisade through which access is gained via four mighty stone gates or torana, each facing one of the four directions of the compass.

The stupa or pilgrimage site of Sanchi includes some of the oldest Buddhist buildings in India.

ELEPHANTA

Location: Island off Mumbai, south-western India (Maharashtra)
Best time to travel: October–March
www.travelmasti.com

The rock sanctuary of Elephanta dedicated to the Hindu god Shiva, one of the most important gods in the Hindu pantheon, is famous for its exquisite stone reliefs that depict the powerful deity in his many incarnations. The sculptures in this 7th-century rock temple are among the best examples of early Hindu art. The 6-m-tall (20-ft) bust of Shiva Mahadeva is especially impressive, showing the god with three faces and splendid headwear. Its dimensions are truly monumental.

At this rock sanctuary, Shiva shows his three faces – as creator, preserver and destroyer.

KHAJURAHO

Location: Central India (Madhya Pradesh)
Best time to travel: October–March
www.mp-tourism.com
www.tourismkhajuraho.org

The roughly 20 temples from the Chandella dynasty preserved in Khajuraho excel thanks to their outstandingly successful marriage of architecture and sculpture. The site is deservedly famous for the explicitly erotic motifs on the outside walls of its temples. Khajuraho is divided into three distinct groups. In the village itself stands a group of Brahma, Vamana and Jawari temples while east of the village are Jain temples that are today still centers of an active cult. In the 10th to 11th centuries, Khajuraho was the cultural capital of the Chandella Rajput dynasty, which is apparent in the ensemble of Lakhshman, Kandariya, Vishvanath and Chitragupta temples. All the temples are built according to similar principles of construction, with their main axis oriented from east to west, so that the first rays of the rising sun could illuminate the interior of the temple. In the west is the entrance gateway followed by a porch, main chamber, a vestibule and the sanctuary, or cella. The roof rises like a series of towers above the individual sections of the buildings, getting steadily higher towards the cella. The latter symbolizes the world mountain of Meru, the seat of the deity, and it holds the god's image.

The temples of Khajuraho are lavishly decorated with a profusion of sculptures that are masterpieces of Indian art and attract attention with their explicit erotic motifs. Faithful to detail and lively, the unambiguous images of sexual union symbolize fertility and the regeneration of the world.

BODH GAYA

Location: North-eastern India (Bihar)
Best time to travel: October–March
www.buddhisttoursindia.com

The first great empire in India's history was founded by Emperor Ashoka (272–231 BC). After converting to Buddhism, he built a temple on the site where the Buddha was said to have attained supreme enlightenment under a Bodhi tree. The present 50-m-high (164-ft) Mahabodhi Temple was built during the Gupta Dynasty (AD 320–540), when Buddhism was being promoted as the state religion.

The Mahabodhi temple complex is closely linked with the life of the Buddha and the religious history of the country. Tens of thousands of pilgrims visit it every year.

PATTADAKAL

Location: South-western India (Karnataka)
Best time to travel: October–March
www.shubhyatra.com

As well as the tolerance of Chalukya rulers, it is the location in the border region between northern and southern India that has made Pattadakal into a melting pot of architectural styles. The northern Indian style is represented by the small Kashi Vishwanath Temple whose special feature is the structural unity of the shikhara tower and the cella, preceded by an entrance hall. The main cult image in the cella can only be walked around outside the building. Typical of the southern style is a corridor built around the cella.

The temples in Pattadakal are lavishly decorated with reliefs.

HAMPI

Location: South-western India (Karnataka)
Best time to travel: October–March
www.hampi.in

This former capital, founded in the 14th century, is akin to an open-air museum of southern Indian architecture. It is surrounded by circular walls and includes a number of palaces and temples of the Dravidian princes. The Vittala Temple, begun in the first half of the 16th century but never completed, is impressive thanks to a number of sculptures standing in front of the pillars and an 8-m-high (26-ft) temple chariot cut from a single block of stone. The highlight of the Virupaksha Temple, aside from its lavish figurative decoration, is the more than 50-m-high (164-ft) gopura (the gate tower in southern Indian architecture). Dedicated to the god Shiva, Virupaksha was built on a former place of worship as early as the 9th century. The temples are concentrated in the northern half of the city, the palaces are mostly found in the south.

All the temples and palaces have different ornamental features. Particularly famous is the temple chariot cut from a monolith in the Vijayanagar temple district.

KERALA (KOCHI)

Location: South-western India
Best time to travel: October–March
www.kerala.gov.in

The federal state of Kerala stretches for 550 km (342 mi) along the Malabar Coast. In 1498, the Portuguese navigator Vasco da Gama landed in Calicut, officially discovering the sea route to India for the Europeans. In around 1500, Cochin (now called Kochi) became the first European settlement in India. The port city is spread across several islands off the coast of its mainland sister town, Ernakulam. On the isle of Mattancherry, the St Francis Church was the first Christian church in India, built in 1510. Mattancherry Palace was constructed by the Portuguese in 1567. In 1663, the Dutch renovated the palace, which has been known as the "Dutch Palace" ever since. The nearby Jew Town is usually very lively, with antiques and souvenir shops in the narrow alleyways.

During the Theyyam Festival in Kochi, temple dancers sport imaginative and colourful costumes and their faces are artistically adorned with paint (top; below: fishing nets on the shore near Kochi and a Keralan thali, a meal of several little dishes, served on a banana leaf).

KAZIRANGA NATIONAL PARK

Location: Eastern India (Assam)
Best time to travel: November–March
www.kazirangananationalpark.com

Kaziranga National Park is defined by the boisterous fluctuations of the Brahmaputra River. During the monsoon rains in July and August, two-thirds of the park are flooded on a regular basis. The animals are then forced to escape to higher ground, sometimes outside the park.

Protection of the Indian rhinoceros has always been at the heart of animal conservation efforts here. When its population was so severely decimated that no further hunting licenses were issued. In 1908, the area was declared a forest preserve. In 1950, it became a game reserve, and in 1974 a national park. Today, there are again an estimated 1,500 rhinos. Animals from the park were recently resettled in the nearby Manas Game Reserve In order to renew the population there.

The Kaziranga National Park is a veritable nature paradise. The main attractions are the Indian rhinoceroses (top right) roaming through the grassland. But elephants and wild water buffalo all feel at home in this national park. The sambar (above left) is the largest species of deer after the moose and the red deer. During the day it prefers to stay in the dense undergrowth.

SUNDARBARNS NATIONAL PARK

Location: Eastern India/Bangladesh
Best time to travel: November–Marz
www.india-wildlife.com

Two very large rivers, the Ganga and the Brahmaputra, as well as their combined estuary region, the Meghna, form the natural basis for the Sundarban National Park. This wetland ecosystem is a transitional zone between saltwater and freshwater that offers an ideal habitat for a wide range of animals including the common otter, water snakes, tortoises, water monitors, crocodiles, storks, herons, cormorants, curlews, seagulls and terns.

The Sundarbans are the largest mangrove habitat on Earth and a refuge for the Bengal tiger, an endangered species.

MANAS

Location: Eastern India (Assam)
Best time to travel: November–March
www.manasassam.org

This reservation in Assam is named after the raging Manas River. Grassland makes up about sixty percent of the territory and it is home to, among other species, wild buffalo and the pygmy hog, considered extinct in Assam but then rediscovered in Manas. The swamp deer, or barasingha, the leopard cat and pangolins also find refuge here. Grass savannah, forests and rivers also offer a habitat to many bird species such as blue-breasted quail, drongo cuckoo and forest eagle owl.

Langurs belong to the family of Old World Monkeys. In the park, both the golden langur (left) and the capped langur occur.

MADURAI

Location: South-eastern India (Tamil Nadu)
Best time to travel: October–March
www.madurai.com

No other federal state in India has as many temples as Tamil Nadu, and nowhere else do the gods reside in such splendor as here. The former Chola residence of Chidambaram boasts the Temple of the Dancing Shiva (Nataraja), who is depicted on two of four gate towers (Gopurams) in 108 poses of Cosmic Dance. When the gods dance, it is believed, the dancers become mediators between Heaven and Earth. Classic Indian dance does not allow for improvisation. Every movement of the body, every expression of the face, even every twitch of a muscle have their own meanings. The oldest source for the classic Indian dance is the "Natya Shastra", a collection of texts in Sanskrit dating from the second century. Allegedly it originated from the wise sage Bharata, who is also credited with one of the oldest solo dances in India, from the Tamil Nadu region: the Bharata Natyam ("Bharata's Dance"), which is performed regularly as part of religious rites, court ceremonies, weddings and other social events.
The tall towers of the Sri Meenakshi Temple in Madurai, covered with a profusion of painted images of gods and demons, can be seen from afar.

The lavishly decorated Sri Meenakshi Temple (right, and a decorative detail opposite bottom) is one of the largest and most fascinating temple complexes in all of India. The Temple of the Dancing Shiva in Chidambaram (opposite top) is believed to have been founded originally by Brahmins from Kashmir around 500. The present building, though, dates only from around 1000.

MAHABALIPURAM

Location: South-eastern India (Tamil Nadu)
Best time to travel: October–February
www.mahabalipuram.co.in

Unlike most conquerors, the Pallavan Prince Narasimhavarman I, who reigned from 625 to 645, also had quite a thirst for knowledge and scholarly pursuits. During the conquest of other cities in the area, he became acquainted with the breathtaking architecture of the Chalukya rulers, and subsequently ordered that his own town, Mahabalipuram, be similarly beautified. Some of the most attractive structures of Dravidian architecture were created at his behest, and their forms became the standard for architecture all over southern India.

As part of his experimentation with the different possibilities for cult worship architecture, Narasimhavarman had five rathas built. They were not temples in the true sense, but rather colossal sculptures cut straight from the bedrock. Ratha No. 1 still looked fairly plain, but Ratha No. 5 became the prototype for other Dravidian temples.

The vast bas-relief "Descent of the Ganges" in the Mahabalipuram temple district tells the story of the descent of the sacred Ganges River. On a rock in a cleft Shiva is depicted, allowing the the river waters to run through his tresses.

THANJAVUR

Location: Southern India (Tamil Nadu)
Best time to travel: October–February
www.thanjavur.org.in

Southern India was ruled by the Chola dynasty from the 9th until the 12th century. Thanjavur, 350 km (217 mi) south of Chennai, was the capital of the Chola empire. The Chola rulers modeled it on the southern Indian style of the Pallava princes from Mahabalipuram. Several outstanding temples from this time are preserved – the most impressive of these is the Brihadeeswarar Temple of Thanjavur, built by King Raja Chola I and completed around 1010.

Realistic stone sculptures greet visitors to the Brihadishvara Temple in Thanjavur.

KONARAK

Location: Eastern India (Orissa)
Best time to travel: November–March
http://konark.nic.in

Surya, the sun god, together with Agni, the god of fire, and Indra, the god of thunder, formed a divine trinity. Surya, for his part, has always been highly worshipped by Hindus as the giver of life, steering a chariot in heaven pulled by seven horses – much like Apollo in Greek mythology. The temple in Konarak, with its 75-m-high (246-ft) pyramid-like Shikhara Tower and the cella below it, is an image of the chariot-turned-stone, which the god drives across the firmament every day.

Colossal sun wheels, embellished with great detail, are characteristic of the complex which was completed in the 13th century.

DAMBULLA

Location: Central Sri Lanka
Best time to travel: December–March, July/August
www.srilanka.travel

The first of three documented periods of construction on the slopes of the "Black Rock" began in the early 1st century BC under King Vattagamani Abhaya, who had fled Anuradhapura before the second large influx of Tamil people. During his fourteen years in exile, he found refuge in the granite rock caves of Dambulla where a number of temples were built. The sanctuary was then forgotten and not rediscovered and expanded until the 12th century. The third period came during the reign of King Sri Kirti Rajasinha in the late 18th century. The first cave, the "Cave of the Divine King" (Devaraja Vihara), has a stunning, 14-m-long (46-ft) reclining Buddha. The largest cave, the "Temple of the Great Kings" (Maharaja Vihara), boasts a number of statues and paintings of outstanding quality. The "Great New Monastery" (Maha Alut Vihara) is the third cave and was commissioned by King Sri Kirti Rajasinha. The fourth is the oldest, dating back to the 1st century BC, and the fifth temple was more recently renovated in the style of 1820.

The five cave temples of Dambulla, comprising countless statues and frescoes, date back to the beginnings of Buddhism in Sri Lanka.

ANURADHAPURA

Location: Central Sri Lanka
Best time to travel: February–July
www.srilanka.travel
www.srilankatourism.org

In the year 244 BC, Sanghamitta, a Buddhist nun, brought to Sri Lanka the branch of a tree under which the Buddha once meditated on his path to enlightenment. The tree is now 2,200 years old and the oldest in the world. The Isurumuniya rock temple is said to date back to the Bodhi branch. It houses one of the loveliest reliefs in Sri Lanka and the dome of the Ruwanveli Dagoba (2nd C. BC) is 110 m (361 ft) high.

Anuradhapura is known as the cradle of Buddhism in Sri Lanka. The "Reclingin Buddha" in the rock monastery of Isurumuni Vihara (left) was probably created as early as the 7th or 8th century.

POLONNARUWA

Location: Central Sri Lanka
Best time to travel: February–July
www.lanka.com
www.tourslanka.com

Polonnaruwa first became the seat of the government in the 8th century. When Anuradhapura was destroyed in 1017, it was declared the permanent capital; Indian and Singhalese kings took turns to rule it. The most important Singhalese ruler was Parakramabahu I (1153–86) during whose reign temples, schools, hospitals, irrigation systems and a magnificent palace were built, including a council chamber, royal bathing pool, the "Moonstone" and the "House of Eight Relics". The city was abandoned in the 13th century.

The medieval royal residence of Polonnaruwa is famous for its colossal statues of the Buddha.

SIGIRIYA

Location: Central Sri Lanka
Best time to travel: February–July
http://sigiriya.org

The fortress of the kings of Anuradhapura rests high upon on the Sigiriya, or "Lion's Rock", which rises straight out of the tropical vegetation. As can be seen from the enchanting and often well-preserved frescoes of nymphs with fashionable haircuts and opulent jewelry that line the path leading up the steep hill, it was built as both a defensive structure and a royal pleasure palace.
The path to the summit originally began at the Lion's Gate, of which today only the gigantic paws remain. The citadel itself is but a ruin these days, but it is still easy to make out what is left of the chambers, baths, bridges, gardens and fountains that once adorned the complex. Planned in the 5th century by King Dhatusena, Sigiriya was actually inhabited by his son Kassapa, who usurped the royal throne by killing his father and expelling his half-brother Moggallana. The return of Moggallana eighteen years later led to a decisive battle during whlch Kassapa took his own life.

The kings of Anuradhapura built their mountain fortress and capital on the "Lion's Rock", a 200-m-high (656-ft), weather-beaten and worn volcano towering above a plain and visible from afar. A path leads up the steep hill via ledges and narrow steps. The many images of bare breasted, elegantly clad women, the thc Sigiriya maidens, are a highlight of ancient Indian art. "Apsaras" – or divine nymphs – emerge from the clouds scattering flowers to greet the king.

KANDY

Location: Central Sri Lanka
Best time to travel: December–March (July/August: "Perahara Kandy")
www.kandycity.org

Founded by King Vikrama Bahu III (r. 1357 to 1374), the essential buildings of the religious metropolis however date back to King Vikrama Rajasinha (r. 1798–1815), the most important ruler at Kandy. He also commissioned the wooden audience chamber in the old palace and the large Kandy Lake in the middle of the city. The origins of the lake are said to stem from the fact that the king wished to get from his palace to the Malwatte Temple to the south with dry feet. He therefore had a dam built across the rice paddies. Soon a pond started to form behind the dam which so delighted the king that he had it enlarged to a handsome lake of some 4 km (2.5 mi) in circumference. The most important pilgrimage destination for Sri Lankan Buddhists is the "Temple of the Tooth" (Dalada Maligawa): According to legend, four teeth and a collarbone were saved from the ashes when the body of the religious leader Siddhartha Gautama was cremated in 480 BC. Many myths are woven around the subsequent odyssey these relics experienced. The tooth in Kandy, for example, is said to have arrived concealed in the hair of a Buddhist nun. The highpoint of the Perahara Kandy, a two-week celebration that takes place every year in July/August in honor of the relic, is a great festival procession.

The "Temple of the Tooth", the shrine of the valuable Buddha, is carefully guarded.

KATHMANDU

Location: Central Nepal
Best time to travel: November–April
www.see-nepal.com

The fascinating ambience of the Kathmandu Valley is difficult to describe, but the pagoda-like roofs of the palaces, temples and houses, the wealth of exquisite carvings, and the opulence of the golden treasures in the temples all contribute greatly to the place. It is the whole package here that is so stunning, manifested in an atmosphere created by the inhabitants long before the first capital was founded in 723. Nepal's capital, the royal city of Kathmandu, is at an elevation of 1,300 m (4,265 ft) and is the focal point of the valley. The heart of the city is formed by Durbar Square, which the Nepalese call "Hanuman Dhoka". It is the site of Buddhist and Hindu temples and shrines as well as the home of the former royal palace. The Malla and Shah kings resided here for centuries. The Boudhanath stupa, the largest sanctuary for Tibetan Nepalese people, is about 5 km (3 mi) outside of the heart of the city. The fascinating Swayambuna temple complex is situated in the north-west of the Old Town and is well worth a visit.

The roughly 40-m-high (130-ft) Boudhanath stupa rests on a hemisphere which itself sits on three accessible plinths.

MOUNT EVEREST/SAGARMATHA

Location: Southern Nepal/Tibet
Best time to travel: May–July
www.everestnews.com

The highest mountain on earth is known to the Nepalese as Sagarmatha, or "Goddess of the Skies". The Tibetans call the mountain Chomolungma, "Mother Goddess of the Universe". Sagarmatha National Park, founded in 1976, not only contains three of the world's 8,000-m (26,000-ft) peaks (Mount Everest, Lhotse and Cho Oyu), making it the highest mountain region on Earth. The mountain's southern slopes are only snow-free for a short period in summer, a time when a variety of carnations, gentians and cruciferous plants blossom at elevations of up to 6,000 m (19,686 ft). Only very undemanding soil fungi are able to survive in the higher zones, while alpine plants such as edelweiss, irises and shrubs flourish in the lower regions. Deciduous and coniferous forests reach elevations of up to 4,000 m (13,124 ft). The national park is inhabited by some thirty mammal species and the skies are ruled by majestic raptors. The existence of the Yeti, however, still remains to be proven.

A majestic mountain landscape can be enjoyed in the grandiose Sagarmatha National Park (above; top: a view from the Khumbu Valley towards the summits of Mount Everest and Lhotse).

MYANMAR

Location: State in the north-west of mainland South-East Asia
Best time to travel: November–April
www.myanmars.net

Located right next to India, present-day Myanmar came under Buddhist influence early on. Between the 11th and the 13th centuries thousands of Buddhist monuments were built in Bagan – the capital of the first united kingdom of present Myanmar –, and many of these can still be seen today. Bagan developed into one of the largest Buddhist metropolises in the world very soon after it was founded in 1057, but the city on the left bank of the Irrawaddy River was destroyed by the Mongols in 1287.
Buddha himself is said to have predicted that Mandalay would one day become a hub not only of Burmese culture but also of Buddhism. Legend has it that the Buddha (Siddhartha Gautama, c. 560 to 480 BC) and his student, Ananda, once visited Mandalay Hill where they encountered a female demon upon whom the Enlightened One made such an impression that she cut off her breasts with the intention of giving them to Buddha. The latter is alleged to have smiled and, pointing to the foot of the hill, said: "There, one day, 2,400 years after my death, a descendant of this demon will found a city that will blossom into a center of my teaching". In accordance with this prophecy, King Mindon laid the foundation stone for a new city, Mandalay, in February 1857, and it was to be the capital of the Burmese kingdom until 1885.
Situated on the Shan Plateau in eastern Myanmar at an altitude of almost 1,000 m (3,281 ft), Inle Lake is about 145 sq km (56 sq mi) in size and a constant source of amazement due to both its idyllic mountain location and the traditional

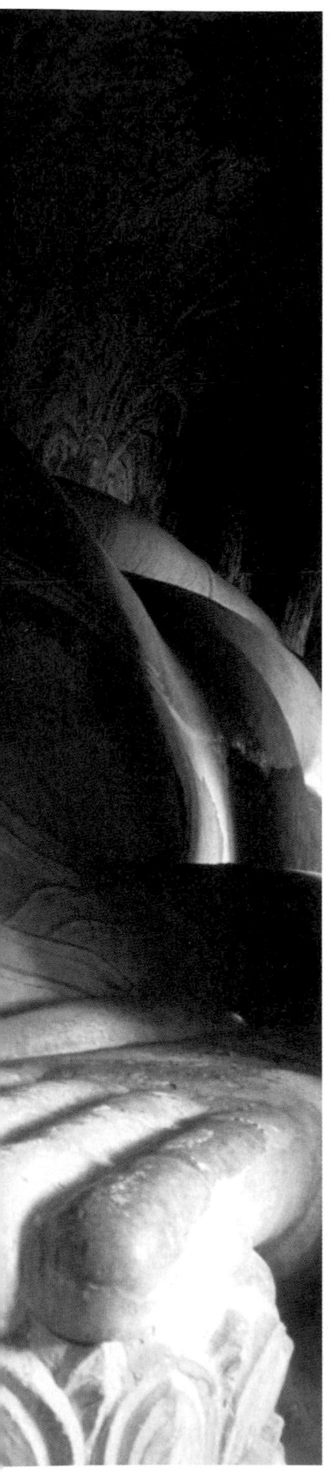

local culture. The ethnic groups living here, particularly the Inthas, or "Sons of the Lake", are a people who originally lived in the southern part of the country but later retreated to this region where they originally established just four settlements along the lake. The lake's name, "Inle", means "Lake of the Four" (villages).

The small town of Kyaiktiyo in southern Myanmar is perched precariously atop Golden Rock Mountain at a height of 1,100 m (3,609 ft). Legend has it that a reliquary in the pagoda on top of the gilded granite formation holds one hair of Buddha and it is this single hair that ensures the necessary balance to keep the rock from falling.

The landmark of the country and the most important religious site in Myanmar is the Shwedagon Pagoda in Yangon, built on a hill north of the historical heart of the former capital. The origins of the 116-m-high (381-ft) structure, which has been decorated time and again with gold and precious stones over the centuries, are said to go back to the Buddha, Siddhartha Gautama (ca. 560 to 480 BC). Apparently, the pagoda contains eight hairs from his head. The building stands on a marble platform measuring 60,000 sq m (645,600 sq ft), with numerous small pagodas scattered around its octagonal base, which has a circumference of 413 m (4,445 sq ft). Its canopied roof is made of gilded mesh decorated with thousands of precious stones, at the top of which is a 76-carat diamond symbolizing enlightenment.

Large picture: the Reclining Buddha in the Shwesandaw Pagoda, Bagan. This page from the top: the Golden Rock Mountain near Kyaiktiyo; the Shwedagon Pagoda in Yangon; a typical "led rower" on the Inle Lake; and the Royal Palace of Mandalay, unfortunately reconstructed not entirely faithful to the original.

ALTAI

Location: Southern Russia/ Kazakhstan, Mongolia, China
Best time to travel: June–September
www.altai.in
www.altaitravels.com

Russia's Altai Republic in southern Siberia is part of a mountain system in Asia that also includes the Mongolian and the Gobi Altai Mountains. From the steppes up to the alpine zone, Altai boasts the most comprehensive sequence of vegetation zones in all of Central Siberia. The plant diversity is enormous, with more than 2,000 genera having been identified, including 212 endemic plant species. The diverse animal world is characteristic of the Siberian forest fauna with over seventy mammal, 300 bird, eleven reptile and amphibian, and more than twenty fish species. Some of the indigenous mammals and many of the bird species are listed as endangered in Russia.

The region around the 4,506-m-high (14,784-ft) Belukha (above) in the Altai region on the Russian border with Kazakhstan is a majestic, isolated high mountain landscape with stunningly clear mountain lakes such as the Ak Kam Lake (top), which reflect the surrounding mountains.

LAKE BAIKAL

Location: Southern Russia
Best time to travel: April–October
http://baikal.irkutsk.org
www.baikalex.com

Baikal, 650 km (404 mi) long and on average almost 50 km (31 mi) wide, is situated in southern Siberia near the city of Irkutsk. This seismically active zone experiences frequent earthquakes but also features some splendid resorts around the hot springs that rise from fissures on the lakeshore.

In Buryat, Baikal means "rich lake", an apt name for its diverse flora and fauna. Over 1,200 animal species, many endemic, have been identified in the lake alone, such as the Baikal Seal and the Golomyanka, a fish that gives birth to live offspring. Some 600 plant species grow in the area around Lake Baikal.

Lake Baikal boasts many superlatives. The freshwater lake with the greatest depth and the largest volume of water, it is – at around 25 million years old – also the world's oldest lake. Nature around the tranquil Peschanaya Bay is as yet almost untouched (top and above right). One of the flowers flourishing on Lake Baikal is Sibbaldia altaica (above left).

KAMCHATKA

Location: South-eastern Russia
Best time to travel: April–October
www.kamchatka.org.ru
www.kamchatkapeninsula.com

The Kamchatka Peninsula extends over a length of 1,200 km (746 mi) and is up to 480 km (298 mi) wide, between the Sea of Okhotsk in the west and the Pacific Ocean and the Bering Sea in the east. It is traversed by two parallel mountain ranges that are divided by the Kamchatka River Valley. The west or central range is up to 2,000-m-high (6,562-ft) and dominated by extinct volcanoes, while the east range transforms into a plateau with a number of active volcanoes. The west coast features expansive marshlands while the east is characterized by steep cliffs. The lower-lying zones are mostly covered with deciduous forest, the region providing a habitat for many primeval indigenous plants.

Kamchatka is located in a subduction zone where the Pacific tectonic plate moves under the Eurasian plate. This caused numerous stratovolcanoes to emerge here as part of the volcanic chain forming the "Pacific Ring of Fire" (top from the left: Karymsky, Avachinsky, Kronotsky), which frequently erupt. Its geographic location across the Pacific from the Americas meant that Kamchatka was a prohibited area until the end of the Cold War in 1990. This period provided ideal conditions for the local fauna to thrive relatively undisturbed. Its most spectacular representative is the Kamchatka brown bear (Ursus arctos beringianus), a subspecies of the brown bear (above).

WRANGEL ISLAND

Location: Island in the Arctic Ocean, north-eastern Russia
Best time to travel: June–August
http://heritage-expeditions.com

The 7,500-sq km (2,895-sq mi) Wrangel Island – named after the Baltic German admiral and Siberian explorer Ferdinand von Wrangel – is situated far north of the Arctic Circle on the western edge of Chukchi Sea. It boasts a great diversity of geological formations and habitats, each with differing microclimates that make them unique. Its mountainous terrain meant that it was never entirely covered in glaciers during the Ice Age, the result of which is that many plant and animal species exist here where elsewhere they have become extinct. Wrangel Island consequently has more than 400 species and subspecies of vascular plants alone, twice as many as in any other tundra region of comparable size. These also include twenty-three indigenous species. The island is home to the world's largest population of Pacific walrus, numbering up to 100,000 specimens, and boasts the greatest density of polar bear caves in the world. Musk oxen also graze in the Arctic tundra landscape. Gray whales come here from Mexico to feed in these rich waters, and around 100 migrant bird species come here to breed. The large number of lemmings exhibit behavioral patterns that set them apart from other Arctic populations.

The tundra and mountain landscape of Wrangel Island is dotted with snowfields and watercourses (top). The musk oxen (above) are the offspring of animals that have been returned to the wild.

UVS NUUR BASIN

Location: North-western Mongolia
Best time to travel: April/May, August/September
www.legendtour.ru
www.visitmongolia.com

The Uvs Nuur region extends as far as the autonomous Republic of Tuva in Russia. It measures over 600 km (373 mi) from west to east and over 160 km (99 mi) from north to south. What makes it so extraordinary is the fact that all of Central Asia's major ecosystems are represented in this one comparatively small area: wetlands, desert, various steppe formations and forest types, rivers, freshwater lakes, alpine habitats and permafrost. The national park also includes bizarre, often pillow-shaped, weathered mountains, cliffs and granite rocks.

The region's grasslands have been used by nomads for thousands of years. Due to its ecological consistency the Uvs Nuur Basin is also used for monitoring global warming and climate change. The different ecosystems include indigenous plants and invertebrate animals, as well as endangered mammal species such as the snow leopard and Asiatic ibex.

Nomads track with their animals from place to place in the Uvs Nuur Basin, living in traditional yurts with little impact on their surroundings. The region is named after the non-draining Uvs Nuur saltwater lake in northern Mongolia.

ORKHON VALLEY

Location: Central and northern Mongolia
Best time to travel: May–October
www.mongolei.com
www.mongoliatourism.gov.mn

The Orkhon Valley lies in the Changai Mountains, the so-called cradle of the Mongolian nation. During the 13th and 14th centuries, Kharkhorin (Karakorum in English) was the capital of the Mongolian khans who descended from Genghis Khan and once ruled over a vast world empire. The Orkhon Valley had actually been settled much earlier, however, and is said to have been a political hub for large parts of Central Asia since the sixth century, during which time symbiotic relationships developed between the nomadic tribes and the political, religious and cultural centers. The region is still inhabited by nomads. The Mongolian form of Buddhist Lamaism also has its roots in the Orkhon Valley, at the Erdene Zuu Monastery. It was built in 1586 by Abtai Sain Khan, a prince of the Chalcha Mongols. During its heyday, some 10,000 monks lived at the Erdene Zuu Monastery.

The Orkhon is the lifeline of Mongolia. During excavations this tone tortoise was found as well as gold jewelry and various seals. The Erdene Zuu Monastery near Karakorum has been a place of worship again since 1990.

BEIJING

Location: North-eastern China
Best time to travel: all year
www.ebeijing.gov.cn

Beijing, which means "northern capital", was founded during the Jin Dynasty (1115–1234) before being laid to waste and rebuilt by the Mongols. The city was then once again built up by the Ming emperors between 1368 and 1420 based on plans from the original city. The town was to be a mirror image of the cosmos, whose laws were reflected in the city's layout.

The old city center is formed by the Forbidden City, which straddles Beijing's main north-south axis. The modern center of Beijing is dominated by the vast Square of Heavenly Peace, named after the Gate of Heavenly Peace (Tiananmen), and is just to the south. It was here that Mao Zedong proclaimed the People's Republic of China in 1949.

On the square stand the Monument to the People's Heroes and the Mao Zedong Memorial Hall. On the western side it is bordered by the Great Hall of the People, and on the eastern side by the Museum of Chinese History and the Museum of the Chinese Revolution.

Outside the Forbidden City is Chang'an Avenue, which runs from east to west across the city.

The 40-km (25-mi) road is roughly 120 m (394 ft) wide at Tiananmen Square and was another of Mao Zedong's projects from the 1950s. Today, the glamorous boulevard is lined with government buildings, multinational company headquarters and modern hotels.

The inner-city districts essentially make up the historic center.

So-called "hutong", houses built around courtyards and narrow alleyways, once characterized the older neighborhoods. Now only a few of them remain, for example around the Drum Tower, and these have

been fully restored. Most were demolished to make room for new roads and massive residential blocks. At the beginning of the socialist era, many inner-city districts were also peppered with iron and steel works, car and machine manufacturing facilities, locomotive and train car plants, and factories for the production of electronics and agricultural machines. These dramatic construction projects were meant to transform the bourgeois consumer town of the imperial age into a productive modern city. The result was that Beijing developed into the largest industrial center in China.

The historic ring of fortifications around the center was sacrificed for the enlargement of the city and construction of new roads, but the main axes of the road network follow the wall's former course.

Beijing also boasts a number of large parks. One of the best-known and largest – covering an area of 270 ha (667 acres) – is the park that houses the Temple of Heaven (Tian Tan), which contains the Hall of Prayer for Good Harvest and the Altar of Heaven. Both were built at the beginning of the 15th century.

For the Summer Olympic Games in 2008, the city's infrastructure was once again dramatically transformed, the most prominent new architectural feature being the national stadium. Designed by Swiss architects Herzog & de Meuron, it is 330 m (1,083 ft) long, 220 m (722 ft) wide, 69 m (227 ft) tall and has capacity for around 80,000 spectators. The stadium is north of the city about 9 km (6 mi) along the extension of the Forbidden City's northern axis in the Olympic Park.

In the Hall of Supreme Harmony (top), the emperor was once seated on the Dragon Throne. Bottom from left: the Imperial Palace, protected by a moat; and the Gate of Heavenly Peace, once the access to the Forbidden City.

THE GREAT WALL OF CHINA

Location: north-eastern China
Best time to travel: all year
www.thegreatwall.com.cn

Ancient China's giant border structure was the largest construction project in pre-modern history. It took nearly 2,000 years to build, yet even so, the wall ultimately failed to protect the empire from invasion by hostile forces.

First mention of the building of a "long wall" on China's northern border was made in 214 BC. The territory had been united shortly before that by the Emperor Qin Shi Huang and the wall was intended to keep the nomadic people of the north at bay. Indeed, the problem of protecting Chinese interests became a recurring theme over the 1,900 years that followed.

The fortifications eventually fell into disrepair and were rebuilt on several occasions over the centuries. During the Ming Dynasty, in the 15th and 16th centuries, the wall was not only repaired but expanded to become a larger and more solid construction than ever before. The result is what we see today: a 6,000-km (3,728-mi) colossus, 2,000 km (1,243 mi) of which are an average of 7–10 m (23–26 ft) high and 6 m (6.5 yds) wide between the Bohai Sea and the Yellow River, or Huang He. The watchtowers also served as soldiers' quarters and enabled the rapid communication of messages by means of beacons. The by far best-preserved and/or restored section of the wall is to be found near Badaling, north-west of Beijing.

At its beginnings in the fifth century BC, the Great Wall, or "Wanli Changcheng" ("Ten Thousand Li Long Wall"), as it is known in Chinese, was built mainly from rammed earth. Only later was its strengthened with bricks.

MOGAO

Location: Northern China (Gansu)
Best time to travel: all year
www.travelchinaguide.com

For more than a thousand years, merchants, army generals, wealthy widows and simple monks alike gathered in the prosperous oasis of Dunhuang to convey their prayers, gratitude and hopes of salvation to the deities of the day by carving grottoes into a nearby cliff and decorating them with scenes from the life of the Buddha, Siddhartha Gautama. Their offerings included images of paradise, worldly scenes and elaborate ornaments. The result of their efforts has today become the largest collection of Buddhist imagery in the world.

The precious wall frescoes also depict historical personalities, such as here, the king of Yutia..

PING YAO

Location: North-eastern China (Shanxi)
Best time to travel: all year
www.chinaculture.org

Founded in pre-Christian times, Ping Yao's real rise to power and expansion took place in the 14th century. Today it is considered a prime example of Chinese architecture from the Ming and Qing eras.
The historical heart of Ping Yao was enclosed in 1370 by an imposing, 12-m-high (39-ft) city wall that averages a width of 5 m (16 ft). Forming a gigantic square with an overall length of more than 6 km (4 mi), it contains an elaborate ensemble of established shopping streets with well-preserved commercial and banking buildings.

Black tiles houses characterize the heart of the Old Town of Ping Yao.

CHENGDE

Location: North-eastern China (Hebei)
Best time to travel: all year
www.chengdetour.com

It was in Chengde – on the way to the imperial hunting grounds – that the Manchu emperors found refuge from the summer heat in Beijing. The abundance of water allowed them to build an extravagant garden landscape to offset the palace buildings, which were of a more modest design than those in Beijing. Magnificent Buddhist temples and monasteries were later built outside the walled palace grounds.

The most impressive of the so-called "Eight Outer Temples" in the area of the imperial summer residence near is the "Temple for Universal Happiness and Longevity of the Sumeru Mountain".

YIN XU

Location: eastern China (Henan)
Best time to travel: September–June
www.cnto.org

Yin Xu was the capital of the late Shang Dynasty from around 1300 to 1066 BC. Yin went into rapid decline following the dynasty's demise and became Yin Xu, the ruined city, where jade workshops, bronze foundries, palaces, tombs as well as countless labelled bones have been found. The area measures around 30 sq km (12 sq mi) and encompasses sections to the north and south of the Yellow River. The main find is the grave of Fu Hao, the only one of the Shang dynasty to have been preserved in its entirety.

The tomb of Fu Hao, the wife of the Shang King Wu Ding, featured a wealth of funerary objects.

YUNGANG

Location: Eastern China (Shanxi)
Best time to travel: all year
www.bergerfoundation.ch

The emperors of the Wei Dynasty established Buddhism as the official religion, but Emperor Tai Wudi suddenly banned it in 446 for fear of it threatening his authority. He died unexpectedly shortly thereafter. His grandson, Wen Chengdi, saw this as a sign from heaven and had the Yungang Grottoes carved out of the rocks in the Wuzhou Mountains. Today the 252 Yungang Grottoes are the largest man-made caves in the world and a masterpiece of Chinese Buddhist cave art. The statues of Buddha measure between 2 cm (¾ in) and 17 m (56 ft) in height.

Some pf the Buddha statues in Yungang even bear the facial features of the Wei emperors.

LONGMEN

Location: Eastern China (Henan)
Best time to travel: September–June
www.longmen.com

Over 2,000 grottoes and niches line the steep slopes of Dragon Mountain above the Yi River in Hénán Province. Covering about 1 km (0.6 mi), the grottoes served as a cult worship site and contain a number of valuable inscriptions as well as more than 100,000 stone Buddhist statues and elaborately carved ceilings and wall decorations.

The cloak of the Bodhisattva at the entrance to the Fengxian Temple is richly arranged in folds, a typical feature of Tang Period (618–906) sculptures. To his right, a world guardian crushes a demon underfoot. On his left is a Lishi, a protector of Buddhist teachings.

THE TOMB OF CHINA'S FIRST EMPEROR

Location: Eastern China
Best time to travel: all year
www.cnto.org

Immediately after having united the territory, China's first emperor, Qin Shi Huang, began construction of his own burial site. It was to be one befitting of his station and located some 30 km (19 mi) north-east of Xi'an, then the imperial capital and a major center on the Silk Route. The fact that the tomb comprised more than just the prominent burial mound became evident only in 1974, when farmers digging for water came across fragments of the larger of the warrior statues. They form just a small part of a still unfinished excavation of an army of about 7,600 soldiers.

Arranged in underground chambers, the army was intended to protect both the tomb and empire of the deceased emperor from evil forces in the afterlife, as well as document the emperor's elevated status.

China's most impressive tomb complex was not unearthed until 1974. More than 2,000 years ago, the Emperor Qin Shihuangdi was laid to rest here, surrouned by thousands of individually made terracotta figures, a portrayal of the military and courtly organization of the day.

IMPERIAL BURIAL SITES OF THE MING AND QING DYNASTIES

Location: Eastern China
Best time to travel: all year
www.cnto.org

The royal burial sites of the Ming (1368–1644) and Qing (1644–1911) dynasties represent more than five hundred years of feudal Chinese rule, the prevailing world view of those times, and the overwhelming power of the emperors. The Xianling Mausoleum in Hubei Province, for example, is the largest single Ming tomb and contains both the old and new burial chambers. The Jiajing Emperor, who ruled from 1521–1567, had his father's grave converted into a large imperial-style tomb complex comprising a total of thirty buildings.

The imposing Qing dynasty tombs are located at two sites, each about 100 km (62 mi) from Beijing. The eastern group of Qing Dynasty tombs near Zunhua were consecrated in 1663 and consist of fifteen graves. The western portion was built in 1723 south-west of Beijing, near Baoding. The actual sites, chosen by Feng Shui masters, are situated in remote and very picturesque mountain regions.

Only three of the imperial Ming tombs can be visited today, among them the Changling complex. Behind the Stele Pavilion begins the Sacred Way lined with stone statues along which the emperors were carried to their tombs.

WUDANG

Location: Eastern China (Hubei)
Best time to travel: all year
www.wudanggongfu.com

Taoist hermits began retreating to this remote but not inhospitable mountain region in north-west Hubei Province at the latest during the Eastern Han Era, (AD 25–220). During the Tang Era (618–907), legends that the Emperor of the Northern Heaven had once lived here inspired the monks to establish the monasteries that transformed the Wudang Mountains into a popular pilgrimage destination.

In 1214, motivated by political aims, Yongle, the third emperor of the Ming dynasty, began building new monasteries of palatial proportions. They were elaborately decorated and required the efforts of some 300,000 workers. A total of 129 of the religious sites survived, albeit mostly as ruins.

The 72 peaks of the enchanted Wudang Mountains are sacred and the cradle of Taosim. Among their many temples, monasteries, shrines, caves and hermitages is the "Supreme Harmony Temple" (top). The pilgrims' destination is usually the monastic town on top the summit of the 1,612-m-high (5,889-ft) Tianzhu (above left; above right: the Golden Hall which holds the statues of King Zhen Wun as well as the sculptures of the Immortals of Taoism).

LUSHAN

Location: southern China (Jiangxi)
Best time to travel: September–May
www.china-lushan.com

Few mountains have had their praises sung as often as Lushan. Most Chinese poets have revered it with a visit, leaving behind inscriptions, as did philosophers, painters, monks and politicians. The "Mountain of the Supernatural Being" has also long been a popular pilgrimage site for Taoists and Buddhists. It was here that Zhu Xi (1130–1200), the most influential supporter of Neo-Confucian philosophy, taught at the Bailudong Academy.

The enchanting beauty of the Lushan mountains, with their many temples and pagodas sited high above the Yangtze, is the cradle of Chinese landscape painting.

SUZHOU

Location: Southern China (Jiangsu)
Best time to travel: September–-May
www.suzhou.gov.cn

Situated just to the west of Shanghai, Suzhou owes much of its prosperity to the Grand Canal. The numerous waterways, some spanned by old stone bridges, are still an important means of transport within this "Venice of the East". Suzhou is primarily known for its gardens, however, which help to preserve some of the atmosphere of the old city with their ponds, creative rock formations and highly symbolic yet sparing vegetation.

Pagodas were often integrated into the beautiful garden complexes of Suzhou. Among the most attractive of the former house gardens is the "Humble Administrator's Garden".

HUANGSHAN

Location: Southern China (Anhui)
Best time to travel: September–May
www.sacredsites.com

"Anyone who has ever seen Huangshan will never need to regret not seeing another mountain range," says a Chinese proverb referring to the mountains that have inspired painters and poets throughout the ages. Covering a surprisingly small area of less than 150 sq km (58 sq mi), the Huangshan Range (or Yellow Mountain) in Anui Province boasts seventy-seven peaks from 1,000 to 1,849 m (3,281 to 6,067 ft).
The mist that fills the steep canyons on around 250 days of the year is so thick that from above the landscape looks like a sea spotted with islands. Over the centuries, a number of pavilions have been built in order to enjoy the beautiful scenery that has come to embody the Chinese landscape ideal. The Huangshan aesthetic, which had a strong influence on China's classic scholarly culture, is perfected by the ancient pines growing out of the rock crevasses.

The Huangshan, with its bizarrely shaped rocks and gnarled pine trees (top), is one of China's most famous mountain regions. This "Ideal-typical" mountain range includes the "Celestial Capital Peak" (above right) and the Lotus Peak, which is accessed via the breathtaking One Hundred Step Cloud Stairs (above left).

SHANGHAI

Location: Eastern China
Best time to travel: all year
www.shanghaihighlights.com
www.entershanghai.info

Shanghai roughly means "settlement above the sea". Once no more than a mooring place for Junks, at the confluence of two rivers – the Yangtze and the Huangpu – and by the sea, that was then enclosed by a protective wall in the 16th century. Today a ring road still follows the oval outline of the wall. The Yu Garden in the northern part of the Old Town Nanshi is worth a visit.
During the Ming Period (1368–1644) Shanghai had already gained economic significance. Modern Shanghai dates back to the Treaty of Nanjing (1842), which granted the right of domicile to Europeans and forced the city to open to foreign trade. In the 20th century, Shanghai has become an important port town with multinational companies, banks, villas, factories and artisan quarters. The Huangpu District is on the north side of the Old Town and contains rich collection of interesting 20th-century colonial buildings along the Bund.

Shanghai grows not only horizontally, sprawling across the delta of the Yangtzekiang, it rises mainly vertically; the number of high-rises and skyscrapers seems to increase almost on a daily basis (top: the skyscrapers of Pudong District, a special economic zone since 1990). One of the spectacular flyovers on the Huangpu River meant to cope with ever-increasing traffic from the Old Town to new Shanghai (right; center: the modern façade of the City Museum; far right: the Bund, the embankment in the historical heart of Shanghai). Opposite page: China's most famous shopping street, the Nanjing Lu.

AURORA

WUYI

Location: southern China (Fujian)
Best time to travel: September–May
www.amoymagic.com

The biodiversity of the ancient subtropical forests in the Wuyi region makes it a paradise for rare plants and animals. The steep cliffs and crystal clear rivers also give it a special aesthetic appeal. Almost 2,500 plant species as well as around 5,000 insects and 475 vertebrate species have been counted here, with the Wuyishan providing an important sanctuary in densely populated China. The average altitude is no more than 350 m (1,148 ft) and consequently the temperatures here are relatively mild, even in winter.

Literary fgures and scholars once withdrew to the isolated Wuyi mountain landscape.

WULINGYUAN

Location: Zhangjiajie, southern China (Hunan)
Best time to travel: September–May
www.hillmanwonders.com

More than 3,000 overgrown sandstone pillars rise majestically out of the valleys in this stunning nature park. They were shaped by erosion from a 500-m-thick (1,641-ft) layer of sediment. The canyons between them are so narrow that agriculture is impossible, a fact that has made the region virtually uninhabitable. Almost all of the prominent formations have floral names. The region is known for its many rivers and its 3,000 or so plant species.

The labyrinth of rocks in the Wulingyuan National Park was submerged under the sea as recently as 100 million years ago.

DAZU

Location: Chongqing, central China
Best time to travel: September–May
www.cq.gov.cn

The various cliff faces here, which range in height from about 7 to 30 m (30 and 98 ft) and are up to 500 m (55 yds) in length, offer a kaleidoscope of Buddhist sculptures going back some 1,000 years. Unlike the large, ancient cliff temple complexes in northern China, which were mainly built in man-made grottoes, a majority of the vibrant Dazu sculptures and reliefs are actually outside. The figure of Buddha, for example, which is recognizable by the simple monk's attire, is an especially common motif along with the Bodhisattvas, who sacrificed their entry to Nirvana in order to to save man from the earthly Vale of Tears. Scenes from Buddhist version of paradise illustrate the happiness that awaits pious believers. Sentinel deities, scenes of hell and even secular motifs are also to be found. The latter provide an insight into the modes of dress and everyday life at the time the works were created. The roughly 10,000 sculptures on Treasure Peak were created by a single monk.

Among the stone reliefs at in Dazu are numerous depictions of the Buddha and a giant demon holdinf the wheel of life in his fangs.

HUANGLONG

Location: Central China (Sichuan)
Best time to travel: September–May
www.huanglong.com

In addition to the fascinating mountain and glacial landscape, visitors to Huanglong Scenic and Historic Interest Area will find a long series of limestone terraces extending roughly 4 km (2.5 mi) through a beautiful forested valley. The water collected in the pools is rich in algae and bacteria which makes it shimmer in an amazing array of color.

The terraced pools were formed during the Ice Age when the area was covered by a glacier. Rich in minerals, the glacial water eroded basins and caves into the soft limestone cliffs, in which water now collects, flowing from one basin to the next.

JIUZHAIGOU

Location: Central China (Sichuan)
Best time to travel: September–May
www.jiuzhai.com

From an altitude of 2,000 m (6,562 ft), three densely wooded Y-shaped gullies climb up, merging into each other, dominated by snow-covered peaks up to 4,700 m (15,420 ft) high. The karst subsoil enriches the water with calcium carbonate, which reappears in the shape of large chalk sediment terraces.

Jiuzhaigou means "Valley of the Nine Villages", a reference to the nine Tibetan villages located on the 60,000-ha (148,260-acre) area. Nearly 120 lakes (top) shimmer in different colors depending on the time of year. They feed waterfalls (right) that crash down into basins and create new lakes.

LIJIANG

Location: Central China (Yunnan)
Best time to travel: October–May
www.travelchinaguide.com

Lijiang is situated in the strategically important transition zone between central and south Asia, not far from the border with Myanmar, and was once a remote outpost of the Chinese Empire. The historic Old Town with its narrow streets and buildings is one of the best-preserved in China. For centuries Lijiang has boasted a unique irrigation system fed by three canals, the result being that a babbling brook flows past almost every building in the city.

At the foot of Xiangshan Mountain lies the Black Dragon Pond Park, affording stunning views over the Jade Dragon Snow Mountains. An artificial waterfalls roars underneath the Shuocui Bridge.

GUILIN

Location: Southern China (Guangxi)
Best time to travel: September–May
www.visitguilin.org

As a consequence of carbonic acid reactions, distinctive weathered rock forms, so-called karsts, appeared here forms of in China's tropical south. The names of the mountains on both sides of the river resonate with the poetry of this unusual region (Mountain of the Waiting Wife; Old Man at the Mill Stone; Climbing Tortoise; Green Lotus Peak) while groves of Phoenix tail bamboo grow on the river banks, water buffalo doze in the shallow water along the shores and cormorants go about their fishing.

Guilin's romantic scenery is characterized by its distinctive karst cones along the Li River.

SANQINGSHAN

Location: Southern China (Jiangxi)
Best time to travel: September–May
www.gotohangzhou.com

The Mount Sanqingshan National Park in China's Jiangxi Province is located in the western part of the Huyaiyu mountain range. The region was declared a main sight of the state as early as 1988 and has been a major tourist attraction since. The area measures just under 230 sq km (90 sq mi) and is situated at an average elevation of between 1,000 and 1,800 m (3,280 and 5,906 ft) above sea level, with the 1,817-m-high (5,962-ft) Mount Huyaiyu its highest peak. Because of the range of elevations it covers, the national park has both subtropical areas and those influenced by a maritime climate with rain and pine forests extending over about 145 sq km

FUJIAN TULOU

Location: South-eastern China (Fujian)
Best time to travel: September–May
www.discoverfujian.com

The Hakka settlements are situated in the midst of rice, tobacco and tea plantations in Fujian Province, a mountainous region of south-western China. The large round or square mud houses, known as Tulou, illustrate the Hakka's ability to adapt their way of life and their building methods to the conditions in the region, in particular to the threat of hostile attacks during the Ming and Qing dynasties.

The impressive Fujian earth houses, huge, perfectly round and between two and five floors high, were built as fortified housing complexes from the 12th to the 20th centuries.

(56 sq mi). The lush forests are a habitat for more than 300 animal and more than 1,000 plant species. Between the peaks and gorges are numerous lakes, sources and up to 60-m-high (200-ft) waterfalls. Among the main attractions are the unique granite formations of the Huyaiyu mountains. Many of the altogether 48 rocks and 89 columns resemble a person or an animal in shape. The effect is strengthened by cloud banks and wafts of mist, creating a steadily changing landscape and unusual lighting effects such as the so-called white rainbow.
The oldest rock layers are around 1.6 billion years old and provide important indicators of the Earth's geological development.

This national park in south-eastern China boasts a landscape of fascinating beauty that is characterized by dense forests and bizarre lifelike rock formations.

KAIPING

Location: Southern China (Guangdong)
Best time to travel: September–May
www.icm.gov.mo

The residential towers of the city of Kaiping and the surrounding villages present a bizarre sight in this rural area. Chinese nationals returning from abroad combined the European, American and other elements of their former host countries with local traditions in building the residential towers. Three types of towers can be distinguished: communal towers inhabited by several families, more ostentatious towers owned by individual, wealthier families, and watchtowers.

Most of Kaiping's residential towers were built of reinforced concrete during the 1920s.

HONGKONG

Location: Southern China
Best time to travel: all year
www.discoverhongkong.com
http://hong-kong.tourism-asia.net

The name Hong Kong means "Fragrant Harbor". The rocky island at the mouth of the Pearl River was named as such on account of the incense sticks produced there. On the other side of the river is the Kowloon Peninsula which owes its name of "Nine Dragons" to the hilly landscape. Hong Kong became a British colony in 1842 and it was from here that the British ran their profitable opium trade, encroaching on Kowloon in 1860. The so-called Unequal Treaties of 1898 gave the British a 99-year lease on the New Territories along with 235 islands. The Crown Colony at the gateway to China eventually devel-

MACAO

Location: Southern China
Best time to travel: all year
www.macautourism.gov.mo
www.olamacauguide.com

Fishermen have lived by the sheltered bay of the Yu-Jiang Delta since long before the Portuguese came to what they referred to as Macao. Seafarers navigating the Chinese coast would often stop here due to its convenient location. The Portuguese began settling this area from 1557, making Macao the oldest city in the Far East to have been continuously inhabited by Europeans. These colonialists first erected a number of Catholic churches as well as simple houses made using wattle and daub masonry. They then fortified their city in the early 17th century to protect it from attacks, but Chinese authorities prevented the city from experi-

oped into one of the most densely populated and financially powerful trading hubs in the world. It has been a Special Administrative Region of China since July 1, 1997, a status that will last for 50 years, with its own currency, own economy and left-hand driving. Until the year 2047, Hong Kong's far-ranging autonomy and the currently existing economic and social systems are therefore guaranteed: "One state – two systems" is the new motto handed out for Hong Kong. Crossing the border from China into Hong Kong or Macao, however, is considered as leaving the country and the re-entry into the Middle Kingdom has to be approved by a visa.

Hong Kong's skyline presents a breathtaking panorama with its nighttime illuminations. The center of the city is divided into two halves by the Victoria Harbour.

encing any kind of boom until Macao became an independent port city in 1848. It belonged to Portugal after 1849. Macao was a hub for major trade routes: raw silk, silk fabrics, porcelain and herbs were shipped from China, silver was brought from Japan, wine from Portugal, industrial goods from Flanders, crystal glass and clocks from England. Many foreign companies established branch offices here. Towards the end of the 19th century, developed into an enclave of the rich and beautiful. After 1949, Macao became a sanctuary for anyone fleeing the mainland, and in 1999 the city with the oldest Western-style university in China was returned to the People's Republic.

With its mosaic-adorned floors and façades, Largo do Senado, Macao's central square, has a Portuguese flair, a reminder of its former colonial power.

TIBET

Location: Western China
Best time to travel: Ovtober–May
www.tibet-tours.cn
www.visittibet.com

Lhasa ("Place of the Gods") lies on the Kyichu RIver at an altitude of almost 3,700 m (12,140 ft). Founded in the 7th century as the residential seat of the Tibetan kings (7th to 9th centuries), the capital of the Tibet Autonomous Region (TAR) became the seat of government of the Lamaist theocracy in the 15th century, ruled by the Dalai Lamas. For hundreds of years, Lhasa was a "forbidden city" for foreigners.
The 7th-century two-floor Jokhang Temple stands in the Old Town. It is the oldest Buddhist monastery in Tibet as well as a sort of Tibetan national sanctuary. All of the roads in Lhasa therefore lead to it.
Almost as old as the Jokhang Temple is the Ramoche Temple with its mighty outer walls. Unfortunately, the temple's many statues were either destroyed or confiscated by the Red Guards during the Cultural Revolution. With thirteen floors it rises 110 m (362 ft) above the city. Its façade alone is 360 m (1,000 ft) long, behind which are said to be 999 rooms covering an area of 130,000 sq m (1,398,800 sq ft). Opposite is the Drolha Lubuk grotto temple with images of Buddhist deities. Norbulingka, the Dalai Lama's summer palace in the west of Lhasa, is even larger.
For Hindus, Buddhists and followers of the ancient Tibetan Bön and the Indian Jain religions, the 6,714-m (22,029-ft) Kailash is the most sacred mountain in the world. Located in the western Tibetan Transhimalaya mountain range, it is believed to be the seat of the gods. Its summit must not be climbed. Walking around it on the nearly 55-km-long (34-mi) "kora", one of the most difficult pilgrimage paths in the world at an altitude of 4,600 to 5,700 m (15,000 to 18,700 ft), usually takes three to four days. A kora represents a rotation of the wheel of life from birth to death, according to Tibetan belief redeeming all the sins that the pilgrim had committed in his life to that day. Very devoted Tibetans repeatedly throw themselves on the ground during the walk, measuring the distance in body lengths.

The whitewashed part of the Potala Palace (large picture) houses administrative and storage rooms. The red-painted area was the Dalai Lama's residence up to his escape in 1959. The whole palace is now a museum. Top left: the Kailash. Top right: monks in the Ramoche Temple, dating back to the Chinese Princess Wencheng.

KYONGJU

Location: Eastern South Korea
Best time to travel: October–April
www.lifeinkorea.com

From the 1st century, the rulers of the Silla Empire were buried in 200 earth mounds in Kyongju and surroundings. The checkerboard grid of the roads and the remains of historic buildings and palaces are vestiges of the capital's expansion after the unification of the empire in the 7th century.

As the "Golden City" (Kumsong) of the Unified Silla realm, Kyongju was the hub of the first centralized Korean state. The historic Kyongju region also includes the area around Namsan Mountain with its monumental Buddha carvings. It is said to be the birthplace of Hyokkose, the founder of the Silla Dynasty.

SOKKURAM, PULGUKSA

Location: Eastern South Korea
Best time to travel: September–June
http://stone.buddhism.org

The "Temple of the Buddha Land" (Pulguksa) and the Sokkuram Grotto were donated by a top-ranking official in the 8th century. Sokkuram was created from granite blocks as an artificial cave temple. It holds one of the most important Buddhist sculptures. Among the treasures of the Pulguksa Temple is the most famous pair of pagodas in Korea: the modest Shakyamuni Pagoda stands symbolic for the peace of the Buddha, while the opulently adorned Treasure Pagoda symbolizes the rich "inner world" of the faithful.

This bronze Buddha is also venerated at the Pulguksa Temple.

HAEINSA

Location: Southern South Korea
Best time to travel: September–June
http://english.visitkorea.or.kr

Haeinsa, on Mount Kaya in South Kyongsang province, is home to an artifact venerated by Buddhists : the Tripitaka Koreana ("Teaching of the three baskets"), 81,258 wooden blocks that make up the most comprehensive collection of Buddhist texts. They are stored on the shelves of two depositories called Changgyong Pango. The blocks are carved on both sides, creating a total of 162,516 pages. Two hundred monks spent twelve years working on the blocks, finishing them in 1248.

The climate inside the Changgyong Pango depositories built in 1488 is perfectly suited for the printing plates that are stored there.

CHONGMYO

Location: Seoul, north-western South Korea
Best time to travel: September–May
www.jongmyo.net

Ancestral worship plays a major role in Confucian rituals, and so the last Korean rulers who were oriented towards China and who made neo-Confucianism the official state and moral philosophy built a central place for the veneration of their own ancestors. Chongmyo, the "Shrine of the Royal Ancestors", dates back to Yi Songgye, the founder of the Choson dynasty. The building received its present look in around 1600. Inside are the ancestral plates of the 19 most significant Yi kings.

The rituals of worship practiced by the monks have changed little in the last 500 years.

TOKYO

Location: Honshu Island
Best time to travel: all year
www.tokyoessentials.com
www.tourism.metro.tokyo.jp

Tokyo is a city of superlatives: Japan's largest city, by area and number of inhabitants It is also one of the megacity's on Earth. More than eight million people live in the Japanese metropolis, which also forms the economic and cultural center of the country.

Tokyo became the capital of Japan in 1868, after the overthrow of the Tokugawa Dynasty. The increase in political importance brought about a rapid expansion. The city mostly recovered quickly from the occasional earthquake and large fire. And the damage sustained in World War II could also quickly be repaired. In the summer of 1964, Tokyo hosted the Olympic Games.

For many people travelling by air to Japan, Tokyo is the first stop. During the peak travel times especially, there is not getting through in the city for in addition to the city dwellers, several million commuters are also on the road. Yet the public transport system works excellently. The center is traversed by a dense network of underground train lines, the Shinkansen high-speed rail line (aka the "Bullet Train") links Tokyo with other large cities in Japan, and the international airport is a hub for the air traffic in the Far East.

An excellent way to acquaint yourself with the city and explore Tokyo in all its diversity is taking a boat trip on the Sumida River. Although the historic buildings in Tokyo do not compete with the quantity and magnificence of the ancient imperial city of Kyoto, it still has some historic sights worth visiting.

One of the most important structures in the center is the imperial palace den, which is surrounded by extensive gardens. The palace is

open to the public only twice a year – on New Year's Day and on the current emperor's birthday, which is always a national holiday. Only the eastern section of the gardens is freely accessible. Among the most significant religious buildings in the city are the Senso-ji (Asakusa Kannon) Temple and Tokyo's main Shinto shrine, the Meiji Shrine, the tomb of Emperor Meiji. The Ginza district is ideal for shopping. Since the late 19th century, it has been systematically developed as a modern district in the Western style, offering for sale anything that the heart of a local or a visitor might desire. Vast department stores and small stores, arts and crafts shops and galleries, bars and restaurants determine the ambience. In the dark, especially, the district presents itself in every possible neon hue.

Entertainment too is of the highest importance in Tokyo. The Tokyo National Museum houses the most comprehensive collection of Japanese art as well as archaeological objects. Stadiums, halls and stages offer wide-ranging program of events. Yet despite its great love of all things 21st century – as everywhere else in Japan, the capital too honors its traditions: the Kabuki theaters are always busy.

The Rainbow Bridge, completed in the year 1993 and spanning the harbor of Tokyo, measures 798 m (2,618 ft) in total – 570 m (1,870 ft) between the two abutments (top; on the right in the picture in the striking Tokyo Tower, which at an elevation of 333 m (1,093 ft) towers 9 m (30 ft) above its clearly recognizable model, the 224-m-high (735-ft) Eiffel Tower in Paris). Bottom: Tokyo's countless skyscrapers can be recognized from afar (left: the Shinjuko Don Avenue in the Shunjuku shopping district; right: the neon lights in the main business and entertainment quarter, Ginza).

MOUNT FUJI

Location: Honshu Island
Best time to travel: July/August
www.japan-guide.com

The islands of Japan form part of the so-called Ring of Fire, a string of seismically and volcanically active regions that encircles the Pacific Ocean. One of the many manifestations of the tectonic peculiarity of this region, which is one of die geologically most active on Earth is earthquakes, and Japan gets plenty of them. Although the Japanese use state-of-the-art technology in the construction of their buildings and transport network, even they are not able to combat the forces at work below the earth's surface.
Mount Fuji, a glorious result of the Ring of Fire's powers, rises up from the island in stoic silence. It is not only Japan's highest mountain, but also the country's undisputed icon –

BANDAI-ASAHI

Location: Honshu Island
Best time to travel: May–September
www.biodic.go.jp

Honshu, the largest of Japan's four main islands, possesses many of the country's most beautiful natural features, and the important elements of its biodiversity are protected in a series of truly stunning parks. Bandai-Asahi National Park, founded on September 5, 1950, and covering an area of 1,870 sq km (722 sq mi), is divided into separate sections that are isolated geographically: to the west is Mount Iide at 2,105 m (6,907 ft); to the north is the Asahi Range with the holy Dewa Sanzan mountain shrines; to the east are the Bandai Azuma mountains; and Lake Inawashiro is to the south. Japan's fourth-largest lake, Inawashiro-ko was dammed by

the pride of an entire nation. At a towering 3,776 m (12,38 ft), Fuji is crowned by a massive crater 600 m (1,900 ft) across and 150 m (492 ft) deep. Temples, cabins, a weather station and a radar station are based on its rim. Every year up to 400,000 people make the ascent in the summer season (July and August). There are five lakes – Motosu-ko, Shoji-ko, Sai-ko, Kawaguchi-ko and Ymanaka-ko – on the north side of the mountain. Japan's sacred mountain last erupted on December 16, 1707. That eruption lasted for about two weeks. and a further crater and a second peak appeared at about half its height as a consequence.

Covered with snow into the summer, the perfectly symmetrically shaped volcanic cone of Mount Fuji rises in the south-east of Honshu Island. On very clear days it can be seen even from Tokyo, which is a good 100 km (62 mi) away.

masses of lava from Bandai Volcano. Its water is so clear that the lake is also known as "Heavenly Mirror". On its north shores are several inviting beaches for bathing and relaxing.

The park is accessible via panoramic toll roads including the Bandai Azuma Skyline, which is open from April to November and is one of the busiest routes. Like many other regions on Honshu there are hot springs in the park, Tsuchiyu-Onsen being one of the most popular. The Tsuchiyu Pass, on the access road between Inawashiro-ko and Fukushima provides an enchanting view.

Since Japan's landscapes are much smaller than those in European countries, the national parks here are often divided into several unconnected sections. This is also the case with the Bandai Asahi National Park (left an autumn scene at Lake Hibara).

SHIRAKAMI-SANCHI

Location: Honshu Island
Best time to travel: May–September
www.jnto.go.jp

The largest primeval beech forest in East Asia is an important refuge for the world's most northerly monkey population, the Asian black bear, the Japanese serow (a goat species) and eighty-seven bird species including the endangered black woodpecker.

More than 500 plant species flourish in the Shirakami Forest, including rare orchids. The mountain landscape, which rises to an elevation of 1,243 m (4,078 ft) and is the origin of fifteen rivers, is mostly impassable.

In Shirakama-Sanchi, the Japanese macaque or snow monkey, an endemic species, has found a refuge.

HORYU-JI

Location: Honshu Island
Best time to travel: May–September
www.horyuji.or.jp

Horyu-ji dates back to the very beginning of Japanese Buddhism, which was declared the national religion at the start of the 7th century. Construction began in 607 on the orders of Prince Regent Shotoku (573–621).

The original Chinese-style temple burned almost completely to the ground in 670, but the buildings here today are still considered the oldest wooden constructions in the world and were built by about 710, the start of the Nara Period. They include the main hall (Golden Hall), the five-floor pagoda, the middle gate and the adjoining gallery.

Among the treasures of Horyu-ji are gilded wooden sculptures.

KYOTO

Location: Honshu Island
Best time to travel: all year
www.city.kyoto.lg.jp

No other city displays Japan's cultural wealth as well as Kyoto, where architecture, sculpture and painting flourished for centuries.
Many Japanese people are of the opinion that their country can only really be understood by strolling through the former imperial city of Kyoto, capital of Japan for more than 1,000 years from 794 to 1868 – and almost without interruption. The administrative seat permanently moved to Tokyo at that point. Despite the loss of political power, however, Kyoto remained the cultural and spiritual hub of Japan, renowned for architecture and theater, handicrafts and kimono collections, and traditional fan manufacturing and festivals. The city boasts nearly 2,000 magnificent palaces, temples and shrines that give entire districts a great ambience. Stunning examples include the Kiyomizu-dera temple and the Heian and Fushimi Shrines.

Dominating the town from up high is the Kiyomizu-dera Temple (top left). It has been visited by pilgrims for more than 1,000 years. The Heian Shrine (above left) – a smaller copy of the first imperial palace from 794 – was not built until 1894, for the 1,100th anniversary of the foundation of Kyoto. The Fushimi Shrine, dating from 711, is one of the most significant structures in the old imperial city of Kyoto. It is dedicated to the goddess of rice cultivation. Worth seeing is also the roughly 4-km-long (2.5-mi) avenue of red Shinto gates ("torii") leading to the heart of the complex (above right).

ITSUKUSHIMA

Location: Miyajima Island
Best time to travel: all year
www.visitjapan.jp

Itsukushima was a holy site very early on and could only be accessed by priests up until the 11th century. There is no cemetery on the island to this day, a measure to ensure that the purity of the religious site is preserved. Although the main buildings date from the period 1556 to 1571, the overall complex with its glistening red paintwork retains the distinct style of the Heian Period (8th–12th centuries), when a similar version was first built.

The red Torii made from camphor wood off Miyajima Island (the "Shrine Island"), seen here in a yellow light, was made as a copy of an older gate. It is surrounded by water only during high tide.

HIROSHIMA

Location: Honshu Island
Best time to travel: all year
www.gethiroshima.com

August 6, 1945, was a day that changed the world. The United States made the fateful decision to use a newly developed weapon to force the Japanese Empire into unconditional surrender. The first atom bomb, "Little Boy", was dropped by the B29 bomber Enola Gay and exploded 570 m (1,870 ft) above the heart of the port of Hiroshima. Every form of life within a radius of 4 km (2.5 mi) was destroyed in an instant.

Since 1945, the former Chamber of Trade and Industry with its burnt-out dome has been a symbol for the horror of modern warfare. The Peace Memorial Museum nearby documents in detail the consequences of the Hiroshima bomb.

NARA

Location: Honshu Island
Best time to travel: all year
www.city.nara.nara.jp

The temple and shrines of the first permanent imperial residence mark the beginning of the aristocratic period and the first peak of Japanese Buddhist art. Based on the Chinese Tang city of Chang'an, the new Japanese capital of Nara was built in just four years and features a checkerboard grid pattern as its road layout. To the north of the city is a magnificent imperial palace that hosted seven emperors up until the end of the Nara period (710–784). From there a wide arterial road leading south divides the city into two equal rectangles. The Buddhist schools that had only been introduced to Japan shortly before that time then set up temples and monasteries in the new capital. The main hall of the Toshodai-ji Temple from 759 was part of the imperial palace and is considered the most important building in Nara. One of the world's largest wooden buildings is located near the Todai-ji temple (728), seat of the influential Kegon sect. The dimensions of the Great Buddha Hall (Daibutsu) are colossal: 58 m (180 ft) long, 51 m (160 ft) wide and 49 m (161 ft) high. The building, which was reconstructed in 1708, is smaller than the original, however.

The giant, 16-m-tall (-ft) Daibutsu ("The Big Buddha of Nara") in the Todai-ji Temple of Nara is considered to be the largest Buddha statue on Earth made from gold-bronze. This impressive figure consists of 437 metric tons of bronze, into which has been mixed about 130 kg (287 lbs) pure gold.

HALONG

Location: Northern Vietnam
Best time to travel: November–April
http://halongtours.com

The limestone cliffs in Halong can be up to 100 m (328 ft) high and most of them are covered with dense vegetation. Reminiscent of Chinese landscape paintings, these cliffs and mountains come in a wide variety of shapes ranging from broad-based pyramids and high, arched "elephant backs" to thin, towering needles of rock. The island landscape has often been perceived as more of a mythical spectacle than as a natural phenomenon: A dragon (Ha Long) descended from the mountains (or from heaven) is said to have created this natural wonder when it destroyed an army of enemy invaders with blows from its mighty tail – or was it that the dragon had been disturbed and therefore angered? The water displaced by the dragon as it dived under the sea then spilled into the resulting channels and canyons. The geological reality is somewhat more down-to-earth: Following the last Ice Age the coastal landscape forming part of the south-west Chinese limestone plateau sank and was flooded. It was erosion which ultimately formed the bizarre-shaped cones of rock.

The archipelago in the Bay of Halong consists of around 2000 islands and limestone cliffs.

HUE

Location: Central Vietnam
Beste Reisezeit: February–July
www.relaxindochina.com

Vietnam's capital from 1802 until 1945, Hue is still one of the country's cultural, religious, political and intellectual centers. Nguyen Anh, who reunited a fragmented Vietnam in 1802 and ascended the throne as Emperor Gia Long, commissioned a fortified residence in the city center that reflects Chinese palatial styles. His desire to emulate Chinese imperial architecture is exemplified by details such as the design of the roof decoration. Seven of the Nguyen emperors had their tombs built outside Hue.

This superb gate forms the access into the main temple in the Thien Mu Pagoda or the "Pagoda of the Heavenly Woman".

HOI AN

Location: Central Vietnam
Best time to travel: February–July
www.visithoian.com

The port city of Hoi An was an important trading hub from the 15th to the 19th centuries. Both Asian and European influences overlap in the city's layout, buildings and temples. The first Portuguese landed on the coast of Vietnam in 1516, followed soon after by Jesuit missionaries. The Portuguese quickly established a trading post in Hoi An in 1535, developing it into a vibrant city. Chinese, Japanese and later other Europeans, especially the Dutch, then settled as traders in the city, also known as Phai Fu, each nationality taking over its own district within the city.

The Japanese Bridge links the Chinese and Japanese quarters.

MY SON

Location: Central Vietnam
Best time to travel: February–July
www.vietnamtourism.com

The kingdom of the Champa or Cham, a Malayo-Indonesian people, dates back to the year 192 when, following the collapse of the Han dynasty in China, the local Han governor founded his own kingdom in the area around present-day Hue. The first wooden temple was built in My Son by Prince Bhadravarman. The first brick temple was erected by a successor in the seventh century, and was the beginning of an architectural tradition that continued into the 13th century.

At the foot of the "Beautiful Mountain" (My Son), the Cham worshipped the Hindu god Shiva. Pillars, friezes and statues of deities adorn the outside of the temple towers.

HO CHI MIN CITY

Location: Southern Vietnam
Best time to travel:
December–April
www.hochiminhcity.gov.vn

While Hanoi is the country's political hub, Ho Chi Min City (in Vietnamese: Thanh Pho Ho Chi Minh, and formerly Saigon), is considered to be the industrial and economic heart of Vietnam. Modernization has indeed left its traces on the urban look and feel here, but the past still manages to shine through in some places. The colonial-style buildings, for example, and the road-side kiosks selling baguettes add a touch of the French colonial atmosphere to some of the city's neighborhoods.

The town hall was also built at the beginning of the 20th century in the French colonial style.

MEKONG DELTA

Location: South-western Vietnam
Best time to travel: December–April
www.visit-mekong.com
www.waytomekong.com

South of Ho Chi Minh City is a series of rolling hills that gives way to an almost perfectly flat expanse – the Mekong Delta. Rice paddy after rice paddy stretches between the countless channels where much of the daily activity takes place. The delta is formed by the accumulated sedimentary deposits of the Mekong River, a process that is ongoing today. The coastline along the river mouth extends further into the sea by around 80 m (262 ft) every year. This fertile land is used intensively for agriculture, making the region Vietnam's undisputed rice bowl. This area is also one of the most densely populated in the country. The constant danger of flooding means that almost all of the houses here are built on stilts. Trading takes to the water during periods of flooding, when the vibrant river markets take place.

In the south of Vietnam lies one of the most expansive river estuaries on Earth: the roughly 70,000 sq km (27,020 sq mi) wide, much frequented delta of the Mekong. Lotus flowers are here considered a symbol of purity – although they flourish in swampy areas, the still appear perfectly clean in their singular surface structure.

WAT PHU AND CHAMPASAK

Location: Southern Laos
Best time to travel: October–April
www.visitlaos.co.uk

The Wat Phu temple complex represents an important historical legacy going back to the first century, harmonizing beautifully with the ancient cultural landscape of Champasak in the south-west of Laos. In the fifth century this was the site of the capital of a pre-Angkorian kingdom. Between the 10th and 13th centuries, Champasak formed part of the Khmer kingdom of Angkor, the territory under its control extending up the Mekong as far as Viang Chan (present-day Vientiane). At that time the region between the holy mountain Kao and the plain was used for organized rice farming, with irrigation systems, temple complexes and two cities on the banks of the Mekong. All this still reflects the pre-Angkorian Hindu worldview of the unity between the universe, nature and man. The Wat Phu temple complex, with "landscape pyramids" of temples, shrines, canals, roads and water pools built in the 10th century under the Angkor ruler Jayavarman IV, forms part of this legacy.

From the temple ruins at the foot of the Phu Kao, the path leads via 90 steep steps to the former Shiva sanctuary on the summit (avove right the impressive main temple). Today, the formerly Hindu Wat Phu ("Temple on the Mountain") is a Buddhist temple as is revealed by the statues, which are clad in monks' robes. These statues date from the seventh century.

LUANG PRABANG

Location: Northern Laos
Best time to travel: October–March
www.luangprabangcity.com

More than any other city, Luang Prabang is the embodiment of traditional Laos. Even though political power has been based in Vientiane (Wiang Chan) since the French colonial era, Luang Prabang remains the country's cultural hub. This city at the mouth of the Nam Khan on the upper reaches of the Mekong got its name at the end of the 15th century from the popular, almost 1-m-high (3-ft) Phra Bang Buddha statue dating from the 14th century and for which a separate temple was built. At that time, as Muong Swa, Luang Prabang had already been the center of one of three Lao kingdoms, the "Land of a million elephants" (Lan Chang), for over a century. The former royal city still boasts numerous Buddhist temples and monasteries with magnificent art treasures. The most imposing of these complexes is the 16th-century royal temple Wat Xieng Thong. The temples are built of stone and the secular buildings of wood. The Old Town beneath Phu Si hill is characterized by traditional buildings and French colonial architecture.

Wat Xieng Thong was named after a Bodhi tree (Thong), which is depicted in a glass mosaic on the back of the Sim. Inside, where monks are saying their prayers in front of a giant Buddha statue, the walls and columns are also adorned with vivid glass mosaics.

ANGKOR

Location: Northern Cambodia
Best time to travel:
October–April
www.visitangkortemples.com

The Khmer culture was strongly influenced by the Indian peoples that migrated to Southeast Asia in the first millennium. They prospered particularly after shaking off the domination of the Funan Empire (2nd–6th centuries), which was also heavily influenced by Indian culture. The founder of the Khmer empire was Jayavarman II, who ascended the throne in 802. As the god king of Angkor with absolute religious and secular power, he acted as intermediary between heaven and earth. The Khmer rulers were Hindu-orientated until the beginning of the 13th century and were venerated in the form of Linga (the phallus of Shiva, creator and destroyer of the world), then later as an incarnation of Bodhisattva. A clear indication of this change can be found in the Bayon Temple of Angkor Thom. Here, a total of 54 towers were built during the reign of Jayavarman VII (1181 to 1218), from each of which a 4-m-high (13-ft) monumental face of the Bodhisattva Avalokiteshvara looked into the four cardinal directions. Since the temple became the tomb of the god king after his death, every Khmer king built a sanctuary for himself so that their number around Angkor grew steadily. The most impressive complex is Angkor Wat, the temple of Suryavarman II (1113–50), under whom the Khmer culture reached its zenith.

Angkor Wat is the largest temple complex in the ancient capital of the Khmer. Since its was abandoned, nature has reclaimed the complex with its prangs (temple towers) and reliefs. A 100-m-long (328-ft) stone dam leads to the main entrance of the site.

SUKHOTHAI

Location: Northern Thailand
Best time to travel: December–March
www.su.ac.th
www.tourismthailand.org

"May the land of Sukhothai thrive and prosper" – that is the stone inscription on the tomb of King Ramkhamhaeng the Great (ruled 1279–98) that is now housed in the National Museum in Bangkok. Sukhothai was the Siamese kingdom's first capital and it indeed enjoyed its greatest period of prosperity under him. The first independent kingdom of Siam expanded as far as present-day Laos and, for a few decades, to the Malay Peninsula after the retreat of the Khmer around 1238. A "golden age" prevailed until the end of the 14th century, one that saw the development of the Thai alphabet as well as the

KAMPHAENG PHET

Location: Northern Thailand
Best time to travel: December–March
www.moohin.com

The city on the Ping Rover was founded in 1347 during the reign of King Liu Thai as an outpost of the Sukhothai empire, and after its fall (1376) it remained an important garrison town for the kings of Ayutthaya. Toward the end of the 16th century, the Burmese raided the city. Aside from the remains of the city walls, once surrounded by tall mounds, an impressive collection of temple ruins was preserved in the area of the Kamphaeng Phet Historical Park to the north.

These slightly weathered Buddha statues can be found in the Kamphaeng Phet Historical Park.

creation of the loveliest Siamese works of art. Following its decline in the 14th century, however, it was largely forgotten until restoration work on the ruins began in 1977 and the Sukhothai National Historical Park was opened. The park includes several dozen temples both inside and outside the original Sukhothai city walls. Monumental Buddha statues look over Wat Sra Sri, with its bell-shaped, Sri Lankan-style chedi. Wat Sorasak, with its bell-shaped chedi surrounded by twenty-five stone elephants is a special highlight in Sukhothai.

Wat Mahathat, the "Temple of the Great Relic", was the religious center of ancient Sukhothai. The historic complex whose architectural style was greatly influenced by the Khmer, extends over an area of about 2 by 1.5 km (2,187 by 1,640 yds) and is surrounded by earth walls and water ditches.

SI SATCHANALAI

Location: Northern Thailand
Best time to travel: December–March
www.reocities.com

Si Satchanalai was built in around 1250, at about the same time as Sukhothai. It became the second seat of the first king of Thailand as well as the seat of the viceroy after two Thai princes from the surrounding area had defeated the Khmer governor of Sukhothai in a bloody battle. In the 17th century Si Satchanalai became part of the kingdom of Ayutthaya, which was abandoned by its inhabitants when the Burmese reached the city gates in the 18th century.

Today, the Buddha statues in Si Satchanalai are still the object of veneration by the faithful.

THUNG YAI, HUAI KHA KHAENG

Location: Northern Thailand
Best time to travel: December–March
http://thailand.tourism-asia.net

The two nature reserves in western Thailand make up one of the largest wildlife sanctuaries in South-East Asia, with a total area of around 6,100 sq km (2,355 sq mi). The highlands on the border with Myanmar are traversed by rivers and streams and alternate between savannah-like plateaus and dense forests.

The grasslands and evergreen forests of the reserve are home to the hog deer, so named because it does not leap over obstacles like most other deer but instead runs in a hog-like manner through the undergrowth with its head hung low.

KHAO YAI

Location: Central Thailand
Best time to travel: December–March
www.dnp.go.th

The Khao Yai National Park covers an area of 2,168 sq km (837 sq mi) at the edge of the Khorat Plateau. The most populous wildlife reserve in Thailand, it is traversed by a total of around 40 km (25 mi) of hiking trails. In the dense evergreen mountain forests, however, it is often only the sounds of the primeval forest that are perceptible – the singing of the cicadas, for example, and the characteristic sound of the great hornbill concealed in the tree tops.

The park's rainforest is a superb refuge for the great hornbill and the rhesus macaque, among others. Waterfalls like the Nam Tok Haeo Suwat are a popular atttraction.

AYUTTHAYA

Location: Central Thailand
Best time to travel: December–March
www.moohin.com

The Siamese empire's second capital was founded in 1350 by King U-Thong (Thibodi I) on the east bank of the Chao Phraya River. Today it has been converted into a magnificent open-air museum of ancient Buddhist culture. The monasteries, chedis, prangs as well as the numerous monumental sculptures are testimony to its former glory.
At the height of its power, "The Invincible" – as the name Ayutthaya translates – was a cosmopolitan city with one million inhabitants, 375 monasteries and temples, ninety-four city gates and twenty-nine fortresses. The city was not ultimately invincible, however, and fell to the Burmese in 1767. Up until that point Ayutthaya had been the political and, more importantly, the cultural hub of a kingdom that had inherited the spectacular legacy of Angkor under thirty-three kings for more than 400 years. Excavated in 1956, the former royal city was restored with UNESCO support and the most important monuments are now assembled in the center of the ruined city.

Aside from the corn cob-like prangs and the bell-shaped chedis, dozens of Buddha statues characterize the temple ruins of Ayutthaya. On the site you will also come across a Buddha head that is entangled with the aerial roots of a Bodhi tree. In Ayutthaya, too, the Buddha is venerated in the shape of countless statues. These mostly fall into four postures or asanas: standing, walking, sitting, reclining. The Buddha statues in Ayutthaya, which depict the Buddha mostly in a seated position, are wrapped in orange monks' habits.

KO SAMUI

Location: Island off south-eastern Thailand
Best time to travel: December–April
www.kohsamui.org

Where holiday dreams come true: miles of immaculate white-sand beaches and idyllic bays; crystal-clear, turquoise water; palms waving in the warm breeze; rainforests and waterfalls; picturesque cliffs; and unspoilt fishing villages. These are the things that make Ko Samui, Thailand's third-largest island after Phuket and Ko Chang, one of the country's most popular travel destinations. Swimming, snorkelling and diving are usually at the top of the wishlist of activities for visitors.

Life is a(n island) dream: Coral Cove Bay on the "Coconut Island", as Ko Samui is also often called.

PHUKET

Location: Island off south-western Thailand
Best time to travel: December–March
www.phuket.com

Phuket is Thailand's largest island (543 sq km/210 sq mi). It is connected to the mainland in the north by a 700-m-long (2,475-ft) bridge. Both town and island offer a wealth of nature, culture and folklore to explore. Phuket's original wealth derived from tin mining and the magnificent villas in Phuket's Chinese-Portuguese heart still recall that time. The Vegetarian Festival is also originally Chinese.

Setting sail on the Andaman Sea from Phuket in a longtail boat is an unforgettable experience. The boats are steered by means of a propeller shaft (longtail) with a motor attached to it.

KRABI AND KO PHI PHI

Location: Coast and island in south-western Thailand
Best time to travel: December–April
www.moohin.com
http://phi-phi.com

The bays around the port of Krabi boast some of Thailand's finest beaches and clearest waters. The village lies at the mouth of the Krabi River where it flows into the Andaman Sea. Smooth sandy beaches, rocky bays, caves and a magnificent underwater world are all at your disposal south of Krabi in the 390-sq km (150-sq mi) Hat Noppharat Thara – Mu Ko Phi Phi National Park.

The most famous island group in the park is Ko Phi Phi thanks to Danny Boyle's film of Alex Garland's cult novel The Beach.

AO PHANG-NGA

Location: South-western Thailand
Best time to travel: December–March
www.dnp.go.th

The bizarre rock formations, cones and pyramids tower out of the water in Phang Nga Bay like the backs of prehistoric dragons. These visible peaks of limestone reef in the Andaman Sea, which once extended from northern Malaysia as far as Central China, were formed over the course of 100 million years. An area covering roughly 400 sq km (154 sq mi) was used to create Ao Phang-nga National Park in 1981 and was primarily intended to protect the mangroves in the northern part of the bay – the largest in Thailand.

The Nail Island cliffs were made famous by the James Bond film The Man with the Golden Gun.

KUALA LUMPUR, BATU CAVES

Location: Western Malaysia
Best time to travel: January/February, June–September
http://visitkualalumpur.com
www.kuala-lumpur.ws

Malaysia's largest city is also the political and economic center of this Southeast Asian country. At this point, however, there is nothing about the capital today that is reminiscent of a "muddy estuary", which is what the name means. No other city in the country manifests so consistently the will of Malaysia to present itself internationally as an up-and-coming industrial nation, and it does so impressively with modern high-rise complexes such as the Petronas Towers, the administrative offices of multinational companies, banks and institutions as well as the numerous hotels.
Kuala Lumpur's appeal derives primarily from its vibrant ambience, the plentiful green spaces in the city center, the relaxing parks on the periphery, and particularly from the harmonious multicultural population mix – Chinese, Malay and Indian being the main ethnic groups – with their diverse cultures, traditions and ways of life.
The modern skyline is interspersed with the older parts of the city: the administrative buildings of the former British colonial administration and the villas of the tin barons as well as the traditional residential areas of the Indians and Chinese who live here.
The Batu Caves are located around 15 km (9 mi) north of the capital on the road to Kuantan and are among the most frequently visited attractions in the Kuala Lumpur area. The enormous limestone caves form part of a vast labyrinth of rock openings and passageways that stretch over 1 km (0.6 mi).

At 452 m (1,483 ft), the Petronas Towers (above center and left) are among the tallest buildings in the world and have become the main landmark of Kuala Lumpur, visible from afar. Designed by Cesar Pelli and inaugrurated in 1998, the two towers are linked by a 58.4-m-long (192-ft) "sky bridge" at an altitude of 170 m (558 ft).
Thousands of visitors travel to the Batu Caves for the full moon in the Tamil month of Thai (January/February) every year when the two-day Thaipusam Festival takes place. The highlight of the festivities is a procession of penitents who have metal hooks pushed into their backs and their chests (above right).
The shrine (above left) that was established in the main Batu cave back in 1892 has made this one of the most important pilgrimage destinations in the country for Malaysia's Hindu population.

KINABALU

Location: Eastern Malaysia (Borneo)
Best time to travel: April–September
www.mount-kinabalu-borneo.com

Kinabalu Park, founded in 1964, is situated in the Malaysian province of Sabah, at the northern end of the island of Borneo. It is known mainly for its primeval vegetation and for Mount Kinabalu, the impressive focal point of the park and – at 4,095 m (13,436 ft) – the highest mountain between the Himalayas and New Guinea. It is characterized by very diverse plant life that constantly changes between the different zones and extends as far as the barren, rocky summit region. A tropical rainforest extends in the lowlands.

The mountain range has its highest elevation in Mount Kinabalu.

GUNUNG MULU

Location: Eastern Malaysia (Borneo)
Best time to travel: April–September
www.mulupark.com

The formation of this craggy landscape began around thirty million years ago when pulverized volcanic rock formed the sand and sediment that made up what was then still a seabed. Coral and other marine fauna then formed the limestone over millions of years. Uplifting and a drop in sea levels about five million years ago led to the creation of the mountain range that forms today the protected national park territory.

The Gunung Mulu National Park comprises sharp-edged limestone formations and the largest cave complex on Earth (right: Wind Cave) in a tropical karst landscape.

SINGAPORE

Location: Island south of Malaysia
Best time to travel: all year
www.yoursingapore.com
www.visitsingapore.org

The city-state of Singapore is on a small island at the south end of the Malaysian Peninsula on the Strait of Malacca. The city was founded in 1819 as a trading post and rose to become Southeast Asia's most important transport, financial and economical hub within just a few decades. It is here that modernity and the future co-exist peacefully with history and tradition.
Singapore is considered the cleanest of Asian cities, with the best air quality of any city in the world. This is ensured by high penalties for littering, for instance, as well as high road charges, extreme vehicle taxes and severely limited licensing regulations for new vehicles. These seemingly draconian measures have managed to keep cars away from the city for many years, however, and the outstanding public transport system means that any point within the city is easily and quickly accessible. The population is composed of two-thirds Chinese together with a mix of Indians and Malays. In colonial times, each ethnic group had their own district, all of which have undergone extensive renovations in recent years. The markets shops and restaurants are full of atmosphere, particularly in the evenings, the most vibrant of which can be found in Little India.

Singapore is a city of superlatives: in the Financial District (top; left: Orchard Road), one futuristic skyscraper towers next to another, the airport is one of the largest in Asia and the container port one of the biggest in the world. Yet it also boasts many historic buildings that keep alive the memory of the Singapore of old.

IFUGAO (LUZÓN)

Location: Northern Philippines (Luzon Island)
Best time to travel: December–April
www.ifugao.org

Deepwater rice cultivation is one of the most important cultural accomplishments in Asian history and the Ifugao – an indigenous mountain people living in the province of the same name in the Philippine Cordillera – are especially gifted in this ancient skill. The rice terraces, laboriously built by hand, literally cling to the steep slopes. Irrigation is provided to each terrace by a sophisticated system of bamboo pipes, canals and small sluices.

In the mountains of northern Luzón, the Ifugao, an Igorot people, have cultivated rice on emerald-green terraces for about 2,000 years.

PUERTO PRINCESA SUBTERRANEAN RIVER NATIONAL PARK (PALAWAN)

Location: Western Philippines (Palawan Island)
Best time to travel: December–April
http://visitpuertoprincesa.com

This park is about 80 km (50 mi) north-west of Puerto Princesa, the capital of Palawan. Among its attractions are the limestone formations of the St Paul Mountain Range. The main scenic attraction is the 8 km (5 mi) Puerto Princesa Subterranean River, the longest navigable underground river on earth.

The underground river has created a gigantic cave complex.

TROPICAL RAIN FORESTS OF SUMATRA

Location: Western Indonesia
Best time to travel: January–July
www.sumatra-indonesia.com

One of the last continuous rain forest areas on earth is protected by three national parks on the island of Sumatra: Gunung Leuser in the north, Kerinci Seblat in the center and Bukit Barisan Selatan further to the south. Some 10,000 plant species flourish in this region, including seventeen endemic genera. The flowering plants here comprise more than fifty percent of the species on Sumatra.
Also enormously diverse, the animal world has until now only been partially researched by scientists. Over 580 bird species alone have been discovered, twenty-one of these endemic. The most spectacular of the local animal species are the orang-utans, tigers, rhinos, elephants, serow, tapirs and the clouded leopard. This high level of biodiversity is matched only by the wealth of geological formations and habitats.

Orang-utans (top) are natives of the rain forests of Sumatra and Borneo. Males grow to 80 kg (176 lbs in weight, making them one of the heaviest tree dwellers that also spend the night in their tree nests. Above from left: a titan arum (the plant with the largest inflorescence in the world – up to 3 m/10 ft); a giant rafflesia (the largest, solitary, fleshy flower in the world – its five red petals attain a diameter of up to 1 m/ 3ft); tropical rain forest in the Gunung Leuser National Park.

BOROBUDUR

Location: Southern Indonesia (Java Island)
Best time to travel: May–October
www.borobudurpark.co.id

This temple complex built in the eighth century on the main Indonesian island of Java is the most important Buddhist sanctuary outside India. Buddha himself is said to have determined the design of the stupa here by folding his mendicant robes into a mound, placing his alms bowl on the top, and then crowning it with a staff.

The temple complex of Borobudur, built on a hill, a shrine and a place of pilgrimage, symbolizes the cosmic view of the Meru world mountain in its various levels of meditation: the "world of desire", the "world of names and shapes" and the "formless world".

PRAMBANAN

Location: Southern Indonesia (Java Island)
Best time to travel: May–October
www.borobudurpark.co.id
www.borobudur.tv

The one-time most important Hindu religious site on Java was originally dedicated to the gods Brahma, Vishnu and Shiva, but the main temple, Loro Jonggrang, is said to have been completed only in around 915. It is dedicated to Shiva, the Indian god of virility and called "Maha Deva" here. He is the most powerful of the three deities, signalled by the omnipresence of his symbol, the phallus (lingam). Brahma and Vishnu each have their own smaller temples.

Construction on the complex's high temple towers, known as prangs and visible from afar, probably began in the eighth century.

BROMO-TENGGER-SEMERU

Location: Southern Indonesia (Java Island)
Best time to travel: May–October
www.eastjava.com

Gunung Bromo in Bromo-Tengger-Semeru National Park is 2,392 m (7,848 ft) high and the most frequently visited of all volcanoes on Java due to its unique setting. This remote region is inhabited by the Tengger people, who retreated to these mountains when Islam spread across Java. They have managed to maintain their Hindu traditions to the present day.

The country's highest volcano, Semeru, at a gigantic 3,676 m (12,061 ft), towers above the park, which covers an area of about 58,000 ha (143,318 acres).

BALI, LOMBOK

Location: Southern Indonesia
Best time to travel: April–November
www.dipardabali.com
www.lombok-network.com

In the Indonesian holiday paradise of Bali, the north and west are dominated by narrow, dark beaches, whereas in the south of the island are magnificent sandy beaches and picturesque bays. The rice terraces in the center of the island are the work of generations of farmers who made the steep slopes arable. The summit of Gunung Agung offers a magnificent view of the adjacent island of Lombok. At its west coast visitors will find temples and palaces and picture-postcard sandy palm beaches.

Balinese dancers are lavishly adorned for their (danced) veneration of the deities.

The solitude of the sand desert, the fires of the Virunga volcanoes, the raging waters of Victoria Falls, the majesty of Mount Kilimanjaro, the pyramids of Egypt, the palaces of Morocco, and the monasteries of Ethiopia. The Serengeti, Masai Mara, Okavango Delta, Chobe. Tuareg, Nuba, Samburu, Zulus. The diversity in Africa is hard to beat. Main picture: Quiver trees, endemic aloe plants in the southern Namibian desert.

RABAT

Location: North Morocco
Best time to travel: all year
www.mairiederabat.com
www.visitrabat.com

In 1956, Rabat became the capital of independent Morocco with its historic center built around the kasbah of the Udayas on a hill above the Bou Regreg River. The 12th-century Bab Al-Oudayas gate, with magnificent stone carvings, leads into a maze of partly covered alleyways that end at the "platform", where you get a view of the neighboring city of Salé.

East of the kasbah, 200 column stumps and the minaret of a mosque, the Mosque of Hassan, can be seen. The mosque was planned by Yacoub el-Mansour, but never completed after the death of the sultan in 1199.

TETOUAN

Location: North Morocco
Best time to travel: all year
www.gotetouan.com
www.visitmorocco.com

Tétouan, located in the foothills of the Rif Mountains, is known as the "white dove" because of its white-washed houses. Until Morocco gained its independence in 1956, this, the largest town in the Rif, was under Spanish rule. The medina is completely surrounded by fortified walls; it has countless vaulted alleyways and houses whose windows have wrought-iron grilles. Tétouan's souk is the fourth-largest in Morocco. On market days, many farmers come from the Rif Mountains to sell their produce in town.

In the alleyways of the medina, you can still encounter traditionally dressed women from the Rif.

CASABLANCA

Location: North Morocco
Best time to travel: all year
www.casablanca.ma
www.visitcasablanca.ma

A visit to this city of three million inhabitants is worthwhile especially to see the Hassan II Mosque. The mosque's prayer hall can accommodate 25,000 faithful, and 80,000 can fit on the forecourt under the shade of the 200-m-high (656-ft) minaret. A laser beam at the top of the minaret points toward Mecca at all times. The mosque is the only house of god in Morocco that may be visited by non-Muslims.

Dedicated by the king in 1993, more than 3,000 artisans were involved in adorning the Hassan II Mosque with traditional majolica mosaics, stucco, inlay work and dark-cedar wood carvings.

EL JADIDA

Location: North Morocco
Best time to travel: all year
www.eljadida.ma
www.visitmorocco.com

The story of El Jadida began around the year 1500, when the Portuguese set up their fortress there on the Atlantic coast just 100 km (62 mi) south of present-day Casablanca. It was not until the end of the 18th century that the Moroccans managed to conquer the fortress. Arab tribes and the Jewish community then settled there. Over time, a new town began to emerge, called El Jadida, "the new one".

The Portuguese Cistern of El-Jadida is an impressive complex of three chambers and four towers. The cross-vaulting of the main chamber rests on twelve round columns and thirteen pillars.

FÈZ

Location: North Morocco
Best time to travel: all year
www.visit-fez.com

Fèz was founded by the Idrisid rulers as a twin city on an important trading route from the Sahara Desert to the Mediterranean Sea. The oldest part of the town, Fes el-Bali, was settled by Andalusian refugees from the Moorish region of Spain as well as by families from present-day Kairouan in Tunisia. The Kairaouine Mosque, which goes back to these settlers, provides room for more than 20,000 worshippers. It is also the center of the highly regarded university that was founded in the year 959. Andalusia Mosque also dates back to the early days of the town. Fes el-Bali is surrounded by city walls with twelve gates.
Féz experienced a time of great prosperity in the 14th century under the Marinid rulers. The Royal Palace, the Bou Inania Medersa and the Mellah (the Jewish Quarter) all date from that time. Qur'anic schools, mosques and the tombs of the Marinids testify to the importance of this part of town, Fès el-Djedid ("New Fes") – a district of artisans and merchants. The French conquered the city in 1911.

Time seems to have stood still in the old town (right: the Bab Bou Jeloud gate).

Opposite from the top: Nejjarine Square, near the carpenters' souk, has one of the most beautiful fountains in the city; in the tanneries' district, visitors can see the densely packed vats filled with natural tannins and dyes; the Moulay Idriss II Mausoleum also includes a mosque and a courtyard; the Madrassa es-Sharij was named after the large fountain shaped like a water basin in the middle of its inner courtyard.

ESSAOUIRA

Location: West Morocco
Best time to travel: all year
www.essaouiranet.com

The fortification walls that surround the Old Town of Essaouira, the former Portuguese fortress of Mogador, are greatly influenced by European military architecture. Mogador was rebuilt in the middle of the 18th century during the reign of Sultan Sidi Mohammed Ben Abdallah, who entrusted the work to architect Théodore Cornut. The latter based his design on the French town of Saint-Malo, which explains the European look of the center. Built on a rectangular grid, it features arcades and white houses with blue doors and window frames.

When Morocco gaied independence, the city was renamed Essaouira ("the Beautifully Designed").

VOLUBILIS

Location: near Meknès, North Morocco
Best time to travel: all year
www.sitedevolubilis.com

Volubilis was once the most important Roman settlement in what is now Morocco. Founded during the rule of Carthage, the city was in corporated into the Roman Empire in AD 44. In the years that followed, magnificent secular and religious buildings were erected here, particularly during the reign of Emperor Septimius Severus, who ruled from 193 to 211 and bequeathed many architectural gems upon North Africa.

Residences like the vast Gordian Palace and private mansions such as the "House of the Cortège of Venus", with its beautiful mosaic floors, give insight into the everyday life of the Roman governor.

THE HIGH ATLAS

Location: South Morocco
Best time to travel: March–May, September/October
www.atlasvoyages.com

Rising up between Middle Atlas and Anti-Atlas, the High Atlas range forms the border between fertile Morocco and the desert. Its highest mountain is Jbel Toubkal (4,167 m/ 13,672ft). The Cascades d'Ouzoud are the most impressive natural spectacle. In the deep, narrow Todra and Dades Gorges of the High Atlas, farmers make use of every tiny scrap of fertile land.

The Todra River which rises in the High Atlas cuts through the Todra Gorge. In the Berber language, Ouzoud means "olives", and the 110-m (361-ft) Ouzoud waterfalls are named after the olive trees that thrive in the vicinity.

MEKNÈS

Location: North-east Morocco
Best time to travel: all year
www.visitmorocco.com

Meknès, which developed around an earlier Berber fortress, was conquered a number of times by Almoravid, Almohad and Marinid rulers. It enjoyed its greatest prosperity under the Alaouite Sultan Moulay Ismail (1672–1727) who turned Meknès into a "Moroccan Versailles". Even his European contemporaries were impressed. Moulay Ismail's architectural legacy is indeed extraordinary, although a large number of Moroccan and Christian slaves were forced to work for the despot. Only parts of his "Ville Impériale" are still preserved today.

Near the "Ville Impériale" stands Sultan Moulay Ismail's mausoleum (left: the antechamber).

MARRAKESH

Location: Central Morocco
Best time to travel: all year
http://visitmarrakech.net

The oasis city, Marrakesh – or "mar-our-kouch" as it is known in the Berber language, meaning "Land of Transit" – was once an important center for the trans-Saharan trade and served as a capital for the rulers of several dynasties.

Among the structures from the early period of the medina, the roughly 10-km (6-mi) town walls and the gates and towers, some of which were added later, are preserved today. The mosque and its minaret, built in the year 1153 by the Almohad sultans, is one of the most attractive buildings in the city. Together with the Giralda of Seville and the Hassan Tower of Rabat, the nearly 80-m (262-ft) masterpiece is a mixture of Spanish and Moorish architecture that quickly became a model for minarets all around the country. Just behind the beautiful mosque is the tomb of the city's founder, Yusuf ibn Tashfin.

Visitors enter the ancient fortified town of the Almohads, referred to as a kasbah, via the 12th-century Bab Agnaou, Marrakesh's most beautiful city gate. Another architectural gem is the Ben Youssef Madrassa, built in the 14th century under the "Black Sultan" – a Marinid ruler. The 16th century was another period of great building activity, and the elaborate Saad tombs date back to this period. The inner rooms of the well-preserved necropolis are splendidly decorated with cedar, stuccowork and mosaics.

In the heart of Marrakesh is Djemaa el-Fna, the "Square of the Beheaded". At night, after the sun has set, large crowds throng around the numerous cook shops, the snake charmers, storytellers, acrobats and other entertainers.

GHARDAÏA

Location: Central Algeria
Best time to travel: all year
http://ghardaiatourisme.com

Five fortified settlements (ksour) were built by the Mozabites of the Ibadi community in the valley of the Oued M'zab, which carries water only once a year. They include El Atteuf, Bou Noura, the holy town of Beni Isguen, Melika and Ghardaïa. The youngest and largest of these is Ghardaïa. Like the other settlements, it was built around a mosque on top of a hill and encircled by walls. The mosque's minaret was also a watchtower. The mosque itself was conceived as an independent entity, with grain storage silos and an arsenal of weapons.

The earth-colored buildings of Ghardaïa are perfectly adapted to the desert climate.

ALGIERS

Location: North Algeria
Best time to travel: all year
www.algeria.com

Originally founded by the Phoenicians and later known as "Icosium" during the days of Roman rule, the settlement that is now Algiers only developed into an important trading post after the Arab conquest. It repeatedly attracted foreign powers, however. In the 16th century the Spanish conquered the town, which in response called upon the pirate Khair ad-Din, aka Barbarossa, an Ottoman admiral. When he had reconquered Algiers, Khair ad-Din submitted to the Ottoman Sultan. For a long time, Algiers remained a haven of piracy fought over by the European powers. From 1830 to 1962, the French had occupied the strategically important city. Not until the end of the 19th century did

TASSILI N'AJJER

Location: South-east Algeria
Best time to travel: September–March
www.algeria.com

In one of the most inhospitable areas of the Sahara Desert, close to the borders with Libya and Niger, the Tassili-n'Ajjer Plateau extends. The region resembles a lunar landscape, with eroded rocks rising from the sands like giant stalagmites. In this barren setting, countless rock paintings were discovered 1933.

On the Tassili-n'Ajjer Plateau, known as the "Louvre of the Sahara", rock art thousands of years old tells of the life of hunter-gatherers and shepherds when a humid climate still defined the savannah-like landscape. The painting on the left was produced during the "Bovidian Period" (4000–1500 BC).

Algiers grow beyond the confines of the city walls that enclosed the original kasbah and citadel.
Most of the buildings in the kasbah are from the Ottoman period. Only the Djemaa el-Kebir, or Great Mosque, is older – it was built on the site of a Christian basilica in the Almoravid style. The minbar, built in 1017, boasts splendid carvings, and the minaret is from 1323. The New Mosque from 1660 is another important monument.

On a walk through the twisted lanes and narrow alleyways of Algiers, it is the house entrances that especially impress the visitor. Designed with an immense love of and attention to detail, the "builders of the kasbah have created a masterpiece of architecture and town planning", is how the famous Swiss-French architect Le Corbusier enthused after seeing the old town of Algiers.

KAIROUAN

Location: North Tunisia
Best time to travel: all year
www.commune-tunis.gov.tn

The town of Kairouan, around 150 km (230 mi) south of Tunis, was founded in about 670 by the Uqba ibn Nafi of the Omayyad Dynasty as an outpost for the conquering Arab army. The mosque named after him is the oldest in North Africa and also one of the most attractive religious structures in Tunisia. The town experienced its heyday in the ninth century during the rule of the Aghlabids Dynasty of emirs.

Today, Kairouan is still one of the most important religious centers for Muslims in North Africa. Particularly worth seeing is the Great Mosque or Sidi Uqba Mosque in the old town (right), whose prayer hall is subdivided by Roman columns (below).

TUNIS

Location: North Tunesia
Best time to travel: all year
www.commune-tunis.gov.tn

Around two million people live in greater Tunis where the suburbs spread like the tentacles of an octopus along the Bay of Tunis, from Bou Kornine Mountain to the saline lakes of the lagoon. The history of the city goes back to the ninth century BC. When the Phoenicians founded Carthage, a settlement established by the indigenous Numidians and originally known as Tunes already existed there. It wasn't until 894, however, that Tunis finally became the capital during Aghlabid rule.

The Es-Zitouna Mosque (left: the minaret seen from a terrace in the medina) owes its name to an olive tree with miraculous powers that once was said to have stood here.

EL DJEM

Location: North-east Tunisia
Best time to travel: all year
www.tunisia.com

The Roman amphitheater of El Djem in Central Tunisia was built in about AD 230 and remodeled as a fortress after the withdrawal of the Romans. During the seventh century it served as a sanctuary for the female Berber leader Dahia al-Kahina in her futile battle against the Arab conquerors. Measuring 148 by 122 m (450 by 375 ft) and a good 40 m (131 ft) high, the massive oval building can seat 30,000 spectators and was one of the largest amphitheaters in the entire former Roman Empire. It is so well preserved that it compares well with the Coliseum.

Sports contests, gladiator spectacles and animal baiting once took place in the El Djem amphitheater.

GHADAMES

Location: West Libya
Best time to travel: all year
www.visitlibya.com

The ancient city of Cydamus was founded as a Roman garrison before becoming a Byzantine bishop's see and finally being converted to Islam by Arab conquerors in the 8th century. This crossroads town traded along the Saharan caravan routes from Timbuktu to the coast of Morocco. Today, most people live in the new city, but in the summer many move back to the old town as the two-story adobe houses are better suited to the hot desert climate. The house façades in the old town are often beautifully embellished with decorative patterns.

The tall walls either side of the lanes in Ghadames resemble fortified city walls.

CYRENE

Location: North-east Libya
Best time to travel: all year
www.cyrenaica.org

The former Greek colony of Cyrene on the Mediterranean coast is the origin of Cyrenaica, now Libya. Until the 4th century it was one of the largest cities in Africa. From the Greek period date a partially restored Temple of Zeus, the Temple of Apollo built on the site of an earlier structure and the Temple of Artemis. The Greek theater was converted as an amphitheater during Hadrian's reign. The Greek agora (marketplace) features the monument of Battos, the legendary founder of the city, and is lined with remains of buildings from Hellenic days.

A round temple with statues of the gods Demeter and Kore has been found in the agora of Cyrene.

LEPTIS MAGNA

Location: North Libya
Best time to travel: all year
www.visitlibya.com

Leptis Magna, located at the estuary of the Wadi Labdah some 100 km (62 mi) east of Tripoli, was administered by Carthage. A trading hub and export port for grain and olives, it came under Roman influence from the first century BC and was awarded the status of "colonia" with full rights by Emperor Trajan.

Founded by the Phoenicians, Leptis Magna was one of the most beautiful cities in the Roman Empire. This fact is made apparent by its splendid ruins, which include the impressive market building, the triumphal arch of Septimius Severus and the vast Forum of Severus, whose arcades were once decorated by Medusa heads.

SABRATHA

Location: North-west Libya
Best time to travel: all year
www.libyantravels.com

Sabratha, about 70 km (43 mi) west of the present-day Libyan city of Tripoli (the ancient Oea), today still features many well-preserved remains from Roman times including the theater built around 200; the Forum which is surrounded by columns; the Temple of Antonius and Faustina; the Temple of Jupiter; the 1st-century Basilica; public baths; and fountains, latrines and various other secular and religious structures. In the early Christian period a church was built into the Roman law court basilica.

The most impressive structure in Sabratha is the theater with its grand stage wall and beautiful reliefs on the proscenium frieze.

CAIRO

Location: North-east Egypt
Best time to travel: all year
www.egypt.travel

"He who has not seen Cairo has not seen the world," it says in the tales of One Thousand and One Nights. Today, nearly one in four of the just under 80 million Egyptians live in Africa's largest city. The glitter of the metropolis on the Nile may have faded a little since the days of Scheherazade, but Cairo is much more than just the undisputed political, spiritual and economic heart of the country. It is also the epitome of an Oriental fairytale city and as such it continues to fascinate visitors.

Al Qahira – the "Triumphant One", a name that was later corrupted to Cairo by Italian merchants, was founded in the year 969 by Shiite rulers, the Fatimids, near the ancient Arabic settlement of Fustat. Initially it served as a palace city, but it was Saladin, founder of the Ayyubid dynasty, who finally opened the royal enclave to the public.

Around 1900 Cairo counted some half million inhabitants. Since then, its population has grown more than thirtyfold. In districts like Shubra and Bab ash-Sharya, more than 150,000 people live crowded together per square kilometer (388,600 per sq mi). Of course, to call this situation untenable would be to underestimate the Egyptians' considerable talent for improvisation and regeneration. Recently, much progress was made in upgrading the infrastructure, and in addition, a dynamic middle class is developing whose members enjoy all the staples of Western comfort in modern apartment blocks.

Cairo is also known as the "City of a Thousand Minarets". In this picture, the towers of the 14th-century Sultan Hassan Mosque appear side by side with the Er Rifai Mosque dating from 1912.

GIZA, MEMPHIS, SAKKARA

Location: North-east Egypt
Best time to travel: all year
www.egypt.travel

Closely linked with Cairo is the provincial capital of Giza on the west bank of the Nile. On a limestone plateau above the town stand the three large pyramids of the pharaohs (kings) Khufu, Khafre and Menkaure. Built in the 3rd millennium BC they were to survive as tombs for all eternity. Each of the blocks used to build the vast mount of the Great (or Khufu) Pyramid weigh an average of two tons. During his campaign in the year 1798, Napoleon had the calculations made that these blocks would suffice to build a 3-m-high (10-ft) wall around all of France. It is a majestic and awe-inspiring sight, even without the finely polished casing originally used to enshroud the structure's core. After completion, the pyramid was almost 147 m (482 ft) tall, but today it is some 10 m (33 ft) shorter because Cairo builders during the Middle Ages felt justified in helping themselves to the free materials. The adjacent Khafre Pyramid has preserved some of its outer casing. The pyramid of Menkaure is markedly smaller – about half the size – at only 65.5 m (215 ft) in height, a rather modest attempt when compared with the neighboring giants.

The Great Sphinx lies to the east of the three monuments. Hewn from natural rock, it is a representation of the Sun God. The Sphinx Temple stands in front of the statue's giant paws, a veneration temple also carved from rock. Beside it is a valley temple built by Khafre and clad in rose granite and alabaster.

About 20 km (12.5 mi) to the south of Giza is Memphis, the capital of the Old Kingdom whose origins date back to the fifth millennium BC.

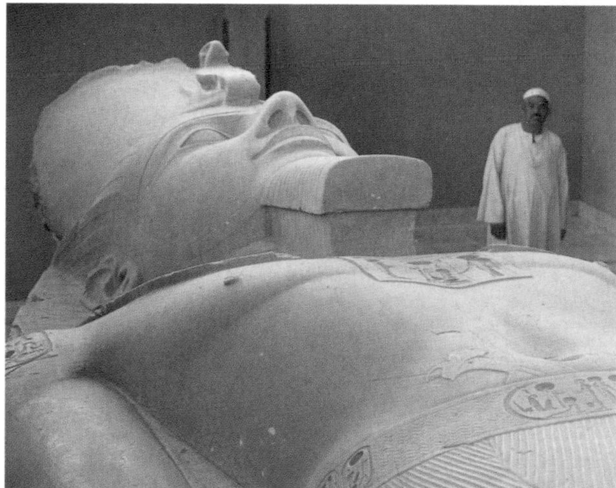

It remained an important military base into the days of the Greek and Roman empires. Memphis has played many roles in its long history: Egypt's first capital, administrative center, largest garrison town, and sanctuary of the God Ptah. Today, however, not a lot is left of this former metropolis. The palaces and mansions made from clay tiles have vanished and reverted to fertile agricultural land. Only the colossal figure of Ramses II and an alabaster sphinx testify to its former glory. They are located in the open-air museum in a palm grove close to the small village of Mitrahina on the south-western margins of Giza. Much more impressive is the ancient cemetery of Sakkara, Ancient Egypt's largest necropolis. In the middle of this vast complex stands the burial precinct of King Djoser, whose 4,600-year-old step pyramid is today widely believed to be the oldest stone structure in the history of humankind.
With their fascinating relief pictures, the many mastabas (tombs) offer superb insight into the everyday life not only of high-ranking officials but also of farmers, artisans and fishermen. They also depict the fauna and flora of the time.

In a hollow in front of the Khafre pyramid sits a sphinx (large picture). The more than 70-m-long (77-yd) and 20-m-high (65-ft) creature, half human and half lion, is thought to be both a guardian and a representation of the sun god.

The Pyramids of Giza are the only remaining one of the Seven Wonders of the Ancient World – "a structure of which time itself is afraid; while otherwise all here on earth fear time", it is said in Scheherazade's tales of One Thousand and One Nights (this page top; center: the beautiful monumental figure of Ramses II in Memphis; bottom: the famous step pyramid of Sakkara).

LUXOR

Location: East Egypt
Best time to travel: October–April
www.touregypt.net

The town of Luxor on the east bank, counting some 200,000 inhabitants, combines with the temple city of Karnak and the necropolis of Thebes on the west bank of the Nile to form a focal point of ancient Egyptian culture. They are the main attractions of any visit to Upper Egypt. The foundation stone for the central temple complex, which stands in the heart of the urban area right on the river promenade, was laid as early as 1380 BC by Amenophis III (or Amenhotep III). A symbol of power in the New Kingdom, the temple was dedicated to the trinity of gods in Thebes: Amun, Mut and Chons. Today it still presents an amazing wealth of giant statues, obelisks, pylons and papyrus columns all lined up over a length of 260 m (853 ft). The smaller artifacts from there and other excavation sites have all been taken to the local museum where they are expertly displayed.

The creation of the vast temple and courtyard complex at Luxor with its overwhelming colonnaded entrance dates back to Amenophis III (or Amenhotep III). During the reign of Ramses II the complex was once more enlarged – the new courtyard, lined by columns and statues, is now entered through a pylon next to an obelisk.

KARNAK

Location: East Egypt
Best time to travel: October–April
www.karnak-egypt.com

For many centuries, the temple complex of Karnak, north of Luxor's city center, was Egypt's main spiritual sanctuary. It is dedicated to Amun, the "Hidden One", an ancient divinity mentioned as far back as the Old Kingdom; he became the imperial god Amun-Ra of Thebes only in 2000 BC. The complex originally boasted ten entrance gates, known as pylons. Today, the main entrance to the compound of ruins leads through an avenue lined with ram-headed sphinxes. From there to the Precinct of Mut, more than half a mile away, visitors are faced with one superlative after the other: the tallest obelisk at 30 m (98 ft) weighing 323 tons; the largest columned hall with 134 petrified umbels and papyrus plants, each up to 10 m (33 ft) in circumference; and the largest pylon at 113 m (3,652 ft) wide, 43 m (141 ft) tall and about 15m (49 ft) deep).

A temple was viewed as the image of the world, its columns symbolically supporting the firmament. The penetralia, which even the king could only enter after strict cleansing, lay in darkness.

NILE CRUISE FROM LUXOR TO ASWAN

Location: East Egypt
Best time to travel: October–April
www.min-travel.com

A cruise on the Nile in Upper Egypt reveals a seductively idyllic and constant world – despite the ships having to jostle for position between Luxor and Aswan in high season. The riverbanks are lined with children at play and women tending to their washing; with water buffalo, ibises, and the odd camel; with sand dunes and rock faces, deep green sugarcane fields and date palm groves; with villages with mud huts and thatched roofs, and the ever-fascinating tombs and temples all forming the backdrop for this picturesque scene. The finishing point of every Nile cruise to the south, and indeed the most southerly large settlement in the country, is Aswan. The town, which has now grown to way more than half a million inhabitants, was in antiquity the gateway to the interior of Africa and an important trading hub. Here ended the caravan routes from Nubia, and from here the Ancient Egyptians began their military expeditions into the deep south. The city was once known as Jebu, "Land of the Elephants" – possibly because here the Egyptians first encountered the pachyderms from the south; or because of the ivory that was once shipped from here.

One of the loveliest things to do on a late afternoon is to take a cruise through the island world of the cataract (top) on board one of the large-sailed feluccas. Center: A granite threshold cuts through the river valley here, defining the surrounding landscape. Bottom: The Sanctuary of Isis at Philae on Agilkia Island is full of magic.

THEBES WEST

Location: South-east Egypt
Best time to travel: October–April
www.thebanmappingproject.com

In the days of the pharaohs, the east bank of the Nile was the bank of life. It was in Thebes, the "City of a Hundred Towers", as it was known to the Greeks, where people established their settlements. It is also where the rulers' palaces and the monumental temples stood. The opposite bank, meanwhile, where the sun sets, belonged to the dead. Vast funerary sanctuaries and necropolises were erected there in Thebes West.

Hatshepsut was the only female pharaoh in Ancient Egypt. Her mortuary temple in the Valley of Deir el-Bahai extends over several levels linked by ramps and can be seen from as far away as Karnak.

VALLEY OF THE KINGS

Location: East Egypt
Best time to travel: October–April
www.touregypt.net

Howard Carter believed that there were still more treasures to be discovered in the Valley of the Kings, and in 1922, the British archeologist was vindicated when he found the legendary treasure of Tutankhamun. Since then, researchers have uncovered more than sixty Pharaonic tombs in the rocky valley on the northern fringes of the Nile's west bank, but less than one-third is open to the general public.

In Tomb No. 62 in the Valley of the Kings, Tutankhamun rests in a sarcophagus of red quartzite. The pharaoh died aged barely eighteen under as yet unknown circumstances.

ABU SIMBEL

Location: South Egypt
Best time to travel: October–April
www.sis.gov.eg

They are certainly among the more lasting memories of any Nile cruise: The four 20-m tall (66-ft) colossal statues of King Ramses II. Commissioned by the pharaoh to be hewn straight out of the rock formation on the west bank of the Nile, between the First and the Second Cataract, these giant reliefs are at the gable end of the Great Temple dedicated to Amun-Ra and Re-Harakhte and were completed in the 13th century BC. No less impressive is the "Small" Temple next to it, dedicated to the goddess Hathor and containing three 10-m- (33-ft) giant figures of Ramses II and his wife Nefertari. When the two giants were in endangered by the future Lake Nasser, UNESCO had them moved 60 m (200 ft) higher up – a massive effort that took four years to complete. To achieve this, the temples had to be sawn up into 1,000 individual components, numbered, transported to their new locations and reassembled – luckily for the visitors who can now again visit this incomparable site.

The Great Temple of Ramses II would have been swallowed forever by Lake Nasser had it not been cut into 20-ton stone blocks and reassembled higher up (large picture; opposite page top). Four colossal statues of the king dominate the pylon-like façade. One of these was soon heavily damaged by an earthquake; a part of the head now lies at its feet. Behind the entrance to the Great Temple is a columned hall with further giant figures of Ramses II (opposite page bottom). Ramses dedicated the smaller temple (opposite page center) to the goddess Hathor and to his wife Nefertari.

ST CATHERINE'S MONASTERY

Location: North-east Egypt (Sinai)
Best time to travel: all year
www.sinaimonastery.com

The St Catherine's Monastery is set between the steep rock faces of the Wadi Araba, a valley at 1,500 m (4,922 ft) where the Israelites are said to have danced around the Golden Calf. Covering an area of 84 by 74 m (276 by 243 ft), it is the smallest diocese in the world as well as one of the oldest monasteries in all of Christendom. Its history goes back to the year 330, when Helena, the Empress of Byzantium, and her husband Justinian built a small chapel here.

The St Catherine's Monastery is concealed behind fortress-like walls. Its most sacred place is the the Chapel of the Burning Bush, established in 1216.

RAS MUHAMMAD

Location: North-east Egypt (Sinai)
Best time to travel: all year
www.red-sea-shadow.com

The Râs Muhammad National Park at the southern tip of the Sinai Peninsula protects some 480 sq km (sq mi) of land and sea habitats. The coastal strip of Sharm el-Sheik was also subsumed in the park which protects against urban sprawl. An insignificant fishing village only one generation ago, the town has developed into a popular seaside and diving resort. The underwater world enchants the senses – even a snorkeling trip gives a good impression of its wonders.

The island and most of the shores in the vicinity, particularly around Ras Muhammad, are nature reserves protected by guardians.

MOUNT SINAI

Location: North-east Egypt (Sinai)
Best time to travel: all year
http://st-katherine.net

St Catherine's Monastery receives around 50,000 visitors each year. More than half of these, it is estimated, climb the adjacent peak on which, according to the Bible, Yahweh is said to have given the Tablets of Law with their Ten Commandments to the Prophet. "...and they arrived in the desert of Sinai, and they [...] encamped there opposite the mountain", it is written in the Old Testament.

Several routes lead up the 2,285-m-high (7,497-ft) Mount Sinai, the most direct of which has a staircase with more than 3,000 stone steps. Legend has it that it was built by a single monk honoring a vow.

THE RED SEA

Location: between North-east Africa and the Arab Peninsula
Best time to travel: all year
www.redseatourism.com

The Sinai Peninsula forms a 60,000 sq km (23,160 sq mi) "hinge" between Asia and Africa. It is mostly shapeless and flat in the north, where it has served as a gateway for almost all of Egypt's invaders, from the Hyksos and the Persians to the British. Toward the south, however, the scenery becomes more dramatic, culminating in the 2,600-m-high (8,530-ft) mountainous region around the St Catherine's Monastery.

Fascinating underwater world: The riffs located between Sharm el-Sheikh and the border city of Taba in the Gulf of Aqaba make for one of the most beautiful diving areas on earth.

KSOUR – NORTH AFRICAN FORTIFICATIONS

Location: Mauretania
Best time to travel: September–April
www.palinstravels.co.uk

These four fortified towns, known as ksar (plural: ksour) on the caravan routes of the North African Sahara, are testimonies to a great history. Oualata in the far south-east of the Mauritanian Sahel, Tichitt, an important trading city halfway between Timbuktu and the Atlantic, Ouadane, once an important post for the camel caravans, and Chinguetti the most famous historic desert settlement in the country's interior.

The manuscript library in Chinguetti is housed in a traditional mud brick house.

DJENNE

Location: Central Mali
Best time to travel: October–May
www.visit-mali.com

For centuries Djenné, a town situated on a branch of the Bani River, a tributary of the Niger, maintained a very close trading relationship with Timbuktu, which could be reached on the river. Even after Djenné had been integrated into the Songhai Empire in the 15th century, it continued to flourish both economically and culturally. The oldest city districts still have the classic houses of merchants and artisans from the 16th to the 19th centuries. The Great Mosque was rebuilt.

Typical of Djenné is the old town with its mud brick houses and the Great Mosque, which appears like a fortress. A market is held on the square in front of it every Monday.

BANDIAGARA

Location: Central Mali
Best time to travel: October–May
www.visit-mali.com

East of Mopti is a rocky mountain range extends for about 150 km (93 mi). It is the home of the Dogon, a people famous for their cliff buildings and creative masks. In the Dogon's worldview, all elements in the universe are linked with each other by a tight network of symbolic relationships. The construction style for their homes, cult buildings and gathering places reflects this and is characterized by religious and mythological notions.

A product of the highly developed carving traditions among the Dogon are their masks. Mud box houses cling to the rock faces of Bandiagara like birds' nests and some can only be reached by ladders.

TIMBUKTU

Location: Central Mali
Best time to travel: November–March **www.chiff.com**
www.visit-mali.com

By 1330, Timbuktu (or Tomboucto) had become one of the most important centers of trade and culture in West Africa. During its heyday in the 15th century, this town on the Niger was the main transhipment center for Saharan trade as well as a focal point for Islamic scholarship. The main sights in the northern districts are the medieval university and the Sankoré Mosque with its pyramid-shaped minaret, built in traditional mud-brick and wood. The Djinguereber is the oldest mosque; the Sidi Yahya mosque is the smallest (1440).

The Sankoré Mosque became the model for many Islamic buildings in sub-Saharan Africa.

AÏR AND TÉNÉRÉ

Location: North Niger
Best time to travel: October–April
http://us-africa.tripod.com

This nature reserve is the largest in Africa and covers just under 80,000 sq km (30,880 sq mi). One of the most impressive landscapes to be experienced here is the transitional area between Aïr and Ténéré, where rock formations and sandy desert meet to create a fascinating contrast. The Aïr Mountains in north-western Niger stretch over 400 km (249 mi) from north to south. It is an eroded plateau punctuated by a series of flat granite peaks of volcanic origin that are on average 700 m (2,297 ft) high. They feature series of individual peaks that are separated from one other by dune valleys or koris that are at their highest up on Mont Gréboun. In the Ténéré Desert to the east, shallow gravel and sandy plains give way to a sea of dunes. Often there is no rainfall here for years, and the range of temperatures is extreme. The humid south-western slopes of the Aïr Mountains feature grassy plains, for example. The koris store groundwater allowing palm trees and acacia shrub to flourish, while wild olive trees and cypresses grow up in the mountains. Barbary sheep, wild asses and fennec foxes live here. In the northern parts of the mountains prehistoric humans created superb rock paintings. The oldest paintings here indicate a much wetter savannah climate and date from the Neolithic period when people began herding cattle. In the early Tertiary, some parts of the Ténéré were a shallow inland sea and it is this era that produced the many fossils here (dinosaurs, tortoises, crocodiles, extinct fishes). Arrowheads from 7000 to 3000 BC indicate the early existence of hunting and farming cultures.

In the Montagnes Bleues, the "Blue Mountains", in the border region between the Aïr and Ténéré national parks in Niger, visitors come across a bizarre seeming world of sand and rock formations (left). Prehistoric rock drawings, as were found here near Tiguidit (above) and Arakaou on the limits between Aïr and Ténéré, as well as the discovery of arrowheads and axe blades at various sites, tell us that, thousands of years ago, the region had not yet entirely turned to desert and big game, such as giraffes, could still graze here. It is believed that that the Aïr Mountains were settled by humans at least 30,000 years ago.

NIMBA

Location: Guinea, Liberia, Côte d'Ivoire
Best time to travel: October–April
www.greenpassage.org

The 180-sq km (70-sq mi) nature reserve is located in the border triangle of Liberia, Guinea and Côte d'Ivoire. Its highest elevation and most distinctive landmark is the 1,752-m-high (5,748-ft) Mount Nimba Massif, which straddles the border of Côte d'Ivoire and Guinea. It is covered by a virtually uninterrupted blanket of forest. On the lower slopes it is mostly still deciduous, while above 1,000 m (3,281 ft) a montane forest dominates, and the summit is characterized by savannah. Forty indigenous plants and more than 200 animal species thrive here.

Mugger crocodile romp around in the waters of the national park.

COMOÉ

Location: Côte d'Ivoire
Best time to travel: October–March
www.africannaturalheritage.org

The largest most species-rich nature reserve in Côte d'Ivoire is Comoé National Park, in the north-east of the country straddling the transitional zone from savannah to rainforest. The park covers roughly 11,500 sq km (4,439 sq mi) and owes its name to the Comoé River, which is between 100 and 200 m (328 and 650 ft) wide and runs north-south through the park for over 230 km (143 mi). It carries sufficient water even during the dry season and is fringed by dense gallery forests. Near the water's edge you are likely to find many animals.

Predators such as leopards also prowl about here, but their populations are now quite small.

TAÏ

Location: Ghana, Côte d'Ivoire, Liberia, Sierra Leone
Best time to travel: October–March
www.africannaturalheritage.org

Taï National Park comprises a large part of Africa's remaining tropical rainforests that once covered the countries of Ghana, Côte d'Ivoire, Liberia and Sierra Leone. The dense tropical vegetation in this 3,300-sq-km (1,274-sq-mi) nature reserve in south-western Côte d'Ivoire is characterized by a number of endemic and more than 50-m-tall (164-ft) trees whose dense foliage and vines allow little sunlight to penetrate down to the forest floor. Aside from many bird species, this is also a habitat for larger mammals.

Four subspecies of the chimpanzee – here seen in the Taï National Park – live in West and Central Africa.

VIRUNGA

Location: Democratic Republic of Congo
Best time to travel: October–March
http://gorillacd.org

Virunga National Park covers a vast expanse of just under 8,000 sq km (3,088 sq mi). It extends along the Great African Rift Valley, to the north and south of Lake Rutanzige (Lake Edward) in the north-eastern section of the Democratic Republic of the Congo on the border with Uganda and Rwanda. Formerly known as Albert National Park, which was Africa's first national park founded in 1925, Virunga is home to leopards, okapis and several species of antelopes and a number of primates.

Around half of the remaining few hundred mountain gorillas live in the Virunga National Park in the Democratic Republic of Congo.

SIMIEN, AKSUM, OMO

Location: North (Simien, Aksum) and South-west Ethiopia
Best time to travel: October–March
www.tourismethiopia.org

Due to heavy erosion, the Simien Mountains developed into one of the most spectacular landscapes on earth. The peaks reach heights of 4,500 m (14,765 ft), while raging torrents course through rugged basalt gorges that are up to 1,500 m (4,922 ft) deep. Simien National Park, named after the mountain range, offers a refuge to some extremely rare animal species.
The kingdom of Aksum in the heart of ancient Ethiopia existed in the first century and was converted to Christianity in the fourth century. The Omo River is roughly about 800 km (497 mi) long and carries water throughout the year to its final destination, Lake Turkana, on Ethiopia's southern border. The lower reaches of the river have gained recognition as an archaeological excavation site for prehistoric remains. Two skulls and other skeletal remains ("Omo I" and "Omo II") that were found in 1967 by the U.S. paleoanthropologist Richard Leakey near Kibish are likely to be 195,000 years old.

Among the peoples who live in the Omo Valley, the Karo tribe is well known for its artistic hair and body decorations (large picture).

This page: The 4,620-m (15,158-ft) Ras Dashan in the Simien mountain range is the fourth-highest mountain in Africa. The rare Ethiopian wolf also roams the Simien National Park. The monoliths of Aksum were replicas of the "ghost homes" in the ancient Hadramaut region, where immigrants arrived in Ethiopia in the seventh century.

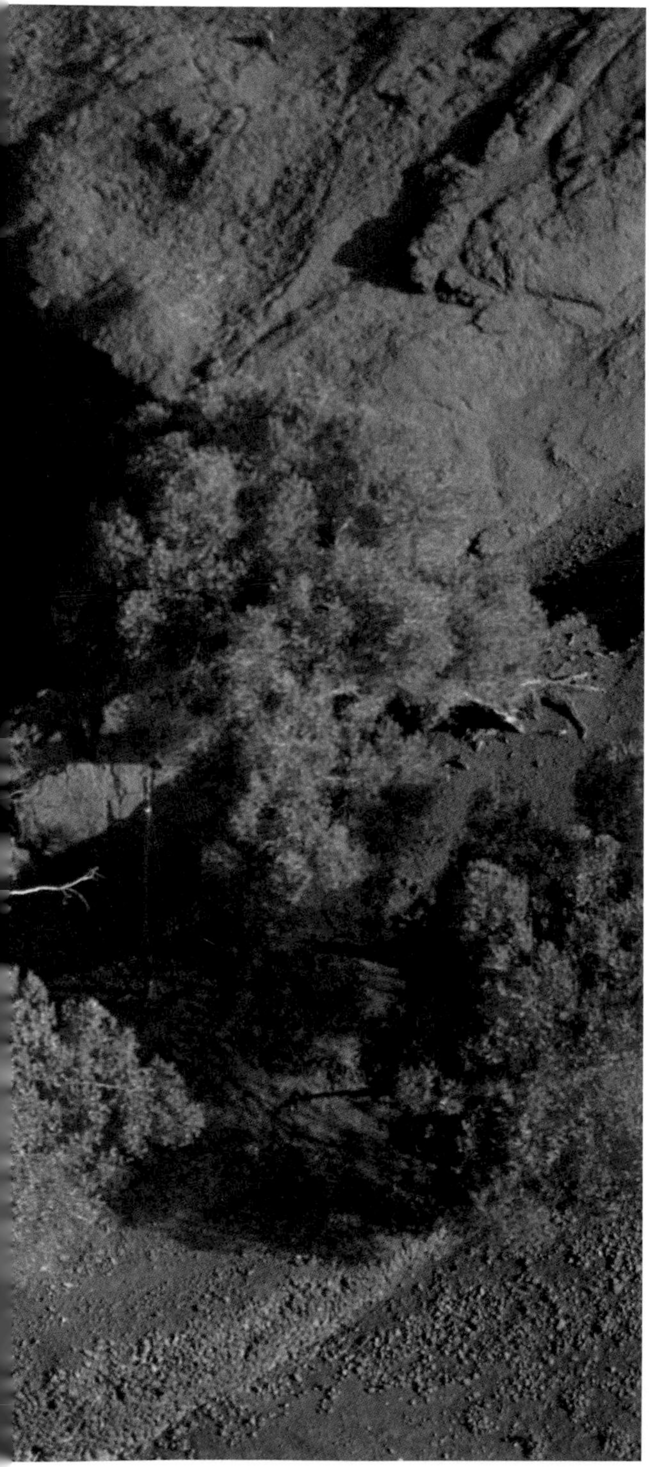

LALIBELA

Location: North Ethiopia
Best time to travel: October–March
www.ethiopiantreasures.co.uk
www.greatbuildings.com

Situated at an elevation of around 2,600 m (8,531 ft), the rock-hewn churches of Lalibela were built from the end of the 12th century during the reign of Gebre Mesqel Lalibela. He was the most important king of the Zagwe Dynasty, and Roha, as the capital was formerly known, was renamed Lalibela in his honor. The eleven churches are architecturally among the most beautiful places of worship in Africa. They are monolithic churches, that is, they were cut from straight the volcanic rock over the course of several decades and linked by a maze of paths and tunnels that have been dug out of the rock.
The most popular destination for pilgrims traveling to Lalibela is the Bete Maryam, or Saint Mary's Church. Bete Medhane Alem is the largest monolithic church in the world, featuring a total of five naves. The best-known church is Bete Giyorgis, modeled after a Greek Orthodox cross. Inside Lalibela's churches priests guard the many art treasures that include valuable manuscripts, crucifixes and murals.

God himself had commanded King Lailbela, so the legend goes, to build this place – today named after the king – and to make it a likelihood of the "divine Jerusalem". Heavenly assistance was provided. Thus, the angels are said not only to have assisted the master-builders with their work, but also to have taken the chisel in hand themselves during the night in order to ensure that the eleven church around Lalibela would be completed in – allegedly – only 23 years of construction. Bete Giyorgis (left) is probably the best-preserved among them. Four of the eleven church in Lalibela are monolithic churches, including Bete Medhane Alem (above pilgrims during a religious service). They were separated from the surrounding rocks by wide corridors – which makes them look like structures that have been sunk into the solid rock. The other places of worship are churches built into natural caves, whose structure may include rockfaces.

AMBOSELI, TSAVO, MASAI MARA

Location: South-west Kenya
Best time to travel: October–March
www.kws.go.ke
www.amboselilodge.co.uk
www.wdpa.org

Kenya's most frequented national park owes its popularity to the breathtaking beauty of Mount Kilimanjaro as a backdrop. The relatively small nature reserve, covering an area of only 392 sq km (151 sq mi), boasts an astonishing diversity of species, especially around Lake Amboseli, which attracts large herds with its juicy savannah grass. Fascinating sightings of black rhino, elephant, buffalo, leopard and lion are likely in Amboseli National Park.

Covering 20,800 sq km (8,029 sq mi), Kenya's largest national park is divided into an eastern and a western part by the parallel road and rail tracks that run through it. While sparse vegetation with thorn bushes and open scrubland predominate in Tsavo East, Tsavo West features denser vegetation. The rolling Taita Hills make the countryside here more attractive, but they also make it more difficult to observe the wildlife.

The Masai Mara Reserve consists of open, hilly grassland and is situated at an elevation of between 1,500 and 1,700 m (4,922 and 5,578 ft). The Mara and Talek rivers flow through the area year-round, providing an important habitat for hippopotamuses and crocodiles while Burchell's zebra, buffaloes, giraffes and hartebeest graze in the open savannah. From June to October they are joined by 250,000 Burchell's zebra and 1.3 million wildebeests migrating north from the Serengeti. Aside from the 520-sq km (200-sq mi) interior, the Masai Mara Reserve is not reserved for animals alone. The Masai, in whose traditional grounds the reserve has been established, may continue their semi-nomadic life on the perimeter of the park. The guides in the lodges know the area well. It is best to join an organized safari to be sure you see the "big five" (elephants, rhinos, lions, leopards and buffalo) on your trip.

Up to 4 m (13 ft) tall and weighing up to 8 tons, the African elephant (large picture: in the Amboseli National Park) is the largest mammal living on land.

Above: inhabitant of the Masai Mara Reserve

BWINDI

Location: Uganda
Best time to travel: October–March
www.uwa.or.ug
www.visituganda.com

Bwindi Impenetrable National Park is located in a remote transitional area between steppe and mountains. More than 100 species of ferns exist here, and no fewer than 160 tree species form the montane forest of the national park. Of the approximately 300 bird species that have been documented so far, the woodland birds make up about two-thirds and they are joined by about 200 types of butterflies. The nature reserve is famous for its mountain gorillas and the park's higher altitudes are home to about 300 of them. They live in peaceful family communities led by an older male or silverback.

Bwindi in the far south-west of Uganda is famous for its great diversity of tree and fern species as well as for its rare birds and butterflies. The monate forests are also one of the last remaining refuges of the endangered mountain gorillas.

RUWENZORI

Location: Uganda, Congo
Best time to travel: October–March
www.summitpost.org

This roughly 120-km-long (75-mi) and 50-km-wide (31-mi) mountain range was created by movements in the earth's crust and is situated on the border between the Democratic Republic of the Congo and Uganda. Its highest peak is Mount Stanley at 5,109 m (16,763 ft). The national park comprises a mountain territory covering roughly 1,000 sq km (6,214 sq mi) in south-western Uganda and, aside from glaciers, lakes and waterfalls at the higher altitudes there are also vast marshes and swamps in the valleys and foothills of the Rwenzori Mountains, where tall plant species such as papyrus offer protection to the elephants. The volcanic craters are covered in lush grasses that provide food for gazelles, antelopes and buffaloes. Bamboo even grows at elevations of about 2,000 m (6,562 ft). This is the natural habitat of the leopard. At higher elevations, the montane forests are mostly shrouded in mist and feature flora of unusual sizes.

The montane forests and marsh areas of the Ugandan Ruwenzori Mountains offer plentiful living space and protection for many endangered species of animal and plants of often giant sizes, such as this giant lobelia (top left).

SERENGETI, NGORONGORO

Location: South Kenya, North Tanzania
Best time to travel: October–April
www.serengeti.org
www.tanzaniaparks.com

The Serengeti, a vast savannah east of Lake Victoria, extends from northwestern Tanzania all the way to neighboring Kenya. The "kopjes" (Dutch for "little heads") that rise everywhere from the otherwise flat grasslands (above) are gneiss and quartzite rocks that once lay below the surface of the soil. Laid open by erosion over thousands of years, they now serve as viewpoints for people as well as animals, but they also provide protection from enemies and the often blazing hot sun. Around 15,000 sq km (5,790 sq mi) of Tanzanian territory have been turned into a national park which is now the setting for an annual mass migration of animals. The Ngorongoro Conservation Area covers 8,000 sq km (3,088 sq mi) of the Ngorongoro crater floor in northern Tanzania. Against the backdrop of an impressive natural landscape, thousands of wild animals roam freely, representing a cross-section of the biodiversity here.

Siringitu, meaning "endless plain", is what the Masai, who also live in the north of Tanzania, call the wide savannah. Twice a year the grass-eaters, led by the gnus, start their long migration in search of water and fresh greenery from here in vast herds. The African buffalo too traverse the Serengeti in great numbers (large picture). Here as in the Ngorongoro game reserve, the close encounter with the animal world makes for one of the most exciting of all travel experiences (opposite from top to bottom: giraffes, elephants, zebras, lions).

KILIMANJARO

Location: North Tanzania
Best time to travel: October–April
www.kilimanjaro.com

Mount Kilimanjaro comprises three main cones and numerous smaller peaks of volcanic origin. In the west is the 4,000-m-high (13,124-ft) Shira; in the middle is Kibo at 5,895 m (19,341 ft), the highest point in Africa; and in the east is the 5,148-m (16,891-ft) Mawenzi. The lesser peaks are lined up along a crevasse that runs from south-east to north-west. Although it is situated not far from the Equator, the peaks of Kilimanjaro are often covered with snow. The massif in the heart of the savannah features a great range of climate and vegetation zones. Above the savannah is a cultivated agricultural belt and former woodland savannah that today remains only on the northern slopes. This zone blends into the deciduous montane forest that goes up to 3,000 m (9,843 ft). It is followed by an extensive ericaceous and alpine belt, which itself gives way to the ice-capped summit region. The national park provides a habitat for numerous animals including gazelles, rhinoceroses, Cape buffalo, elephants and leopards, some of them endangered species.

Africa's tallest mountain can be climbed in a strenuous five-day tour, starting from Marangu in Tanzania. Hikers cross new vegetation and climate zones every day, right up to the snow-capped peak of the "Mountain of God".

GREAT ZIMBABWE

Location: Central Zimbabwe
Best time to travel: April–October
www.zimbabwetourism.co.zw

In 1871, German explorer Karl Mauch discovered the ruins of Great Zimbabwe. For a long time it was believed that foreign peoples such as the Phoenicians or Arabic tribes might have been the founders of this former trading metropolis, but archaeological research ultimately showed that the remains originate from the Shona culture. This ethnic group, belonging to the larger Bantu community, first settled the region in the 11th century.

The best-preserved part of the nearly 80-ha (200-acre) complex is the Great Enclosure, an elliptical wall. Defensive corridors extend in between the walls.

MANA POOLS

Location: West Zimbabwe
Best time to travel: April–October
www.zimparks.com

This national park on the southern shores of the Zambezi River and the two adjacent safari parks of Sapi and Chewore are a paradise for animals. The three parks in the border region between Zimbabwe, Zambia and Mozambique cover an area of just under 7,000 sq km (2,702 sq mi), with Chewore occupying about half of this. In the north the Zambezi forms the natural boundary of the park. The river regularly floods the reserves – Mana Pools is the name of four of the Zambezi's main basins.

This hippopotamus is hard to detect among the water hyacinths. During the rainy season, the Zambezi bursts its banks and a landscape of lakes appears.

VICTORIA FALLS

Location: Zimbabwe/Zambia
Best time to travel: April–October
www.zambiatourism.com
www.gotovictoriafalls.com

Victoria Falls are among the most spectacular waterfalls in the world. The first harbinger of these gigantic falls is the cloud of mist rising to a height of up to 300 m (1,000 ft), which can be seen from as far away as 20 km (12.5 mi) or so. With ear-shattering force, the Zambezi River, which forms the border between Zambia and Zimbabwe, plunges about 110 m (361 ft) into the abyss, a natural spectacle reflected in the falls' local name: "Mosi-oa-Tunya", or "Smoke that Thunders". During the spring floods in March and April, the falls grow into a nearly 2-km-wide (1.2-mi) wide curtain of water with up to 10,000 cu m (353,147 cu ft) of water plummeting over the edge every second. During the rest of the year, when the Zambezi carries less water, the individual falls separate out again, with the Rainbow Falls the highest among them. The land around the waterfalls is also a habitat for about 30 mammal, 65 reptile as well as 21 amphibian species.
David Livingstone was the first European to see the falls, in 1855, and he named them for Queen Victoria of England.

During the rainy season, the Victoria Falls – comprising the Devil's Cataract, the Main Falls, the Horseshoe Falls, the Rainbow Falls and the Eastern Cataract – form the largest single sheet of falling water in the world. Beyond the waterfalls, the Zambezi squeezes itself through the Boiling Pot Gorge (top) and overcomes further rapids before finally pouring itself into the Kariba Lake. The deep gorge, into which the Zambezi plunges over the edge of the Victoria Falls, was dug by the river itself over the course of millions of years (right). Today still, the waters of the Zambezi continue to wear away the soft rock – the Victoria Falls "walk" upstream.

MAKGA-DIKGADI

Location: North Botswana
Best time to travel: April–October
www.botswanatourism.co.bw
www.game-reserve.com

Unlike in the Namib, the sand dunes of the Kalahari run in long, narrow, parallel ribs. These are fossil dunes whose base became petrified a long time ago and which do not shift. In the dune valleys, water exists close to the surface. It is connected with the Okavango inland delta by a subterranean network of channels. When the delta is full of water, the overflow extends into the far corners of the network. When it has dried up, it draws the water back out. This process guarantees a relatively high humidity to the Kalahari. The beauty of this continuous alternation between desert and greenery certainly rivals

OKAVANGO DELTA

Location: North Botswana
Best time to travel: April–October
www.okavango-delta.net

The delta is a unique natural habitat in the Kalahari Desert. The Okavango River rises in the Angolan highlands and ultimately flows through Namibia and northern Botswana before evaporating and seeping away in this inland delta. The delta floods each year in June when the waters of the Cuando River arrive after the rainy season. It is a mostly flat terrain with only few high spots. These become islands in the floods and the previously dry Kalahari is transformed into a lush green paradise.

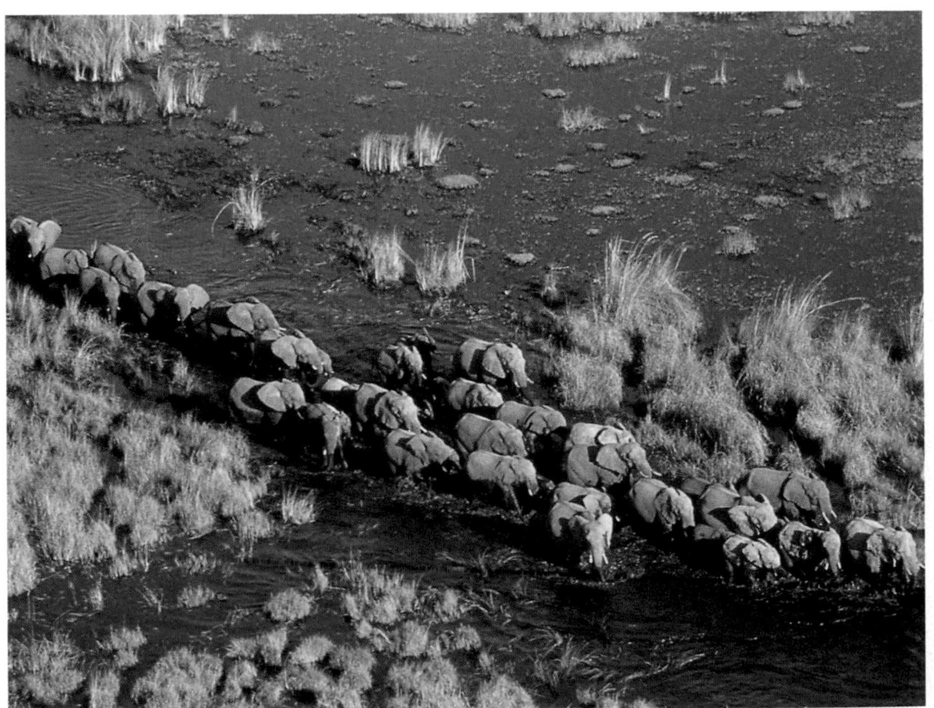

A herd of elephants arrives to drink at one of the many-branched water channels in the delta.

the majestic appeal of the Sossusvlei dunes. Saltpans of all sizes make up the core of the Makgadikgadi. In an area covering about 12,000 sq km (4,362 sq mi) they are not only the largest of their kind in the world but also the most recognizable feature of this part of the Kalahari Desert. During the rains the hard salt crust softens and turns into a treacherous sludge that is impassable for vehicles; the 165-km (103-mi) route across the Makgadikgadi Pan to Kubu Island is therefore only open during the dry season.

Although they appear to be utterly hostile to any form of life, the Makgadikgadi saltpans are in fact a veritable paradise for certain creatures. Depending on the season, colonies of zebra and herds of antelope (left) settle around their margins along with pink flamingos and a number of other animals.

CHOBE

Location: North Botswana
Best time to travel: April–October
www.botswanatourism.co.bw

Chobe National Park, which has existed in its present size since 1968, covers about 12,000 sq km (4,362 sq mi) of land, ranging from the Chobe riverfront, which features dense vegetation, to open woodland savannah and barren desert-like terrain. Aside from the riverbanks, the Savuti Marshes in the southwest of the park offer the greatest variety of wildlife and habitats.

The Chobe River hugs the border between Botswana and Namibia; its gallery forests and the southern thornbush savannah are the home of great herds of elephants. As well as the grey giants, lions (left) too enjoy a drink from the river, here during a thunderstorm.

ETOSHA

Location: North Namibia
Best time to travel: April–October
www.nwr.com.na
www.met.gov.na

Etosha means "Great White Place" and refers to the vast saltpans in the 22,275-sq km (8,598 sq mi) Etosha National Park. Located on the north-western margins of the Kalahari Basin, they provide a sanctuary for the numerous animal species. Elephants, which were nearly extinct in the area, have been able to reproduce here in great numbers, and the park's population of black and white rhinoceroses is one of the largest in Africa. Cheetahs, lions, leopards, hyenas, bat-eared foxes and jackals find a gluttonous menu including vast herds of antelopes, gazelles, zebras and giraffes. The birds here are similarly fascinating, ranging from bizarre marabou storks to yellow-beaked tokos. Flamingos even arrive after the rains.

"Nature is relentless and unchangeable, and it is indifferent as to whether its hidden reasons and actions are understandable to man or not", observed Galileo Galilei. And here the queens of the animal world are killing a Kudu calf; after their meal the lionesses are languid and sated.

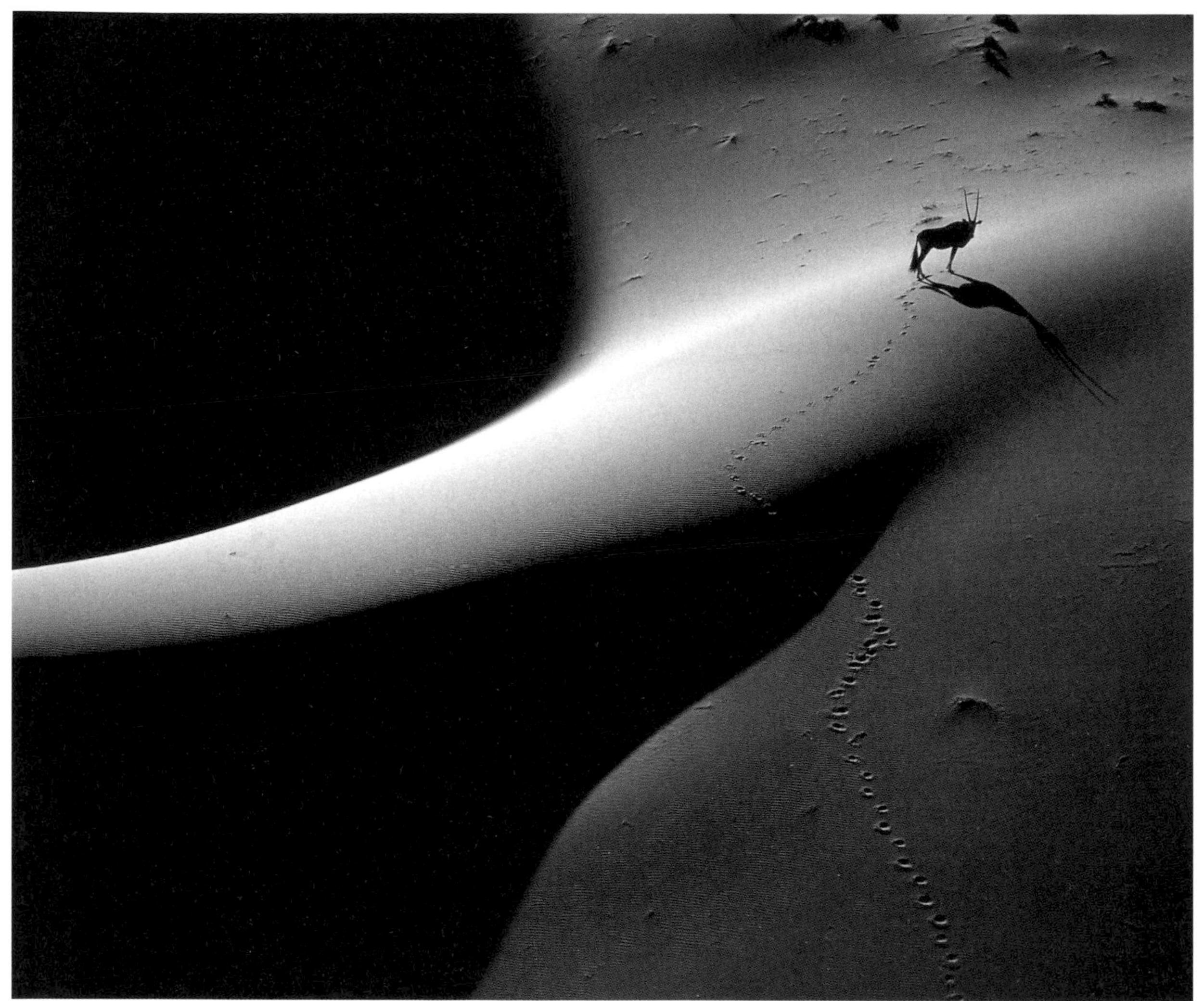

NAMIB NAUKLUFT, SOSSUSVLEI

Location: West Namibia
Best time to travel: April–October
www.nwr.com.na
www.met.gov.na
www.sossusvleilodge.com

Covering a vast area of 50,000 sq km (19,300 sq mi), Namib Naukluft National Park is one of the largest nature reserves in the world. It comprises the Naukluft Range and a large portion of the Namib Desert, which goes straight down to the coast and is about 1,500 km (932 mi) long and 80 to 130 km (50 to 81 mi) wide. Although the area is nothing but subtropical desert landscape, it nevertheless boasts great species diversity. The geological features range from blackish gravel plains and regions of eroded island mountains to dune seas in the Central Namib.
The Naukluft Range has rugged peaks that reach nearly 2,000 m (6,562 ft) and dramatic valleys that together form a unique ecosystem. First and foremost, there is sufficient water here to provide for a diverse range of flora and fauna – mountain zebra, baboons, jackals and springboks coexist with a number of bird species including Nubian vultures, dune larks and Gray's larks.

The main attraction in the Namib Naukluft National Park is the Sossusvlei – the epitome of a fascinatingly sensual dune landscape, with smooth waves extending to the horizon. An Oryx antelope takes in the air full of concentration (above). What it can scent is the humid air current that blows in from the Atlantic – the animal needs this precious water to survive. In order to obtain it, the antelope stands on top of a dune ridge and waits for the fog banks that will soon drift inland. At that point, it will lick the condensing moisture from its nostrils.

FISH RIVER CANYON

Location: South Namibia
Best time to travel: April–October
www.canyonnaturepark.com

With a length of 161 km (100 mi) and a depth of 450 to 550 m (1,476 to 1,805 ft), this is the second largest gorge in the world after the Grand Canyon. From above it is easy to make out the two different levels of the canyon. The first canyon, on a north-south axis, is a rift valley about 20 km (12 mi) wide that was created by tectonic shifting in the plateau during the Paleozoic about 500 million years ago. During an ice age some 200 million years later, the glaciers further deepened this valley. For the last 50 million years or so, since the Tertiary, the Fish River has carved its course into the canyon, further eroding it over time and in the process creating the second portion of the canyon, which is also the narrowest and deepest section. From the vista point, a steep, exposed path takes visitors down to the valley floor.

Hiking the Fish River Canyon is a challenge, however. The trail leads from Hikers' View to the Ai-Ais Hot Springs resort about 85 km (53 mi) away at the southern exit from the canyon. The trek lasts a good four days and takes you across the more or less dry riverbed several times. Encounters with baboons, Hartmann's mountain zebras and klipspringers are not uncommon. The glorious conclusion to the hike, which is only permitted during the cool time of year, are the hot springs of Ai-Ais. The name comes from the Nama language and means "hot water" – the thermal springs have a surface temperature of 60 °C (140 °F).

Fish River Canyon in Namibia is the largest gorge in Africa.

CAPE TOWN, TABLE MOUNTAIN

Location: South-west South Africa
Best time to travel: all year
www.tourismcapetown.co.za
www.capetown.gov.za

Framed in by Table Mountain and its auxiliary peaks on one side and the ocean on the other, Cape Town's historical and multicultural essence is plainly evidenced in the former colonial buildings. It is also considered one of the most attractive urban centers in the world. Since it was founded by Jan van Riebeeck in 1652, the city has steadily increased in size and population.
The Castle of Good Hope, built in around 1679, reflects colonial history in its Victorian and Cape Dutch architecture. Former suburbs like Bo Kaap now have a distinctly Asian flair to them. Steep and narrow lanes are lined with low houses painted in pastel hues; here and there, the minaret of a mosque can be glimpsed. Bo Kaap is home to the descendants of slaves who had been imported in the 17th and 18th centuries from Indonesia, Sri Lanka, India and Malaysia. Most of them are Muslims and have preserved the languages and the cultures of their home countries. As an instrument of communication across cultural and linguistic divides, Afrikaans developed, the lingua franca of southern Africa. The main attraction for night owls is the Victoria & Alfred Waterfront. The area around the east pier in Cape Town's port had long been abandoned to decay, but toward the end of the 1980s an elegant shopping and entertainment district was created here, following the model of Fisherman's Wharf in San Francisco.

The yachts and fishing boats in the marina significantly contribute to the charming ambience of the Victoria & Albert Waterfront.

WINELANDS, GARDEN ROUTE

Location: South South Africa
Best time to travel: all year
www.winelands.co.za
www.gardenroute.co.za

Jan van Riebeeck, the Dutch founder and first administrator of the Cape colony, also planted a few grapevines, and in 1654 he was able to harvest the first grapes and taste the locally produced Muscadet wine. Today, the vineyards north-east of Cape Town produce top wines, often in cooperation with renowned European winemakers.
South Africa's most famous road, the Garden Route, runs for about 200 km (124 mi) from Mossel Bay to Storm River along the Indian Ocean coastline with its many charming bays and coves. Among the best-known sights along the way is Knysna Lagoon, which is best viewed from the rocky cliffs of Knysna Head. Plettenberg Bay is probably the most popular beach resort on the Garden Route, where upscale hotels and elegant beach villas belonging to wealthy South Africans line the powdery white beaches. During the winter months, whales come into the bay to calve. A section of the coast here is covered in dense primeval forest and protected within Tsitsikamma National Park.

The king protea (top right) is the national flower of South Africa. Mossel Bay is the real start of the Garden Route in the Cape – the Outeniqua Choo-Tjoe Train (bottom right) is a good way to travel from one bay to the next.

Opposite page from top: Vineyards such as Boschendal and Lanzerac Manor enjoy a worldwide reputation. The Kooperatiewe Wijnbouwers Vereeniging (KWV), the former cooperative of winemakers, has its headquarters In Paarl.

DRAKENSBERG RANGE

Location: East South Africa
Best time to travel: all year
www.lhwp.org.ls
www.drakensberg-tourism.com

The Drakensberg Range forms a boundary between the South African interior plateau and the east coast over a distance of more than one thousand kilometers. Its northern section, the Transvaal Drakensberg, is protected by the Blyde River Canyon Nature Reserve while the southern region, known as Natal Drakensberg, features mountains that rise to an impressive 3,377 m (11,080 ft) amidst quaint lakes. The range was declared a national park and named uKhahlamba Drakensberg Park.

The greatest treasure in the park are the age-old rock image created by bushmen – the San people.

ISIMANGALISO WETLAND PARK

Location: East South Africa
Best time to travel: all year
www.stlucia.org.za
www.kzn.org.za

The 380-sq km (147-sq mi) St Lucia Lake forms the heart of this national park, which covers about 2,500 sq km (965 sq mi). This shallow body of water is separated from the Indian Ocean by only a belt of dunes. Fed by several rivers and ocean tides, St Lucia's salt content draws a number of bird species that are attracted by the rich food supply they find in the shallow brackish lake.

If the mining companies had been given a carte blanche to pursue their own interests, there would be neither hippopotamuses (right) nor crocodiles in Lake St Lucia and its environs today.

KWA NDEBELE

Location: North-east South Africa
Best time to travel: all year
www.southafrica.net

The Ndebele people arrived in South Africa in about the 16th century. Under the yoke of Apartheid they were assigned KwaNdebele as a "homeland" north of Pretoria, the capital. Many of the around 400,000 Ndebele still live there. Most of the billages are inhabited only by women, children and elderly people – the men of working age have to move to the industrial centers. Despite numerous restrictions, the traditions of the Ndebele have still prevailed, especially their love of artistic body and wall painting and colorful clothing.

Abstract patterns and bright colors distinguish the traditional clothes of the Ndebele women.

KRUGER

Location: North-east South Africa
Best time to travel: all year
www.krugerpark.co.za

What is now Kruger National Park was created around the turn of the 20th century. It now boasts the most animals of any African park. Some 2,000 km (mi) of tracks and made-up roads traverse the 2,000 sq km (1,242 sq mi) of wilderness; fifteen rest camps, from simple tents to a luxury lodge, offer accommodation. As you move south from the thorny savannahs in the north vegetation becomes more plentiful, featuring Mopane woods, expansive, grass-covered plains and thick acacia forests that form a habitat for a fascinating world roughly 500 different bird and mammal species.

Encounters with leopards are not that unusual in the park.

MADAGASCAR

Location: island state off the east coast of Mozambique
Best time to travel: April–October
www.visitmadagascar.com

Madagascar's appeal lies in its exceptional flora and fauna, dazzling coral reefs, bizarre limestone formations, volcanic craters, endless sandy beaches and the relics of ancient civilizations. The island is tropical, with the exception of its very southern tip. Its length of 1,580 km (982 mi), means that the climate and vegetation zones differ greatly between the north and the south. The backbone of the landscape is formed by mountain ranges and volcanoes that run nearly the entire length of the island. The eastern highlands drop steeply down to the Indian Ocean coast while in the west they drop off into the coastal lowlands along the Mozambique Channel. The west coast is much drier and more fragmented with coves and promontories than the east coast and is dominated by a savannah landscape that features impressive, towering baobab trees. Influenced by the south-easterly

trade winds, the east side of Madagascar is covered with lush rainforest. In addition, there are a number of islands off Madagascar's nearly 5,000-km (3,107-mi) coast which are surrounded by coral reefs that make them prized swimming and diving territory. Altogether, Madagascar appears like a natural paradise; but in reality this paradise is under threat. The "Indri Indri" ("there he is"), for example, one of about 30 prosimian species (lemurs) endemic to Madagascar, is in danger of becoming extinct. This is because nearly half the rainforest has been felled or slashed and burned in the last few decades.

Madagascar separated from the African mainland some 130 million years ago; since then, fauna and flora have been able to develop completely independently. The pictures on this double page show clockwise from top left: lemurs on the needle-sharp rock points in the Ankarana reservation; the Andringitra National Park; prehistoric seeming chameleons; the breathtaking karst rocks in the Tsingy de Bemaraha National Park.

SEYCHELLES

Location: island state off the east coast of Kenya
Best time to travel: April–October
www.seychelles.com
www.virtualseychelles.sc

This group of islands, "discovered" in the western Indian Ocean by Vasco da Gama in 1501, comprises more than one hundred individual islands, fewer than half of which are actually inhabited. While many of the islands are no more than coral reefs or atolls (covering a total surface area of about 210 sq km/81 sq mi), the main islands of Mahé, Praslin, Silhouette and La Digue are quite mountainous with the peaks on Mahé, the largest island at 158 sq km (61 sq mi), reaching an altitude of up to 905 m (2,969 ft) and featuring only very sparse vegetation. The tropical oceanic climate means that the year is divided into a dry, and relatively cool, season (from May to September) and a hot, rainy north-west monsoon season (from December to March). Some 98 per cent of the population are Christians, with a mix of Asian, African and European ancestors. The brisk tourist trade means that residents of the Seychelles have the highest per capita income of all the African countries; about ninety percent – around 72,000 people – of the population live on Mahé. Picard, Polymnie, Malabar and Grande Terre, four of the coral islands in the Aldabra Atoll, the largest atoll in the world, are not accessible to the general public. Together they form the most westerly group of islands in the Seychelles in the Indian Ocean. Thanks to their great isolation it has been possible to preserve here a natural landscape untouched by humans. The atoll is famous for its large population of Aldabra giant tortoises, a type of Seychelles tortoise. These reptiles are among the largest worldwide – they can weigh up to 250 kg (550 lbs) and reach an age of more than 100 years.

The Seychelles present the ideal image of a tropical island paradise. Below is the rocky Anse Soleil beach in the bay of the same name, on the main island, Mahé. Mahé's urban center, Victoria, is often described as the smallest capital in the world.

MAURITIUS AND LA RÉUNION

Location: islands east of Madagascar
Best time to travel: April–October
www.tourism-mauritius.mu
www.reunion.fr

The small islands of Mauritius and Réunion belong to the Mascarene Islands, a group of islands around 850 km (528 mi) east of Madagascar. The first European to discover the islands was a Portuguese mariner named Pedro Mascarenhas at the beginning of the 16th century. Both islands were formed by a hotspot in the earth's crust – at eight million years old Mauritius is the oldest island in the group while Réunion is only three million years old.
Réunion's rugged mountainous landscape is dominated by the 3,070-m (10,073-ft) volcano Piton de Neiges, with its wild yet dormant calderas (cirques), while its smaller neighbor, the 2,632-m (8,636-ft) Piton de la Fournaise, is one of the most active volcanoes in the world. A lovely trail to the Trois Bassins of St-Gilles-les-Hautes on the west coast of the island leads to the Bassin des Aigrettes, where several waterfalls cascade over steep cliffs.
A ring of coral reefs has formed in the warm tropical waters of the Indian Ocean around the volcanic heart of Mauritius, producing ideal conditions for a rich underwater world. On land the original tropical vegetation is now only found in a few places in the south-west while most of the island, which otherwise features just a few mountains, is taken up with sugar cane fields.

The Portuguese explorer Pedro de Mascarenhas was one of the first Europeans to explore Mauritius (above: Tamarin Bay) in c. 1510. Together with Réunion, it now forms the Macarene Islands which were named after him.

The land of "Dreamtime"... and dreamy landscapes. From the azure blue of the Barrier Reef to the sated dark green of the rainforests in the Wet Tropics, from the glowing red of the rock monoliths in Uluru National Park to the rusty red of the sand dunes in the Simpson Desert, the fifth continent mirrors the earth's fascinating colors and variety. The view of the Caroline Islands, the largest group of islands in Micronesia, is also unforgettable. They comprise 963 islands and atolls, most of which are volcanic in origin.

KAKADU

Location: North Australia (Northern Territory)
Best time to travel: May–October
www.kakadu.com.au

Situated about 250 km (155 mi) east of Darwin, Kakadu National Park, having been extended a number of times to its present size of around 20,000 sq km (7,720 sq mi), actually encompasses five different ecological zones with their respective distinctive flora and fauna. The national park became known on an international level in the middle of the 20th century when excavations revealed stone implements that were at least 30,000 years old. More than 5,000 Aborigine rock paintings were also discovered here as well. The motifs, which were either scratched or painted, depict episodes from what Aboriginals consider mythical primordial times. A special feature is the so-called x-ray style which illustrates not only the visible body but also parts of the skeleton and the organs as well. They depict myths and legends, including that of "Namarrkun", the "Lightning Man", who carries a lightning jolt on his shoulders and creates thunderclaps in the clouds with stone axes that are tied to his knees, elbows and head.

Mangrove trees with stilt-like roots have anchored themselves in the mud of tidal rivers and serve to protect the hinterland from the destructive effects of wave action (below). During the rainy season from November to April – known as "the Wet" in Australia – coastal areas are transformed into a vibrant carpet of lotuses, water lilies and floating ferns. The adjacent hilly landscape with its diverse vegetation consists of open tropical forests, savannah and grassy plains and extends over most of the park. It provides a haven for endangered animal species such as dingoes and wallabies. A number of rare kangaroo species live on the sandstone plateau of Arnhem Land as well as on the Arnhem Escarpment (bottom right), a steep bluff around 500 km (311 mi) long that traverses the park from the south-west to the north-east (bottom left: Aboriginal rock art in the national park).

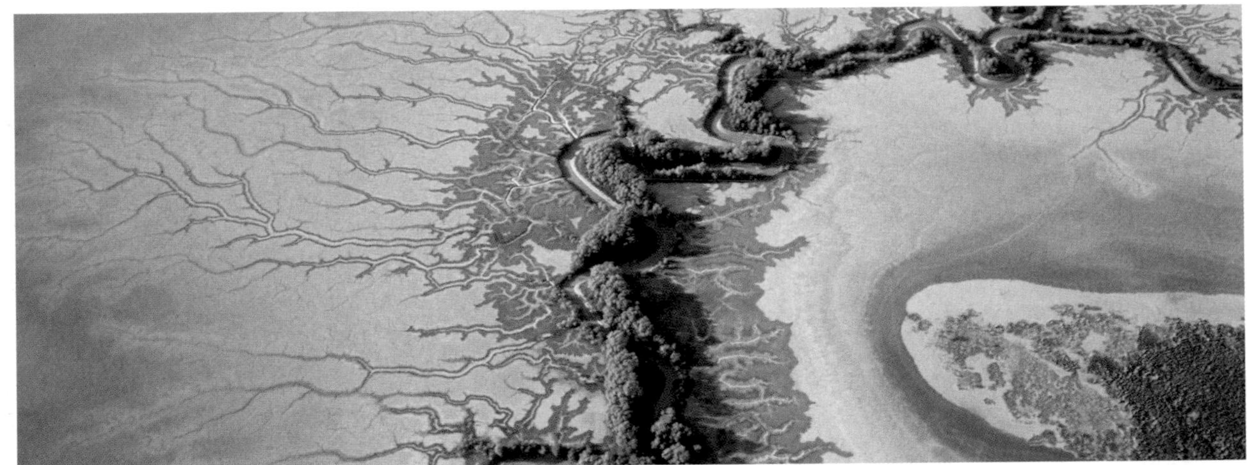

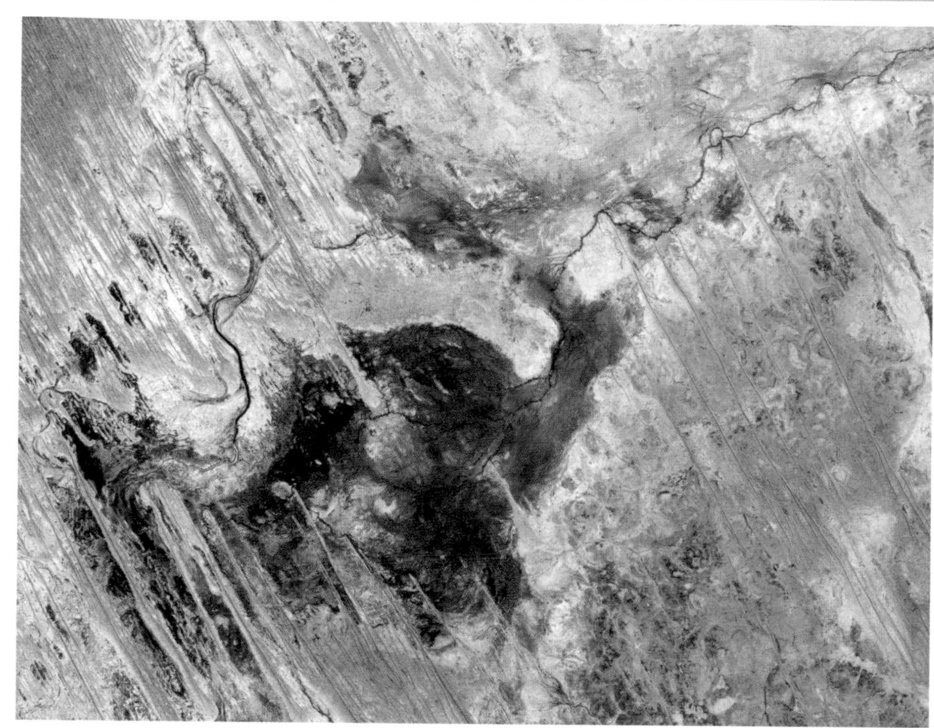

SIMPSON DESERT

Location: Central Australia (Queensland)
Best time to travel: May–December
www.derm.qld.gov.au

It was only mapped from the air in 1929. The first non-vehicular crossing was undertaken forty-four years later, in 1973, and another four years later by writer Robin Davidson, who started in South Australia on camelback. She managed to find the Oodnadatta Track, a stretch of outback covering more than 615 km (382 mi) that was named after the tiny outpost of Oodnadatta on the south-western edge of the Simpson Desert.

The dunes of the Simpson Desert (left: a satellite photograph), one of the last remaining wildernesses on earth, extend up to 300 km (186 mi) to the north-west.

NITMILUK

Location: North Australia (Northern Territory)
Best time to travel: April–October
www.nt.gov.au

Over millions of years the Katherine River has worked itself deep into the Arnhem Plateau over a stretch of 12 km (7 mi), creating canyons as deep as 13 to 100 m (43 to 328 ft) which can be viewed by boat or canoe. During the rainy season the Katherine River becomes a raging torrent and can therefore only really be negotiated safely during the dry season (April to October).

A canoeing trip through the gorges of the national park is an unforgettable experience. From the water, an awesome view opens up of the up to 100-m-high (33-ft) reddish brown rock face.

ULURU AND KATA TJUTA

Location: Central Australia (Northern Territory)
Best time to travel: May–December
www.environment.gov.au
http://en.travelnt.com

The Uluru and Kata Tjuta National Park is situated in a vast area of sparse, dry savannah. The iconic red rocks were discovered almost simultaneously in 1873 by the two explorers William Gosse and Ernest Giles. They named Ayers Rock after Henry Ayers, the prime minister of South Australia at the time – to which the Northern Territory then belonged.
Unlike the surrounding rock, the cliffs are very resistant and weathered very slowly, today towering above the plain as magnificent petrified witnesses of the Paleozoic. Despite the inhospitable surroundings, the Anangu have been living in this area for thousands of years. Although the white invaders used unambiguous terms ("ab origine" meaning "from the beginning"), it took more than 200 years before the Australian High Court decided that to overthrow the legal fiction of the "terra nullius", or "empty land", "land belonging to nobody", that was applied by the British Crown when it claimed the sovereignty and ownership of the land. In fact, the ancestors of the indigenous Australians probably arrived 50,000 years ago from southern Asia at "Terra Australis Incognita", the myth-enshrouded southern lands, separated from the world that was known at the time by a belt of fire and the dangerous seas, a land that had been thought a necessity by the ancient Greeks for reasons of symmetry, aa a counterweight to the northern half the world.

Indigenous Australians called their holy mountain Uluru and this is now its official name.

GREAT BARRIER REEF

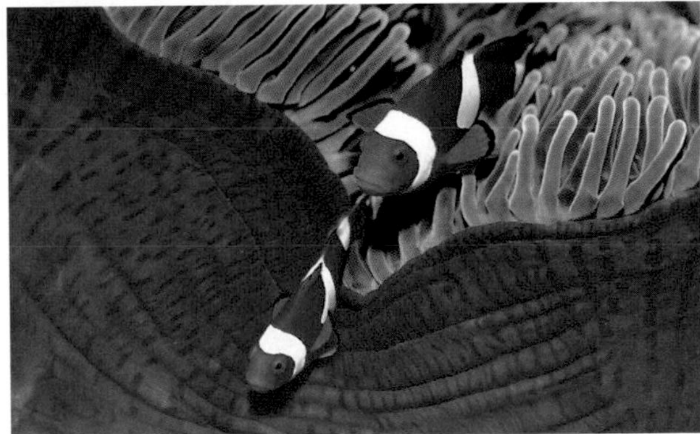

Location: Barrier reef north-east off Australia
Best time to travel: May–October
www.gbrmpa.gov.au
www.cultureandrecreation.gov.au

The longest living coral reef on earth extends from the Tropic of Capricorn to the mouth of the Fly River (New Guinea). The reef, comprised of around 2,500 individual reefs and 500 coral islands, follows more than 2,000 km (1,243 mi) of the north-eastern coast of Australia at a distance from the mainland of 15 to 200 km (9 to 124 mi).
The reef was formed by coral polyps who live together with blue-green algae. The polyp larvae hatch in the spring and are already able to swim at birth. They then attach themselves to the reef close to the surface of the water, slowly developing their skeletons and forming colonies with other members of their species. After a short while they die off and their calcium carbonate tubes are ground into fine sand. The algae then "cake" the sand into a new reef layer on which new young polyps are able to settle the following year. This is how the reefs and islands have developed over thousands of years.

One of the most beautiful section of the Great Barrier Reef can be found off the Whitsunday Islands (large picture).
For about 8,000 years coral polyps (top) have been constructing this largest natural an "building" in the world. The bright clownfish (above) is also at home here.

GONDWANA

Location: East Australia (Queensland/New South Wales)
Best time to travel: May–December
www.bigvolcano.com.au

The Gondwana Rainforests of Australia are a UNESCO World Heritage Site that essentially comprise fifteen national parks and various other protected zones in Queensland and New South Wales. The name refers to Gondwana, the former supercontinent in the southern hemisphere that broke up towards the end of the Mesozoic Period to form the continents as we know them today.

Temperate rainforest in the valley floors characterizes the Barrington Tops National Park, which is part of the Gondwana site. These rainbow lorikeets are two of the rainforest inhabitants.

FRASER ISLAND

Location: Island off East Australia (Queensland)
Best time to travel: April–November
www.fraserisland.net
http://environment.gov.au

Fraser Island is the largest sand island on Earth, and the crescent-shaped dunes are up to 250 m (820 ft) high. The sand came from the northern mesa of New South Wales. There is blows into the river valleys, is then transported by the currents as by tides, and finally deposited on Fraser Island. The continual south-easterly trade winds shaped the sand into bizarre structures such as the Cathedrals and the Pinnacles. Fraser Island also features many crystal-clear streams and lakes.

The Indigenous Australian name of Fraser Island is K'gari ("Paradise").

WET TROPICS

Location: North-east Australia (Queensland)
Best time to travel: April–November
www.wettropics.gov.au

Much of Australia used to be covered with tropical rainforest. Today only part remain on the mountain ridge in the Great Dividing Range, the Great Escarpment depressions and of the coast in Queensland, where the tropical climate has been stable over millions of years. A rich diversity of animals and plants has evolved largely undisturbed here. Under the canopy of the up to 50-m-tall (164-ft) tree giants, which allow almost no light to penetrate to the forst floor, more than 350 different vascular plants have developed.

Tree ferns up to 20 m tall (66 ft) thrive in the Wet Tropics.

BLUE MOUNTAINS

Location: South-east Australia (New South Wales)
Best time to travel: April–November
www.bmwhi.org.au

Despite their low altitude of 600 to 1,000 m (1,969 and 3,2181 ft), the mountains are very rugged, with much of the area still untouched by humans. In the dense forests, 132 endemic plant species thrive; among them the Wollemi pine, discovered only in 1994. It is regarded as a living fossil whose origins date back at least 90 million years.

Charles Darwin, described the view from the rocky ledges (left: the Valley of the Waters) as "fantastic". Essential eucalyptus oils create a light bluish mist here – hence the name.

SYDNEY

Location: South-east Australia (New South Wales)
Best time to travel: all year
www.cityofsydney.nsw.gov.au

At least since the Olympic Games of 2000, Sydney has been viewed as a world metropolis like Paris, Cape Town and Bangkok. And the view of Sydney Harbor with the bridge and the opera house is famous throughout the world. The latter has a surprising history. In 1955, a largely unknown Danish architect named Jörn Utzon won the contest for the opera house design. He submitted no more than sketches as plans but these convinced the judges. It was only much later, in 1959, once the foundations had been built, that any thought was given to how the roof was actually to be structured. Pouring it in one piece proved too costly. And thus the conches were

MELBOURNE

Location: South Australia (Victoria)
Best time to travel: all year
www.visitmelbourne.com
www.melbourne.vic.gov.au

Melbourne, located on the Yarra River, is considered Australia's most British city, although with the large numbers of immigrants living here it could also be called one of the largest Greek or Italian cities in the world. For a long time Melbourne was the largest and most important city in Australia, a status it developed during the area's gold rush in the mid-19th century. It was here that the first inner-city transportation services went into operation in 1869: initially a horse-drawn omnibus, then cable cars based on the example of San Francisco with miles of steel cable, and ultimately electric trams. The trams still give the city an appealing flair today and some of

made from individual, pre-cast ribs that were then linked. Other problems occurred during the tiling and glazing. Utzon withdrew in 1966, and the opera house was not completed until 1973. Admittedly, instead of the budgeted seven million Australian dollars, it had actually cost 102 million. Today Sydney is a vibrant, self-confident and cosmopolitan port town with charm and joie de vivre to spare. Of its four million inhabitants about 250,000 own a boat. Beyond the restored old town (The Rocks) with its colonial-era houses, many shops, galleries, pubs, restaurants and hotels, the modern city reaches into the sky; the Monorail runs 5.5 m (18 ft) above the road from the inner city to Darling Harbour.

Some 1400 workers built Harbour Bridge. Today visitors can appreciate the entire structure and the view from it on a "Bridge Climb".

them have been in service for more than fifty years. Melbourne was actually Australia's capital for a quarter of a century, before this role was given to Canberra, a city that created on the drawing board. Today still some Melbourners look down with some disdain on Sydney which they consider happy-go-lucky. And, indeed, Melbourne boasts an inner city that is richer in history as well as two complexes built by Joseph Reed for the international exhibitions of 1880 and 1888: the Royal Exhibition Building and Carlton Gardens surrounding it.

The bridge over the Yarra River provides a view of the city center with Flinders Street Station (left), the railway station built in 1905. Towering over the city's modern skyline is the Eureka Tower (far left), completed in 2006. At an elevation of 297.3 m (975 ft) it is Melbourne's tallest building.

MUNGO

Location: South Australia (New South Wales)
Best time to travel: all year
www.environment.nsw.gov.au
www.visitnsw.com

Mungo National Park forms part of the "Willandra Lakes" UNESCO World Natural and Cultural Heritage Site. The landscape of Mungo National Park was overgrazed by sheep in the 19th century, lumber was taken for houses and barns, and the loose soil was then carried away by the wind. But 15,000 years ago the entire area was under water and traces of settlements around 40,000 years old have now been found along the shores of the former lake – including some petrified human remains. DNA analysis indicated they are the oldest traces of Homo sapiens in Australia.
In addition to three different kangaroo species, the spiny anteater lives in the semi-desert. It has a small head and a tube-like snout with a tiny mouth opening from which its long, sticky tongue darts out to lick up ants. Bird lovers visit the park to observe parakeets, zebra finches, crested pigeons and emus.

This lunette in Mungo National Park, which once formed the shore of the fried-up lake, is known as "Walls of China". Erosion has created a fragile environment of finely rippled formations on whose back sand dunes have deposited.

GREAT OCEAN ROAD

Location: South Australia (Victoria)
Best time to travel: all year
www.greatoceanrd.org.au

The Great Ocean Road begins south of Geelong and heads westwards before joining the Princes Highway. The route covers around 300 km (186 mi), much of which is along the coast. The cold winds from the Antarctic can be felt here in autumn and winter. The tall mountains are a deep green and densely forested. Off the spectacular shore is one of the largest ship graveyards in the world – this is a region defined by prevailing westerlies and the Roaring Forties. The consistent waves are a magical draw for surfers. In Otway National Park rainforests of evergreen eucalyptus and tall tree ferns thrive which seem primeval in appearance. The most spectacular section of this route takes you through Port Campbell National Park with the rusty-red sandstone cliffs known as the Twelve Apostles. These too will eventually be eroded by the surf, in the future that will be close in geological terms.

Landscape in transformation – the most famous landmark of Port Campbell National Park on the stunningly beautiful Great Ocean Road at Victoria's south coast are the Twelve Apostles. Breathtaking breakers roar against the up to 65-m-tall (213-ft) rock formations, constantly changing due to the forces of wind and waves.

TASMANIA

Location: Island south-east off Australia
Best time to travel: all year
www.tas.gov.au

Australia's largest island is at the same time its smallest federal state. Tasmania, the vacation island of the "mainlanders", covers an area of only about 68,000 sq km (26,248 sq mi), but with its wild mountains and rivers, dense forests and attractive bays it offers as much diversity as an entire continent. Fewer than half a million people live here, about half of these in the main town, Hobart. It is easy to imagine then that large areas of the island are virtually untouched. Here you can still find the last remaining large forested areas of the temperate climate zone. In contrast to the largely uninhabited west coast, Tasmania's east coast is more easily accessible and can be reached on the Tasman Highway. Part of the east coast is formed by the Tasman Peninsula, where the former Port Arthur penal colony is situated. The former convict settlement with its ghostly church and the infamous "model prison" has since become one of Australia's most important tourist attractions. Between 1833 and 1877, more than 12,000 prisoners lived here in inhumane conditions, doing forced labor.

There are five important protected areas along the east coast: Tasman National Park, Maria Island National Park, Freycinet National Park with Wineglass Bay, Douglas Apsley National Park, and Mount William National Park, virtually on the northern tip of the island.

Tasmanian Wilderness is the official name of the World Heritage Site in West and South-west Tasmania as defined by UNESCO. This protected area essentially includes the national parks of Cradle Mountain–Lake St Clair, Southwest, Franklin Lower

Gordon Wild Rivers as well as three smaller areas. The wild, romantic landscape was formed by glaciers during the last ice age and is characterized by a great many lakes and waterfalls. The island receives up to 2,500 mm (98 in) of annual rain, facilitating the growth of temperate rainforests. They look familiar from a distance and close up we recognize them: a place of sub-Antarctic and Australian shapes. Only the gums, types of eucalyptus, reveal that we are still in Australia. Tasmania's most famous animals are the unique duck-billed platypus and the Tasmanian devil.

Mount Ossa, at 1,617 m (5,305 ft) the highest mountain in Tasmania, consists of dolerite, just like Cradle Mountain, so called because of its shape. Dolerite is an extremely hard magnetic rock, which about 165 million years ago pushed itself in between much older sedimentary rock layers and hardened there. The rugged mountain peaks, moraine lakes and trough valleys of the Cradle Mountain Lake St Clair National Park, however, were only formed by glaciers during the last Ice Age. Here you will find signposted hiking trails; the most famous of these is the five- to eight-day Overland Trail, and it is possible to stay in huts overnight. Lake St Clair, in which live rainbow trout, is the deepest natural freshwater lake in Tasmania (more than 200m/656 ft deep). The indigenous people here call the lake Leeawuleena, meaning "Sleeping Water".

Flinders Island lies to the north-east of Tasmania in the Bass Strait. It forms part of the Furneaux Group – thought to be the remains of a former land bridge between Tasmania and the Australian continent.

South Cape: Tasmania boasts one of the last remaining undisturbed ecosystems on the planet featuring sandy scrubland on the coast, buttongrass plains and forests.

CAPE REINGA

Location: North-west of New Zealand's North Island
Best time to travel: all year
www.doc.govt.nz

New Zealand's North Cape can be visited on a day trip from the Bay of Islands. Visitors and locals alike consider Cape Reinga, where the Tasman Sea and the Pacific converge, to be New Zealand's northernmost point, but the claim in fact belongs to the Surville Cliffs to the north-east of the cape. When the weather is right, it is possible to see the Three Kings Islands, which owe their name to Dutchman Abel Tasman who anchored there on Three Kings Day (the Twelfth Day of Christmas) in 1643. It was also here in 1902 that the Elingamite steamship sank with forty-three crew members and a hoard of gold. To this day, only a portion of the ship

BAY OF ISLANDS

Location: North-east of New Zealand's North Island
Best time to travel: all year
www.bay-of-islands.co.nz
www.bayofislands.net

The former Maori settlements around the Bay of Islands were a focal point of the early colonization of New Zealand and therefore considered the cradle of the nation. On Waitangi Peninsula, in 1840, Maori chiefs signed the Treaty of Waitangi with delegates from England. It is considered the founding document of an independent New Zealand. The first white settlement was founded in Russell in 1809 and became New Zealand's first capital in 1840.

The unmistakable carvings of the Maori in the Whare Waka (boat house) of Waitangi.

and its treasure have been recovered. The way to the Cape takes you past Houhora Heads where the Wagener Museum provides information on Maori art, Kauri resin and whaling. Nearby Spirits Bay is home to an ancient, weathered Pohutukawa tree. The Maori believe the souls of the dead slide down its roots into the ocean. On the journey back to the Cape you will pass Kaitaia, the northernmost town in New Zealand.

For the Maori, whose ancestors began to colonize the uninhabited Pacific region some 6,000 years ago, this is a magical place. They see themselves as the direct descendants of deities who embody the forces of nature. For them, life is a journey that does not end in death. On the steep coast of Cape Reinga their souls plunge into the sea to begin the homeward journey to the mystical Hawaiki homeland from where they came.

ROTORUA

Location: Center of New Zealand's North Island
Best time to travel: all year
www.rotoruanz.com

The geothermal center of the North Island boasts geysers, bubbling mud pools, hot springs, ten lakes and an abundance of Maori folklore. It attracts many tourists, coming to the spas or for various watersports.

Let's do tongues: Sticking out the tongue only happens at traditional dances. It is meant to deter evil spirits and to symbolize fearlessness. "Moko", the tattooing of the faces (today the patterns are mostly painted on), differs from one Maori to the next just like a fingerprint. In the past, only the supreme leaders of the Maori were entitled to wear a full face tattoo; it was a sign of superiority.

TONGARIRO

Location: Center of New Zealand's North Island
Best time to travel: all year
www.doc.govt.nz

Tongariro, the oldest national park in New Zealand, was donated by New Zealand's original population, the Maori. In 1887, Chief Te Heuheu Tukino gave the Maori's sacred land around the Tongariro volcano to the New Zealand government with the specific condition that it be protected for all humankind.

The national park encompasses three active volcano systems within a total area of around 750 sq km (290 sq mi): Tongariro, after which the park is named; Ngauruhoe (right, with Tongariro in the background); and Ruapehu, the highest mountain on the North Island at 2,797 m (9,177 ft).

AORAKI/ MOUNT COOK

Location: West of New Zealand's South Island
Best time to travel: all year (climbing: January/February)
www.doc.govt.nz
www.mtcooknz.com

Aoraki/Mount Cook National Park, which covers a vast area of about 700 sq km (270 sq m), is home to all of New Zealand's 3,000-m (9,843-ft) peaks, with the exception of Mount Aspiring. The highest of the peaks is Mount Cook at 3,754 m (12,317 ft), known to the Maori as "Aoraki", which can be roughly translated as "Cloud Piercer". (The Maori call New Zealand "Aotea-roa" which is usually translated as "Land of the Long, White Cloud".) A rockslide in 1991 reduced the height of Aoraki to 3,754 m (12,317 ft), but it still towers a few hundred meters over

EGMONT

Location: West of New Zealand's Noth Island
Best time to travel: all year
www.newzealand.com

Egmont National Park encompasses the last primeval forest areas around the volcanic mountain Taranaki, which has been dormant for the last 300 years. Asphalt roads bring visitors to rest points at an altitude of roughly 1,100 m (3,609 ft) above sea level, while short hiking trails provide access to fabulous, fairytale-like forests.

For the Maori, the snow-covered peak of New Zealand's famous mountain (left: Taranaki) symbolizes the sacred heads of their ancestors. Every Maori tribe had its "own" mountain. When two tribes made peace their mountains were also symbolically wed.

its number two, Mount Tasman, at 3,498 m (11,477 ft). Once the training ground for Sir Edmund Hillary, the Auckland-born mountaineer who managed the first ascent of Mount Everest, Mount Tasman is accessible from the east via a 60-km (37-mi) access road that takes you along the shores of Lake Pukaki. New Zealand's most formidable ice field, the Tasman Glacier, is 29 km (18 mi) long, up to 3 km (1.8 mi) wide and nearly 600 m (1,969 ft) thick in places. In addition to the cheeky Kea mountain parrot, the flora and fauna in this national park include rare falcon and owl species, while the star amongst the plants is the Mount Cook Lily.

The hiking trail through Hooker Valley takes you across the valley floor on wooden planks and crosses the Hooker River glacier by means of rope bridges. The routes over ice and snow are more strenuous.

WESTLAND

Location: West of New Zealand's South Island
Best time to travel: all year
www.wcrc.govt.nz
www.west-coast.co.nz

It is out on the bright sheets of ice that the mountain world of the Westland National Park reveals its full allure. Its magnificent main glaciers, Franz Josef in the north and Fox in the south, flow down the steep valleys from the main alpine ridge around Mount Cook and end in the rainforests around 13 km (8 mi) from the South Island's coast.

While the easily accessible glacier snouts of the Fox Glacier (right) and of the Franz Josef Glacier attract about 350,000 visitors each year, you will often enjoy complete solitude on other tracks in the Westland National Park.

MOUNT ASPIRING

Location: West of New Zealand's South Island
Best time to travel: all year (climbing: January/February)
www.doc.govt.nz
www.newzealand.com

Mount Aspiring National Park was founded in 1964 and covers an area of 3,550 sq km (1,370 sq mi). Its northern border of is formed by the mighty Haast River, which flows into the Tasman Sea close to the town of the same name. It then extends south as far as Fiordland National Park. The focal point of the park is Mount Aspiring at 3,027 m (9,932 ft) – the only 3,000-m (9,843-ft) peak outside of Mount Cook National Park.

Hikers will find mostly challenging routes in this park, such as the Routeburn Track (right).

FIORDLAND

Location: South-west of New Zealand's South Island
Best time to travel: all year (climbing: January/February)
www.fiordland.com
www.doc.govt.nz

Covering around 12,520 sq km (4,833 sq mi), New Zealand's largest national park is also considered the country's loveliest. Snow-covered mountains provide the backdrop for vast beech forests with giant, moss-covered trees that are often centuries old. The wide valleys formed by retreating glaciers feature a plethora of crystal clear rivers and serene lakes. The park is home to around 700 endemic plants and rare animals, and owes its name to the fiords on the west coast that form underwater valleys reaching up to 400 m (1,312 ft) in depth. Only one of them, the Milford Sound, is accessible by road. The glacial landscape here receives up to 1,000 cm (394 in) of rain annually, providing ideal conditions for the temperate forests to flourish. This area is still home to many plant and animal species that already existed millions of years ago on Gondwana, the supercontinent that was once located in the southern hemisphere. The main threat is from introduced species.

Four days are required to complete the just under 54-km-long (34-mi) Milford Track from the north shore of Lake Te Anau via New Zealand's Southern Alps to the Tasman Sea, crossing the Fiordland National Park (bottom: the Mackay Falls) to the Milford Sound (below).

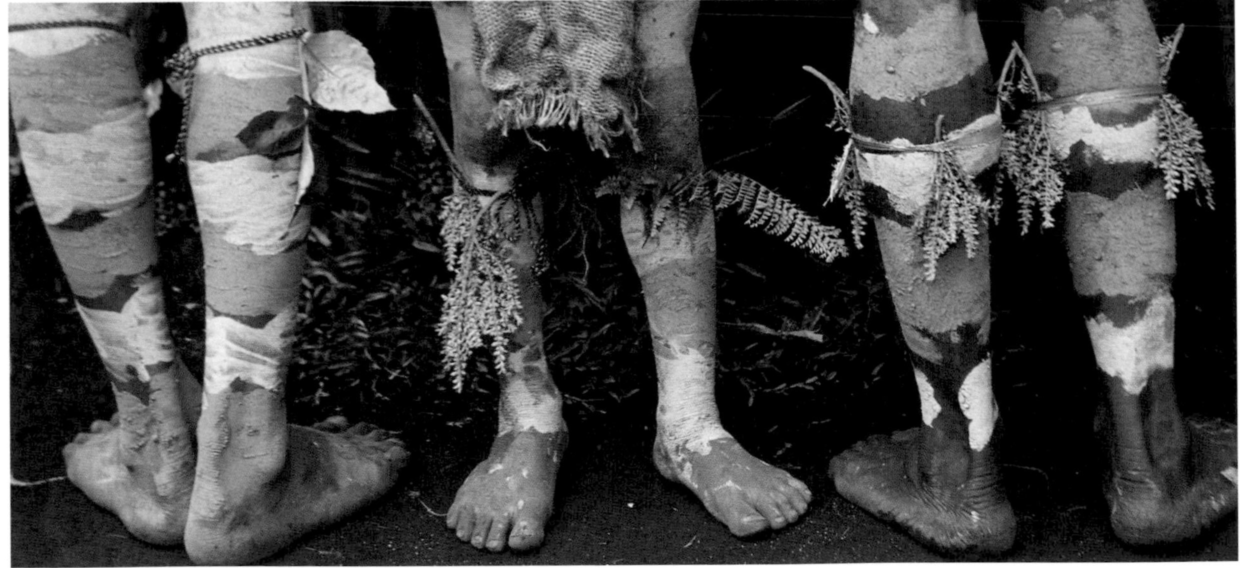

PAPUA NEW GUINEA

Location: Island state in the Pacific (Melanesia)
Best time to travel: June – September
www.pngtourism.org.pg

Papua New Guinea is only about 150 km (93 mi) off the Cape York Peninsula of northern Australia. The country comprises roughly 85 percent of the eastern part of the island of New Guinea while the rest is spread over a further 600 islands, the largest of which are New England and New Ireland.

In the southern highlands at an elevation of around 1,500 m (4,922 ft) is the Kuk Swamp. Archeological excavations document that the soil here was cultivated by humans as much as 7,000 years ago – long before any known influence on the island from south-east Asia. In the rural regions of Papua New Guinea, "taro" is grown, a root vegetable also known as eddoe and one of the oldest known agricultural crops. Kuk provides the proof that agriculture developed on Earth more often than assumed in areas independently of each other.

The substantial differences in elevation – one quarter of the country lies above 1,000 m (3,281 ft) – account for the vast range of vegetation that exists here. Oak trees,

bay trees and conifers dominate the mountains, while the low-lying areas boast palms, climbing plants, ferns and orchids.
Papua New Guinea's cultural diversity is also unique on the planet: Around 95 percent of the population is made up of Melanesians, who are divided into ever-smaller clans that speak several hundred, often mutually unintelligible languages. There are also small groups of Papuans (the island's indigenous inhabitants), splinter groups from Micronesia and Polynesia, and about 20,000 foreigners.
The Western Highland Province is inhabited by hundreds of traditional clans who gather in the provincial capital Mount Hagen every August for a festival of song and dance.

Because of their elaborate headgear the Huli, Papua New Guinea's most popular inhabitants, are often also known as "the wig men". Their rich jewelry and bright body paint (opposite bottom) are an expression of a great artistic tradition that always impressed visitors. Opposite top: stilt villages on the Sepik River. Above: festival participants sporting their traditional red face paint and white stripes during the annual song and dance festival in Mount Hagen.

FRENCH POLYNESIA

Location: Island state on the Pacific (Oceania)
Best time to travel: April–June, October/November
www.tahiti-tourisme.com

The six archipelagoes of French Polynesia (Society, Tuamotu, Marquesas, Austral, Gambier and Bass) are located in eastern Polynesia and their 118 islands cover a total area of about 4.5 million sq km (1,737,000 sq mi). One of the largest of the thirteen Marquesa islands is Nuku Hiva, which has dramatic coastal formations that drop nearly vertically into the sea. The highest volcano is Poitanui on Uapu (1,232 m/4,042 ft). The Tuamotu archipelago, which consists exclusively of atoll reefs, is more than 1,000 km (621 mi) to the southwest. The best-known island group

FIJI ISLANDS

Location: Island state in the South Pacific
Best time to travel: April–June, October/November
www.fijime.com
www.tourismfiji.com

The majority of Fiji's islands are relatively close to each other compared to other similar groups in the South Pacific: within a radius of only 250 km (155 mi). The two main islands, Viti Levu and Vanua Levu, are volcanic and feature high, jagged ranges that dot the interior. The climate is predominantly tropical, with the windward side on the southeast recording a hefty 3,000 to 5,000 mm (118 to 197 in) of annual rainfall. This feeds the dense mountain forests as well as the coastal mangroves and coconut palms. Meanwhile, less than half as much rain falls in areas protected from

is the Society Islands, some 1,500 km (932 mi) west of Tuamotu. It comprises by far the largest island, Tahiti, as well as Raiatea, Bora Bora and Moorea.

Tahiti, in the geographic heart of Polynesia, is also the economic and cultural center of the French overseas territory. Tahiti was made a French protectorate in 1842, and in 1880 a French colony. The other islands were taken into French possession by 1881. The islands are divided into the "Windward Islands" and "Leeward Islands", depending on their exposure to the south-east trade winds. Volcanic in origin, they boast lush tropical vegetation surrounded by rich coral reefs.

Left: a dance performance in Papeete, French Polynesia. Far left: the ideal image of a South Sea scene – here the lagoon of Bora Bora where resorts have many over-water hotels on stilts.

the wind. There, grasses dominate the landscape and cane sugar is a major crop. The largest island, Viti Levu, boasts bubbling hot springs and a number of rivers. Fiji is also famous for its coral reefs, which lie at a great depth. The islands are a mecca for soft coral diving.

The first humans are said to have settled on Fiji at least 3,500 years ago. It is unclear where these people came from but a legend tells that at one time, three god-like chiefs coming form Africa landed in the west of Viti Levus and founded the village of Vuda. Then, it is said, a large flood came and spread the people all over the islands.

In 1643 Abel Tasman was the first European to set foot on the Fiji Islands. Today, their gleaming white beaches and the clear turquoise sea attract swimmers and divers – and surfers too find ideal conditions here.

THE AMERICAS

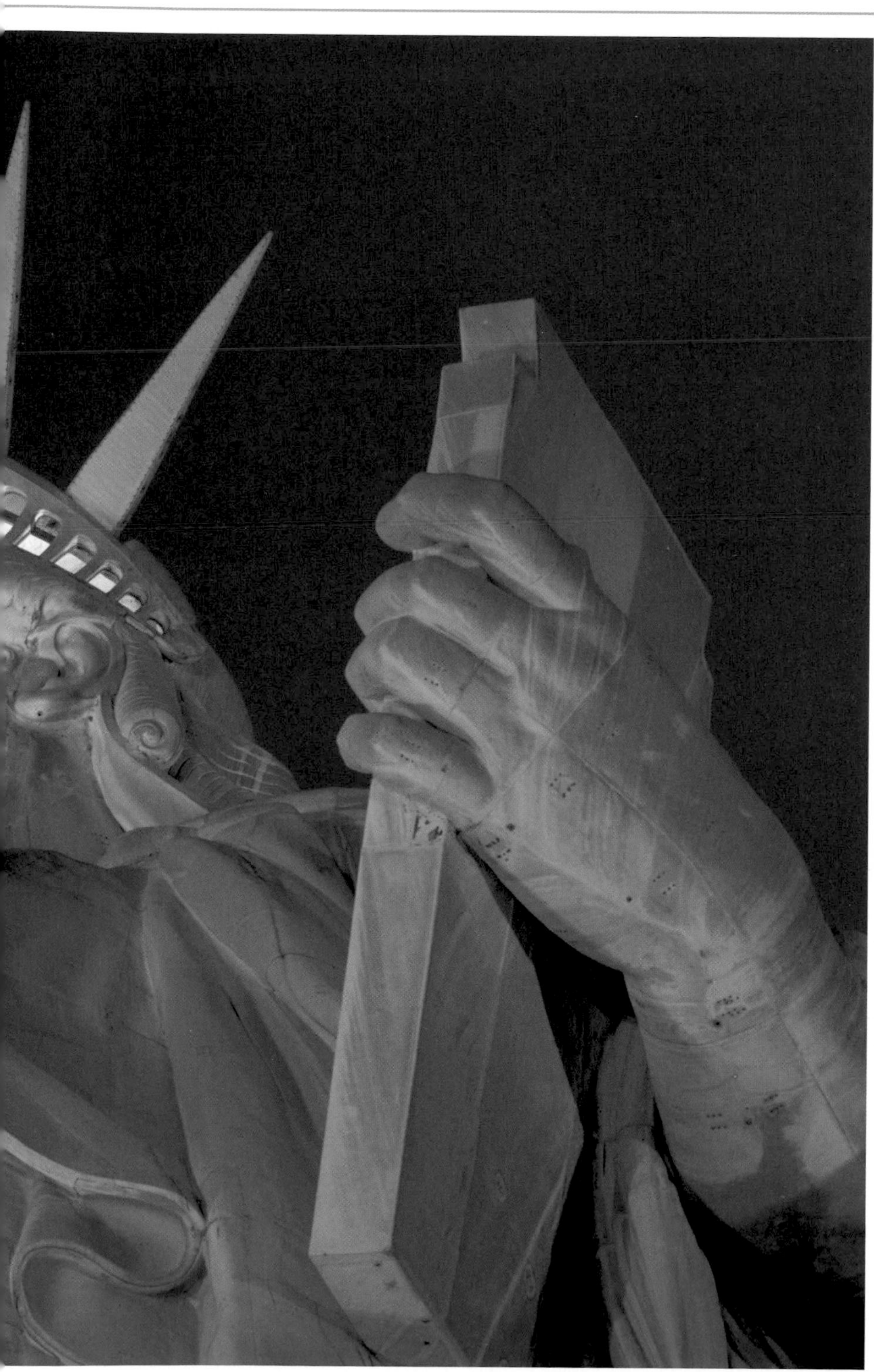

The Golden Gate and the sparkling San Francisco skyline, the red sandstone towers of Monument Valley, the grandiose gorges of the Grand Canyon, the endless expanse of the prairie, the legacy of the Aztecs and Mayans, the baroque pomp at the Popocatépetl, Highway 1 and Route 66, the "capital of the world" New York (left: the Statue of Liberty on Liberty Island off the southern tip of Manhattan)...from the green jungles of the Amazon and the ice caps of the world's highest volcano to the immense glaciers of Patagonia, the mysterious ruins of the Incas and the colonial heritage of the European explorers...the list of marvelous sites to visit and enjoy seems to be never-ending. Welcome to the Americas!

JASPER

Location: South-west Canada (Alberta)
Best time to travel: April–September
www.jaspernationalpark.com

Within its boundaries there are more than 800 lakes, most of which are fed by the surrounding glaciers. Lac Beauvert, for example, is a jade-green glacial lake situated near the town of Jasper, home of the famous Jasper Park Lodge, built by the former Grand Trunk Railroad to compete with the nearby Banff Springs Hotel. Jasper is not as overrun by visitors as Banff. A mountain train takes you up the popular Whistler Mountain, where breathtaking views of the region unfold below.

Numerous trails explore the beauty and wilderness of the national park (right: Maligne Lake).

WOOD BUFFALO

Location: Central Canada (Alberta/North-West Territories)
Best time to travel: April–September
www.woodbuffalo.ab.ca

Two-thirds of Canada's largest national park, which covers about 44,802 sq km (17,294 sq mi), are located in Alberta; the other third is in the Northwest Territories. The park was founded in 1922 to protect the breeding grounds of the endangered whooping crane and the last remaining wood buffalos. The bison population (wood as well as prairie bison released here) is estimated at about 6,000 animals – the largest group of bison living in the wild anywhere in the world.

The powerful animals with their big heads and massive bodies grow to 3 m (10 ft) long and weigh 1 ton.

KOOTENAY

Location: South-west Canada (British Columbia)
Best time to travel: April–September
www.pc.gc.ca
www.hellobc.com

The picturesque Kootenay and Vermillion valleys traverse through the park, and the informative Fireweed Trail leads through a landscape that was destroyed by fires in 1968, but has since been replanted with young trees and fireweed (rosebay willow herb). Marble Canyon is an impressive, 70-m-deep (230-ft) gorge cut through jagged limestone. The Paint Pots feature multicolored ochre that was used as sacred paint by the Ktunaxa Native Americans.

Kootenay National Park comprises an impressive mountain scenery as well as rivers and lakes.

BANFF

Location: South-west Canada (Alberta)
Best time to travel: April–September
www.banff.ca

Banff National Park on the border of Alberta and British Columbia features snow-covered peaks, huge glaciers, silent valleys, crystal-clear rivers – all still largely untouched despite the five million annual visitors. The elegant town of Banff, center of this most popular Canadian national park, sits at the confluence of Bow and Spray rivers, below the distinctive "tipped" peak of the 2,950-m-high (9,679-ft) Mount Rundle and the mighty, 2,998-m-high (9,836-ft) Cascade Mountain.

Dense vegetation spreads in the sheltered areas during summer in the Banff National Park.

VANCOUVER, VANCOUVER ISLAND

Location: South-west Canada (British Columbia)
Best time to travel: all year
www.tourismvancouver.com
www.vancouver.ca
www.vancouverisland.com

Vancouver is simply one of the loveliest cities in the world. Superbly situated on the idyllic northern Pacific Coast and surrounded by picturesque bays and the majestic mountains of the nearby Coast Range, this modern metropolis also has its share of glass skyscrapers, a quaint Old Town, spacious Stanley Park, sandy beaches, the Lion's Gate Bridge, as well as the futuristic Canada Place. Few cities harmonize so comfortably with the inviting wilderness nearby. Granville Island is an artificial leisure island under

TORONTO

Location: South-east Canada (Ontario)
Best time to travel: all year
www.toronto.ca
www.torontoinfocenter.com

Toronto is a surprisingly lively city. The metropolis on Lake Ontario owes its cosmopolitan character to the large number of immigrants, who arrived here after World War II and gave the city its European–Asian feel. Ambitious construction projects indicate dynamic development, while traditional buildings such as Holy Trinity Church are protected heritage sites. Particularly worth seeing are Ontario Place, a futuristic leisure and shopping area on Lake Ontario that hosts rotating exhibitions and the Harbourfront Centre, a contemporary arts and cultural center in converted warehouses located on the piers with

the highway bridges out on False Creek. The converted warehouses here were reassigned as restaurants, bars and shops, with artists and craftspeople working in their galleries. The past still shines brightly in Gastown while vibrant, exotic restaurants and shops are the focus in Chinatown. Off the coast is Vancouver Island – one of the last remaining paradises on earth and a beacon of hope for all those who wish to enjoy a stunning natural environment away from the urban bustle nearby, and yet in close proximity to the comforts of a city.

One of the loveliest places on Earth, the city of Vancouver is spread across a narrow peninsula, bordered in the north by the Burrard Inlet, in the west by the English Bay and in the south by False Creek. Left: False Creek, with the Coast Range mountains forming a stunning backdrop.

shops, restaurants, waterfront cafés, art galleries and theaters as well as the Queen's Quay and York Quay Promenades. Toronto Islands, linked with the city by ferry, is a tranquil sanctuary featuring quiet canals, gentle strolls and a historic amusement park for children. The CN Tower is the city's emblem and is visible from vast distances. The viewing platform offers superb views over the city and its surroundings. Other highlights include the BCE Place, a bold skyscraper with a light-flooded atrium, the 19th-century Holy Trinity Church and the urban district Yorkville, Toronto's "Greenwich Village".

The CN Tower dominates the city of Toronto. At 555.3 m (1,822 ft) it is one of the tallest free-standing buildings in the world. "CN" is short for "Canadian National", the railway company that had it built in a record 40 months.

QUÉBEC CITY

Location: East Canada (Quebec)
Best time to travel: all year
www.quebecregion.com
www.telegraphe.com

The capital of the province of the same name is the heart of francophone Canada. More than ninety percent of the roughly 170,000 residents here speak French and the cityscape exhibits strong European influences. In fact, Québec City is the only North American metropolis with an intact city wall, while the Old Town's narrow alleyways are somewhat reminiscent of old Paris.

Originally founded on the banks of the St Lawrence River in 1608, the buildings in the settlement beneath Cap Diamant have burned down on several occasions, forcing the residents to retreat to the promontory and build Haute-Ville, the "Upper Town", which is linked via cog railway with the Lower Town.

Sightseeing attractions include the Escalier Casse-Cou, a harrowingly steep staircase linking the Haute-Ville with the Quartier Petit-Champlain in the Basse-Ville, and the Place Royale, a former marketplace in the Lower Town. The Musée de la Civilisation provides insight into the city's history. La Citadelle, which dates from the early 19th century, is located at the east end of the city wall in Haute-Ville and has been a base for the only French unit of the Canadian Army since 1920. The Cathédrale Notre-Dame was built in 1647 and recalls French rule. The Maison Chevalier gives an indication of how the city's wealthy families lived in the 18th and 19th centuries. The luxury hotel Château Frontenac, built in 1893, resembles an oversized European castle. The Parc des Champs-de-Bataille, once the scene of a legendary battle between the English and the French on September 13, 1759, is today one of the largest municipal parks in North America. The narrow alleyway Rue du Trésor adds a touch of Parisian charm to Canada.

Château Frontenac, the luxury hotel built in 1893 by the Canadian Pacific railway, sits high above the Saint Lawrence River in Québec City. The river, which rises in Lake Ontario and is an important transportation route, is about 1 km (0.6 mi) wide in Quebec.

MONTREAL

Location: East Canada (Quebec)
Best time to travel: all year
www.quebecregion.com
http://ville.montreal.qc.ca

Montreal was founded by French Catholics in 1642. Today, seventy-five percent of the city's residents can still claim French ancestry.

Situated at the confluence of the St Lawrence and Ottawa Rivers, Montreal quickly grew into a prosperous center of trade. The French influence remains strong in Vieux-Montreal, the lovely Old Town featuring a good number of historical buildings and narrow streets on the southern slopes of Mont Royal, while an air of cosmopolitan urban life prevails in the inner city.

After Paris, Montreal is the second-largest city in the world where French is spoken. In the winter, residents take refuge in the underground city – "la ville souterraine" – with its network of tunnels, passageways and shopping malls. The Basilique Notre-Dame, a splendid Catholic church, was built by the prominent Protestant architect James O'Donnell.

The lights of the big city: a view from the 223-m-tall (732-ft) city mountain Mont-Royal across the glittering lights of Montreal.

NIAGARA FALLS

Location: South-east Canada (Ontario)/North USA (New York)
Best time to travel: April–September
www.niagarafalls.ca
www.infoniagara.com

Niagara Falls – a very popular travel destination for honeymooners – are located on the Niagara River between Lake Erie and Lake Ontario. The border between the USA and Canada runs through the middle of the falls.

The first white man to see Niagara was a Jesuit priest by the name of Louis Hennepin, who came in December 1678. Since then they have been known as one of the greatest natural wonders on Earth. The huge volume of water drops more than 50 m (164 ft) over the escarpment in a massive cloud of mist and spray. The river is actually split into two channels by tiny Goat Island: the large Horseshoe Falls are on the Canadian side and the smaller American Falls are on the U.S. side. The 290-m-long (951-ft) Rainbow Bridge links the two countries.

Table Rock to the west, next to the horseshoe-shaped falls, or the Minolta Tower, are recommended as observation points. The best view is afforded by the "Maid of the Mist" which sails right past the falls. You can also take a "Journey Behind the Falls", a particularly impressive and unforgettable experience.

The Niagara Falls straddle the border between the United States and Canada. They are divided into two by the tiny Goat Island. The falls' water flow is on average 4,200 cu m/sec (148,322 cu ft/sec). With ear-shattering noise, the water masses plunge down the Horseshoe Falls, the Canadian side of the Niagara Falls (right, known for centuries by Native Americans as "Thundering Water").

ALASKA

Location: North-west USA
Best time to travel: June–August
www.travelalaska.com

Alaska is almost a continent, which disappears into the hardly visible horizon. Endless deserts of ice, treeless tundras, silent woods, deep gorges, a maze of rivers and bubbling brooks. Snow-covered mountains are mirrored in the crystal-clear lakes, giant glaciers wallow from the rugged slopes. The valleys of the Kobuk River located north of the Arctic Circle recall the days when ancestors of the Inuits and Native Americans arrived in Alaska via the landbridge from Siberia. Some 12,000 years ago they migrated to North America, when the same vegetation grew in the Kobuk Valley as today in the tundra, but at the time it had not yet been flooded by the ocean separating the continents.

In northern Alaska, two particularly striking peaks rise up like silent guardians from the Brooks Range to form a natural barrier between the valleys of the south and the endless plains of the north. Robert Marshall, a scientist and explorer who lived on the Koyukuk River as well as in North Fork between 1929 and 1939, named them the peaks "Frigid Crags" and "Boreal", but they are better known as the "Gates of the Arctic", also the name of the national park that was founded here in 1980 and extends to the north beyond the giant mountains. It is a vast area of mountains, rivers, lakes and wholly untamed nature, home to only a few Inuit. Mount McKinley and the surrounding glaciers, forests and lakes were all placed under protection back in 1917. In those days only a few adventurers were able to enjoy the beauty of the park, but when the Denali Highway was completed in 1957, ordinary folks could also discover the glory of the park founded as Mount McKinley National Park but renamed Denali National Park in 1980, after the indigenous word "denali" ("the high one"). In fact, Mount McKinley (6,194 m/20,323 ft) is the highest peak in North America. Wrangell-St Elias is the largest national park in the United States and is also home to the country's second-highest peak after Mount McKinley: Mount St Elias, at 5,489 m (18,009 ft). More than one hundred glaciers here form the largest ice field south of the Arctic Circle. The Wrangell-St Elias wilderness area features impressive gorges and raging torrents; people live only in the two copper towns, McCarthy and Kenicott.

The majestic bald eagle, the emblem of the United States since 1782, is at home mainly in Alaska. With a wingspan of up to 2.4 m (8 ft), it is one of the north's most impressive animals (left). Top: snow and ice in the Glacier Bay National Park.

MOUNT ST HELENS, MOUNT RAINIER, OLYMPIC

Location: West USA/North-west USA (California/Washington)
Best time to travel: May–September
www.visitmtsthelens.com
www.nps.gov
www.olympic.national-park.com

On the morning of May 18, 1980, the earth quakes around Mount St Helens – in a massive volcanic eruption a large section of the mountain blasted away, and the ash that was expelled made night out of day for nearly a week. As a result, the mountain slumped to a height of 2,550 m (8,367 ft) and the glacial melt devastated entire forests. The area has been protected since 1982. Mount Rainier is 4,392 m (14,410 ft) high and boasts the largest mass of ice in a single mountain range in the continental United States (not including Alaska and Hawaii). For Native Americans it is a holy mountain. William Fraser Tolmie, a brave physician in search of healing herbs, was allegedly the first white man to have ventured into its foothills.

From its majestic mountains all the way to the rugged coast, Olympic National Park offers a spectacular alpine scenery, with jagged peaks, lakes and waterfalls, the wildly romantic Pacific seaboard with its craggy cliffs and sandy beaches, and also a dense temperate rain forest unique within the United States.

Mount St Helens (right) is still active. In the Mount Rainier National Park (top), nature has not changed much since the arrival of the first white settlers. Hoh Rain Forest (above) is the largest temperate rainforest in the western hemisphere.

SAN FRANCISCO, REDWOOD

Location: West USA (California)
Best time to travel: all yesr (San Francisco), March–October (Redwood)
www.onlyinsanfrancisco.com
www.nps.gov

The "City on the seven hills" is one of the most attractive metropolises in the world. Founded in 1776 by Spanish explorers and originally called Yerba Buena, it received its present name in 1847, after Mission San Francisco de Asis founded by Father Serra. The first gold discoveries in January 1848 brought on the rise of the city as an important trading center and seaport. Three nature reserves in northern California – Jedediah Smith, Del Norte Coast and Prairie Creek – owe their existence to a nature conservation movement focused primarily on saving the redwoods. Together with Redwood National Park, located some 500 km (310 mi) north of San Francisco, they form a unified reserve.

The tall Art Deco double piers of the Golden Gate Bridge (large picture) can be seen from almost any higher point in the city. The distinctive Transamerica Pyramid (top) is another landmark of the cityscape in the bay. The Redwoods (above), close relatives of the sequoias, reach heights of more than 100 m (328 ft).

HIGHWAY 1, LOS ANGELES

Location: West USA (California)
Best time to travel: March–October (Highway 1),
all year (Los Angeles),
www.losangeles.com
www.cahighways.org

Author Robert Louis Stevenson called this place the "most beautiful convergence of land and sea on earth". Highway 1 is a spectacular route, particularly the stretch between San Francisco and Los Angeles. Secluded sandy beaches, rugged coastlines, romantic mission churches and picturesque towns line this coastal road, covering more than a thousand miles from Washington and Oregon in the north down to the California-Mexico border. Sections of it follow the historic El Camino Real, which once linked the old fortresses of Christianity. Los Angeles is the second-largest city in the United States. In terms of surface area, however, it has no rivals. Greater Los Angeles covers 1,200 sq km (463 sq mi). The "City of Angels", founded in 1781 as "Pueblo de los Angeles" and still a relatively insignificant town throughout the 19th century, has never become a melting pot like New York City. Instead, it was and still is made up of autonomous towns. Mann's Chinese Theater, a movie palace built in 1927 by Sid Grauman that resembles an ornate Chinese temple, recalls the golden years of Hollywood. A location for many a festive film premiere, legendary stars including Elizabeth Taylor, Humphrey Bogart and John Wayne are immortalized here in the cement with their hand or footprints.

Right: Cypress Point on Highway 1. Top: The legendary Sunset Boulevard in Los Angeles.

YOSEMITE

Location: West USA (California)
Best time to travel: March–October
www.ohranger.com

The Merced River has dug itself deeply into the primeval landscape of this glorious park and formed a deep, elongated valley, which also has a visitor center and some lodges. Powerful natural forces shapes this valley, giving form to the granite. Aside from the vast rock formations Half Dome and El Capitan, the Yosemite Falls and Bridal Veil waterfalls are also worth seeing.

The first areas were made a national park as early as the 1860s, and in 1905 the Yosemite National Park (right: El Capitan, lit by the setting evening sun, with the Merced River in the foreground) attained its present extent.

JOSHUA TREE

Location: West USA (California)
Best time to travel: March–October
www.nps.gov

The true beauty of this national park can best be appreciated on a hike through the hinterland where Joshua trees are silhouetted against the often breathtakingly blue sky north-east of Palm Springs. Related to the Yucca tree, these cactus-like plants can reach heights of up to 12 m (39 ft).Mormons named the tree after an image of the Prophet Joshua praying with raised hands – the irregular branches reminded them of their prophet, who promised to show them the way to Paradise.

In the evenings, the play of light and colors make the Mormon "god trees" seem like the silent guardians of the high desert.

DEATH VALLEY

Location: West USA (California)
Best time to travel: October–May
www.death.valley.national-park.com

The first white men to enter the valley came in 1849 as part of a wagon train headed for the riches of the California Goldrush. After taking what was meant to be a shortcut, they got stranded in the blistering heat. They persevered for twenty days before being rescued. One of the settlers is said to have shouted, "Goodbye, Death Valley!", which explains the name of the valley.

One-fifth of Death Valley lies at sea level or below; near Badwater is the lowest point anywhere on the North American subcontinent, at 86 m (282 ft) below sea level. Temperatures in summer of can reach more than 50 °C (122 °F).

LAS VEGAS

Location: West USA (Nevada)
Best time to travel: all year
www.visitlasvegas.com
www.lasvegastourism.com

Las Vegas, the glittering gambling metropolis in the Nevada desert, has fascinated visitors since the 1940s with its casinos and flashing neon lights. In those days, Bugsy Siegel, an infamous underworld boss from the East Coast, opened the first gambling palace in this otherwise desolate expanse: the Flamingo Hotel. Gambling was legalized in Las Vegas as early as 1931.

Vast hotels such as the Egyptian-themed Luxor are glittering entertainment palaces with gigantic casinos. There is only one thing visitors won't find in these noble guesthouses: clocks, for Las Vegas is open around the clock!

YELLOWSTONE

Location: North-west USA (Wyoming)
Best time to travel: April–September
www.yellowstonenationalpark-lodges.com

The earth below the park is in an ongoing state of upheaval. The Grand Canyon of Yellowstone and the bubbling geysers recall ancient volcanic eruptions. There are more than 300 hot springs within the park. Members of the Washburn-Langford-Doane expedition began exploring the region in 1870. Finally, in 1872, Yellowstone was declared the first national park of the United States.

The White Dome Geysir's water is heated underground, then squirted out (right). The vibrant colors of the Grand Prismatic Spring (opposite page) are caused by microorganisms.

CANYONLANDS

Location: West USA (Utah)
Best time to travel: September–May
www.nps.gov
www.canyonlands.national-park.com

The Canyonlands in southern Utah are among the most exciting landscapes on our planet. Accessible only to Native Americans and skilled riders during the first half of the 20th century, this terrain was declared a national park in 1964. Many trails lead through deep gorges and hidden valleys. It is a fairytale world of colorful rock formations with the Green and Colorado rivers flowing through the park like green ribbons. The full beauty of the region can really only be appreciated on foot.

A 450-m-long (492-ft) trail takes you up to the Mesa Arch.

ZION

Location: West USA (Utah)
Best time to travel: September–May
www.zion.national-park.com

Zion National Park features breathtaking high plateaus, deep gorges and massive plateaus. The Virgin River has carved its way into the colorful stone, forming Zion Canyon, which was given its Biblical name by the Mormons, who were the first to settle in the area. They had been searching for fertile farming country and believed they had found Heaven on Earth. They named the impressive rock formations after the Bible too, using names such as East and West Temple or Great White Throne.

Zion has been a national park since 1919. A road runs through the canyon along the Virgin River, a tributary of the Colorado.

BRYCE CANYON

Location: West USA (Utah)
Best time to travel: September–May
http://brycecanyon.com

John Wesley Powell was the first white man to explore the Canyon in about 1870. The national park owes its name to Ebenezer Bryce, who built a farm in Bryce Canyon but soon moved on to Arizona. It seems that the arduous task of spending weeks on end trying to find his cattle in the nooks and crannies here finally got to him. Bryce Canyon has been a national park since 1924. Native Americans have a more interesting name for the area: "red rocks standing like men in a bowl-shaped canyon".

The Bryce Amphitheater is one of the great sights – the actual canyon with its red-rock organ pipes.

DEAD HORSE POINT

Location: West USA (Utah)
Best time to travel: September–May
http://stateparks.utah.gov

The forces of nature needed more than 150 million years to fashion this geological spectacle. Before the 20th century, giant herds of mustangs still grazed on the surrounding mesas, but were driven onto the peninsula by cowboys, caught by lasso and broken in. Legend has it some horses died of thirst on the plateau, despite being able to see the river, because they couldn't find a way down.

From atop the 600-m-high (1,969-ft) outcropping of a huge escarpment, superb views of the Colorado River unfold, as it meanders through magnificent colorful rock formations and labyrinthine canyons.

MONUMENT VALLEY

Location: West USA (Utah)
Best time to travel: September–May
www.monumentvalley.com

Arguably the most beautiful valley in the world, Monument Valley, the "eighth wonder", is indeed a magical world of red rock formations the symbol of the American Southwest. The countless films that have been shot here have transformed it into a near-mythical landscape. Three rock needles standing in a line, once known as the "Three Sisters", have been renamed as "Big W" for John Wayne, who shot so many films here. They form a giant W when silhouetted against the sky.

Monument Valley has been protected since 1960 as a tribal park of the Navajo Native Americans.

GRAND CANYON

Location: South USA (Arizona)
Best time to travel: April–October
www.grand.canyon.national-park.com
www.nps.gov

In 1540, the Spaniard López de Cárdenas was the first European to see the magnificent panorama of the Grand Canyon, but it took until the mid-19th century before the vast area was accurately mapped.
The origins of the Grand Canyon are still not entirely clear. Presumably, the Colorado River began to carve a path through the rocky plateau around six million years ago and, over the course of time, the gorge grew. über die der passionierte John Muir, an influential and passionate naturalist, called it the "grandest of God's terrestrial cities". Wind and weather obviously contributed to the shaping of rock cliffs and bizarre rock formations, and the sequence of sedimentary layers in the stone documents the various geological periods. Fossils that were found in the canyon provide important information on life in primeval times.
Temperatures in the canyon can rise to 50 °C (122 °F), and only a few exceptionally resilient plants and animals are capable of withstanding this heat including some species of cacti and thorn bushes. Rattlesnakes, black widow spiders and scorpions also call it home.

For 446 km (277 mi) the Colorado River meanders through this stunning gorge, which is between 5.5 and 30 km (3.5 and 19 mi) wide and up to 1,800 m (5,906 ft) deep (right; top: the Havasu Falls).

MESA VERDE

Location: Central USA (Colorado)
Best time to travel: April–October
www.mesa.verde.national-park.com

The oldest and best-preserved adobe houses of the Anasazi, or Ancient Pueblo Peoples, can be found on the long, flat mountain called Mesa Verde (Spanish for "Green Table"), which is about 2,600 m (8,530 ft) high. The area was made into a national park back in 1906, and archeologists have found and restored entire villages in and among the gorges and cliffs on this plateau.

The Anasazi rock houses are the visible proof of the amazing skill of the Puebloans, who mysteriously disappeared from history, to build solid homes into the rock in very extreme locations.

CHACO CANYON

Location: South USA (New Mexico)
Best time to travel: April–October
www.chacoarchive.org

The term "Chaco Culture" denotes the period of greatest prosperity for the Anasazi, an Ancestral Pueblo People. In Chaco Canyon there are twelve large pueblos and numerous smaller settlements that housed a total of between 6,000 and 10,000 people. Half-sunken round and oval buildings are known as "pit houses", while kivas are round ceremonial chambers with a diameter of up to 22 m (72 ft). The best-known is Pueblo Bonito, which was built on a semicircular area covering about 12,000 sq m (129,120 sq ft) and had space for thirty-six kivas. The Pueblo Bonito had 800 rooms on four levels.

In the Chaco Canyon are also rock engravings by the Anasazi.

TAOS PUEBLO

Location: South USA (New Mexico)
Best time to travel: April–October
www.taospueblo.com
http://sccc.acomaskycity.org

The Spanish named the Native Americans they found in the Four Corners region of the Southwest "Puebloans" because of their vast settlements, or pueblos, with terraced slopes and interconnected dwellings which, presumably for security reasons, could only be accessed via ladders and through hatches in the roof. The Puebloans include a number of culturally related tribes such as the Tiwa, Keresan, Hopi and Zuni who believe themselves to be descendants of the Ancient Pueblo Peoples.

The Taos Pueblo, just 5 km (3 mi) outside Taos, the "Soul of the Southwest", has been there for 1,000 years without changing much.

SANTA FE

Location: South USA (New Mexico)
Best time to travel: April–October
www.santafenm.gov
www.santafe.org

Santa Fe, the capital of New Mexico and the second-oldest town in the U.S. after St Augustine, Florida, still has a strong Spanish character. The heart of this artists' paradise is the Plaza, a square enclosed by adobe houses with galleries and workshops where Puebloans spread their blankets under the porch roofs to sell local turquoise jewelry. The historic flavor of the city can best be appreciated in the Palace of the Governors, the oldest public building in the United States.

Spanish joie de vivre and Puebloan traditional culture have harmoniously intermingled in Santa Fe.

CHICAGO

Location: Midwest of the USA (Illinois)
Best time to travel: all year
www.gochicago.com
www.ci.chi.il.us

Chicago was already an important transport and trading hub in the state of Illinois back in the 19th century. During the "Roaring 1920s", Al Capone's "Windy City" gained a deservedly dubious reputation as a metropolis of gangsters. For two days in October of 1871, a devastating fire destroyed almost the entire city. From among the many old buildings, only the historic Water Tower still stands today. The new Chicago was built on top of the charred ruins of the former city, and proved a perfect chance to show the enterprising spirit of the inhabitants. Aside from New York, no other city in the United States has a more impressive cityscape and so many skyscrapers than Chicago.

The Loop, an area of downtown Chicago encircled by the "L" (elevated mass transit railway), is bordered by the Chicago River in the north and the west, Michigan Avenue in the east and Roosevelt Avenue in the south. It is basically the heart of this fascinating metropolis. State Street, the largest pedestrian zone in the world, lures visitors with its department stores, boutiques, restaurants, cinemas and theaters. Even the sidewalk is full of surprises, among them the City of Chicago Public Art Program's 16-m-high (53-ft) untitled sculpture by Pablo Picasso at the Richard J. Daley Civic Center Plaza; the "Flamingo, Alexander Calder's giant spider in front of the Chicago Federal Center; the "Universe", a giant mobile by the same artist that hangs in the lobby of the Sears Tower; and "The Four Seasons", a 20-m-long (66-ft) mosaic wall by Marc Chagall in what is now the Chase Tower Plaza.

Chicago is also a musical city. Gifted artists such as Muddy Waters, Howlin' Wolf, Elmore James and Little Walter all left a permanent mark on the Chicago Blues and their music is still popular today. As a genre, it forms part of the soundtrack for a journey through African American history, when the blues developed as an independent style from popular traditional songs. Like the rock 'n' roll of the 1950s, the Chicago Blues also emerged from the Mississippi Delta Blues of the Southern states.

Before World War II, Chicago already boasted a lively music scene firmly rooted in Glenn Miller's big band swing sound, but it was less rootsy than the Chicago blues that would soon develop. Muddy Waters brought his version of the "dirty" blues from Clarksdale, spicing it up with a bit of electric guitar. Later blues greats including John Lee Hooker from nearby Detroit and Howlin' Wolf from Memphis, Tennessee, followed in his footsteps and helping to create a sound that greatly influenced a number of styles including rhythm and blues, country, rock 'n' roll and jazz, a genre that is unthinkable without the "blue notes", or worried notes. Jazz and blues still characterize the sound of the city in Chicago today. The Chicago Blues Festival, born in 1984, is the largest blues festival in the world.

A metropolis of millions on Lake Michigan – Chicago is the third-largest city of the United States. Since the election victory of the current U.S. President, whose political career took him from here to the White House in Washington, it is also known as "Obama City". After the destruction wrought by the fire of 1871, the city became an El Dorado for architects. Today, still, architects have more of a free hand here than in New York or San Francisco.

OAK ALLEY PLANTATION

Location: South-east USA (Louisiana)
Best time to travel: April–October
www.oakalleyplantation.com

Before the Civil War ended slavery, there were countless cotton and sugarcane plantations scattered along the Mississippi whose owners commissioned grandiose estates for themselves known as "Plantation Houses". These mansions exude the kind of nostalgia that is evoked when people speak of the "Old South", perhaps thinking of the successful film of the book "Gone with the Wind" by Margaret Mitchell. Locally, however, they are not usually referred to as plantation houses but "antebellum homes", meaning pre-war houses. Since many of the owners had made their fortune on

NASHVILLE

Location: South-east USA (Tennessee)
Best time to travel: all year
www.nashville.com

Nashville, in northern Tennessee, is a city that lives off of country music – in both emotional and economic terms. All the key record companies, music publishers and studios are all based on Music Row and most visitors and tourists flock to Broadway which, after costly renovation work, has been restored to its former splendor. Even Tootsie's is buzzing once more, the legendary bar where country luminaries like Hank Williams and George Jones once drank their beer. Right next to it is the, the "Grand Ole Opry", the legendary temple of country music.

At night, music can be heard at (nearly) every corner in Nashville.

the backs of slaves, the number of plantations declined rapidly after the Civil War.
Famous Plantation Houses that are open to visitors for most of the year include Rosemont Plantation, where Jefferson Davis spent his youth before becoming the president of the southern states during the Secession; Houmas House Plantation; and most of all Oak Alley Plantation, which is considered the emblem of the southern states. It owes its fame and its name to the 400-m-long (1,312-ft) avenue of twenty-eight old and gnarled live oaks whose branches form a leafy green canopy over the road. At the end of the oak alley after which the property has been named stands the plantation home, built in gleaming snow-white Greek Revival Style in 1839.

The avenue leading to the Oak Alley Plantation is framed by live oaks planted some 300 years ago.

MEMPHIS

Location: South-east USA (Tennessee)
Best time to travel: all year
www.memphistravel.com
www.memphistn.gov

Most people visit Memphis in the south-western corner of Tennessee because of the music. Famous Beale Street, for example, which was named after a forgotten war hero, is lined with restaurants and music clubs. The city's main draw, however, is Graceland, the former country mansion of Elvis Aaron Presley, the "King of Rock 'n' Roll", today a museum open to the public.

The U.S. singer-songwriter Marc Cohn immortalized di Beale Street (left) in his hit "Walking in Memphis": "Then I'm walking in Memphis / Walking with my feet ten feet off of Beal …"

ACADIA

Location: North-east USA (Maine)
Best time to travel: April–October
www.acadia.national-park.com

Visitors arrive in large numbers on Mount Desert Island, especially in the fall when large swaths of forest transform into a sea of magical autumn colors. The changing leaves in fall are something of an event, with news of the current status broadcast via telephone and the Internet. The 19th-century Bass Harbor Lighthouse in Acadia National Park is one of the most attractive lighthouses on the New England coast. The structure was built in the 19th century. From there, the journey continues to the dreamy port of Bass Harbor, a romantic port. Then a drive along the asphalted Park Loop Road and up Cadillac Mountain takes you to Thunder Hole on Sand Beach, where the Atlantic Ocean roars deep into caverns in the rock cliffs. und After that it's on to Jordan Pond, a large, serene lake. Paved roads take you into the wooded hinterland, and far from the circuit road you can hear the mysterious call of the loon, a diving bird also known as the "Nightingale of the North".

Mount Desert Island, the main part of the national park, is covered by light woods of firs and birches, blue lupines, green ferns and many wild flowers. The Bass Harbour Lighthouse was built in 1858.

CAPE COD

Location: North-east USA (Massachusetts)
Best time to travel: April–October
www.capecodchamber.org

This Massachusetts peninsula thrives on the rugged charm of the Atlantic Ocean and the hustle and bustle of popular resort towns like Hyannis. Provincetown, known locally as just "P-town", is a romantic village with narrow lanes and flower-bedecked houses that once belonged to former ships' captains. Pilgrim Monument, an impressive granite tower, commemorates the first pilgrims to set foot on American soil here. "Old King's Highway" winds along the coast past quaint villages, antiques shops and bed & breakfasts reminiscent of historic New England. In between there are wonderful expanses of marshland, dotted with fields and ponds. On the southern Cape Cod coast there is noticeably more activity where locals and holidaymakers are attracted to Hyannis by the hotels, golf courses, go-carting tracks and restaurants.

One of the most attractive landscapes on the Cape Cod Peninsula is the Cape Cod National Seashore. Far from the main road, the quiet dunes offer a charming contrast from the hustle and bustle. The peninsula was given its name by the English explorer Bartholomew Gosnold – in the year 1602 he found the cod in the sea here particularly plentiful.

NEW YORK

Location: East USA (New York)
Best time to travel: all year
www.nycgo.com

In the early 17th century, when European towns like London and Paris had long become famous world cities, New York was still an unknown village inhabited by Native Americans, and Nieuw Amsterdam then did not grow into an important economic and financial hub until the late 18th century. At that time, the city had become a receptacle for numerous immigrants who had to leave Europe because of great economic need or political pressures and wished to start a new life in America. New York was a symbol of an unbroken hope and optimism that inspired poor and rich alike – even if many immigrants had to scrape a meager leaving in subhuman conditions on the Lower East Side.
New York, New York. The lights on Times Square, Broadway, the Empire State Building; vast temples of culture such as the Met(ropolitan Opera) and the MoMA (Museum of Modern Art); Fifth Avenue and Christopher Street; three-starred restaurants and gigantic department stores; a stream of yellow taxis and, in front of the harbor entrance, the Statue of Liberty, the symbol of freedom. In its history, the city has had to live through many a downturn, but even in its hardest hours New York was able to rely on the unbroken dynamism and the pioneering spirit of its inhabitants. New York is not a place for nostalgia; the look back over the shoulder is no more than the ned for reassurance that tomorrow, today will already be the past, that nothing is as certain as change…

"It was … so huge, intricate, unfathomable and beautiful in its distance, smoking, window-flashing, canyon-shadowed realness…" (Jack Kerouac).

MIAMI, MIAMI BEACH, FLORIDA KEYS

Location: South-east USA, island chain off South-east USA (Florida)
Best time to travel: all year, November–May (Florida Keys)
www.miami.com
www.fla-keys.com

Miami is avant-garde and futuristic, as well as being a gateway to the Spanish-speaking world of the Caribbean and South America. The Latin American influence gives it a cosmopolitan feel and more than 50 percent of the population speaks Spanish. Miami is international – quite "un-American" compared with cities like Denver and San Diego. Out on Key Biscayne, Miami turns tropical. The island was christened the "Little South Seas" in the old days because it served as the back-drop for Hollywood films meant to be set in Hawaii and Tahiti. From Rickenbacker Causeway there are superb views of the cityscape. Coco-nut Grove, with its elegant bou-tiques and southern street cafés, is the place to see and be seen In the evening, the most popular spot is South Beach. When the sun sets in the ocean, the pastel-shaded Art Deco hotels on Ocean Drive are splendidly illuminated and Ocean Drive turns into a catwalk.

Right from the top: The beach is only a few minutes away from the office, a fact that defines the city. In the Miami Beach Art Deco district, the styles of the Viennese Secession harmonize – appropriately, so close to the Caribbean – with stylized flamingos and tropical features. Key West, where the Nobel Prize-winning author Ernest Hemingway once lived in a house in Whitehead Street that today is a museum, has meanwhile become a busy holiday resort with a Caribbean feel.

CAPE CANAVERAL

Location: South-east USA (Florida)
Best time to travel: all year
www.nps.gov

NASA (the National Aeronautics and Space Administration), an organization set up for the peaceful exploration of space, was established on October 1, 1958. Eleven years earlier, on July 8, 1947, the former Ministry of War had moved its rocket test center to Florida's east coast. Apollo 11, the first expedition to the Moon, was launched from Complex 39 on Merritt Island, just adjacent to Cape Canaveral and the permanent home of the Kennedy Space Center from 1964.

A new era of space exploration began on April 12, 1981, with the maiden flight of a Space Shuttle launched in Cape Canaveral.

WALT DISNEY WORLD

Location: South-east USA (Florida)
Best time to travel: all year
http://disneyworld.disney.go.com

Near Orlando, Mickey Mouse & Co. now reign over an entire empire: the "Magic Kingdom", which is the actual theme park with Mickey and his friends; the "Epcot Center", where technological experiments are demonstrated in a playful and very entertaining way; and the "Disney MGM Studios", a mixture of a theme park and real film and TV studio. Additional attractions include leisure facilities such as the "Walt Disney World Village", three separate aquatic parks, as well as "Pleasure Island", which features nightclubs, cinemas and shops.

The giant golfball is "Spaceship Earth" at the Epcot Center.

EVERGLADES

Location: South-east-USA (Florida)
Best time to travel: November–May
www.florida-everglades.com

The Everglades, in Miami's "front yard", cover an overall area of 5,661 sq km (2,185 sq mi) that extends from the Tamiami Trail in the north to Florida Bay in the south, and from the Florida Keys in the east to the Gulf of Mexico in the west. Mangrove woods and marshes overgrown with sawgrass form a unique ecosystem in southern Florida and offer a perfect habitat for a fascinating range of animal and plant life.
The robust, evergreen mangroves profit from the nutritious mix of freshwater and saltwater that is found along the coasts. With their woven network of roots, small islets and ever-winding waterways they gradually form a transitional landscape between the mainland and the sea. Beyond the mangrove woods the sawgrass grows so abundantly that Native Americans originally referred to the area as "pay-hay-okee", meaning the "sea of grass". The conservationist Marjorie Stoneman Douglas, who has campaigned for the preservation of the Everglades, referred to this when she spoke of a "river of grass". And indeed, the Everglades could be described as a roughly 80-km-wide (50-mi), but only between 10 cm (4 in) and just under 1 m (3-ft) deep river. Every day, the precious, life-giving liquid flows out of Florida's largest lake, Lake Okeechobee, via the Shark River Slough

into the Everglades. In addition, the low altitude and lack of natural drainage have caused the region's high precipitation to collect here, which ultimately formed a vast network of swamps.

Swamp cypresses grow vertically from the water, forming horizontal root "knees" which act as snorkels and supply them with oxygen. Widely branched waterways run through the swamps. In between the hammocks – islet-like mounds covered in tropical woods – in the "river of grass", it is usually possible to observe many species of birds. In the dry winter months especially, when many migratory birds make a stopover here on their way from South to North America, the Everglades become a veritable paradise for birdwatchers.

Unfortunately, the complex ecosystem of the Everglades is seriously threatened by intensive agriculture, ever-growing drinking water consumption in local towns and even overfishing. Thus, the fauna and flora are still endangered despite extensive preservation efforts. In the last fifty years alone, up to 90 percent of bird and 80 percent of fish species have died out.

The Everglades provide ideal living conditions for animals that are endangered elsewhere because of a loss of habitat. This includes many aquatic birds, such as the snowy egret (above left). Another animal very much at home in the swampy waters of the Everglades is the giant American alligator (above right), which can grow up to 6 m (20 ft) long.

HAWAII

Location: Island chain in the Pacific (USA)
Best time to travel: all year
www.gohawaii.com

The Polynesians, who came to Hawaii as early as 500 BC, called the islands "Heaven" or "Paradise". They would still be right. It is indeed a Garden of Eden for locals as well as visitors seeking a bit of tropical sunshine on the volcanic islands, comprising Oahu, Kauai, Molokai, Lanai, Kahoolawe, Maui, and the Hawaiis. All visitors are greeted with a smile and a "lei", the trad itional Polynesian flower garlands. At the time of the kings, who ruled the islands before they were overthrown by the settlers from the United States and Europe, traditional "chants", were still sung, romantic songs that told of life in the villages. Today, the hula, a dance in honor of the gods that was originally exclusively for men is still performed at various celebrations.

"Pele, the goddess of fire, is angry", so it is said on Hawaii when the lava. There is nowhere else on Earth where volcanic activity can be observed as well as on Hawaii's "Big Island". The Hawaii Volcanoes National Park (right) includes to of the ost active volcanoes worldwide. Today still, lava emerges squirts out overground from the depths of the sea. Above: Excursion boats on the most famous beach in Hawaii, Waikiki in Honolulu on the island of Oahu and a waterfall pouring itself into the greenery on Kauai.

MEXICO CITY

Location: South Mexico
Best time to travel: all year
www.mexicocity.gob.mx
www.allaboutmexicocity.com

According to unofficial figures, Mexico's capital is one of the fastest growing metropolitan areas in the world today. The metropolis lies at an altitude of 2,240 m (7,349 ft) above sea level, in a wide basin in the central highlands and on the site of the pre-Columbian city of Tenochtitlán.

The former Aztec capital was founded in about 1370 on a number of islands in the Lago de Texcoco. Following the conquest of Tenochtitlán the city was almost completely destroyed by Spanish conquistadors in 1521. They then built their churches and colonial buildings on the ruins of where Aztec temples, palaces and sanctuaries once stood. Aztec artefacts continue to be unearthed during construction work in the historical heart of Mexico. A number of Mexico City's most significant historic buildings are grouped around the main square of Zócalo. The Templo Mayor, dedicated to the Aztec gods Tlaloc and Huitzilopochtli, is the most important relic from that era. The National Palace has been the scene of key political events and now serves as the president's residence. Paintings by Diego Rivera (1886–1957) depicting scenes from Mexico's history can be seen on the staircase and in an upstairs gallery. The cathedral has a mix of styles from Renaissance to neoclassical. Magnificent patrician houses such as the Palacio de Marqués de Jaral de Berrio document Mexico's economic advancement. Architectural highlights of the 20th century include the Art Nouveau Palace of Fine Arts, built between 1901 and 1934, and the opera house (1937).

The first university in Latin America was founded in Mexico City in 1551

by King Philip II. Prior to being awarded autonomous status in 1929, the university originally comprised a collection of separate buildings in the historic heart of the city. It was only during the 1930s that plans were drawn up to building a university campus combining all of the institutes in one complex. The final plans were implemented from 1949 to 1952 at the Pedregal de San Ángel, then located outside the city. The master plan for the university's design was the work of architects Mario Pani and Enrique del Moral. Although they consistently applied the principles of contemporary architecture and modern urban development, they also managed to incorporate local traditions and building materials. Particularly remarkable is the successful integration within the architecture of works by artists such as Diego Rivera, José David Alfaro Siqueiros and others.

The "floating gardens" (chinampas, meaning "place of flower fields") in Xochimilco, a village located to the south of Mexico City, today still recall the man-made water landscape created by the Aztecs in their capital Tenochtitlán. In order to gain artificial cultivation ground from the lake, rafts were woven from reeds, and then filled with mud and fertile soil. Everything was held in place to the outside walls with the help of willows and then planted with flowers and vegetables whose roots soon took "anchor" in the shallow lake bottom. Today tourists can go boating on the canals and there is an ecological park.

The Catedral Metropolitana (top) is the second largest church in the Americas. It towers over the Zócalo, one of the largest open squares in an inner city worldwide. El Ángel (bottom left), the golden angel on the Monumento a la Independencia, flies high above the Paseo de la Reforma.

EL VIZCAÍNO, BAJA CALIFORNIA

Location: North-west Mexico (Baja California)
Best time to travel: September–June
www.parkswatch.org
www.llbean.com
www.baja.com
www.bajacalifornia.gob.mx

There is a unique marine habitat comprising the lagoons Ojo de Liebre and San Ignacio as well as several coastal lakes that extends along the Pacific Coast about halfway along the Baja California peninsula. Countless gray whales cavort here between December and March after travelling about 8,000 km (4,971 mi) from their summer territory, the Arctic Bering Sea, in order to mate and give birth in these warmer, calmer waters. Almost half of all gray whales worldwide are born in the waters of Baja California.

Blue whales, humpback whales, seals, sea lions and elephant seals also frolic here. Five of the seven sea turtle species still in existence worldwide are found here as well, while thousands of migratory birds come to spend the winter in the coastal regions each year.

The Baja California (Lower California) peninsula extends over 1,150 km (715 mi) from north to south, from Ensenada to Cabo San Lucas. It runs parallel to the Mexican coast, thus separating the Gulf of California from the Pacific Ocean. With a maximum width of 240 km (149 mi), the peninsula is divided into two federal states: Baja California Norte and Baja California Sur, north and south, respectively. The landscape of this sparsely inhabited region is mostly impassable, inhospitable and barely accessible in many areas – but it is an Eldorado for naturalists.

As well as the gray whales, blue whales and humpback whales (right) also come up near the shores of El Vizcaíno.

Baja California is dominated by succulents and cacti like the giant cardon cactus (top). The islands off the coast attract many birds, including the world's largest population of blue-footed boobies (below).

TEOTIHUACÁN

Location: South Mexico (México)
Best time to travel: September–June
www.visitmexico.com

With around 150,000 residents, the city was easily the largest in the Americas by the year 350. Its wealth was based on mining obsidian, a volcanic rock used to make tools. The decline of Teotihuacán began in the seventh century and the city was finally abandoned in about 750. The most important constructions include the more than 2-km-long (1.2-mi) and 40-m-wide (125-ft) Street of the Dead, the around 65-m-high (213-ft) Pyramid of the Sun, the somewhat smaller Pyramid of the Moon and the Temple of Quetzalcoatl.

The Pyramid of the Sun in the middle of Teotihuacán covers 222 by 225 m (728 by 738 ft) on plan.

XOCHICALCO

Location: South Mexico (Morelos)
Best time to travel: September–June
www.visitmexico.com

The pre-Columbian ruins known as Xochicalco are around 100 km (62 mi) south of Mexico City. The fortified complex, which experienced its heyday during the Epiclassic period (650–900) following the downfall of Teotihuacán, was an important political and cultural center that reflected a variety of ethnic influences. Interestingly, however, it has not yet been possible to assign Xochicalco to a specific civilization. The city was abandoned in the tenth century.

The Temple of the Feathered Serpent, dedicated to the supreme deity, stands on a plinth decorated with human figures. They are surrounded by serpents.

EL TAJÍN

Location: South-east Mexico (Veracruz)
Best time to travel: September–June
www.manos-de-oaxaca.com

El Tajín is thought to have been a center for pelota, a ball game played as a tribute to the storm god, to whom the losing players were sacrificed. The ball could only be moved with the hips, knees or elbows and thrown through a ring. Archaeological discoveries indicate a close relationship with Teotihuacán. El Tajín reached the zenith of its power following the fall of the latter in 800. The city was destroyed and abandoned about 400 years later, in around 1200.

Friezes and columns along the southern ball-game ground of Tajín display detailed reliefs depicting, here, the sacrifice of a pelota player.

MORELIA

Location: South-west Mexico (Michoacán)
Best time to travel: September–June
www.visitmorelia.com

Morelia, the capital of Michoacán located about 250 km (155 mi) west of Mexico City, enjoyed a rapid rise shortly after being founded by the viceroy of New Spain in 1541. Its first church, the Renaissance Iglesia de San Francisco, was consecrated in 1546. The building was attached to a monastery that today houses a museum of handicrafts. Twenty other churches were subsequently built and several historical colleges are also testimony to Morelia's role as an important intellectual center.

The 18th-century Palacio de Gobierno in Morelia has a beautiful patio with arcades on two levels.

CAMPECHE

Location: South-east Mexico
Best time to travel: November–April
www.campeche.ca

Campeche was founded in 1540 and served as the starting point for the Spanish crown's conquest of the Yucatán Peninsula. The hexagonal, over 2.5-km (1.8-mi) city wall was built between 1668 and 1704. Exports of the red fabric dye, palo de tinte, inspired Campeche's second golden age in the 19th century and many magnificent buildings from this era have survived: stunning city palaces, the Teatro Toro and the Catedrál de la Concepción (built in 1540–1705 on the site where the first mass is said to have been held in the New World in 1517).

The lanes in Campeche the Old Town are particularly charming.

OAXACA

Location: South-west Mexico
Best time to travel: September–June
www.go-oaxaca.com

The city of Oaxaca has a wealth of colonial-era grandeur as well as Zapotec and Mixtec culture on offer. There is a large indigenous population here. The Plaza de Armas, which is the site of the cathedral, was rebuilt after an earthquake in 1730. The Iglesia de Santo Domingo is smaller and seems inconspicuous from outside, but the interior furnishings are breathtaking.

Santo Domingo is Oaxaca's most beautiful baroque church. Once a Dominican monastery (today the Centro Cultural Santo Domingo) formed part of this church, which was largely rebuilt in the early 1700s following a huge earthquake.

POPOCATÉPETL

Location: Central Mexico (México)
Best time to travel: September–June
www.volcano.si.edu

At 5,465 m (17,931 ft), the snow-covered "smoking mountain" is the second highest peak in Mexico after Citlaltépetl at 5,700 m (18,702 ft). This stratovolcano has been unusually active again since 1994 and often emits a plume of smoke. Gas and ash from eruptions have hindered air traffic and public life in Ciudad de México on several occasions in recent years – most recently on December 1 and 2, 2007.

The construction of monasteries on Popocatépetl (left: the Church of Nuestra Señora de los Remedios Monastery) was the signal for the country's Christianization by Franciscans, Dominicans and Augustines.

MONTE ALBÁN

Location: Near the city of Oaxaca, south-west Mexico
Best time to travel: September–June
http://oaxaca-travel.com

The region around the city of Oaxaca has been settled since the sixth century BC. It was originally the Olmec people who excavated the mountain above Oaxaca Valley, but the resulting city, Monte Albán, later became the religious center of the Zapotec, who were highly developed in mathematics and writing. As Monte Albán came under the increased influence of ancient pre-Spanish city of Teotihuacán, it lost importance as a major cult site and was gradually abandoned by its up to 20,000 inhabitants after the year 800.

The pyramids and palaces of Monte Albán extend across a vast plateau.

UXMAL

Location: South-east Mexico (Yucatán)
Best time to travel: November–April
http://mayaruins.com

The ruins in Uxmal and the buildings of the sites of Kabah, Labná und Sayil, located nearby, about 80 km (50 mi) south of Mérida, are stunning highlights of classic Mayan architecure. Uxmal, like the town adjacent to it, was an important urban and ceremonial center from the eighth to the 10th centuries. The central building is the almost 40 m (131 ft) high Pyramid of the Magician. The imposing construction, which was dedicated to the rain god Chac, is in fact the fourth building to have been constructed on this site of former temples. The expansive Governor's Palace stands on a 15-m-high (49-ft) platform decorated with a

PALENQUE

Location: South-east Mexico (Chiapas)
Best time to travel: November–April
http://mayaruins.com

Palenque, a Mayan city that reached the zenith of its influence between the sixth and eighth centuries, was built between the third and the fifth centuries, when most important structures were erected. The glyphs in the Temple of the Inscriptions have been deciphered and constitute the most significant written records of Mayan culture. The untouched burial chamber of the Mayan Prince Pacal was discovered in the pyramid in 1952.
Inside the most famous temple, the 20-m-high (66-ft) Templo de las Inscripciones (Temple of the Inscriptions), are sixty steps leading into the crypt at a depth of 25 m (80 ft).

particularly impressive stone mosaic frieze. The front elevations of the Nunnery, the House of the Tortoises and the Dovecote also feature detailed stone mosaics. The peculiar features of the friezes on the façade of the great palace of Sayil are surpassed only by those of the pillar ornaments. The triumphal arches over the once cobbled streets in Labná and Kabah are rare Mayan architectural treasures. The Palace of the Masks in Kabah owes its name to the roughly 250 stone masks of the god Chac that can be seen on the front elevation.

A masterpiece of the Mayan art of building is the Governor's Palace (left, in the foreground of the picture), which sits on a giant platform. Behind it rises the Pyramid of the Soothsayer. Uxmal lost its importance after the 11th century, and it was abandoned by about the year 1200.

Similar to the Egyptians, the Palenque pyramids were also burial chambers, the valuable objects from which are now on display in the Museo Nacional de Antropologíca in Mexico City. Opposite the Temple of the Inscriptions stands the palace where the royal family lived. Its 15-m (49-ft) tower was used for astronomy while a tabletop on the upper floor functioned as an altar.

The ruins of one of the most impressive Mayan cities rise from the middle of the tropical jungle of Chiapas in southern Mexico. Although it had been discovered in 1784, Palenque was not systematically excavated and researched until the 20th century. From the so-called palace, the main structure in Palenque, a tower rises that was probably used as an observatory (far left). Almost all the buildings are decorated with lavish reliefs (left).

CHICHÉN ITZÁ

Location: South-east Mexico (Yucatán)
Best time to travel: November–April
www.chichenitza.com

These ruins extend over an area of 300 ha (741 acres) in the northern Yucatán and are the legacy of two pre-Columbian civilizations: the Maya and the Toltec. The cult site is thought to have been founded by the Maya in roughly 450. Large constructions followed in characteristically grand Mayan style such as the Complex of the Nuns or the main church. Groups influenced by the Toltec eventually moved into the abandoned Maya cult center in the 10th century and initiated a second golden age that lasted around 200 years. The transition to a Toltec-influenced sculptural and relief style that featured warrior figures and graphic atlases is clearly recognizable. The observatory (Caracol) and the Quetzalcoatl pyramid known as the Castillo are representative of this epoch and have other monumental structures (Temple of the Jaguar) as well as a variety of ball courts grouped around them.

On March 21 and September 21, the sun's rays hit the vast El Castillo pyramid in Chichén Itzá in such a way that a shadow shaped like a serpent winds its way down the stairs to meet the giant stone head of a serpent at the bottom (top right; right: the observatory).

In Chichén Itzá, the styles of ancient local Mexican cultures have combined with those of the Maya, as in this reclining figure with a bowl in the Temple of the Warrior, called "Chac-Mool" (top). The skulls of those that had been sacrificed were displayed on a tzompantli, a wall decorated with skull reliefs (below).

BELIZE BARRIER REEF

Location: Barreer reef off Belize
Best time to travel: November–April
www.travelbelize.org

The longest-living barrier reef in the northern hemisphere is located off the coast of Belize on the edge of the continental shelf. It is made up of a variety of reef types comprising around sixty-five different coral species, their bizarrely shaped thickets and columns creating an ideal habitat for countless creatures. In addition to almost 250 species of aquatic plant this fantastic diversity also includes around 350 mollusk species, sponges, shellfish and about 500 fish species (above), from eagle rays to goliath groupers. Heavily endangered aquatic creatures such as manatees, hawksbill turtles and loggerhead sea turtles also inhabit this protected area.

The islands (cayes) off the coast are mostly covered with either mangroves or palms. Accessible cayes in the area include Ambergris Caye, 58 km (36 mi) north of Belize City, and the Turneffe Islands. In addition to the underwater world, which often affords visibility of up to 30 m (65 ft), the reef's other attractions inclu-de the bird sanctuary on Half Moon Caye and the Blue Hole, a collapsed underwater cave that was found in the mid-1970s by the French marine scientist Jacques-Yves Cousteau with the help of a decommissioned minesweeper (Calypso).

The Blue Hole in the Belize Barrier Reef is located some 80 km (50 mi) east of Belize City. The coral reefs were described as early as 1842 by the Charles Darwin. About 10,000 years ago, an underwater cave had collapsed here and the land sank to the seafloor. The circular Blue Hole has a diameter of about 300 m (984 ft) and is 125 m (410 ft) deep.

ANTIGUA GUATEMALA

Location: South Guatemala
Best time to travel: November–April
www.roadtoantigua.com

The Spanish conquerors founded the "noble" and "royal" city of Antigua in the highlands of Guatemala at the foot of three volcanoes in 1543. During the decades that followed, the capital of the Spanish colonial empire in Mesoamerica, situated at an altitude of 1,500 m (4,922 ft), developed into a virtual metropolis with up to 70,000 inhabitants. San Carlos de Borromeo, the first papal university in Central America, was founded here in 1675. Built in Italian Renaissance style, Antigua, with its checkerboard layout, flourished for two centuries before being destroyed by an earthquake in 1773. The impressive ruins and rebuilt churches, cathedrals, monasteries, palaces and townhouses are testimony to the city's former economic, cultural and clerical significance. Today, the grandiose baroque colonial buildings still make it possible to see why Antigua was considered the loveliest capital in the New World.

The Agua volcano rises steeply from its surroundings. Despite damaged sustained during an earthquake, the former capital of Guatemala (top: an Easter procession) is still one of the most attractive cities built in the Spanish colonial style.

TIKAL

Location: North Guatemala
Best time to travel: November–April
www.tikalpark.com

The site was first settled in around 800 BC. A giant complex of temples and palaces was built starting in the third century. During Tikal's golden age (550–900), up to 90,000 people lived in this temple city. To date, more than 3,000 buildings and complexes have been excavated in the 15-sq-km (6-sq-mi) area that was the city center – magnificent palaces as well as simple huts and ball courts. The most spectacular are the five huge temple pyramids, one of which is 65 m (213 ft) high, the highest of all Maya constructions.

This fragment of a vase is proof of the high standard of artisanship among the Maya.

QUIRIGUÁ

Location: East Guatemala
Best time to travel: November–April
www.enjoyguatemala.com
www.authenticmaya.com

This Mayan city reached the height of its prosperity until the eighth and ninth centuries, a fact that is reflected in a wealth of art treasures. The majority of the famous monumental stelae, which have made Quiriguá famous, date from this golden age. The elaborate and finely worked sculptures on the monolithic sandstone blocks are sculptural masterpieces and depict political and military events – including the execution of the ruler Copán on the main square in 738.

Like many other sculptures, Stele D depicts Quiriguá's most powerful ruler, Cauac Sky.

RÍO PLÁTANO

Location: North-east Honduras
Best time to travel: November–April
http://visithonduras.net

The amazingly beautiful Río Plátano Biosphere Reserve, which covers an area of 830,000 ha (2,050,930 acres), extends from the north coast to the interior of Honduras to an elevation of more than 1,300 m (4,265 ft) above sea level. The largely mountainous region covers about seven percent of the country's territory. Lagoons and mangrove forests alternate beyond pristine beaches while coastal savannah with beak rush sedge and other marsh plants meets palms and lowland pines. Tropical and subtropical rainforests with all of their biodiversity can be found deeper in the interior. The reserve's wild inhabitants include jaguars, pumas and ocelots, king vultures and harpy eagles, manatees, tapirs and pacas, as well as a number of monkeys. In addition to the indigenous Miskito, Pech and Tawahka peoples, the Garifuna (an ethnic group of Caribbean and African descent) and Mestize also live here. There are also some archeological sites with Mayan remains as well as traces of another pre-Columbian civilization.

The residents at the biosphere reserve include mantled howler monkeys and white-nosed coati (above left/right).

COPÁN

Location: West-Honduras
Best time to travel: November–April
www.copanhonduras.org

Copán was one of the most important city-states that thrived during the Mayan golden age in around 700. One of the earliest descriptions of Copán is that by Diego García de Palacio from 1570, but the city was not actually excavated until the 19th century. Hundreds of ruins are thought to still exist under the earth mounds in the Copán Valley.
The Acropolis – a complex of interconnected constructions in the shape of pyramids, temples and terraces – forms the center of what has been excavated to date. Altar Q, in which the names of sixteen rulers of Copán are carved, is especially remarkable. The Hieroglyphic Stairway is Copán's most important monument. Close to 2,500 glyphs cover the sixty-three steps and form the longest Mayan text to date. It pays tribute to the achievements of the dynasty from its founding through to the opening of the staircase in the year 755. The ball court with three marker stones, which occurs in this form only in Copán, is also worthy of note.

On the terrain of the site of ruins are elabroately carved eighth-century stelae (above: Stele B). They depict the Maya rulers and their actions and achievements.

COSTA RICA'S SPECTACULAR MOUNTAINS OF FIRE

Location: Central Costa Rica
Best time to travel: December–April
www.visitcostarica.com

Tiny Costa Rica has a number of national parks within a relatively small area that are all still climatically very different: from the humid, tropical Caribbean side to the arid regions in the Pacific side, and from the marsh areas in the east to the rain forests of the central highlands and the dry forests of the northwest with its prickly bushes. Both coasts of the country also serve as breeding grounds for sea turtles. This was the inspiration for setting up the Tortuguero National Park, which is only accessible by boat.

Costa Rica's spectacular mountains of fire are situated east of the island's capital San José, on the edge of the Valle Central. Some of them have crater lakes such as Irazú (3,432 m/11,260 ft) and Poás (2,704 m/8,872 ft), which feature geyser-like eruptions of muddy water and steam. Arenal erupted again in 1968 after being dormant for centuries and the crater now emits a constant plume of smoke.

The Poas volcano has two craters that are filled with water. The water in the top crater is clear and cold, while the lower crater (above) holds an acid lake that is 300 m (984 ft) deep and has a diameter of 1,300 m (4,265 ft).

TALAMANCA AND LA AMISTAD

Location: South Costa Rica/Panama
Best time to travel: December–April
www.infocostarica.com

The cross-border reserve shared by Costa Rica and Panama and covering 800,000 ha (1,976,800 acres) boasts the greatest biodiversity of fauna and flora in the world. It overs the Central Cordillera de Talamanca from southern Costa Rica to western Panama and ranges from sea level all the way up to an elevation of roughly 3,800 m (12,468 ft). The wide spectrum of very diverse habitats and landscapes is predominantly covered with tropical rain forest, which has been growing here for 25,000 years. Above the lowlands are cloud forests and areas of sub-alpine paramo with bushes and grasses as well as areas with evergreen oaks, moors and lakes. Its topographic and climatic variety as well as its geographic location at the juncture between North and South America mean that the park has no shortage of unique flora and fauna. Human beings have also been living in this region for many thousands of years.

The reserve is covered in tropical rainforest, an ideal habitat for birds (top left: a long-tailed silky-flycatcher; below a quetzal) as well as more than 200 species of mammal, including the jaguar (above right), puma and ocelot.

BAHAMAS

Location: Island state in Central America (West Indies)
Best time to travel: all year
www.bahamas.com
www.thebahamasguide.com

"It's better in the Bahamas" was the islands' tourist slogan for many years. Lying on a white sandy beach, forgetting everything under palms waving in the gentle wind, and washing away your cares in the pleasantly warm waters you might be tempted to agree. Pastel-colored houses in the blazing sunshine, vibrant corals and turquoise water. The Bahamas indeed provide the perfect holiday and wellbeing atmosphere. This island nation comprises about 700 islands and has been independent since 1973. Among the best-known islands are New Providence Island with the capital Nassau, Cable Beach and Paradise Island as well as Grand Bahama with Freeport, the islands' economic hub and the home of a great many gambling casinos. The Family or Out Islands are only accessible via light aircraft or by boat. The British influence can still be felt everywhere and, combined with the jet-set atmosphere in Nassau and Freeport and the Caribbean charm of the Family Islands, it contributes to some of the islands' appeal. The water is warm and clear and the reefs off the Bahamas are among the loveliest in the world.

Shipwrecks, not a rarity in the waters around the Bahamas, attract vast shoals of fish – and these are welcome prey for predators such as sharks and barracudas (opposite page).

This page top: a market scene in Freeport; below: starfish off San Salvador, where Columbus is said to have stepped on land during his first voyage to America.

HAVANA, VIÑALES

Location: North Cuba (Havana), North-west Cuba (Viñales)
Best time to travel: all year
www.cuba.com

Havana is not only one of the oldest but also one of the most fascinating cities in the New World. To protect the merchant harbor, where all the gold and silver transports were shipped from the Americas back to Spain, the Spanish built mighty fortifications between the 16th and the 18th centuries.
The Old Town was laid out in a checkerboard plan in which the grid of streets is frequently broken up by spacious squares. The main square, Plaza de Armas, features impressively restored colonial buildings such as the Palacio del Segundo Cabo. One of the most attractive baroque structures is the Palacio de los Capitanes Generales. Among the religious buildings in town, the Cathedral stands out. Completed in 1704, Alejo Carpentier once called it "music that has become stone". A worthwhile detour from Havana is an excursion to the west of the island where traditional forms of agriculture are still practiced in the Viñales Valley.

Bizarre "mogotes" stand in the Viñales Valley, rugged cone-shaped rocks that were formed 150 million years ago. They were once part of an extensive system of caves which collapsed. What remained are the rock formations, which look like giant glacial erratics. Tobacco is grown everywhere in this region.

"Queen of the Caribbean" is just one of Havana's epithets; Lovingly "pimped-up" classic cars serve as taxis in the center; Fidel Castro is still omnipresent; the ladies of the night dance at the Tropicana.

FIDEL

JAMAICA

Location: Island state in Central America (Caribbean)
Best time to travel: all year
www.visitjamaica.com

"Xaymaca" – "the land of forest and water" – is how the indigenous Arawak named their little slice of paradise in the Caribbean Sea. It is a fitting name for this place, which is separated from Cuba by the up to 7,240-m-deep (23,754-ft) Cayman Trough. Discovered by Christopher Columbus for the Spanish Crown in 1492, it has been a parliamentary monarchy within the British Commonwealth since 1962. The partly swampy coastal regions, characterized by mangroves and coconut palms, feature a number of good swimming beaches. About two-thirds of the island is comprised of a very heavily karstified limestone plateau. Jamaica rises in elevation as one travels from west to east, and forms of the tropical cockpit or cone karst can also be found in abundance in Cockpit Country. The eastern Blue Mountains are home to the 2,292-m-high (7,520-ft) peak of the same name, which is also the the island's highest point.

Jamaica offers a wide variety of natural ecosystems with densely overgrown mountains, rolling hills, fern-covered river valleys and breathtakingly beautiful beaches (top right: the north coast). Especially stunning is the sight of the waterfalls gushing from the tropical greenery into the turquoise sea (bottom right: the Dunn's River Falls; center: Cockpit County).

Modern cruise ships resemble floating leisure parks. They lack in nothing, from the department store to the saltwater swimming pool, like here aboard the MV Galaxy in the harbor of Montego Bay (large picture).

SAN JUAN

Location: Island state in Central America (Caribbean)
Best time to travel: all year
http://welcome.topuertorico.org

The island state of Puerto Rico belongs to the West Indies and is associated with the United States. The gigantic fortress jutting into the sea at the tip of the island and visible from afar attests as to the importance that San Juan, Puerto Rico's capital city, once had for the Spanish colonial masters, Dominating the harbor entrance with its more than 40-m-high (131-ft) ramparts, the complex consists of four sections. The first, La Fortaleza or Palacio de Santa Catalina, has been the seat of the Governor of Puerto Rico since 1822. Fort San Felipe del Morro (1539), at the harbor entrance, is the most conspicuous part of the whole complex. A smaller fortress, San Juan de la Cruz (1606), was built in a strategic position in front of Fort San Felipe del Morro, and a fourth fort, San Cristóbal (1634), protected the fortress from inland attack. Despite all the effort, though, it was not possible to stop Puerto Rico becoming part of the United States in 1898, at the end of the Spanish American War, without ever having fought a battle.

San Juan with the El Morro fortress (top) and its historic inner city (below), eternally washed by the Caribbean Sea.

MORNE TROIS PITONS

Location: Island state in Central America (Caribbean)
Best time to travel: October–April
http://tourism.gov.dm
www.dominica.dm

The climax of any visit to the third-largest of the Lesser Antilles is the Morne Trois Pitons National Park, founded in 1975 and featuring beautiful mist and rain forests, as well as numerous lakes and waterfalls. This nature reserve, which covers nearly 7,000 hectares (17,297 acres), offers a unique habitat for a number of plant and animal species. Nearly 150 bird species populate these forests and the various volcanic formations surrounding the still-active Morne Trois Pitons Volcano are of breathtaking beauty. Roughly fifty fumaroles, hot springs and five active volcanic craters can be found between the rugged and densely overgrown canyons. Hot mud bubbles up from one boiling lake. The Emerald Pool (above) also owes its unusual hue to the elementary powers at the center of the earth.

At the feet of the 1,342-m-high (4,403-ft) Morne Trois Pitons on Dominica extends the eponymous national park which enchants visitors with its tropic forests full of animal and plant species and its bizarre volcanic rock formations. Fumaroles, such as these in the Valley of Desolation, reveal the volcanic origins of the environs.

TRINIDAD AND TOBAGO

Location: Island state in Central America (Caribbean)
Best time to travel: January–May
www.gotrinidadandtobago.com

This island republic consisting of the two main islands of Trinidad and Tobago as well as several smaller islands is situated north-east of Venezuela and forms the southern part of the Caribbean island arc. Trinidad, the largest of the Lesser Antilles islands, received its name from the three prominent mountain chains that traverse the island and reach elevations of 941 m (3,087 ft). The considerably smaller island of Tobago is located 32 km (20 mi) to the north-east of Trinidad and is traversed by the densely forested Main Ridge range, this one only reaching elevations of up to 576 m (1,890 ft). Both islands were "discovered" for Spain by Christopher Columbus in 1498. The Spanish had fully colonized Trinidad by 1552, but in 1797 it was taken from them by the British. In 1814, Tobago also became a British colony and in 1888 it was united with Trinidad. In 1962 the state of Trinidad and Tobago gained its independence, and since 1976 it has been a republic within the British Commonwealth. Trinidad and Tobago is particularly famous for its vibrant street carnival.

Nowhere else in the Caribbean can you see such stunning costumes in the first few weeks of the year. Weeks or months before the actual climax of the carnival in February, the lavish costumes are sewn and decorated with palettes and feathers. After the carnival in Rio, for which many of the costumes are actually made in Trinidad and Tobago, this is the second largest carnival in the world.

ST LUCIA

Location: Island state in Central America (Caribbean)
Best time to travel: January–May
www.stlucia.org

St Lucia, the birthplace of Derek Walcott, winner of the Nobel Prize for Literature, has lovingly been called by the British and the French "The beautiful Helena of the West Indies". Indeed, both European nations have had great influence on the history of the island – it changed hands between the two powers fourteen times until it finally became British in the Treaty of Paris in 1815. Since 1979, St Lucia has been independent but it has remained a member state of the British Commonwealth. Even more exciting than a visit to the capital, Castries, is a trip around the island to the Pitons Nature Reserve, an area near Soufrière in the south-west that covers roughly 30 sq km (12 sq mi) and is well worth the time. The nature reserve includes the mountain ridge, a field of solfataras with fumaroles and hot springs as well as some adjacent marine areas. Nearly sixty percent of the underwater area was once covered in coral, but Hurricane "Lenny" (1999) destroyed much of this. The establishment of zones where fishing is forbidden has now led to a recovery of the stocks that has made the area around the Pitons one of the most biodiverse in the entire Caribbean.

The cone-shaped twin peaks of the Gros Piton (770 m/2,526 ft) and Petit Piton (743 m/2,438 ft) form a landmark of the Lesser Antilles that is visible from vast distances. Created during a volcanic eruption, they were described by Walcott as the "Horns of the Caribbean".

SANTA CRUZ DE MOMPOX

Location: North Colombia
Best time to travel: October–April
www.santacruzdemompos-bolivar.gov.co

For a long time, Santa Cruz de Mompox was an important inland port on the trade route to Cartagena. Today the Río Magdalena flows through another riverbed and the town has lost its importance. The historic heart of the city, with its harmonious architecture in Spanish colonial style is more like an open-air museum unique to Colombia. Instead of just one central square, Mompox boasts three squares that form its center, all linked by the Calle de la Albarrada.

The strangest structure is the baroque octagonal tower of Santa Bárbara, with its balcony.

SAN AGUSTIN

Location: South Colombia
Best time to travel: October–April
www.colombia.travel

South of Tierradentro in southern Colombia is the most important archeological site in the country, and one that features the largest collection of religious monuments and megalithic sculptures in South America. The region around the excavation site, in the area where the Río Magdalena rises, was already settled in the 5th century BC. The most impressive discoveries are the idolos: stone figures of humans and animals that recall the statues of the Mayan gods in Central America. Sarcophagi have also been excavated.

Vast anthropomorphic monoliths are the main attraction among the finds in the Park of San Agustín.

TIERRADENTRO

Location: South Colombia
Best time to travel: October–April
www.tierradentro.info
www.turismocolombia.com

The archaeological park of Tierradentro in the Cordillera Central in southern Colombia is littered with superbly decorated subterranean tombs that are unique in South America for their size as well as their unusual access staircases. Above ground, several figures have also been found that were cut into the stone. This site probably had its time of greatest productivity in the years 500 BC to AD 500.

The excavations in the archaeological park (left: a pre-Colombian golden mask) probably date back to a farming culture with a highly developed cult of the dead.

CARTAGENA

Location: North Colombia
Best time to travel: October–April
www.cartagenainfo.com

Founded in 1533, this port city quickly developed into a flourishing center for the trade in gold and slaves thanks to its favorable location on the Caribbean coast. In the middle of the 16th century, however, attacks by pirates became more frequent and so the city was fortified. When the English buccaneer Sir Francis Drake captured Cartagena in 1586, a 12-m-high (39-ft) and up to 18-m-thick (60-ft) defensive wall was built. The largest fortification wall in the New World, it managed to once again withstand attacks by the British in the 18th century.

Cartagena's walls had to withstand many attacks over time.

CANAIMA

Location: South-east Venezuela
Best time to travel: October–April
www.think-venezuela.net

In the language of the Camarocoto Indians who live here, the name "Canaima" represents a somewhat sinister god who manifests all evil within himself. Im By contrast, the national park – which covers about 3 million ha (7.4 million acres), the second-largest in Venezuela – captivates with its overwhelming natural beauty. Located in the south-east of the country, on the borders with Guyana and Brazil, the park extends across the magnificent landscape of the Gran Sabana. It is filled with dense vegetation and spectacular waterfalls such as the Salto Ángel, the Salto Kukenam and the cascades of the Canaima Lagoon, which plunge over breathtaking cliffs.
Between 3,000 and 5,000 species of flowering plants and ferns are said to exist here – many of them endemic. Aside from savannah it also features impenetrable montane forests and scrubland. On the many tepuy, or flat-topped mountains, a special, even enterprising vegetation has developed that includes carnivorous plants. Of the roughly 900 plant species that have been recorded on one of these tepuys, at least one-tenth are endemic. Colorful butterflies, hummingbirds and parrots flutter through these forests while on the ground, mammals like great anteaters, giant armadillos, giant otters, forest dogs and ocelots prowl around. The Catalan Captain Félix Cardona Puig was the first white man to see the powerful Salto Ángel waterfall in 1927. It was ultimately named after the American pilot, Jimmy Angel, however, who flew there in 1933, with his single-engine propeller plane.

The highest waterfall on Earth, the spectacular Salto Ángel plunges 1,000 m (3,281 ft) down down the north-east side of the mighty 2,500-m-high (8,203-ft) Auyántepui (right and top).

CUENCA

Location: South Ecuador
Best time to travel: October–April
www.ecuador.travel

When the Spanish arrived here, it was already an important settlement known as Tomebamba, originally founded by the Cañaris Indians and later taken over by the Inca. But by the time Gil Ramírez Dávalos arrived and established Santa Ana de los Ríos de Cuenca here in 1557, only the ruins of the Inca ruler Huayna Cápac's former metropolis remained. It had been destroyed in the war between the last two Inca kings.
The Spanish built Cuenca using a grid style around a central square, the Plaza Abdón Calderón, and it is here that the heart of the city still beats. The Old Cathedral with its squat bell tower from 1557 stands here. The New Cathedral, just opposite, dominates the cityscape. When the city experienced a period of prosperity in the second half of the 19th century thanks to the sale of quinine and handmade straw hats, many of the old houses were "modernized". Now, the unusual combination of local and European architectural features is what gives the city its special flair.

Many local people regard Cuenca, the "Athens of Ecuador", as the most attractive city in the country (above: the mighty domes of the New Cathedral).

QUITO

Location: South Ecuador
Best time to travel: all year
www.quito.com.ec
www.inquito.com

Quito, located at an elevation of 2,850 m (9,351 ft), is the oldest town in South America. The volcano-fringed upper basin was settled by the Caras Indians in pre-Inca days. Under Huayna Cápac it developed into the second-largest administrative center of the Inca Empire. Spanish conquistadores ultimately destroyed this northernmost outpost of the Incas and in 1534, Spanish Sebastián de Belalcázar founded "San Francisco de Quito" on its ruins. The historic center of Quito today is the place with the highest density of colonial art treasures in South America.

The Church and Convent of San Francisco, the largest and oldest place of worship in the city, was built by the so-called Quito School of Art, which combines the various style influences of Spanish, Italian, Moorish, Flemish and South American indigenous art.

Only a few years after the town had been founded in 1534, the Franciscans already started building San Francisco. The church and convent were completed in 1580, creating Quito's most outstanding architectural treasure as well as the largest preserved historical complex of buildings anywhere in South America.

GALAPAGOS ISLANDS

Location: Island group west of South America
Best time to travel: July–December
www.savegalapagos.org
www.galapagosislands.com

About 1,000 km (625 mi) off the west coast of Ecuador, out in the middle of the Pacific Ocean, is a spot where hot magma from the core of the earth reaches its surface. The oldest in the easternmost part developed some 2.4 to 3 million years ago. Fernandina, in the west of the archipelago, is the youngest island, notching up just 700,000 years. Three major ocean currents flow around the archipelago including the Humboldt Current, which brings cold water from the icy polar regions right up to the Equator. Other currents bring life from the tropical and subtropical regions of Central and South America as well as the Indo-Pacific region, all of which have made the Galapagos Islands a swirling melting pot of the most diverse species. The geographic isolation of the archipelago also offered the best conditions for flora and fauna to develop in complete isolation. Darwin's observation of species of finches that were nearly identical but which had developed different beak shapes according to the specific island they were on allowed him to gain valuable insights for the development of his theory of evolution.

The Galapagos consist of twelve larger and more than 100 smaller volcanic islands. Primeval animals were able to survive here such as the Galapagos land iguana (right). Galapagos giant tortoises (opposite bottom left) are the largest living land tortoises. Marine iguanas (opposite bottom right) feed exclusively from the sea.

MACHU PICCHU

Location: South Peru
Best time to travel: April–September
www.machupicchu.org
www.rediscovermachupicchu.com

The first white person to discover Machu Picchu was the American Hiram Bingham in 1835. Bingham called the settlement Machu Picchu, meaning "Old peak", in reference to its location below the Huayna Picchu, or "Young peak". Simply put, everything seems mysterious about this Inca settlement, which sits like an eagle's eyrie on top of a flat mountain at an altitude of 2,430 m (7,973 ft) and is hidden in the tropical montane forest of the eastern Andes.

What makes this place above the Río Urubamba Valley so fascinating is not just the amazingly well-preserved buildings but also the unique harmony between architecture and nature. The structures are perfectly adapted to the uneven terrain around them.

Speculation continues to this day as to the significance of this town, which was never discovered or even noticed by the Spanish colonists. Perhaps it was no more than an attempt by the Inca to also colonize the easterly slopes of the Andes. All that is certain is that the city was built around 1450 and abandoned again just one hundred years later.

The complex is divided into two areas: the agricultural zone out on the steep mountain slopes, with terraces for arable farming that were integrated into a sophisticated irrigation system, and the unfortified urban district with palaces, temples and residential buildings. Among the most remarkable structures are the Round Tower, the Sun Temple and the Temple of the Three Windows.

One of the most impressive examples of the perfect harmony between architecture and its natural surroundings is the "forgotten city" of Machu Picchu, located in a majestic high mountain landscape. Also known as the "city in the clouds", the Inca settlement was set up on several levels in the form of terraces on a high plateau (right; below: detail of some of the well-preserved structures).

CUZCO

Location: South Peru
Best time to travel: April–September
www.cuzco.info

Cuzco is one of the oldest cities in the New World that still exists today. This region was already settled by farming peoples in about 1000 BC, and about 2,000 years later it became the focal point of the powerful Inca Empire.

According to one creation myth, the city, located at 3,400 m (11,155 ft) above sea level, is said to have been founded in about 1200 by Manco Cápac, the first mythical Inca ruler. Over the 300 years or so that followed, Cuzco developed into the most sumptuous Inca city in the empire and became the political, religious and cultural heart of the ancient realm.

Most of the temples and palaces were built during this imperial period, which began with the accession to power of King Pachacútec (1438). It is said that numerous buildings were clad in gold and copper plates. In 1533, the conquistador Francisco Pizarro brutally conquered the city. missionaries built their churches and monasteries on top of the ruins of the Inca temples. The Santo Domingo Monastery was built on the site of the Temple of the Sun, the central sanctuary of the ancient temple district. The Plaza de Armas, during the Inca period the center of the city and the location of religious ceremonies, has preserved its colonial-era character until the present day. The domed Jesuit La Compañía Church is one of Peru's most beautiful baroque structures.

The block structures in the Sacsayhuamán Inca fortress near Cuzco seem the work of giants. It is a mystery how the Inca moved stones up to 200 tons in weight without wheels or rolls.

AMAZON, MANAUS

Location: Northern half of South America (Amazonia), North-west-Brazil (Manaus)
Best time to travel: June–October
www.manuperuamazon.com

The river is only called the Amazon after its confluence with the Rio Negro 18 km (11 mi) downstream from Manaus. In its middle reaches it is called the Solimõe, into which three tributaries flow: the Maranón, the Huallaga and the Ucayali, all of which rise in the Andes. The other tributaries – the Rio Negro, Rio Madeira, Rio Tapajós and Rio Xingu – are of great size as well. The difference between the ebb and flow in the Amazon can be up to 15 m (49 ft). After Manaus the river is very sluggish and seldom less than 5 km (3 mi) wide, except near Óbidos where it narrows to 2 km (1.2 mi) and can reach depths of 100 m (328 ft). Scientists have theorized that the source of the primeval Amazon was originally in the Sahara. It has been proven that the river once flowed in the opposite direction, namely into the Pacific. South America and Africa, then one continent, began to split apart 70 million years ago. The upthrust of the Andes then began at the same time as the American Plate slid westward under the East Pacific Plate. For a long time the river flowed westward through Guayaquil. The current direction only dates from six million years ago.

The Amazon is by far the largest river system on earth: its catchment area is larger than Europe (large picture).

FUNAI, a governmental agency, protects the interests and culture of the Amazon Indians (opposite top: Kayapó; bottom Yanomami). The ocelot (opposite center) is hunted for its attractive fur.

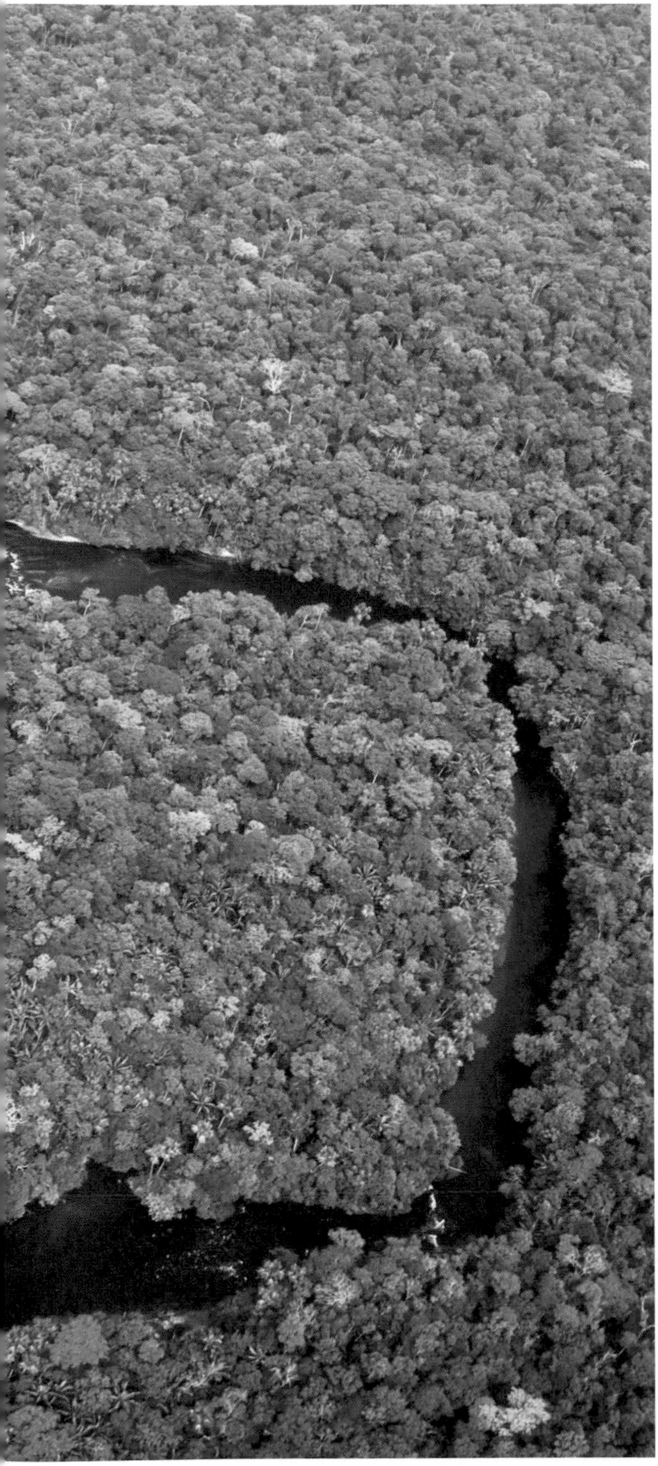

SALVADOR DA BAHIA

Location: East Brazil
Best time to travel: all year
www.bahia.com.br

In 1501, Italian seafarer Amerigo Vespucci landed at this site on the Atlantic coast where fifty years later Salvador da Bahia de Todos los Santos was founded, the city of the "Holy Savior of the Bay of All Saints". The city was Brazil's first capital, a title it held between 1549 and 1763, and it was here at Cafuá das Mercês that the first slave market in the New World took place back in 1558.

The best-preserved buildings from the colonial era are found in the district of Pelourinho, including the Igreja de Nossa Senhora do Rosário dos Pretos (Our Lady of the Rosary of Black People monastery).

OLINDA

Location: East Brazil
Best time to travel: June–October
www.brazil-travel-guide.com

Olinda's Old Town is known as the "Pearl of the Brazilian Baroque" and spans several palm-covered hilltops. "O linda situação para uma vila" was how the Portuguese described this "beautiful location for a city" before founding the settlement on the Atlantic coast in 1535. Around twenty baroque churches and countless "passos" – small chapels – as well as monasteries such as São Francisco and São Bento remain as testimony to the city's tremendous religious significance.

The São Francisco monastery was founded in 1585, making it the oldest Franciscan church in Brazil. The tiles in the sacristy depict scenes from the life of St Francis.

RIO DE JANEIRO

Location: East Brazil
Best time to travel: all year
www.riodejaneiro.com

Very few cities in the world enjoy a location and a backdrop as breathtaking as Rio de Janeiro. When Portuguese seafarer André Gonçalvez arrived with his ships in expansive Guanabara Bay on January 1, 1502, he thought he had discovered an estuary. As a result, he called what he thought to be a river the Rio de Janeiro – January River. Today, Brazil's former capital (since 1960 Brasília in the country's interior has been the capital of Brazil) boasts two of the world's most famous beaches – Copacabana and Ipanema – as well as the flamboyant and enormously sensual Carnival in Rio.

The famous statue of Christ with outstretched arms on top of the 704-m (2,310-ft) Corcovado mountain (top) and the 394-m (1,293-ft) Sugar Loaf mountain (below) are the most recognizable icons in the metropolis.

PANTANAL

Location: West Brazil/Paraguay/ Bolivia
Best time to travel: all year
http://pantanaltourism.com

The Pantanal wetlands are located in the very south-eastern corner of Brazil, close to the border with Bolivia and Paraguay. During the torrential summer rains between November and April the substantial rivers systems of the Rio Cuiabá and Rio Paraguai flood a lowland area that is three times the size of Costa Rica to form a vast expanse of wetlands with shallow lakes, marshes and swamps. These annual floods function well as a natural control mechanism that regulates the exchange of groundwater and freshwater as well as purifying the existing supply. The sediment and nutrients brought by the floodwaters then enable lush grasslands to develop here during the drier winter from the end of April to October, when the rivers once again subside. Pantanal's unique landscape – the largest wetland in the world – is particularly spectacular during these hot, humid months when the sky tends to possess a semi-permanent haze. The rich tropical fauna of this area is also remarkable.

The Pantanal is one of the largest freshwater wetland areas in the world. The flowers and leaves of the Santa Cruz water lily are spread out on the water's surface.

IGUAÇU

Location: South-west Brazil/ Argentina/Paraguay
Best time to travel: all year
www.cataratasdoiguacu.com.br

Iguaçu Falls, where Brazil, Argentina and Paraguay meet, can be heard long before they actually come into view. Initially it is a faint gurgling that quickly swells into a deafening, thunderous roar. The Iguaçu River, lined with dense tropical vegetation and called the Iguazú in Argentina, is about 1 km (0.6 mi) wide where it approaches the horseshoe-shaped precipice. The falls then crash with impressive power over a cliff that is 2,700 m (850 ft) in length – an amazing natural spectacle. More than 270 individual waterfalls have been counted here. After Niagara, it has the second greatest annual flow of any falls in the world.
The adjacent Iguaçu National Park on the Brazilian side covers an area of 1,700 sq km (656 sq mi) and provides refuge for a vast range of endangered species. Parrots and white-bellied nothuras flit around under the protection of dense forests while swifts build their nests in the craggy rocks between the waterfalls. Ocelot, jaguar, tapirs, ant bears and collared peccaries populate the lush greenery of the rainforest.

Local Indians call the largest cataract of the roaring Iguaçu Falls "Garganta del Diablo", meaning Throat of the Devil.

LAKE TITICACA

Location: East Peru/West Bolivia
Best time to travel: all year
www.titicaca.info

With a surface area of 8,300 sq km (204 sq mi), it is the largest lake in South America, and it lies at an elevation of 3,812 m (12,507 ft). The roughly 200-m-high (656-ft) Isla del Sol contains Inca cultural and ritual sites. According to Inca legend, the island is the birthplace of the sun god. Beyond the geological islands on Lake Titicaca, there are also a number of man-made floating islands on the lake. They were created in pre-Inca times by the Uros (Uru), fisher folk who live on these artificial islands.). Initially they used reeds mixed with earth just to build the foundations of their houses on land. The continual rise in the water level, however, meant that they had to keep raising these foundations until some of the houses began floating on the lake during the floods. Since this had advantages for fishing, the Uros made a virtue out of necessity – the concept also afforded them protection from Inca attacks, and some islands have watchtowers. The Uros simply retreated to their floating islands on the lake whenever there was threat of an invasion.

Lake Titicaca is about 190 km (118 mi) long and up to 50 km (31 mi) wide. The state border between Peru and Bolivia runs right across the lake.

TORRES DEL PAINE

Location: South Chile
Best time to travel: all year
www.torresdelpaine.com
www.tourismchile.com

The mountains of the Torres del Paine range rise directly from the expansive, windswept plain. They consist of steep, seemingly impregnable peaks and massive granite formations with the 3,050-m (10,007-ft) Cerro Torre Grande as their highest point. Cerro Torre is then surrounded by the only slightly lower peaks of Paine Chico, Torres del Paine and Cuernos del Paine. This is Chile's adventure paradise and offers a wide range of hiking trails for both short day tours or longer treks that take visitors through the entire park and last several days. All of these fascinating excursions take you along bluish white, milkily opaque glacial lakes on which ice floes float, over the Grey Glacier and along the swift-moving Río Paine river, which cascades into Lago Pehoe lake. Gnarled trees bracing themselves against the wind are a unique feature of the park, as are the colorful plains covered in wildflowers, endangered Andean condors, various waterfowl and endemic guanacos. Any trip to this region requires good preparation.

The steep granite towers of the Chilean Torres del Paine rise up to 3,050 m (10,000 ft) high from the beautiful, wildlfower-strewn plains of southern Patagonia.

ATACAMA

Location: North Chile
Best time to travel: all year
www.explore-atacama.com

The heart of the Atacama Desert is the driest place in the world. The Humboldt Current, an ocean current off the Pacific coast, carries cold water from the Antarctic northward. Due to the lack of wind, the steep coastal mountains then trap fog rising from the ocean – and therefore the moisture – which keeps it from reaching the interior. This results in an extremely dry climate, with some places having never recorded any form of precipitation since records have been taken. To put it mildly, it is an inhospitable environment that can be very warm during the day and uncomfortably cold at night. Yet it is anything but monotonous. The ocher desert mountains and snow-covered volcanoes are as enchanting as the deep blue and green lagoons and the scattered oases. A booming economy does not always require a fertile landscape. The desert, too, has its riches. In this case, these riches made Chile a wealthy country back in the 19th century, initially with saltpeter, an essential raw material for the manufacture of gunpowder and artificial fertilizers. At that time, however, the Atacama did not yet belong to Chile. This vast region was shared by Peru and Bolivia, Chile having become involved in the saltpeter business only through a company in Antofagasta. In 1879, when the Bolivian government made an attempt to expropriate the company, Chile made its move. The army occupied the town, instigating the Saltpeter War. Peru and Bolivia lost the war in 1883 and Chile then enjoyed a saltpeter monopoly. Most of the towns are

derelict nowadays, but new towns continue to appear elsewhere in the desert: Chuquicamata, for instance, not far from Calama. This small town was built up around the world's largest opencast copper mine. The desert also holds other mineral reserves including sulfur, phosphate, gold, silver, manganese, molybdenum, rhenium and lithium.

San Pedro de Atacama is the best jumping off point for exploring this impressive desert region. About 12 km (7.5 mi) to the west is the Valle de la Luna a bizarre, waterless erosion landscape created primarily by wind (since there is no precipitation). "Moon valley" is most impressive at sunset and at full moon when the sandstone glows in all manner of colors, from ocher-yellow and orange to deep red and violet, with everything bathed in pale white moonlight. Almost 100 km (62 mi) north of San Pedro de Atacama is the Géiser el Tatio geyser field. Located at an elevation of 4,300 m (14,100 ft), it is one of the highest geyser fields worldwide. These geysers should be visited before sunrise because it is only at dusk and in the early morning hours that they are at their most active. Bubbling up from dozens of holes in this volcanic landscape, they make for a fascinating spectacle. The salt lake south of San Pedro covers an area of 3,000 sq km (1,158 sq mi). It is no shiny, white salt lake, but rather a crusty, brown-white clay mixture interspersed with salt crystals. There are a number of individual water basins in the lake, however, that form small, clear lagoons.

Top: a salt lake, with several stratovolcanoes in the background; below: the spectacular Géiser el Tatio.

RAPA NUI (EASTER ISLAND)

Location: Island in the south-east Pacific (Chile)
Best time to travel: August–March
www.netaxs.com
www.gonomad.com

Two million years ago the Rano Kau volcano rose up out of the vast Pacific Ocean. The island that this uplifting created originally comprised 77 smaller craters. At a distance of some 3,700 km (2,299 mi) from the South American mainland and around 4,200 km (2,610 mi) from Tahiti, Easter Island) is one of the most isolated places on earth. The island was first settled as early as AD 400. A second wave of settlement is thought to have taken place in the 14th century, when the legendary King Hotu Matua arrived here with his Polynesian followers. The Polynesians called the island Rapa Nui, meaning "Big island". The main testaments to their culture are the several hundred "moais", tuff sculptures, measuring up to 10 m (33 ft) in height and standing on large platforms known as "ahu", as well as the Rongorongo script, a kind of pictorial writing. The significance of the moais has not yet been established. The Dutchman Jacob Roggeveen reached Rapa Nui, which is today inhabited by about 4,000 people, on Easter Monday in the year 1722, which gave the island its present English name.

The Chilean Easter Island covers a mere 164 sq km (63 sq mi) in the Pacific Ocean. It has become famous thanks to the giant moais, also known as "Easter heads". Carved out of a volcanic rock, these silent witnesses of an earlier Polynesian culture are actually complete figures, depicted kneeling on a platform with their hands covering their stomachs.

BUENOS AIRES

Location: East Argentina
Best time to travel: all year
www.easybuenosairescity.com

Porteños – or port residents – is what the residents of Buenos Aires call themselves, referring to the city's location on the western side of the Río de la Plata. Around three million people live in the city of "good air", and almost fourteen million in the greater urban area – about one-third of the entire Argentinean population, which is of largely European descent. Founded by the Spanish in 1536 as Nuestra Señora Santa María del Buen Aire, the city had to be abandoned just five years later following bloody conflicts with indigenous populations. It was founded anew in 1580, was the capital of a Spanish viceroyalty from 1776 to 1810, and has been the capital of Argentina since 1880. The heart of the metropolis, with its grid layout, is the Plaza de Mayo with the Casa Rosada, seat of the state president. The Mothers of the Plaza de Mayo gather there on Thursday afternoons in silent protest against the crimes committed by the military dictatorship.

At night, the Plaza de la Republica is one of the liveliest squares in Buenos Aires (right). At its center stands the 67-m-tall (220-ft) obelisk, which recalls the foundation of the city in 1536.

Buenos Aires became famous as the birthplace of the tango (above) – once described as "a sad thought that is danced".

PEPSI
DESAFIO PEPSI
CABAL
Una tarjeta como la gente
HITACHI
CITIZEN
LT
TICKETS
El nombre de los Tickets
PRIMICIA
Tome
Coca-Cola
Coke
CROWN MUSTANG

LOS GLACIARES

Location: East Argentina
Best time to travel: all year
www.losglaciares.com
www.patagonia-argentina.com

The park's thirteen glaciers form part of the Patagonian Ice Field which, covering 15,000 sq km (5,790 sq mi), is the largest continuous ice mass outside of Antarctica. There are also another forty-seven large glaciers and 200 small ones that are not directly connected to the ice field. The most famous of these is the 30-km-long (19-mi), 5-km-wide (3-mi) Perito Moreno Glacier, which calves into the Lago Argentino. One of only few glaciers in the world that is still growing today, it slowly pushes its "tongue" across a peninsula, cutting off a branch of Lago Argentino every three or four years. The water table rises by up to 30 m (100 ft). When

ANTARCTICA

Location: South Pole
Best time to travel: November to February
www.coolantarctica.com

"It lies there, wilder than any other part of our earth, unseen and untouched," wrote Norwegian Roald Amundsen, the first person to reach the South Pole, in his travel journal in 1911. The Antarctic is a gigantic land mass almost completely covered with snow and ice. Only one-sixtieth of its surface area (with the ice shelf almost 14 million sq km/5.5 million sq mi) is free of ice while the rest is covered by ice with an average thickness of 2,500 m (8,203 ft) – it reaches thicknesses of over 4,500 m (14,765 ft) in areas. This ice expanse is not a flat surface either, but one that is traversed by high mountain ridges. One of the longest ranges on earth is found here, the Trans-

the wall of ice is no longer able to withstand the pressure an amazing natural spectacle ensues: the backed-up mass of water breaks through part of the glacier front and makes its way into the remaining lake area. Also part of the glacial primeval world of this park are the Upsala and Spegazzini glaciers. Further scenic highlights are the virtually inaccessible, up to 3,000 m (9,840 ft) high granite summits of the Cerro Torre and the Monte Fitz Roy in the northern section of the national park, not far from the Lago Viedma. The parks' fauna is dominated by its roughly 100 bird species. They include the lesser rhea, andean condor, torrent duck and white-throated caracara.

The front of the Perito Moreno Glacier rises up to 60 m (200 ft) above Lago Argentino. At regular intervals, individual ice floes break off and plunge into the lake.

antarctic Mountains, which extends diagonally across the entire continent over more than 4,800 km (2,983 miles). Only the highest peaks such as the 4,897-m (16,067-ft) Mount Vinson poke up through the gigantic ice mass.

The Antarctic has never been truly settled by humans. The more than eighty research stations, however, are home to about 4,000 people in the summer and about 1,000 in the winter. And these could hardly be called inviting – at the Russian Vostock Station, located some 1,400 km (mi) inland, the coldest-ever temperature on Earth was measured on July 21, 1983: minus 89.2 °C (-129 °F). The second man to reach the South Pole, the British Antarctic explorer Robert Falcon Scott, reached the South Pole just one month after Roald Amundsen.

Left: Penguins taking a break on an iceberg in Antarctica.

Index

Picture Credits

Abbreviations:
A = Alamy
Akg = akg-images
B = Bilderberg
C = Corbis
G = Getty Images
H = Bildagentur Huber
IB = The Image Bank
Ifa = ifa-Bilderteam
JA = Jon Arnold Images Ltd
L = Laif
M = Mauritius
P = Premium
PC = Photographer´s Choice
RH = Robert Harding
S = Schapowalow

p. 2/3 G/PC/Banana Pancake, 4/5 L/hemis, 6/7 P/Winz, 8/9 G/Panoramic Images, 10/11 G/Riser/Andre Gallant, 12/13 G/PC/Gary Yeowell, 14 t. A/Mikael Utterstöm, 14 b. G/IB/Harald Sund, 15 G/Arctic Images, 16 S, 17 t. A/Phil Degginger, 17 b. H, 18 Erich Spiegelhalter, 18/19 Alimdi.net/Christian Handl, 19 Erich Spiegelhalter, 20 Erich Spiegelhalter, 21 t. Helga Lade Fotagentur/Förster, 21 b. A/OJ-Photos, 22 t. G/IB/Hans Strand, 22 b. F/Achterberg, 23 F1 online/Jan Byra, 24 t. G/IB/Chad Ehlers, 24 b. ifa/F. Chmura, 25 G/Johner, 26 F1 online/Johnér RF, 27 t. B, 27 b. G/Altrendo Panoramic, 28/29 L/Glaescher, 30/31 g/Stone/ Cesar Lucas Abreu, 32 t. A/John Sparks, 32 b. A/imagebroker, 33 G/RH World Imagery/ Reale Clark, 34 Alimdi.net/Whitestar/ Monica Gumm, 35 H/R. Schmid, 36/37 Zielske, 37 t. C/Jim Richardson, 37 M. Zielske, 37 b. Zielske, 38 Zielske, 38/39 P/ImageState, 39 C/Listri, 40 t. A/David Chapman, 40 b. L/RA-PHO, 41 t. A/ImageState, 41 b. G/IB/Guy Edwardes, 42/43 t. A/Jim Zuckermann, 42/43 b. Arco Images/ NPL, 44 t. l. A/David Noble Photography, 44 t. M. Bildarchiv Monheim/ Florian Monheim, 44 t. r. LOOK/Ingolf Pompe, 44 b. A/Jon Gibbs, 45 t. G/IB/Chris Simpson, 45 b. G/Stone/Chris Simpson, 46 t. A/The Photolibrary Wales, 46 M. G/RH World Imagery/Roy Rainford, 46 b. A/BL Images Ltd, 47 t. l. A/David Noton Photography, 47 t. r. A/David Noton Photography, 47 b. l. G/IB/Guy Edwardes, 47 b. r. G/IB/Peter Adams, 48 t. G/Stone/Mike Caldwell, 48 b. L/Hartmut Krinitz, 49 t. A/Arco Images, 49 M. Karl-Heinz Raach, 49 b. A/David Gowans, 50/51 P, 52/53 G/IB/Dennis Flaherty, 54/55 t. H/Massimo Ripani, 54/55 b. L/Zielske, 56/57 G/Digital Vision/RH, 58 t. S/RH, 58 b. C/Bill Ross, 59 t. P, 59 M. P, 59 b. A/negelestock.com, 60 t. A/imagina Photography, 60 b. L/hemis, 61 L/Zenit/Boening, 62/63 L/Meyer, 64 t. L/hemis, 64 b. l. L/hemis, 64 b. r. akg/Joseph Martin, 65 A/JA, 66 t. L/hemis, 66 b. B/Andrej Reiser, 67 L/hemis, 68/69 ifa/JA, 70 t. ifa/Panstock, 70 b. H/G. Simeone, 71 t. Bildarchiv Monheim, 71 b. ifa/Panstock, 72 t. Focus/Harf Zimmermann, 72 b. l. B/Berthold Steinhilber, 72 b. M. L/Kirchner, 72 b. r. L/hemis, 73 L/Kirchner, 74 ifa/Panstock, 75 LOOK/Karl Johaentges, 76 t. l. B/Wolfgang Kunz, 76 t. r. B/Berthold Steinhilber, 76 b. L/Heeb, 77 t. LOOK/Jürgen Richter, 77 b. L/hemis, 78/79 t. ifa/Panstock, 78/79 b. G/RH World Imagery/Ruth Tomlinson, 79 Visum/Cooperphotos, 80 t. ifa/Panstock, 80 M. G/IB/Jeremy Walker, 80 b. ifa/Diaf, 81 t. G/PC/ Scott Stulberg, 81 b. A/images Etc Ltd, 82/83 G/IB/David Madison, 84 G/PC/Peter Adams, 85 A/LOOK/Jürgen Richter, 86 t. G/IB/ Allan Baxter, 86 b. Bridgemanart, 87 t. C/Jon Hicks, 87 b. H/G. Gräfenhain, 88 G/PC/ Peter Adams, 88/89 White Star/Monica Gumm, 89 t. B/Frieder Blickle, 89 b. L/Raach, 90/91 t. P, 90/91 b. Jürgen Richter, 92 t. B/Felipe J. Alcoceba, 92 b. ifa/K. Welsh, 93 t. P/ImageState, 93 b. G/PC/ Marco Cristofori, 94 t. P, 94 b. L/hemis, 95 ifa/Kanzler, 96 t. P, 96 M. Martin Siepmann, 96 b. G/Stone/Manfred Mehlig, 96/97 G/IB/Hans Strand, 98/99 Argus/Schwarzbach, 99 t. G/IB/ Bruno Morandi, 99 M. H/Schmid, 99 b. A/Alandawsonophotography, 100 G/Taxi/Guy Vanderelst, 101 t. G/PC RF/Guy Vanderelst, 101 b. G/PC RF/Guy Vanderelst, 102/103 t. L/Zanettini, 102/103 b. L/hemis, 104 C/Jose Fuste Raga, 105 t. A/photolocation2, 105 b. A/Peter Mc Cabe, 106/107 t. G/PC/Guy Vamderelst, 106/107 b. G/PC/Siegfried Layda, 108 t. B/S. Puschmann, 108 M. G/LOOK/Konrad Wothe, 108 b. P, 109 G/LOOK/Karl Johaentges, 110 Zielske, 111 G/IB/Siegfried Layda, 112 t. Zielske, 112 b. F1 online/Steiner, 113 t. Zielske, 113 b. L/Zielske, 114 t. Zielske, 114 b. Zielske, 115 t. Clemens Zahn, 115 b. l. Wildlife, 115 b. r. Wildlife, 116 L/Zenit/Boening, 117 t. G/Panoramic Images, 117 M. G/IB/Siegfried Layda, 117 b. G/IB/Wilfried Krecichwost, 118 B, 119 Zielske, 120/121 G, 121 t. G/Stone/Michael Busselle, 121 M. ifa, 121 b. L/Zenit/Boening, 122 t. Freyer, 122 b. transit/Thomas Haertrich, 123 t. Zielske, 123 b. Zielske, 124 t. Klammet, 124 b. ifa/Stadler, 125 t. C/Richard T. Nowitz, 125 b. Zielske, 126/127 L/Ingrid Firmhofer, 128 Visum/Alfred Buellesbach, 129 t. A/mediacolors, 129 b. L/Kirchgessner, 130 Visum/Alfred Buellesbach, 130/131 G/Panoramic Images, 131 Visum/Alfred Buellesbach, 132 G/PC RR/ Dan Tucker, 133 A/JA, 134 t. Mediacolors, 134 b. l. S/Sime, 134 b. M. S/Sime, 134 b. r. S/Sime, 135 G/RH World Imagery/Jochen Schlenker, 136/137 S/H, 137 t. G/IB/Hans Wolf, 137 M. A/Interfoto Pressebildagentur, 137 b. A/Wilmar Photography, 138 L/Kirchgessner, 138/139 t. L/Martin Kirchner, 138/139 b. Iris Kürschner, 139 G/LOOK/Ingolf Pompe, 140/141 C/zefa/Fridmara Damm, 141 t. Anzenberger/Yadid Levy, 141 b. Bildarchiv Monheim/Florian Monheim, 142 A/JA, 143 t. A/Woody-Stock, 143 b. G/Riser/Hans Peter Merten, 144 t. l. Arco Images/Rolfes, 144 o .r. A/Woodystock, 144 b. l. Arco Images/Usher, 144 b. r. P/Schuyl/FLPA, 145 t. G/Altrende Panoramic, 145 b. L/hemis, 146 ifa/Lecom, 146/147 t. Das Fotoarchiv/Riedmiller, 146/147 b. ifa/JA, 147 A/Bildarchiv Monheim, 148 t. L/Bialobrzeski, 148 b. L/hemis, 149 t. L/hemis, 149 b. l. P, 149 b. r. G/Taxi/Peter Adams, 150 t. ifa/Alastor Photo, 150 b. L/Galli, 150/151 L/Galli, 151 t. akg/Erich Lessing, 151 b. Bilderberg, 152/153 t. G/PC/Richard Elliott, 152/153 b. G/IB/Macduff Everton, 154/155 G/LOOK/Jan Greune, 154/155 G/Panoramic Images, 156 t. ifa/JA, 156 M. P, 156 b. G/Stone/travelpix Ltd., 157 L/Le Figaro Magazine, 158 t. P, 158 b. L/Kirchner, 159 t. Axel M. Mosler, 159 b. L/Zenit/jan Peter Boening, 160 t. G/PC/Adrian Pope, 160 b. Ernst Wrba, 160/161 L/Celentano, 162 L/Amme, 162/163 t. L/Celentano, 162/163 b. L/Galli, 163 C/David Lees, 164 t. G/National Geographic/t. Louis Mazzatenta, 164 b. L/Celentano, 165 t. B, 165 M. G/RH Worl Imagery/Bruno Morandi, 165 b. Josef H. Neumann, Dortmund, 166 t. G/IB/David Noton, 166 b. P/Image State, 167 t. G/Taxi/David Noton, 167 M. Hubert Stadler, 167 b. P, 168 t. A/JA, 168 b. G/De Agostini, 169 t. G/PC/Peter Adams, 169 b. G/Photodisc/Stefano Stefani, 170 t. L/Zanettini, 170 M. L/Eligio Panon, 170 b. L/Zanettini, 171 t. C/Roger Ressmeyer, 171 M. L/Celentano, 171 b. l. C/Jodice, 171 b. r. L/Celentano, 172/173 P, 173 t. L/Celentano, 173 M. ifa/Harris, 173 b. A/LOOK/Hauke Dressler, 174 L/Harscher, 174/175 t. L/Celentano, 174/175 b. G/IB/Andrea Pistolesi, 175 t. Rainer Hackenberg, 175 b. L/Galli, 176 t. ifa, 176 b. l. A/Cuboimages srl, 176 b. r. L/Celentano, 177 t. A/JA, 177 b. l. L/Martin Kirchner, 177 b. r. L/Kirchgessner, 178 t. Jahreszeiten Verlag/Florian Bolk, 178 b. l. FAN/R. Hackenberg, 178 b. r. C/Jon Hicks, 179 H/Schmid, 180 Das Fotoarchiv/Müller, 180/181 P, 181 A/David Sutherland, 182 G/IB/Siegfried Layda, 183 t. L/Florian Werner, 183 b. P/Buss, 184 t. L/hemis, 184 b. M/Peter Widmann, 185 t. ifa/Strobl, 185 b. A/Magdalena Rehova, 186/187 ifa/JA, 187 t. G/Taxi, 187 M. akg, 187 b. B/Madej, 188 l. L/Hahn, 188 r. L/Hahn, 188/189 H, 189 L/Kristensen, 190 t. L/Kristensen, 190 b. G/PC/Guy Edwardes, 191 t. Vario Images, 191 b. A/Simon Reddy, 192 S, 192/193 C/Jose Fuste Raga, 193 BA-Geduldig, 194 L/Zanettini, 194/195 t. L/hemis/Frank Guiziou, 194/195 b. S/Sime, 196/197 t. H/Johanna Huber, 196/197 b. L/Zanettini, 197 L/Heuer, 198 t. Visum/Ilja C. Hendel, 198 b. Visum, 199 t. A/Sean Sprague, 199 b. L/IML, 200 l. t. Avenue Images/Index Stock/David Ball, 200 l. b. A/JA/Russel Young, 200 r. Still Pictures/Dana Wilson, 201 Naturbildportal/Martin Zwick, 202 M/age, 203 A/Miha Krofel, 204 l. akg, 204 r. G/AFP/Johannes Eisele, 204/205 t. C/P. Saloutos, 204/205 b. L/GAFF/Adenis, 206 t. L/IML, 206 M. M/imagebroker, 206 b. L/IML, 206/207 L/IML, 208 C/J. Hicks, 209 ifa/JA, 210 t. B, 210 b. l. A/David Crossland, 210 b. r. C/S. A., 211 t. G/DEA/A. Garozzo, 211 b. B, 212 L/hemis, 213 A/JA, 214 t. L/IML, 214 b. L/Huber, 215 t. G/Taxi/Maremagnum, 215 b. L/Harscher, 216/217 S, 218/219 P, 219 t. A/Paul Carstairs, 219 M. C/Atlantide, 219 b. B/Klaus Bossemeyer, 220 t. A/John Farnham, 220 b. LOOK/Konrad Wothe, 221 t. A/Blaine Harrington III, 221 b. A/Images &Stories, 222 t. G/RH World Imagery/Bruno Morandi, 222 b. S/Robert Harding, 223 t. Das Fotoarchiv/Manfred Vollmer, 223 b. G/AFP/Ed Oudenaarden, 224 t. L/Raach, 224 b. L, 225 B/Berthold Steinhilber, 226 t. A/JA, 226 M. L/hemis, 226 b. L/Babovic, 226/227 ifa/JA, 228 t. G/National Geographic/Dean Conger, 228 b. C/P. Turnley, 228/229 M, 230 t. M/Ferdinand Hollweck, 230 M. L/Galli, 230 b. G/PC/ Fotoworld, 230/231 t. G/National Geographic/ Richard Durrance, 230/231 b. A/David Crossland, 232/233 mediacolors, 234 t. L/Moleres, 234 b. L/Moleres, 235 l. L/Galli, 235 r. Jupiterimages/ifa/Nowitz, 236 B/Felipe J. Alcoceba, 237 P/Orion Press, 238 M/Michael Obert, 239 t. L/Eid, 239 M. ifa, 239 b. Pictor, 240/241 t. L/K. Hoffmann, 240/241 b. L/Le Figaro Magazine, 241 t. L/Shabi, 241 b. L/Le Figaro Magazine, 242/243 C/Kazuyoshi Nomachi, 243 t. L/Redux, 243 b. C/Kazuyoshi Nomachi, 244 G/PC/Michele Falzone, 244/245 L/Grabka, 246 H/R. Schmid, 246/247 jupiterimages/JA, 247 C/Arne Hodalik, 248/249 t. G/IB/Jochem D. Wijnands, 248/249 b. L/Heeb, 249 t. Imagebroker/Jochen Tack, 249 b. M/A, 250 t. l. B/Christophe Boisvieux, 250 t. M. C/Kazuyoshi Nomachi, 250 t. r. B/Christophe Boisvieux, 250 b. L/Kimmig, 251 t. l. C/JAI/Michele Falzone, 251 t. r. C/Dave Bartruff, 251 b. C/Kazuyoshi Nomachi, 252 C/Michel Setboun, 252/253 t. M/Jeff O´Brien, 252/253 b. C/Michel Setboun, 253 L/hemis, 254 t. A/RH Picture Library Ltd./Jane Sweeney, 254 b. C/Reuters, 254/255 S/RH, 255 l. S/RH, 255 r. C/RH World Imagery/Jane Sweeney, 256 t. G/IB/Toshihiko Chinami, 256 b. A/Michele Falzone, 257 G/IB/Art Wolfe, 258/259 t. A/Roger Cracknell, 258/259 b. C/Macduff Everton, 259 A/Realimage, 260 P, 261 t. l. C/Blaine Harrington III, 261 t. r. A/Jeremy Horner, 261 b. l. A/David Noton Photography, 261 b. r. A/Eastland Photo, 262 t. Okapia, 262 b. l. C/Blaine Harrington III, 262 b. r. C/Travel Ink/Abble Enock, 263 t. l. Okapia, 263 t. M. Blickwinkel/M. Wolke, 263 t. r. Okapia, 263 M. t. Arco Images/Jorens-Belde, 263 M. b. G/Glowimages, 263 b. G/Panoramic Images, 264 t. C/Dave Bartruff, 264 b. A/Yadid Levy, 265 t. C/Freeman, 265 b. L/Harscher, 266 t. G/Panoramic Images, 266 M. l. L/hemis, 266 M. r. Blickwinkel/J. Royan, 266 b. G/Panoramic Images, 267 t. C/Atlantide Phototravel, 267 b. C/Atlantide Phototravel, 268 t. A/Wolfgang Kaehler, 268 b. L/hemis, 269 t. l. L/Celentano, 269 t. r. Still Pictures/Thomas Kelly, 269 b. l. Andia/Mattes, 269 b. r. B/Till Leeser, 270 t. mediacolors/Flueeler, 270 b. l. L/Huber, 270 b. r. L/Lewis, 271 t. P/M. Garcon, 271 b. l. A/David Pearson, 271 b. r. Olaf Krüger, 272 t. l. A/Kevin Schafer, 272 t. r. Okapia, 272 b. l. A/Nature Picture Library, 272 b. r. A/Nature Picture Library, 273 t. A/Louise Murray, 273 b. Okapia, 274/275 G/Riser/Keren Su, 275 t. L/Huber, 275 b. L/Olivier Foellmi, 276 A/travelib india, 277 t. A/Deepak Dogra, 277 b. C/Christophe Boisvieux, 278 A/Peter Horree, 279 t. L/hemis, 279 b. S/RH, 280 t. l. L/hemis, 280 t. r. H, 280 b. l. A/Kumar Sriskandan, 280 b. r. H, 281 C/Christophe Boisvieux, 282 P, 283 t. P, 283 b. A/Robert Preston, 284/285 G/Axiom/Tim Hall, 285.1 G/IB/Jochem D.

Wijnands, 285.2 G/IB/Andrew Geiger, 285.3 G/IB/Daryl Benson, 285.4 G/Stone/Glen Allison, 286 t. M/imagebroker/Konstantin Mikhailov, 286 b. L/Hilger, 287 t. LOOK/Per-Andre Hoffmann, 287 b. l. Arco Images/K. Wothe, 287 b. r. A/imagebroker, 288 t. l. C/Goodshoot, 288 t. M. C/Wolfgang Kaehler, 288 t. r. C/Yann Arthus-Bertrand, 288 u .l. Wildlife, 288 b. r. Wildlife, 289 t. C/Roger Tidman, 289 b. Junior Bildarchiv, 290 C/Wheeler, 291 t. l. A1Pix/D., 291 t. r. Visum/Marc Steinmetz, 291 b. l. Visum/Marc Steinmetz, 291 b. r. Visum/Marc Steinmetz, 292 C/Redlink, 292/293 C/Redlink, 293 A/JLImages, 294/295 Panoramastock/Chu Young, 296 t. C/Pierre Colombei, 296 b. Panoramastock, 297 t. Panoramastock, 297 b. C/Asian Art & Archaeology Inc., 298 t. C/JAI/Demetrio Carrasco, 298 b. C/Wolfgang Kaehler, 299 H, 300 t. A/Martin Probert, 300 b. ifa/Index Stock, 301 t. L/REA, 301 b. l. LOOK/Karl Johaentges, 301 b. r. LOOK/Karl Johaentges, 302 t. A1PIX/PCH, 302 b. A1PIX/PCH, 303 t. L/hemis, 303 b. l. C/Keren Su, 303 b. r. C/Marc Garanger, 304 P/Pixtal, 304/305 t. C/Paul Hardy, 304/305 b. Panoramastock, 305 l. Panoramastock, 305 r. ifa/JA, 306 t. F1 online/Panorama Media, 306 b. Panoramastock/Ru Suichu, 307 l. A1PIX/PCH, 307 r. Panoramastock/Yang Tiejun, 308 t. A1PIX/PCH, 308 M. F1 online/Panorama Media, 308 b. A/China Span/Keren Su, 309 t. A/Sylvia Corday Photo Library, 309 M. l. ifa/JA, 309 M. r. ifa/Int. Stock, 309 b. P/Panoramic Images, 310 t. Das Fotoarchiv/Xinhua, 310 b. Sinupictures/Phototimes, 311 t. Sinupictures/cns, 311 b. C/China Photos/ Reuters, 312 L/Kristensen, 312/313 t. L/Hauser, 312/313 b. L/Marcel & Eva Malherbe, 313 L/hemis, 314/315 C/Rob Howard, 315 l. G/National Geographic/Martin Gray, 315 r. ifa, 316 t. L/Sasse, 316 b. A/Pat Behnke, 317 t. C/Christophe Boisvieux, 317 b. F1 online/Horizon, 318 LOOK/Hauke Dressler, 318/319 G/IB/Tom Bonaventure, 319 G/Stone/Ehlers, 320/321 t. LOOK/age, 320/321 b. C/Image Plan, 322 t. G/National Geographic/Timothy G. Laman, 322 b. A/J Marshall - Tribaleye Images, 323 l. t. ifa/JA, 323 l. b. ifa/JA, 323 r. ifa/JA, 324 t. P, 324 b. L/Redux, 325 Arco Images/R. Philips, 326 t. H/Gräfenhain, 326 b. l. G/National Geographic/Steven L. Raymer, 326 b. r. L/hemis, 327 t. C/Peter M. Wilson, 327 b. A/Paul Panyaiotou, 328 t. Jochen Tack, 328 b. G/IB/Wilfried Krecichwost, 329 t. l. G/Lonely Planet Images/Andres Blomqvist, 329 t. r. C/Steve Raymer, 329 b. l. P/Pacific Stock/K. Su, 329 b. r. M/A, 330 t. l. A/Iconotec, 330 t. r. A/J Marshall - Tribaleye Images, 330 b. l. A/dreamtours, 330 b. r. A/David South, 331 A/Ron Yue, 332 Das Fotoarchiv/Lineair, 332/333 t. G/National Geographic/Steven L. Raymer, 323/333 b. L/hemis, 333 l. Avenue Images/Index Stock/ Angelo Cavalli, 333 r. L/hemis, 334 S, 334/335 t. L/Martin Kirchner, 334/335 b. L/Kirchgessner, 335 t. C. & W. Kunth, 335 b. l. ifa, 335 b. r. C. & W. Kunth, 336 C. & W. Kunth, 336/337 C/Luca I. Tettoni, 337 l. Martin Sasse, 337 r. Martin Sasse, 338 t. Wildlife/A. Schah, 338 M. l. Wildlife, 338 M. r. C. & W. Kunth, 338 b. Arco Images, 339 t. C. & W. Kunth, 339 M. C. & W. Kunth, 339 b. l. C. & W. Kunth, 339 b. r. C. & W. Kunth, 340 t. G/PC/Glen Allison, 340 b. Martin Sasse, 341 t. ifa, 341 b. Martin Sasse, 342/343 G/IB/Paul Souders, 343 l. C/Nik Wheeler, 343 M. ifa/F. Raga, 343 r. C/Dave G. Houser, 344 t. A/Atmotu Images, 344 b. l. WaterFrame/Reinhard Dirscherl, 344 b. r. C/Robert Holmes, 345 t. G/PC/Frank Lukasseck, 345 b. P/Roda, 346 t. l. G/Lonely Planet Images/Richard I´Anson, 346 t. r. G/Lonely Planet Images/Richard I´Anson, 346 b. L/Le Figaro Magazine, 347 t. G/National Geographic/Tim Laman, 347 b. l. A/Photofrenetic, 347 b. M. L/Hoa-Qui, 347 b. r. F1 online/ Horizon, 348 t. G/Asia Images/Jill Gocher, 348 b. A/Mark Lewis, 349 t. ifa, 349 b. L/Emmler, 350/351 P/Delphoto, 352 t. G/Gallo Images/Travel Ink, 352 b. L/Heeb, 353 t. L/hemis, 353 b. G/IB/Walter Bibikow, 354/355 H/Ripani, 355.1 M/Jose Fuste Raga, 355.2 G/IB/Vision, 355.3 L/Hilger, 355.4 L/Reporters, 356 t. A/Tim Mossford, 356 b. A/Nicholas Pitt, 357 t. A/Martin Norris, 357 b. H/Riccardo Spila, 358/359 P, 360 t. Das Fotoarchiv/Lineair, 360 b. L/Bermes, 361 t. C/Pierre Colombel, 361 b. G/Panoramic Images, 362 t. Jupiterimages/ifa/Charles, 362 b. C/zefa/Guenter Rossenbach, 363 t. L/hemis, 363 b. L/Bialobrzeski, 364 t. alimdi.net/Guenter Fischer, 364 b. A/Wolfgang Kaehler, 365 t. L/Sasse, 365 b. H, 366/367 Clemens Emmler, 368/369 P, 369 t. Clemens Emmler, 369 M. Clemens Emmler, 369 b. ifa/JA, 370 Das Fotoarchiv/Riedmiller, 371 Michael Martin, 372 t. G/PC/Sylvian Grandadam, 372 M. Hub/Zoom, 372 b. G/Stone/ Press, 373 t. P/T. Smith, 373 b. P, 374/375 H/F. Damm, 376 t. Michael Martin, 376 b. Clemens Emmler, 377 t. L/Kirchner, 377 b. L/hemis, 378 t. A/Images&Stories, 378 b. A/Yadid Levy, 379 t. l. A/JA, 379 t. r. A/Robert Estall photo agency, 379 b. Visum/Christoph Keller, 380/381 L/Michael Martin, 381 C/Pierre Colombel, 382 t. C/Martin Harvey, 382 b. A/Ann and Steve Toon, 383 t. G/National Geographic/Michael K. Nichols, 383 b. G/National Geographic/Ian Nichols, 384 t. L/Ulutuncok, 384 M. Wildlife, 384 b. L/Torfinn, 384/385 C/Remi Benali, 386/387 C/George Steinmetz, 387 L/Redux/The New York Times, 388 P/Stock Image, 388/389 C/Martin Harvey, 390 Okapia, 391 l. Blickwinkel/Pflanzen, 391 r. Lonely Planet Images/Grant Dixon, 392/393 Mauritius, 393.1 C/Howard, 393.2 C/Harvey, 393.3 G/Sean Russell, 393.4 Okapia, 394 t. C/Yann Arthus-Bertrand, 394 b. ifa/Aberham, 395 t. A/Images of Africa Photobank, 395 b. Eye Ubiquitous/Hutchinson, 396 G/Photonica/Jake Wyman, 396/397 G/Axiom Photographic Agency/Ian Cumming, 398 P, 398/399 G/Gallo Images/Dave Hamman, 399 G/Stone/Paul Souders, 400 t. l. C/Gallo Images, 400 t. r. C. & W. Kunth, 400 b. P, 401 P, 402/403 Clemens Emmler, 404/405 ifa/JA, 406/407 t. Franz Marc Frei, 406/407 b. Das Fotoarchiv, 407 t. Clemens Emmler, 407 M. Clemens Emmler, 407 b. Clemens Emmler, 408 t. Das Fotoarchiv/Markus Matzel, 408 b. L/Riehle, 409 t. L/Emmler, 409 b. P/Joubert/NGS, 410 C/Gallo Images/Martin Harvey, 410/411 t. G/Riser/Michael Melford, 410/411 b. P/Minden, 411 G/Riser/JH Pete Carmichael, 412 L/Le Figaro Magazine, 413 H/G. Simeone, 414/415 C/TSM/Faulkner, 416 t. C/Yann Arthus-Bertrand, 416 b. l. Transglobe/Schmitz, 416 b. r. Clemens Emmler, 417 t. Geospace/Acres, 417 b. C/Jon Sparks, 418/419 P, 420 t. P/Minden, 420 b. G/Chesley, 420/421 Don Fuchs, 422 t. Okapia, 422 b. C/Yann Arthus-Bertrand, 423 t. P, 423 b. Don Fuchs, 424 L/hemis/Herve Hughes, 424/425 ifa/JA, 425 L/Back, 426 t. C/Dave G. Houser, 426 b. Clemens Emmler, 427 P/StockImages, 428/429 C/Yann Arthus-Bertrand, 430 Christian Heeb, 430/431 Tobias Hauser, 431 Bilderberg/Burkard, 432 C/Eurasia Press/Steven Vidler, 432/433 L/Christian Heeb, 433 Tobias Hauser, 434 t. Clemens Emmler, 434 b. Franz Marc Frei, 435 t. G, 435 b. Clemens Emmler, 436 t. A/RH Picture Library Ltd., 436 b. C/Keren Su, 437 C/Charles & Josette Lenars, 438/439 t. C/Yann Arthus-Bertrand, 438/439 b. C/NewSport/Jeff Flindt, 439 C/Darrell Gulin, 440/441 P/Stock Images/S. Harris, 442 t. P/Firstlight, 442 b. G/Taxi/Ambrose, 443 t. Vario Images, 443 b. P, 444/445 t. G/All Canada Photos/Chris Cheadle, 444/445 b. P, 446 L/Raach, 447 L/hemis, 448/449 P/Orion Press, 450/451 C/T. Allofs, 451 P, 452 t. P, 452 b. Christian Heeb, 452/453 P/Raymer, 454/455 G/PC/Michele Falzone, 455 t. P/Kosuge, 455 b. P/Gilchrist, 456 t. Christian Heeb, 456 b. Christian Heeb, 456/457 Christian Heeb, 458 t. G/National Geographic/ Philip Schermeister, 458 b. P, 459 t. P/Image-State, 459 b. G/Stone/George Diebold, 460/461 t. P/Roda, 460/461 b. P, 461 P/Minden/Brandenburg, 462 t. Christian Heeb, 462 b. L/Heeb, 463 t. C/Roberts, 463 b. ifa/Nova-Stock, 464 C/Randklev, 464/465 ifa, 466 t. C/Huey, 466 b. Arco Images/NPL, 467 t. ifa/TPC, 467 b. P/Stock Image/Frilet, 468/469 P, 470 L/Heeb, 470/471 Das Fotoarchive/Moore, 471 Christian Heeb, 472 t. P/Minden/C. Clifton, 472 b. C/Sohm, 473 t. S/Atlantide, 473 b. l. Avenue Images/J. Greenberg, 473 b. r. Avenue Images/G. Ercole, 474/475 Martin Sasse, 476.1 P/Barbudo, 476.2 ifa/JA, 476.3 Avenue Images/W. Metzen, 476.4 L/REA, 477 t. P/Gorsich, 477 b. L/Heeb, 478/479 L/Kristensen, 479 P/Minden/N. Wu, 480 t. L/Heeb, 480 b. P, 480/481 G/Art Wolfe, 482/483 t. G/Stone/Robert Frerck, 482/483 b. P, 484 t. C/George H. H. Huey, 484 b. G/Patricio Robles Gil, 484/485 G/Riser/Kevin Schafer, 486 t. C/Angelo Hornak, 486 b. C/Richard A. Cooke, 487 t. C/Archivo Iconografico, 487 b. A/Aflo Ct. Ltd., 488 t. Andia/Mattes, 488 b. L/Heeb, 489 t. P/Brimberg/NGS, 489 b. Visum/Andreas Sterzing, 490/491 t. ifa/Panstock, 490/491 b. H, 491 L/hemis, 492 t. G/Picture Finders, 492 b. G/Picture Finders, 492/493 t. Marr, 492/493 b. Marr, 494/495 H/Giovanni, 496 t. L/heeb, 496 b. L/Tophoven, 497 t. C/Macduff Everton, 497 b. C/Charles & Josette Lenars, 498 l. Wildlife, 498 r. A/Arco Images, 499 NGS/Garrett, 500 L/Heeb, 501 l. t. A/Kevin Schafer, 501 l. b. Okapia, 501 r. H/Kiedrowski, 502 t. L/Kirchgessner, 502 b. C/Stephen Frink, 503 C/Stephen Frink, 504/505 L/Hauser, 505 t. L/Hauser, 505 M. L/Hauser, 505 b. L/Hauser, 506 t. C/Eye Ubiquitous/David Cumming, 506 M. C/Denis Anthony Valentine, 506 b. C/Eye Ubiquitous/David Cumming, 506/507 L/Sasse, 508 t. P, 508 b. C/Onne van der Wal, 509 Das Fotoarchiv/Babovic, 510 L/hemis/Patrick Frilet, 511 A/Banana Pancake, 512 t. A/Jeremy Horner, 512 b. G/Jane Sweeney, 513 t. C/Archivo Iconografico, 513 b. LOOK/Ingrid Firmhofer, 514 G/Stone/Ke Fisher, 514/515 A/Kevin Schafer, 516 C/Tibor Bognár, 517 A/JA, 518/519 t. A/Wolfgang Kaehler, 518/519 b. P, 519 l. LOOK/Per Andre Hoffmann, 519 r. L/New York Times/Redux, 520 L/Tophoven, 520/521 P, 522/523 L/Gonzales, 524/525 G/Reportage/Daniel Beltra, 525 t. M, 525 M. P, 525 b. P/Pecha, 526 t. L/Heeb, 526 b. Bildagentur-online, 527 t. G/LatinColntent/ SambaPhoto/Cassio Vasconcellos, 527 b. G/National Geographic/Richard T. Nowitz, 528 Okapia/Peter Arnold, 529 t. P/Tansey, 529 b. A/Tibor Bognar, 530 t. C/Houk, 530 b. G/IB/Andrew Geiger, 531 C/Galen Rowell, 532/533 t. digitalvision/Woodhouse, 532/533 P/Hummel, 534/535 L/Malherbe, 536 t. H/Bernhart, 536 b. L/Gonzales, 536/537 S/H, 538/539 t. LOOK/Michael Boyny, 538/539 b. P/Minden/Wiesniewski.

Cover: Mauritius/Super Stock

The publisher made every effort to find all of the copyright holders for the images herein. In some cases this was not possible. Any copyright holders are kindly asked to contact the publisher.

Imprint

This edition is published on behalf of APA Publications GmbH & Co. Verlag KG, Singapore Branch, Singapore
by Verlag Wolfgang GmbH & Co. KG, Munich, Germany

Königinstr. 11
80539 Munich
Tel. (49) 89 45 80 200
Fax (49) 89 45 80 20 21
www.kunth-verlag.de

Distribution of this edition:
GeoCenter International Ltd
Meridian House, Churchill Way West
Basingstoke, Hampshire RG21 6YR
Great Britain
Tel. (44) 1256 817 987
Fax (44) 1256 817 988
sales@geocenter.co.uk
www.insightguides.com

Translation: Silva Editions Ltd., UK; Katherine Taylor
Dtp: Robert Fischer (www.vrb-muenchen.de)

Printed in Slovakia